MODERN CULTURAL ANTHROPOLOGY

an introduction

SECOND EDITION

MODERN CULTURAL ANTHROPOLOGY

an introduction

SECOND EDITION

PHILIP K. BOCK

ALFRED A. KNOPF NEW YORK

To my parents,
Eugene and Clara Bock,
and to the memory
of my teachers
Robert Redfield
and
Clyde Kluckhohn

THIS IS A BORZOI BOOK
PUBLISHED BY ALFRED A. KNOPF, INC.

Second Edition

987654321

 Published in the United States by Alfred A. Knopf, Inc., New York, and simultaneously in Canada by Random House of Canada Limited, Toronto. Distributed by Random House, Inc., New York.

Library of Congress Cataloging in Publication Data
Bock, Philip K.
Modern cultural anthropology.

Includes bibliographical references.
1. Ethnology. I. Title [DNLM: 1. Anthropology, Cultural. 2. Ethnology. GN315 B665m 1974]
GN315.B57 1974 301.2 73-13870
ISBN 0-394-31778-5

Book design by Juli Hopfl

Cover design by Jeheber & Peace

Cover photo by George Holton (Photo Researchers, Inc.)

Acknowledgments are gratefully extended to the following authors and publishers for their kind permission to quote from copyrighted works:

The Clarendon Press for excerpts from *The Nuer* by E. E. Evans-Pritchard.

Northwestern University Press for excerpts from *Dahomean Narrative* by M. J. Herskovits and F. Herskovits.

Manufactured in the United States of America

Preface to the Second Edition

Anyone familiar with the first edition of this text will recognize both continuities and changes. There is a good deal of new material—particularly in the chapters on language, enculturation, and culture change. Some chapters have been reordered, and sections that repeatedly presented problems to students have been clarified or deleted. There are new discussions of ethnic groups and of the social responsibilities of the scientist, and there is an extensive glossary. On the other hand, the basic organizing ideas that served to integrate the text have been preserved; these will soon be made more explicit in my forthcoming book, *The Formal Content of Ethnography*. However, I do not believe that an introduction to a discipline has to deal with the very latest intradisciplinary disputes in order to be relevant or interesting to beginning students. Here, as in *Culture Shock*, I have aimed for a rounded presentation of the major ideas and data of contemporary anthropology.

The wide acceptance of the first edition in English-speaking countries and its translation into German, Spanish, Italian, and Japanese have been very gratifying. I hope that this new edition will continue to assist in making cultural anthropology a significant part of liberal education.

I would like to thank Susan Rothstein of Alfred A. Knopf for her help and kindness. I am also grateful to my students at Stanford and the University of New Mexico, whose responses to the first edition helped in preparing this revision.

Albuquerque, New Mexico
June 1973

PHILIP K. BOCK

Preface

It is hazardous to use the word "modern" in the title of any book, particularly one dealing with a scientific discipline. After all, to our descendants the intellectual fashions of today will doubtless look as absurd as its dress and dwellings. Nevertheless, I have taken the rash step of calling this book *Modern Cultural Anthropology* because I feel that its structure and contents do reflect the major concerns of many anthropologists of the younger generation. Wherever possible, I have introduced current concepts and theories so that the reader can gain some idea of what is happening on the frontiers of our discipline. I have also tried to discuss traditional topics in a way which demonstrates their relevance to contemporary problems.

Rather than an eclectic or encyclopedic introduction, I have tried to present a view of anthropology based on a *unified theory of cultural phenomena.* While conceding that this attempt at unification may be somewhat premature, I nevertheless hope this approach will be useful to the beginning student or interested layman, as well as stimulating to the professional reader. Central to this approach is my conviction that there are valid and important analogies between the structure of language and that of the rest of human culture—analogies which follow from the fact that language is one of several cultural subsystems, all of which share the same fundamental characteristics. My attitude is *not* that linguistics will solve all problems. But I do believe that a careful examination of the relationship between language and culture will point the way to a conceptual framework capable of embracing *all* the forms of customary human behavior.

The conception of culture adopted in this book emphasizes cognitive processes. Whether dealing with language, social structure, technology, or ideology, I have tried to show how persons who share a common culture categorize their experiences and respond in conventional ways to these categorized experiences.

The paired concepts of *category* and *plan* run as a unifying thread through the entire book. Cultural relativism is another persistent theme: that is, both the culturally derived categories and their conventional association with particular plans for action are viewed as partly arbitrary products of historical development—whether the plans are designs for speaking, interacting, valuing, or altering the environment.

As part of this "mentalistic" orientation I have tried to deal in a systematic way with the relation of cultural forms to the *behavior* in which they are manifested. Thus there are discussions of what takes place as language "competence" becomes actual speech, as the abstract social structure is performed in concrete situations by all-too-human role players, and as the technological system is translated into skillful action. Nor does the relativism of my general approach prevent treatment of cultural ecology, cross-cultural comparisons, or theories of cultural evolution, though I have chosen to do so briefly. Many of these ideas are introduced in a section on "The Anthropologist at Work" in which I discuss the methods by which linguists, ethnographers, and archaeologists infer cultural forms and processes from observed regularities in human behavior and the products of behavior. The Epilogue summarizes the argument of the book and raises several central issues of philosophical anthropology.

Due to the conceptual unification of this volume, it is not advisable to skip or rearrange chapters in using it with a class. However, instructors who can (at least heuristically) accept its approach should find it possible to expand upon given chapters or to alter their emphases by assigning supplementary articles or case studies. Many such readings are now available in inexpensive editions. Lists of recommended books and monographs will be found at the end of each chapter.

In closing, I should like to acknowledge several intellectual debts. Earl Lyon taught me about the pleasures and pains of responsible thinking; William Beatty introduced me to the challenge of anthropology; the Woodrow Wilson Foundation made possible a year at the University of Chicago where Robert Redfield confirmed my choice of a career; Clyde Kluckhohn encouraged and stimulated my somewhat deviant interests; and Dell Hymes and Kenneth Pike opened my eyes to the complexities of language and its relationship to culture. Finally, the Department of Anthropology at The University of New Mexico has provided a warm and stimulating setting for my work. To all of these and to my wife, Layeh, who helped in many different ways, many thanks.

P. K. B.

Albuquerque, New Mexico
July 1968

Contents

Anthropology means "the study of man"; therefore, it may seem strange to you that anthropologists have no single, generally accepted answer to the question "What is man?" Many books, articles, and meetings of scholars have been devoted to this question, and the search for an answer continues. It is more important for a beginning student to understand why it is difficult to formulate a definition of man than for him to memorize any single, partial definition.

All definitions have at least two aspects, and any given definition may do a better job with one of these aspects than with the other. The first of these aspects we may call *contrast*: the part of a definition that enables you to set off the thing defined from everything else in the universe. If the contrast aspect of an X is well defined, you should be able to say of any phenomenon: "Yes, that is an X," or, "No, that isn't an X." And anyone who has agreed to use the same definition should agree with you in each case. If you think it is easy to make up a definition that will always do this, try it for some common object—such as a chair—and then think about what you would do with deviant objects such as stools, rocking chairs, electric chairs, benches, or chairs with missing parts.

Assuming that the problem of contrast is solved, there remains the other aspect, which we may call *content*: that is, the definition should tell us something about the nature of the phenomenon being defined—what it means, how it is used, what its possibilities may be. A definition that enabled us always to recognize a chair but that said nothing about the act of sitting would clearly be unsatisfactory.

Many definitions have still another aspect—the emotional satisfaction which they give to the persons employing them. Thus to define man as "the lord of Creation" may make men feel pretty good, but, needless to say, this definition is not at all helpful to a scientific study.

Aristotle defined man as the "political animal," by which he apparently meant "that animal which lives in a *polis* or city-state." While this was quite acceptable to his Greek contemporaries (who, of course, lived in city-states), it would *ex*clude nomadic peoples and, unless "city" were carefully defined, might *in*clude certain social insects. Defining man as a "featherless biped" enables us to contrast him with most animals (except, as has been pointed out, kangaroos or plucked chickens); but besides being emotionally unsatisfactory, this definition tells us nothing about human nature.

There is one brief definition, usually attributed to Benjamin Franklin, that does a surprisingly good job on both contrast and content: "Man is the tool-making animal." By interpreting "toolmaking" precisely yet broadly, we are able to set man off from most other animals by a criterion that is central to human nature—man's

John Nance/Panamin/Magnum

PART I
What Is Man?

ability to shape parts of his environment in accordance with learned techniques. If we adopt this definition, it turns out that we must apply the term *man* to a number of extinct animals who resemble, but are not identical with, modern men and women. In the first chapter we shall consider some of the evidence for human evolution—the development of both man's body and his tool-making abilities. We shall see that these two types of development are closely related to each other. And we shall show how anthropologists have divided up the task of answering the question "What is man?"

CHAPTER 1
The Biological Background

The way that we look and behave and the way the world looks to us are the result of hundreds of millions of years of biological evolution. For example, the fact that there are two human sexes ultimately goes back over a billion years, to the origin of some quite simple, but much improved, life forms. The fact that we are warm-blooded and hairy, rather than cold, clammy, and covered with scales, goes back less than 200 million years, to the origin of the mammals. On the other hand, the fact that we have five digits at the end of each limb is something that we share, not only with our fellow mammals, but with the reptiles as well, indicating a common source much further back.

THE PRIMATE PATTERN

Man is a member of the mammalian order *Primates*—a group of animals whose evolution as a distinct group has been going on for only about 70 million years. There is some important evidence for this affiliation right on the tips of your fingers: only primates (among the mammals) have flat nails, rather than sharp claws, on their fingers. All primates are "grasping" animals; most (apes, monkeys, and a variety of lower primates called prosimians) live in or around trees, and their long, mobile fingers tipped with flat nails are useful for getting a good grip on a tree limb or for manipulating nearby objects.

Unlike the other four-limbed mammals, primates don't trot around on the ground, sniffing and poking at things with snouts.

Man as a primate—a "grasping" animal. *David Margolin*

Rather, they tend to sit up or perch on hind limbs, make noises, look around, and explore with "hands." Life in trees calls for good vision rather than keen scent, and nearly all the primates do have acute color vision; also, primate eyes tend to face forward (rather than out to the sides), and most primates are able to see objects in three dimensions—a handy trick if you are going to go leaping from limb to limb.

Monkeys and apes are noted for their natural curiosity. Recent laboratory experiments have shown that monkeys will do quite a bit of work for no reward other than the chance to manipulate or even gaze at some unfamiliar object.[1] And though they can be stifled by strict training, human infants also demonstrate great amounts of exploratory behavior and curiosity if given a chance. It is not clear whether any of man's direct ancestors ever got around by swinging from branch to branch; but man does share with the apes highly mobile shoulders, arms, and fingers. Of all the animals, only man and the higher primates can throw things accurately.

Another important characteristic of most of the primates who live in groups is their tendency to sort out into what zoologists call *dominance hierarchies.* Within a troop of baboons (a type of monkey in which this characteristic has been carefully studied), each male has an established position in relation to every other male—above, equal, or below, depending on the outcome of a sequence of fights (or bluffs).[2] This is similar to the "pecking order" established among the chickens of every barnyard and also to the prestige systems of human communities, primitive and civilized.

Man's primate ancestors, then, shared the following: long, highly mobile arms and hands; a relatively large brain adapted to control those hands; stereoscopic color vision; various vocal abilities; curiosity; and a tendency to establish dominance within a social group. Surveying this list, S. L. Washburn and V. Avis concluded that "it is no accident that of the many animals which have become bipedal only man has become a tool-maker."[3]

The higher primates also tend to have rather extended "childhoods"—that is, long periods during which they are dependent upon adults of their species for satisfaction of their basic needs. Many young animals are on their own within the first year of life, attaining full physical and social maturity soon afterward. Indeed, the young of many species never even see their "parents." But mammals are born alive, develop slowly, and require the presence of an adult female if they are to survive. This need for care is par-

---

1. H. Fowler, *Curiosity and Exploratory Behavior* (New York: Macmillan, 1965).
2. I. DeVore, ed., *Primate Behavior* (New York: Holt, Rinehart and Winston, 1965).
3. S. L. Washburn and V. Avis, "Evolution of Human Behavior," in A. Roe and G. G. Simpson, *Behavior and Evolution* (New Haven: Yale University Press, 1958), p. 435.

ticularly true in apes and men—a chimpanzee is dependent upon maternal care for about two years and does not reach its adult size until it is eight to twelve years old; comparable figures for human young in most societies are six to eight years of dependency and full growth at the age of about twenty.

This prolonged period of dependence was accentuated by our ancestors' development of a taste for meat. In a tropical environment, getting enough roots or wild fruit is best accomplished by each individual for himself, and tools are only occasionally useful. But a hunting way of life makes the whole group dependent upon the strength, cunning, and tool-making skill of the adult males, as well as upon their willingness to share the kill. A human child must depend upon his parents for both sustenance and knowledge; and his need for food reinforces the learning of group tradition.

Much of what is learned during primate childhood involves ways of getting along with other members of the group. All group-living animals must make some such adjustments to their fellows. In the case of social insects and birds, most of the required behavioral patterns are built into the animal at birth. But primates have few such instincts. Brainy animals that they are, they also "learn to communicate" with one another by means of rather subtle gestures and vocal sounds. Such arbitrary, group-specific, and socially learned signals are not yet language, but they do represent a step in the direction of true speech. In Chapter 2 we shall consider the nature of language and its importance to the human group, keeping in mind the biological background out of which it developed.

THE ORIGIN OF MAN

Our precultural ancestors, then, were curious, communicative, and capable of complex interactions with one another and with their environment. There is no reason to think that they did not make at least sporadic use of tools. Indeed, recent studies of chimpanzees in the wild have revealed that these apes frequently use sticks and other objects in highly intelligent ways learned from other members of the group. Thus, there is no absolute break between the tool-using and tool-making of the apes and that of early men; nevertheless, the ability of our ancestors to shape natural objects into useful forms was carried further and applied to more durable materials. Tool-making is one of the most characteristic activities of man, and one that has had important consequences for the evolution of our species.

If we do define man as the "tool-making animal," it follows

that wherever we find a consistent pattern of tool-making, man has been present. Indeed, this is one of the major advantages of this definition, for tools made of stone are much more likely to persist unchanged for thousands of years than are organic materials like flesh and bones. Most of our evidence for the age and whereabouts of ancient men comes from the tools they left behind them.

The Australopithecinae

The earliest recognizable stone tools are extremely crude, little more than hunks of rock with a few flakes knocked off to produce a sharp edge. Some of these *eoliths* (dawn-stones) may not be tools at all, for there are many natural forces, such as glaciers, landslides, earthquakes, heat, and cold, that can fracture stone; but there are no known natural forces that can transport river pebbles uphill into caves, or that can carry flint, quartz, or obsidian (volcanic glass) dozens of miles from their natural sources and then shape them for cutting and scraping. We will not try to define tools until Chapter 8, but it should be noted that in order to contrast man-made tools with natural objects, we must take account of two things: the *form* of the object and its *distribution* (that is, where it is found).

Among the very earliest recognized tools are the crude choppers known as *Oldowan* pebble-tools. These are found in various parts of East Africa, in early geological contexts, often far away from riverbanks. They are simply pebbles with a few flakes removed to provide a cutting edge. We do not know exactly what they were used for, but they are quite numerous and were evidently made for thousands of years by a technique which was transmitted from generation to generation.

In 1959, Dr. and Mrs. Louis B. Leakey made an important discovery definitely linking an extinct, manlike creature with the manufacture of Oldowan-type stone tools. At Olduvai Gorge in East Africa, Mary Leakey discovered the fossilized skull of a small-brained, bipedal *hominid* (see below), to which her husband gave the name *Zinjanthropus* (East African man).[4] Embedded in the same geological level were stone tools and the fossilized bones of small birds and animals, presumably hunted by Zinjanthropus. Furthermore, the invention of a new technique for dating

4. L. S. B. Leakey, "The Origin of the Genus *Homo*," in S. Tax, ed., *The Evolution of Man* (Chicago: University of Chicago Press, 1960), pp. 17–32. Dr. Leakey later took the position that a fossil form he named *Homo habilis* had lived at the same time as Zinjanthropus and was actually ancestral to modern man; but most anthropologists feel that "*Homo habilis*" and "Zinjanthropus" are only extreme varieties of Australopithecinae.

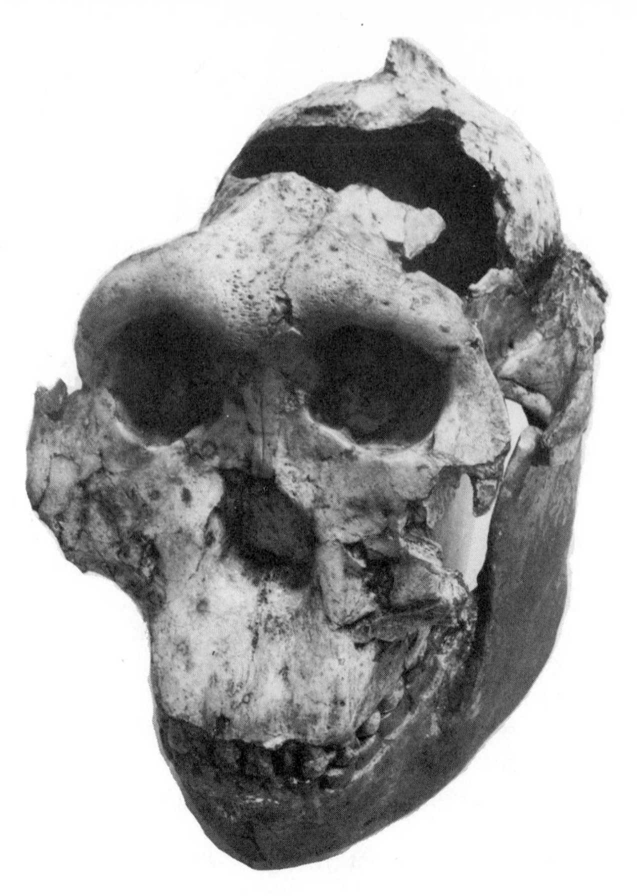

Zinjanthropus* from Bed I of Olduvai Gorge. *Dr. George Gerster/Rapho Guillumette.

ancient deposits (the potassium-argon method) made it possible to show that the level containing fossils and tools was more than 1,750,000 years old! Since this discovery, still older fossils (similar to Zinjanthropus) have been found in various parts of Africa, and it is now believed that these extinct relatives of modern man go back at least five million years.

Man and his extinct relatives are classified in the biological family known as the *Hominidae* (see Figure 1.1). This group of animals (called hominids) shares many anatomical and biochemical features with the family of living and extinct apes, the *Pongidae.* The resemblances are numerous enough that, as Charles Darwin noted, they indicate descent from a common ancestor at some time in the past.[5] However, in the millions of years of their sepa-

5. C. Darwin, *The Descent of Man* (New York: Modern Library, 1949; first published, 1871).

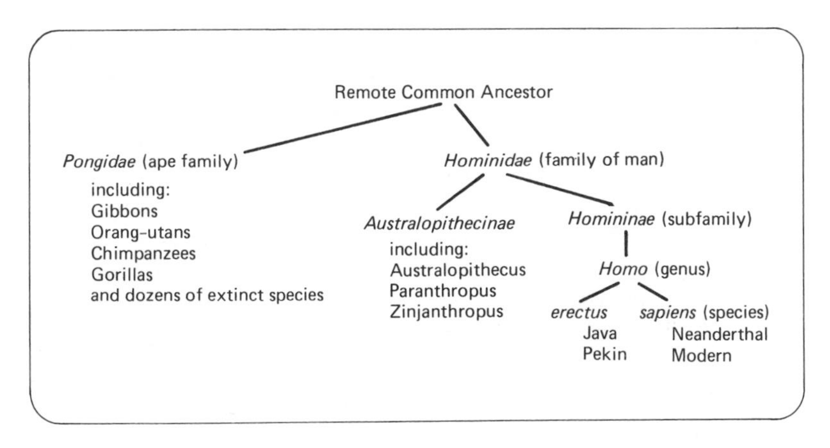

Figure 1.1 **Classification of Man and His Closest Biological Relatives**

rate evolution, apes and men have become sufficiently contrasted so that normally there is little difficulty in telling, say, a chimpanzee from a human being. All members of the Hominidae differ from all members of the Pongidae in three important ways:

1. their brains (those of the Hominidae are larger, relative to body size)
2. their mode of locomotion (that of the Hominidae is primarily bipedal walking rather than brachiating)
3. their teeth (those of the Hominidae are adapted to a mixed diet, unlike those of the apes, who are primarily vegetarian and who have evolved long, pointed canine teeth which are used as weapons).

The exact classification of Zinjanthropus is still disputed, but it is clear that this animal was a member of the family Hominidae and of the subfamily *Australopithecinae*—that is, Zinjanthropus is most similar to two other million-year-old members of his subfamily: *Paranthropus* and *Australopithecus.* All three of these Australopithecinae differ from the apes in relative brain size, locomotion, and dentition; and all three seem to have been toolmakers.

Fossil remains of various Australopithecinae have been found throughout Africa and as far away as the island of Java. The most complete specimens come from limestone caves in South Africa, where the first member of this subfamily was identified in 1924 by Raymond Dart. The type known as Australopithecus was much smaller than the others, and Dart believes it used clubs and spears made of bone and horn to compensate for its small size and lack of fighting teeth. (Australopithecus weighed about ninety pounds and had teeth very much like ours.)[6] Here we can see a significant connection among the three anatomical differences between men and apes. The ability to walk on two hind limbs leaves the forelimbs free for exploring and manipulating parts of the environment; the intellectual improvement which presumably accompanies increased brain size makes possible the shaping and use of tools; and as tools become more effective, the anatomical characteristics which they replace (such as large cutting and tearing teeth) are gradually reduced. This is an oversimplified statement of an extremely complex process: further on, we shall explore other connections among body form, tool-use, and intelligence as we try to understand the meaning of V. G. Childe's dictum: "Man makes himself."[7]

Which (if any) of the Australopithecinae were directly ancestral to more advanced types of men is still an open question. In any case, this group represents a stage in hominid evolution which lasted for several million years. During this stage, although the brain was still comparatively small, upright posture and bipedal locomotion were perfected; this and the use of tools initiated several trends in the evolution of the skull which have resulted in the form characteristic of modern man.

Homo erectus and Homo sapiens

The next stage of human evolution is represented by the fossil remains of *Homo erectus.* These members of our own genus (*Homo*) lived throughout much of the Old World for perhaps as long as half a million years. They were effective tool-makers, manufacturing a variety of stone and bone tools. Below the neck, their skeletons cannot be distinguished from those of living men. Their brains, however, were intermediate in size between those of apes and modern men, and their skulls were quite rugged: the bones were thick, with heavy brow ridges above the eye sockets; the top of the skull was relatively flat and low, leaving no space for forehead; the jaw was large, chinless, and projecting; and the teeth were huge (though clearly human in form). Examples of this stage are the well-known Java and Pekin "ape-men" (formerly classified as the genus *Pithecanthropus*), as well as several more recent discoveries from North and East Africa. *Homo erectus* was

6. R. A. Dart, "The Osteodontokeratic Culture of Australopithecus Prometheus," *Memoir 10* (Transvaal: Transvaal Museum, 1957). Many anthropologists, however, consider Dart's claims to be as unfounded as his designation "Prometheus," which was meant to indicate that some South African Australopithecinae knew how to use fire.

7. V. G. Childe, *Man Makes Himself* (New York: Mentor Books, 1951).

an efficient hunter, and judging by the presence of hearths, charcoal, and charred animal bones in the cave of Pekin man, by about a quarter of a million years ago he had mastered the use of fire.

Let us consider for a moment the importance of the control of fire to the survival and development of man. Though fire is a chemical process rather than a physical object, we may consider its controlled use a special type of tool. This tool provided men with a way of releasing limited amounts of energy from organic substances for purposes of warmth, light, protection against predators, and cooking food. In the hostile environment of the Ice Age, the control of fire was a great aid to survival.

Anthony F. C. Wallace has pointed out some striking implications of the control of fire. Groups of men who had mastered the complex techniques of building, maintaining, and transporting fire had an advantage, not only over wild animals, but over other groups of men who had not mastered these techniques, or who perhaps could not master them because they were less intelligent than the fire-users. Wallace points out that considerable intelligence, foresight, and skill are required to successfully control fire, as are constant subliminal attention and probably some division of labor within a group. Groups which lacked these intellectual abilities would gradually be eliminated; so would individuals within the more successful groups who were incapable of learning the essential skills.[8]

Thus the invention of tools and techniques that required skill and intelligence for their employment reacted back upon the inventors by favoring the skillful and intelligent in the struggle for survival. Without realizing it, man was making himself more intelligent. Before the development of complex tools, nature tended to favor those individuals with greater strength, speed, agility, or natural defenses, with intelligence a helpful but secondary factor. Now, for the first time in the history of life, brains became the key to survival—not automatic reflexes, but learning ability, foresight, and social cooperation, all of which required a large and complex nervous system. The brain of *Homo erectus* expanded until it reached a size equal to that of the smaller-brained men and women of today (see Figure 1.2).

The first well-known representatives of our own species, *Homo sapiens,* date back over a hundred thousand years. These are the *Neanderthal* men. Despite the comic-strip stereotypes, their brains were on the average actually larger than ours. Their skulls show their close relationship to *Homo erectus.* The skulls

---

8. A. F. C. Wallace, *Culture and Personality* (second edition; New York: Random House, 1970), pp. 65–72.

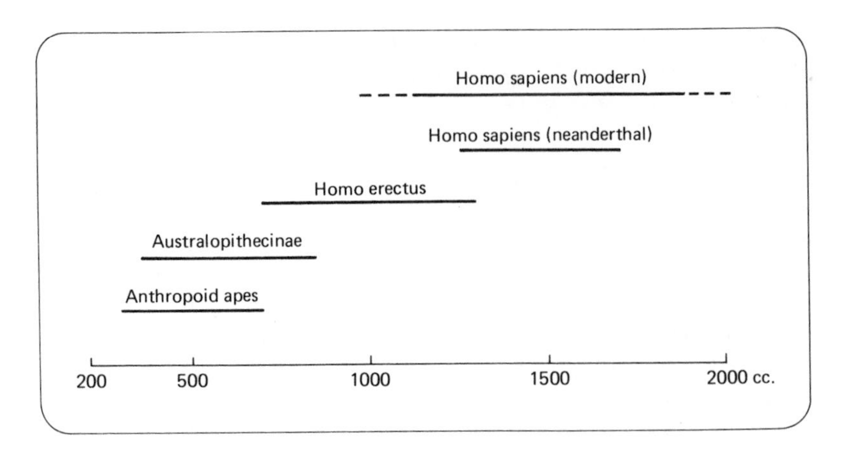

Figure 1.2 **Range of Brain Sizes in Some Living and Fossil Primates (in cubic centimeters)**

of most European Neanderthals were thick and quite flat with heavy brow ridges, while the teeth were large and set into heavy, usually chinless jaws. But Neanderthals had developed an elaborate tool-kit (known as the Mousterian culture), including stone scrapers used for making clothing from animal skins. They also buried their dead and apparently conducted some kind of magical rituals in connection with the skulls of slain bears.[9]

Aside from the heavy brow ridges, which linger on in some races of modern man, the main ways in which the Neanderthal's skull differed from our own were in those parts of the face and jaw associated with his large teeth. As man's tools gradually took over the cutting, tearing, and crushing functions formerly performed by his teeth, his teeth became smaller and the supporting bones of his face and jaw were also reduced and rearranged. The chin, which had been absent in *Homo erectus* and only feebly developed in the Neanderthals, became more prominent, adding strength at a critical point to the jaw, which had become lighter and more fragile.

The earliest known men of a fully modern type date back only thirty to thirty-five thousand years. These are the fossil remains from Combe Capelle and Cro-Magnon in France. The skulls are not radically different from ours, though the Combe Capelle specimen has a rather weak chin and fairly prominent brow ridges. The upper part of the skull has a globular form, encasing the highly developed brain in a thin sheet of bone. The face is almost vertical,

9. For excellent pictures and discussions of man's fossil ancestors see F. C. Howell, *Early Man* (New York: Time-Life Books, 1967).

with the jaws pulled back under the face, causing the nose to stick out in a peculiar way.

These modern-looking hunters lived near the end of the great Ice Age. They pursued their game on both sides of the Mediterranean and in other parts of the Old World. They had a variety of tools made by several new techniques and from numerous natural materials in addition to stone. On pieces of ivory and antler, as well as on the walls of their caves, they have left the first traces of sculpture and pictorial art. Many different interpretations have been ascribed to their works of art; it is probably safest

Detail of cave painting from the Martinshoek Valley depicting a hunt and other events. ***South African Information Service***

to view these as evidence of man's attempt—and probably *not* his first—to portray those aspects of nature which were most important to him and perhaps, through portrayal, to control them.

Since before the time of the Neanderthals, man's body has changed surprisingly little, and most of the changes have been directly related to a limited number of basic inventions. Among these we may list the development of weapons and cutting tools, the control of fire, the use of natural and artificial shelters (including that portable type of shelter called clothing), and the invention of improved ways of getting food by hunting, fishing, and much later, cultivation. All of these inventions have reacted back upon man's body in complex ways; for example, man's relative hairlessness is most likely related to his use of clothing, which makes a hairy body both unnecessary and unsanitary. What man *does* and what man *is* are thus closely connected.[10]

CULTURE AND THE RACES OF MAN

This is a book about cultural anthropology, but the term *culture* has thus far appeared only once in the present chapter. It is important that you realize that the anthropologist uses culture to refer to a much broader range of phenomena than this term covers in ordinary speech. For our purposes, a "culture" includes all of the expectations, understandings, beliefs, or agreements which *influence the behavior* of members of some human group. These shared ideas need not be conscious, but they are always transmitted by social learning, and they constitute one set of solutions to the adaptive problems facing every human society (see Chapter 7).

A classical anthropological definition of culture was suggested by Sir Edward B. Tylor in 1871: "Culture . . . is that complex whole which includes knowledge, belief, art, morals, law, custom, and any other capabilities and habits acquired by man as a member of society."[11] More recently, Robert Redfield has suggested that culture may be briefly defined as: "the conventional understandings, manifest in act and artifact, that characterize societies."[12] In both of these definitions the emphasis is upon the

---

10. M. F. Ashley Montagu, ed., *Culture and the Evolution of Man* (New York: Oxford University Press, 1962).
11. E. B. Tylor, *The Origins of Culture* (New York: Harper Torchbooks, 1958; Part I of *Primitive Culture,* first published in 1871), p. 1.
12. R. Redfield, *The Folk Culture of Yucatan* (Chicago: University of Chicago Press, 1941), p. 132.

ideas and ideals learned and shared by the members of a social group. For Redfield, as for Tylor, the tools and hearths of *Homo erectus* are *not* the culture of these ancient men, though they are *evidence* from which students of prehistory infer the presence of a cultured, tool-making animal. Such objects are the material results of "capabilities and habits" shared within human groups. We cannot "see" the culture. But from regularities in the form and distribution of things we can observe, we are able to infer the existence of "conventional understandings."

The notion of culture will be discussed later many times and with many illustrations. It is introduced here only in order to distinguish between *culturally* regulated behavior, which is transmitted by learning, and *genetically* regulated behavior, which is transmitted by breeding. Some differences among human groups have nothing to do with learning. These are what we call *racial* characteristics; they are a result of biological adaptation to environmental differences and are transmitted genetically in the process of sexual reproduction. Thus, some groups of men have only straight hair, while others have naturally wavy hair; some always have darkly pigmented skin, others (at least during the winter) have little skin pigmentation; some are highly resistant to certain diseases, others are more susceptible; and so on. We cannot always understand the biological advantage conferred by some of these racial characteristics, but the vast majority of racial differences have come about by the same evolutionary processes of adaptation that have produced the millions of forms of life upon our planet.

The difference between genetically and culturally determined characteristics is fundamentally the same as the difference between naturally wavy hair (which you get from the genes of a parent) and artificially waved hair (which you get from the skilled ministrations of a beautician). Superficially they may appear the same, but for scientific purposes it is essential to distinguish them. In one case, persons look or behave as they do because they were "born that way." In the other case, they look or behave as they do because they were "brought up that way." One of the most important jobs of the anthropologist is finding out which is which.

As it turns out, most of the really striking differences among human groups are culturally determined. The language that you speak has nothing to do with the language of your biological parents, except for the fact that you are most likely to be brought up by them or in a group that speaks their language; if you were brought up in a family speaking a different tongue, you would certainly learn this "foster language." Similarly, the tools that you use, the foods that you prefer, the career that you choose, your ideas about the beautiful and the supernatural—all of these depend primarily upon the culture of the group in which you are brought up. Every normal human being has the biological capacity to learn *a* language, *a* technology, and *a* social code; but *which* language, and so forth, he will learn depends upon where and when he is born, not his racial heredity.

Racial differences are of interest in their own right, for when man developed culture he did not cease to evolve biologically. Indeed, part of this chapter has dealt with several ways in which man's inventions have reacted back upon his body by favoring certain kinds of genetically determined characteristics. The physical differences among groups of men must be explained in terms of the different historical experiences of their ancestors: where they lived, what they ate, what diseases they suffered from, and so forth. But the study of human genetic adaptation to natural and cultural conditions requires a firm grasp of biological principles and techniques. Over many generations, each human population becomes adapted to a particular environment; but there is no such thing as "adaptation in general" or "racial superiority." The doctrine of *racism,* which asserts the superiority of one human group over all others, receives *no scientific support* from any of the fields of anthropology. Let us now see what these fields are.

THE FIELDS OF ANTHROPOLOGY

Anthropology may be contrasted with other sciences by virtue of its exclusive and exhaustive concern with man and his works. To the general biologist, man is only one of a large number of interesting organisms, while those human biologists and medical personnel who concentrate on man's body usually do so to the exclusion of his culture. Social sciences such as economics or political science generally select a single broad aspect of man's behavior and limit their study to it. Sociology is probably closest to anthropology in its range of concern with man and his works, but sociology does not have a biological foundation and sociologists generally limit themselves to the study of Western, or at least highly "civilized," peoples.

Anthropology, then, is characterized by its breadth of interest. Ideally, an anthropologist is prepared to study man in all his aspects, and in all times and places. The stereotypes of anthropologists digging in the shadow of pyramids or trekking across deserts and through jungles to measure skulls and ask questions, only to end up in a cannibal's pot—all have some validity. Anthropologists to a greater extent than other social scientists, like to travel to strange places and work with exotic peoples first hand; they like to experience their materials directly; like other natural scientists, they tend to bring back specimens for further study and display. Clyde Kluckhohn used to say that the main difference between anthropology and sociology is that sociologists have no museums.

But such a broad range of interests involves the danger of shallowness, and in an age of specialization it is perhaps inevitable that a division of labor be established within the field of anthropology. The main subdivisions of the field are *physical anthropology* and *cultural anthropology.* Physical anthropologists are primarily human biologists with an interest in the evolutionary history of man (including the process of race formation) and with an appreciation of the relevance of culture to human behavior. Cultural anthropologists, on the other hand, are primarily concerned with man's works—the material and social forms that man has created throughout his history to enable himself to cope with his environment and his fellow men.

Within cultural anthropology are a number of subdivisions. Prehistoric *archaeology* is the subfield that studies the material remains of cultures lacking "written" records, both for their intrinsic interest and with the goal of reconstructing the total pattern of life of men long dead.

Anthropological *linguistics* is concerned with the languages of all peoples, past and present. It looks at language from two general points of view: the *structural* approach is used to find out how languages work by analyzing their parts and describing how these parts go together; the *genetic* approach is employed to reconstruct the form and historical relationships of languages that are no longer spoken. Language is treated in this book as a part of culture; its study can throw light upon many aspects of culture history and culture change.

The rest of cultural anthropology falls under the heading of *general ethnology*—the study of "peoples." It may be divided into three subfields, though these divisions reflect different emphases rather than clear-cut breaks, and there is a great deal of overlap among them. They are: *ethnography,* which deals with the description of ways of life of particular social groups; *ethnology*, which emphasizes the comparison of cultures, the reconstruction of culture history, and the study of culture change; and *social anthropology*, which also emphasizes comparisons of cultures, but with the aim of generalizing about the nature of human societies and the relationships among social groups. (Other subdivisions will be introduced in connection with specified topics.)

Within these fields of anthropology there are vast differences of emphasis: for example, some anthropologists take a historical approach, while others are oriented toward contemporary studies; some try to apply their understanding to practical problems of social change and policy, while others consider such attempts premature or actually harmful to the development of the science. But despite these and other differences of approach and emphasis, most anthropologists hold as an ideal the notion of an integrated approach to man and his works. We believe that man's body, his language, and his way of life "make sense" only when they are seen as integrated wholes and in relation to one another. As Sol Tax put it, "Whether we are archaeologists or linguists, students of the arts or of geography, whether we study the behavior of baboons or the refinements of the human mind, we all call ourselves anthropologists."[13] And all anthropologists are trying to answer the question "What is man?"

RECOMMENDED READING

On physical anthropology:

Alland, A., Jr., *Evolution and Human Behavior.* Garden City, N.Y.: Anchor Books, 1973. A brief, clear, and thoughtful introduction to the study of culture in relation to human evolution.

Howell, F. C., *Early Man.* New York: Time-Life Books, 1967. An authoritative and beautifully illustrated introduction to the study of fossil man.

Hulse, F. S., *The Human Species.* (Second edition) New York: Random House, 1971. A comprehensive and clearly written introduction to physical anthropology.

Pfeiffer, John E., *The Emergence of Man.* New York: Harper and Row, 1969. A good popular introduction to human evolution with materials on primate behavior and the social life of contemporary hunting peoples.

On the fields of anthropology:

Pelto, P. J., *The Nature of Anthropology.* Columbus, Ohio: Charles E. Merrill Books, 1966. A brief overview of the fields and history of anthropology, as well as the major research problems and methods.

13. S. Tax, ed., *Horizons of Anthropology* (Chicago: Aldine Publishing Company, 1964), p. 23.

Shapiro, H. L., ed., *Man, Culture, and Society.* New York: Oxford University Press, 1956. A series of articles by outstanding anthropologists in each of the basic subfields.
Tax, S., ed., *Horizons of Anthropology.* Chicago: Aldine Publishing Company, 1964. Brief articles (originally radio broadcasts) by young anthropologists discussing the future of their respective fields of study.

Human beings are born with an astonishing capacity to learn. By the age of eight, the normal child in any society has developed fantastically complex and subtle modes of behavior. No one really understands what form this knowledge takes within the nervous system, but the child behaves as though he had at his immediate disposal a great many plans for appropriate behavior. These general plans guide him in responding to every kind of object, person, or situation he is likely to meet. And if his response is inappropriate in some particular case, he also has acquired ways of modifying his behavior until it is judged appropriate.

Other animals share some of this learning ability with man, but much of it is unique to our species. In exchange for the flexibility and individuation made possible by these capacities, we have had to pay a price. Human beings are equipped with only a few rudimentary built-in behavior patterns, that is, instincts. Thus men are forced to rely upon the traditions of their societies for the means of satisfying their needs. For example, human infants are supplied with only one set of food-getting instincts: those connected with sucking. All other knowledge of what is edible (or poisonous) and how to secure and prepare it must be learned.

The technical term for the process of learning the traditions of one's society is *enculturation.* It involves many different kinds of learning. To gain some appreciation of the great importance of social learning to typically human behavior, it is useful to consider the daily life of a group of fifty institutionalized "idiots," all of whom had IQ's below 20. C. MacAndrew and R. Edgerton, who studied them, describe them as members of our species whose "capacity for culture is dramatically impaired."[1] Although their behavior is unlike that of any other animal species, the fact that these defectives are so helpless indicates how dependent man has become upon learning to achieve a human level of existence. In the words of Karl Marx, "Man is . . . not only a social animal, but an animal which can develop into an individual only in society."[2]

The everyday routine of these idiots and of the staff assigned to care for them is filled with the mechanical tasks of cleaning, dressing, toileting, and feeding. In addition, the staff is concerned with trying to ensure that the patients do not injure themselves or others. Most members of the group are not toilet-trained, and many individuals cannot feed themselves, while some of the more (physically) competent patients seem barely aware of what is going on.

1. C. MacAndrew and R. Edgerton, "The Everyday Life of Institutionalized 'Idiots,' " *Human Organization,* Vol. 23 (1964), p. 318. This article is reprinted in P. K. Bock, ed., *Culture Shock* (New York: Knopf, 1970).
2. K. Marx, "The Material Forces and the Relations of Production," in T. Parsons *et al.,* eds., *Theories of Society,* Vol. I (New York: Free Press, 1961), p. 137.

John Nance/Panamin/Magnum

PART II
Learning to Be Human

The general impression inside the ward is one of noise and confusion:

> In the background, strange and wondrous sounds originate from all sides. Few words can be distinguished (although many utterances, in their inflection, resemble English speech); rather, screams, howls, grunts, and cries predominate and reverberate in a cacophony of only sometimes human noise.

Outside, in the play yard, though under supervision, the patients are

> left almost entirely to their own singularly limited devices. At least 20 patients do nothing but sit, rock, or lie quietly. The activity of the remaining 30 or so consists of running, pacing, crying, or shouting, and this typically in a manner oblivious of their surroundings. . . . What interaction does occur is almost entirely limited to the tactual: there is occasional cuddling, stroking, huddling together and amorphous, exploratory probing. These interactions . . . are characteristically without relation either to past or future: in a word, they have the appearance of occurring outside of history.

Even this brief description indicates how little human behavior these unfortunate defectives exhibit. Their failure to learn how to control their bodies in socially acceptable ways has an organic basis; but it is also clearly related to their inability to communicate verbally with others, for language is the most important medium of enculturation.

In the next two chapters we shall consider, respectively, the nature of human language and the kinds of learning that take place both before language is acquired and during the later stages of enculturation. In each of these chapters we shall be concerned with the ways in which culture enables man to organize his experiences into manageable units (*categories*) and to deal with these units via learned, socially standardized patterns (*plans*). It will be maintained that every culture consists of a complex set of such categories and associated plans which are learned during the process of enculturation and which enable persons who share them to communicate with one another and to satisfy their needs.

A Note on Categories

Since the notion of "category" will be so important to the rest of this book, it seems wise to make sure that it is clearly understood. Consider the set of objects in Figure II.

Each of these objects differs from each of the others in one or more ways; however, by ignoring some of these differences or by selecting certain resemblances, we are able to form a number of different categories with from zero to six members. For example, the category of "circles" has two members (objects 1 and 2); the category "large objects" has three members (objects 1, 3, and 5); and the category "shaded objects" also has three

3. C. MacAndrew and R. Edgerton, *op cit.*, pp. 314, 315.

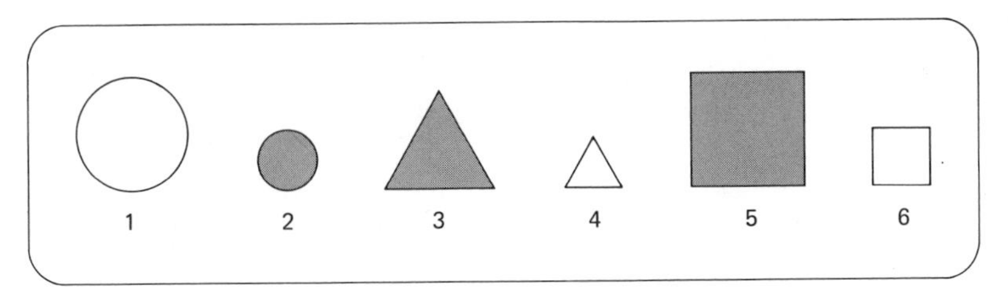

Six Geometrical Objects

members (2, 3, and 5). In forming these categories, we have selected a single *attribute of form* (shape, size, shading) and classed together those figures which share this attribute, while ignoring the other ways in which they differ from one another.

Many different groupings of these six objects can be made by selecting various attributes and combining them in different ways. For example, the category of "large shaded objects" has only two members (3 and 5); "small triangles" has only one member (4); and the category "large shaded circles" has *no* members. It is not even necessary that all members of a category share any single attribute. For example, the *disjunctive* category "empty triangles *or* shaded squares" has two members (4 and 5), but neither of these figures has any attribute in common with the other. Disjunctive categories are particularly difficult to learn and, fortunately, are relatively rare in human cultures.

All of the categories described up to this point have been based upon attributes of form—that is, intrinsic properties of the objects themselves, such as size or shape. But there are also many possible types of nonformal categories. One type consists of categories based upon *distribution*, that is, the position of an object or event in relation to other objects or events. For example, going back to our six objects, we could speak of a category of "objects that occur between two smaller objects" (3 and 5) or "outside objects" (1 and 6). If we regard the six objects as being ordered from left to right (as the numbering implies), then we may speak of the category "objects followed by three or more other objects" (1, 2, and 3). Formal and distributional attributes may be combined to produce a category such as "small objects that are not on the outside" (2 and 4).

Finally, we shall also speak of categories based upon attributes of *function*—that is, the use to which an object may be put, or the purpose of an event. The objects we have been using as examples are not well suited to functional categorization. Some examples of functional categories might include: "objects that can be used to cut wood" (for example, knives, axes, files, saws, chisels); "objects used for transportation" (bicycles, cars, trains, boats, planes); or "ways of getting food" (hunting, fishing, gardening, purchasing, stealing).

A person is said to "have" a category when he is able to *respond* to all members of that category in a distinctive manner. His response may be verbal or nonverbal: he may say, "That's one," or he may push a red button, wink his eye, or clap his hands. Whether or not he can *define* the category by stating its attributes (for example, "large shaded figures"), he "has" the category when his behavior shows consistent responses to its members. Psychologists have amply demonstrated that human beings—and many lower animals—can learn categories without being able to define their attributes.[4]

Two or more people are said to share a category when they are able to respond to all members of the category in distinctive ways. Their responses need not be identical: one may push a red button, another a black button; some may say "small" and still others, "*petit.*" But their consistent behavior shows that they all "have" the same category. In some cases, people may appear to share a category when they are using very *different attributes* in their categorizing. For example, one person may call objects 3 and 5 "zaps" because they are large and shaded, whereas another person responds to them in the same way because they are large and straight sided. In this case we can easily discover whether they are using different bases for categorization by presenting a large shaded circle; the first person will call it a "zap" but the second will not. It is not always this easy to determine what attributes are being used; nor is it essential, for our purposes, to do so.

Once you "have" a category, it is largely a matter of convention what kind of response you attach to it. You may call objects 2, 4, and 6 "small," but you may also label them *petit, klein, zug,* or *dop*; you may raise your hand or stamp your foot when they are presented. Indeed, you can easily learn to switch from one of these responses to another. The conventional nature of the linkage between categories and expected responses (including verbal labels) is an important point to which we shall return again and again.

A fundamental characteristic of human societies is that members of a given society tend to behave in the same general ways under similar circumstances, and that these ways of behaving are learned rather than instinctive. Culture provides both the conventional ways of categorizing experiences and standardized ways of responding to the members of a category, whether they are geometric figures, sound patterns, parts of the envi-

---

4. An excellent introduction to cognitive psychology and the acquisition of categories is J. S. Bruner *et al., A Study of Thinking* (New York: Science Editions, 1962).

ronment, or other people. Man's behavior is not entirely determined by his culture. But shared categories and responses make it possible for him to communicate with other members of his society and to cope with his material environment. They also provide an ideal standard against which he can evaluate his own behavior and that of others. In the following chapters, we shall see how some of these patterns are learned, often unconsciously, quite early in life.

CHAPTER 2
Learning a Language

Among the many remarkable things that happen to a normal human child in the first few years of his life is the *acquisition of language.* Actually, this is a much too passive way of putting it, for though language acquisition is still far from being fully understood, it has become clear that the child plays a very *active* role in the process.

The genetic heritage of every normal child includes the capacity to learn one or more languages. However, *which* language (or languages) he learns depends upon the speech community of his biological parents, and he will learn their language; but there is no *necessary* connection between genetic heredity and speaking any particular language. Thus, if a child born in Germany, to German parents, is brought up among only native speakers of Japanese, he will learn to speak Japanese as his mother tongue; furthermore, in learning to speak or understand German, he will have *no advantage* over other Japanese speakers.

But what does it mean to "learn a language"? To begin with, imagine yourself entering a room where several people are conversing in a tongue completely unfamiliar to you. Instead of rapidly retreating, listen to them and try to understand what is going on. Your first impression—that which tells you that the language being spoken is one you don't know—is that the sounds are very different from English. Quite a few of the individual sounds may be familiar, but there will be some sounds and many combinations of sounds that you have never heard and that you can imitate only with difficulty.

Not only are these people making strange sounds, they also appear to "understand" one another—the sounds they are making are transmitting messages and provoking responses (in the form of further messages, actions, laughter or tears, and so forth). Since as a nonspeaker, you do not know the code, you have no way of understanding these messages, nor can you respond to them appropriately if they are addressed to you. This is a frustrating experience, and you may be tempted to think that they are just making noises to confuse you; but let us assume that they are speaking a real language and see what might happen.

If you listen long enough to such conversation, the sounds will gradually become more familiar and you will begin to hear some repeated *patterns of sounds.* The first ones you are likely to notice and remember will be those patterns which resemble words or phrases in English. For example, you may hear a sound cluster that reminds you of the English syllable *ma* or of its *reduplicated* form *mama.* This would be easy to pick out and to remember. But it would be most dangerous to assume that it carried the English meaning, 'mother,' or even that it was the same *type of word* as the English *ma*. For example, in modern Hebrew the word for 'mother' is pronounced *eema*, but the syllable *ma* at the beginning of an utterance (a stretch of speech) is an interrogative word meaning 'what' or 'how.'

In modern French, the syllable *ma* is neither a noun nor an interrogative: it is a first person possessive pronoun, like English 'my.' But this French form is used to modify only feminine singular nouns. Thus I may say *ma mère,* 'my mother,' but I must say *mon*

American students learn French in a "language laboratory." ***Cornell Capa/ Magnum***

père, 'my father,' because in French 'father' is a masculine noun and the possessive pronoun must agree with it in gender.

If the language being spoken were Russian, you would be correct to assume that *mama* referred to a person's female parent, and with much the same childish overtone that the word has in English. But if the language spoken were that of the Njamal tribe of Australia, you might be astonished to learn that *mama* designates a large category of *male* relatives, including one's father, father's brother, mother's sister's husband, and father's father's brother's son . . . though of course *not* including one's father's father's sister's son, who is called *karna.*

In Mandarin Chinese, the syllable *ma* can mean 'mother,' but only if it is pronounced with a level *tone,* for in this dialect there are four different tones (level, rising, falling, rising then falling), each of which may give a syllable a totally different meaning. Thus, depending on its tone, *ma* can also mean 'horse,' 'hemp,' or 'to scold.' An English speaker would have great difficulty learning to recognize these differences, much less to pronounce them.

In still other languages, *ma* could be unpronounceable, for there are some sound systems (such as Tlingit and Arapaho) which completely lack the *m* sound. In others, *ma* can be pronounced, but it carries no meaning. Or it may function as a prefix indicating noun class (as it does in some Bantu languages), or as a conjunction (as in Italian), and so on. Thus, even if by careful imitation you were able to learn the sounds of a language, you still would have little idea of what they signified or how they should be combined into words or sentences.

Let us now consider the case of a child born into an English-speaking community. He has, in a sense, come into a room full of people speaking a language he does not understand. But unlike adults learning a second language, the child does not even know there *is* such a thing as language; nor does he have any habits of speech which could interfere with his acquisition of English. How, then, does acquisition of language take place?

The general primate characteristics of curiosity, vocalization, and imitation certainly play some part in children's language learning. But unlike apes and monkeys, human children also seem to be born with the capacity to quickly and effectively learn the language of their community. The mere imitation of sounds, though important, is only a small part of what the child must do.

Starting at about six months, the child begins to "babble"—that is, to spontaneously produce sounds such as *ta, nu,* or *gee,* and commonly to reduplicate syllables (*tata, nunu, mama,* and so forth). By the time he is a year to eighteen months old, he usually has a small number of "words" (about twenty); he follows simple commands and responds to "no." At this point, his comprehension of language is not much more advanced than that of a well-trained dog, but by twenty-one months of age a major advance usually takes place: his vocabulary increases tenfold, he understands simple questions, and he speaks two-word phrases of a few characteristic forms, for example, "dada go," "baby up," "see ball."

By two years of age the average child has a vocabulary of 300 to 400 words, and he uses prepositions and pronouns in constructing two- and three-word phrases. The most rapid increase in vocabulary takes place during the following year: by age three many children know a thousand words. But even more important, during this period the child learns to compose a wide variety of sentence types; more and more of his utterances are *free from grammatical errors,* even though they are *unlike anything an adult might say.* This is the truly notable thing about child language: it is *not* just an imitation of adult language with "mistakes." At each stage, the child's verbal productions show patterning and system. It is as if the child is forming "rules" about how to speak and then systematically testing them out, modifying them, and adding new ones until he achieves (unconsciously, of course) a set of rules which adequately guide his speaking and understanding.

Just what is meant by such "rules" will become clear later in this chapter. We can anticipate a little by saying that the rules have to do with categories of sounds, sound combinations, and the association of various sound combinations with different "meanings." The members of a speech community have equivalent sets of rules—plans for speaking—and this makes it possible for them to communicate complex and novel messages. Each child must discover these rules for himself on the basis of a limited and imperfect sample of adult speech, guided only by his innate "language acquisition device" and occasional instruction from adults and peers. This is a remarkable achievement, and it is significant that parental attempts to teach children to speak have relatively little effect upon the speed with which these basic abilities appear. The child learns primarily by listening for recurrent *patterns of sound* and by inferring rules for their combination into larger units.

Let us take one familiar example. In speech and in writing, most English speakers use the words "a" and "an" in regular and predictable ways. As literate adults, you are able to consciously formulate the rule for which of these forms of the indefinite article should be used. But isn't it surprising that four-year-old children use these forms correctly even though they cannot read or write, though they are seldom instructed on this point, and though they do not know the distinction between a vowel and a consonant? Remember, too, that our pronunciation of the word "a" is quite variable: in ordinary fast speech, most Americans say it as a kind of grunted *uh* (technically, a *schwa* sound which linguists represent with the symbol /ə/), but in more careful speech, many people pronounce it as they do the vowel in *hay* (for the linguist, a vowel plus glide: /ey/). Furthermore, the sound of the vowel in the word "an" is like neither of these, but rather like the vowel in *hat* (which linguists, who try to keep these differences straight, write /æ/).

The child (or adult) learning English must learn to distinguish these sounds and to use them in correct combinations. He could, of course, adopt a gambler's strategy: noticing that "a" occurs far more often than "an," he could just say "a" all the time, figuring that he is more likely to be right than wrong. But, interestingly, children do not seem to do this: they seek the *pattern*, and despite mistakes, eventually learn the rule. That is, without being consciously aware of any "reasons," they learn to anticipate the initial sound of the following word (even if it is one they are saying for the first time) and to use the appropriate form of the article.

Before we leave this example, it should be emphasized that there is nothing in human anatomy that makes it *necessary* for English speakers to say "an" before a vowel. This rule is purely conventional, like saluting only with the right hand: we can say "an cup" or "a elephant" without much difficulty, and we can learn quite different conventions in other languages. For example, in French there are also two forms of the indefinite article: *un* and *une*. But which of these is used depends upon the gender of the noun and not upon the sound of the following word; thus, *un père,* 'a father,' but *une mère,* 'a mother.' Our modern English rules for saying "a" or "an" are the result of a long process of language history. In fact, a thousand years ago, Old English had only the form *ān*, 'one,' which was rarely used as an article. This is why we say that linguistic rules are "conventional understandings" and a part of culture.

SOUND SYSTEMS

In trying to understand the *sound system* of a language, we must not be misled by written forms. We have already seen that the letter *a* in the words "a" and "an" may represent three different sounds. Consider the following geographic areas: Africa, Asia, Australia, America, Arctic. How many of these words begin with the same sound? If you carefully pronounce each one of them aloud, you will have to agree that each *a* sounds different from all the others (and different, too, from the first sound in the word "area").

In English (and in many other written languages) a letter may correspond to more than one sound. The converse is also true: a sound may be represented by more than one letter; for example, compare the initial sounds of the words "sir" and "circle," or of "phone" and "fan." A child who is learning to speak English may be completely unaware of the existence of the written language, and yet he does learn to speak and understand, taking account of all the *significant differences* among the sounds used in this language (just as human beings spoke for thousands of years before the invention of writing).

The important thing to learn is which *differences among sounds* always signal *differences of meaning.* Some of these contrasts are clearly represented in traditional spelling: "pat" is different from "bat" in its initial sound, while "bat" and "bet" differ in their vowels, and "bet" differs from "bed" in its final consonant. Since these pairs of words differ only in the quality of a single sound, they are called *minimal pairs.* Other pairs, such as "pat" and "bad" or "pat" and "bed," may differ in several or all of their sounds.

All English speakers agree that these differences are significant and that such phrases as "bat boy" and "bad boy" have different meanings. A few technical terms will actually make the point clearer. Both *t* and *d* are pronounced by *stopping* (and then releasing) the flow of air from the lungs by placing the tip of the tongue just above the teeth; thus these sounds are both called "front stops." But they differ in the quality known as *voicing*: the *d* is said to be "voiced" because the vocal cords are allowed to vibrate as it is pronounced (you can feel the vibration if you place your fingers lightly upon your pharynx); the *t* is "voiceless" because the vocal cords do not vibrate when it is pronounced.

The distinction between voiced and voiceless sounds, together with other differences produced by altering the position and muscular tension of the lips and tongue and by changing the shape of the vocal cavities—these are the basis of all significant sounds in the English language. For example, the sound represented by the letter *k* (and sometimes by *c*) is a voiceless stop, but it differs from the *t* sound in being pronounced with the back of the tongue against the back part of the mouth. The voiced stop produced with the tongue in this position is the *g*. These four sounds, then, are distinguished from one another as shown in Figure 2.1.

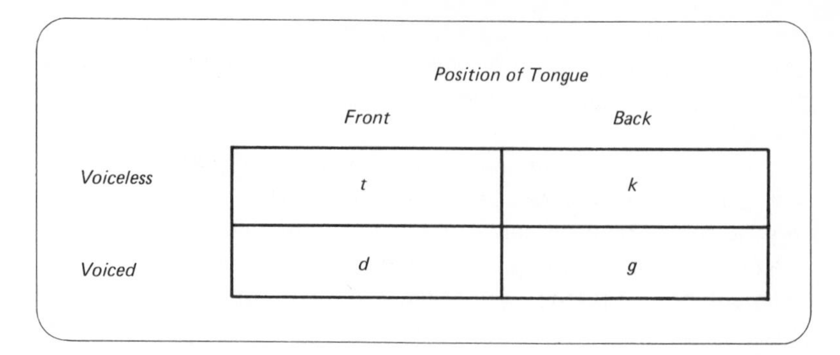

Figure 2.1 **Four English Stops**

Phonemes

The four stops discussed above are actually four *categories of sounds,* defined by the two attributes of tongue position (front or back) and voicing (voiced or voiceless). In English, if all other sounds are held constant, these attributes consistently make a difference in the meaning of words. We can show this by taking the four stops and placing them, one after another, at the beginning or end of certain syllables to produce different words (minimal pairs). Sound categories that can be shown to consistently make a difference in meaning are known as *phonemes.* By convention, the symbols for phonemes are enclosed between slashes (/t/, /d/, /k/, /g/) to distinguish them from the letters of the alphabet (see Figure 2.2).

A similar method can be used to show that our English letter *a* represents no less than five different *vowel phonemes.* If we take the initial sounds in the words "Africa," "Asia," "Australia," "America," and "Arctic," and insert them between the phonemes /t/ and /k/, we find that each change of vowel produces a word with a different meaning (see Figure 2.3).

The phonemes of a language are like the units of a code: they communicate specific meanings only when they are arranged in certain conventional patterns. That is, *although phonemes signal differences of meaning, they are not in themselves meaningful.* The phoneme /t/ has no more meaning than the phoneme /p/ or /æ/, but they may be put together into units that do communicate meanings, e.g., "tap," "pat," or "apt." What is important about a phoneme such as English /d/ is that it is different from all the other English phonemes: /d/ differs from /t/ because it is "voiced"; /d/ differs from /g/ because it is pronounced with the tongue forward; /d/ differs from /k/ on both of these counts; and it differs from all the vowels by virtue of its being a consonant.

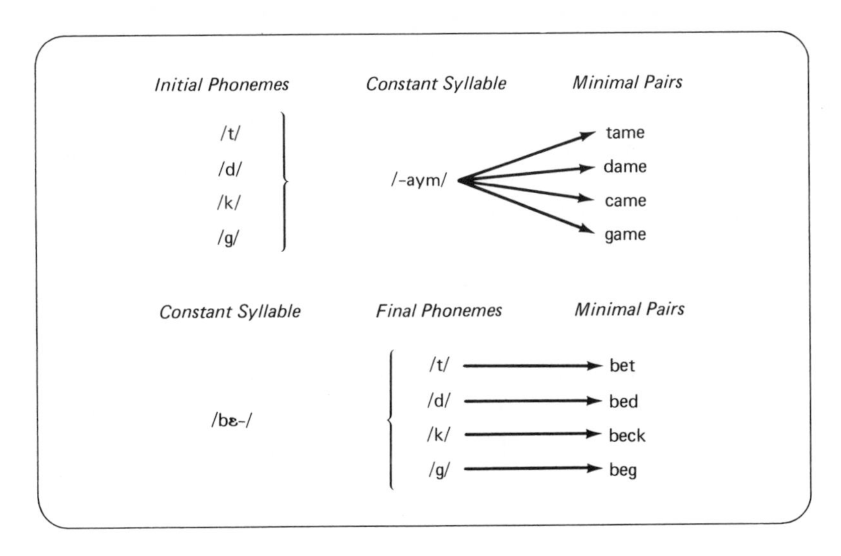

Figure 2.2 **Four English Consonant Phonemes**

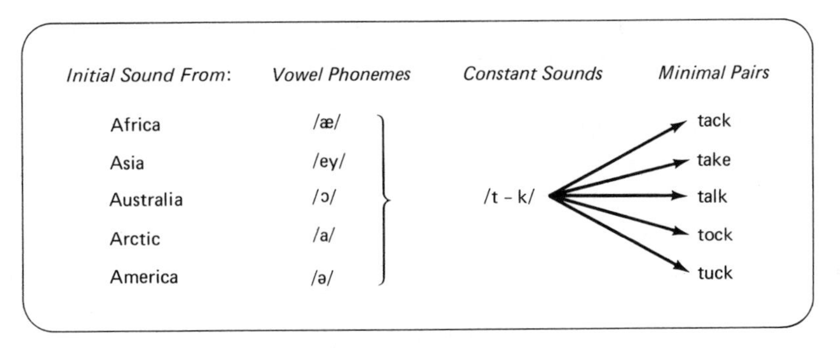

Figure 2.3 **Five English Vowel Phonemes**

Because English speakers have *learned to pay attention* to differences in voicing and tongue position, we are able to attach different meanings to patterns of phonemes such as /bed/ vs. /bet/ and /dot/ vs. /tot/. But /d/ and /t/ do not, in themselves, mean anything, any more than do the dots and dashes of a radio code. The study of sound systems is called *phonology.*

In many languages of Asia, Africa, and Middle America the *tone* or pitch with which parts of a word are pronounced affects its meaning. In Navajo (as in Mandarin Chinese) there are four tones (low, high, rising, and falling), and the Navajo word for "war" differs from their word for "eye" only by the presence of a high tone on the final vowel of the latter. Of course, pitch is also used in English to indicate some differences of meaning (for example, in the command "Go home" versus the question "Go home?"), but we do not use tone to signal differences of meaning between minimal pairs of words.

The voicing of consonants is so fundamental to the English sound system that it is hard for us to believe that other languages might not make use of this quality. Many American Indian languages get along quite well without it. In such languages, if there is a consonant phoneme pronounced with the lips—let us call it /B/—it will sometimes sound to us like a *p* and other times like a *b,* but no consistent difference in meaning will be attached to this variation.

On the other hand, there are many languages that consistently require speakers to make distinctions that are unimportant in English. For example, in English words that start with /t/ followed by a vowel, the /t/ is accompanied by a little extra puff of air. This quality is called *aspiration*: you can detect it by holding a piece of tissue near your mouth as you say the word "till." When the /t/ is preceded by an /s/, however, the aspiration automatically disappears. Compare your pronunciation of "till" and "still." The /t/ in "still" is said to be *unaspirated.* English speakers are not usually aware of this distinction, and it is never used to signal differences of meaning in English; in many other languages, however, aspiration is extremely important.

What does this mean in practice? Let us take four distinct sounds and see how they are classified in two hypothetical languages. All four sounds are frontal stops produced with the tip of the tongue, but two are voiced and two are aspirated:

t	unvoiced; unaspirated
t′	unvoiced; aspirated
d	voiced; unaspirated
d′	voiced; aspirated

In Language I, *voicing is phonemic* but aspiration is not (as in English). In Language II, however, *aspiration is phonemic* while voicing is not. As can be seen in Figure 2.4, each of these two languages will categorize these same four sounds into two phonemes, but each will do it in a different way. It should be obvious that speakers of Language I who try to learn Language II will have some trouble learning to hear the difference in aspiration while learning not to pay attention to the irrelevant difference in voicing. On the other hand, native speakers of Language II who attempt to

---

1. L. Bloomfield, *Language* (London: Allen and Unwin, 1935), p. 116.

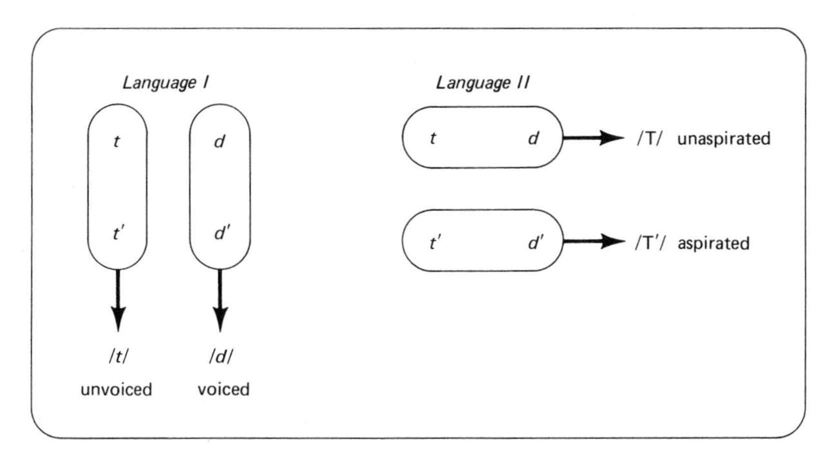

Figure 2.4 **Phoneme Categories in Two Hypothetical Languages**

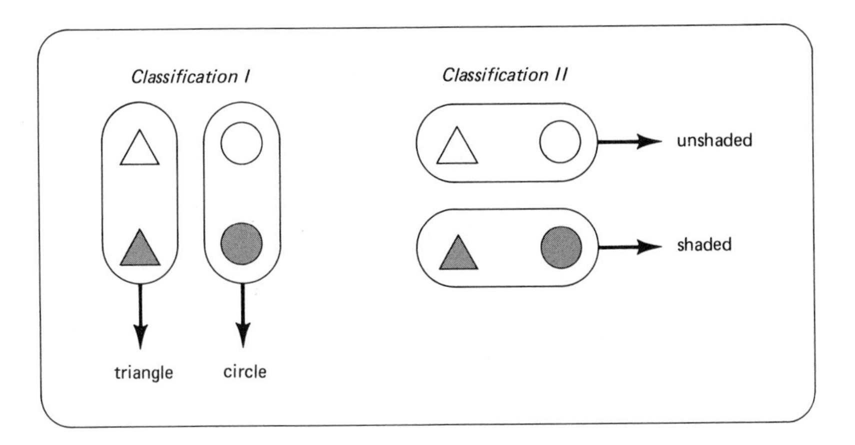

Figure 2.5 **Alternative Categories**

learn Language I will have to learn to hear and control their pronunciation of voiced and unvoiced stops—a feature that signals nothing in their own language.

The grouping of sounds into phonemes is a process of categorization in which certain attributes (qualities) of the sounds are used and others ignored. The example above is identical in principle to the alternative ways of grouping pairs of objects on the basis of their formal attributes, as shown in Figure 2.5. (Compare pp. 22–24, above.) Each of these ways of categorizing is *equally arbitrary* and *equally valid*, for there is nothing natural about the decision to use shape and ignore shading (Classification I) or to use shading and ignore shape (Classification II). Nor is it more natural to use both shape and shading, though these two attributes together would give us a four-way classification of objects equivalent to the classification of English stops in Figure 2.1.

Combinations of Phonemes

The number of phonemes in a natural language is usually between twenty and sixty. (English has about thirty-five). But whether the number of phonemes is large or small, these sound categories are never random selections from the possible vocal noises human beings can produce. Rather, the categories are defined in a *systematic way*: if the attribute of voicing is used to differentiate one pair of phonemes (/t/ vs. /d/), you can be pretty sure that it will be used to differentiate other pairs (/p/ vs. /b/, /k/ vs. /g/, /s/ vs. /z/, and so forth).

The phoneme categories are only one part of the sound system of a language. Along with the system of categories, there must also be a set of *plans*—instructions as to how the phonemes may be put together into larger units. These plans must be learned in the same way as the categories, for even languages that have very similar phonemes do not necessarily allow them to be combined in the same ways. In some languages, sequential clusters of vowels are never allowed; in others, long strings of consonants (which we would consider unpronounceable) are characteristic of most words. (Some consonant clusters occur at the ends of English words that are never found at the beginnings: listen to your own pronunciation of the word "asked" or "tastes.")

The linguist Benjamin Lee Whorf constructed an involved formula that shows exactly which combinations of phonemes are allowed to occur in English words of one syllable.[2] This formula can be shown to predict all English monosyllabic words, with the exception of some recent loans from foreign languages that are still pronounced (by some people) in the foreign way. Even more interesting, however, is the fact that the formula also predicts many words that do not now form part of the English language. Some of these happen to be archaic forms which are no longer used; others are "combining forms" which appear only as parts of larger words; but most of them must be regarded as "potential syllables" which the English sound system would allow to occur alone but which do not happen (at present) to have any generally accepted meanings. Proof of this assertion may be seen in the fact that recently coined monosyllabic words, whether trade names

2. B. L. Whorf, "Linguistics as an Exact Science," in J. Carroll, ed., *Language, Thought, and Reality* (Cambridge: The M.I.T. Press, 1956), pp. 220–232.

("Fab") or slang ("mods"), are all predicted by Whorf's formula, which was originally devised in 1940. It is unlikely that a product designed for English-speaking consumers would be named "Zbulft."

The sound system of a language, then, does two important things: (1) It *selects* from the range of possible human sounds a limited number of qualities (for example, voicing) which are systematically used to define differences among a somewhat larger number of signaling units (phonemes). This defines the categories (of sounds) that a speaker of the language must learn to recognize and to produce. (2) It *limits* the ways in which these categories may be combined by providing rules to govern the construction of larger units. These plans for speaking help to make human behavior more predictable. But while they limit what we may say, they also provide patterns for the creation of new forms.

LANGUAGE AND SPEECH

Before we proceed to a description of the next level of language, two more extremely important distinctions must be made and illustrated. In discussing the nature of sound systems, we have been dealing with abstract categories and plans that are characteristic of *language* as opposed to *speech.* The units of language (phonemes, and so forth) are *inferred* from observations of actual speech, and speech is astonishingly variable. As noted above, careful measurements show that it is impossible to pronounce a word in exactly the same way twice. Thus when we say that two pronunciations of "bat" are the same word, we mean that we recognize the recurrence of three phonemes, /b/, /æ/, and /t/, in the same sequence; but at the same time we are ignoring all kinds of differences in voice qualities such as pitch, loudness, breathiness, and speed. These nonphonemic differences are in the realm of *speech.* By speech we mean that necessarily variable behavior which manifests the abstract categories and plans of the language. The relationship between speech and language is a special case of the relationship between behavior and culture.

In trying to understand the regularities in speech behavior, the linguist distinguishes two kinds of variation. *Free variation* refers to differences in pronunciation for which no rules can be discovered. This includes the uncontrollable variations that creep in even when we try to speak consistently (and that can be detected only with training), as well as the audible variation that seems to have no significance. An example of the latter is the word "economics." There are two audibly different (and equally acceptable) ways of pronouncing the first vowel in this word; some people even switch from one to the other sound in the same sentence; but no detectable difference in meaning is attached to the change.

The second kind is known as *conditioned variation.* This refers to differences in pronunciation of which the speaker may or may not be aware, but for which some kind of rule can be found. The linguist tries to explain as much variation as possible by showing that it is conditioned (regularly caused) by something else in the language system. For example, we have seen that English speakers produce an unaspirated /t/ when this sound follows an /s/ (as in "still"), while in most other positions the /t/ is aspirated. This is an automatic and thus conditioned variation in the phoneme, and so we say that /t/ has two phonetic *allophones, t* and *t'.* (Allophones are audibly different sounds which "belong to" the same phoneme category.) We can go on to state the rule that the allophone *t* follows /s/ and the allophone *t'* is found elsewhere. Another example is seen in the variation of /k/ in the words "keen"—/kin/—and "cool"—/kul/. If you carefully note the position of your tongue while you pronounce these words, you will see that one type of /k/ is pronounced farther back in the mouth than is the other. There is a rule which relates the type of /k/ to the vowel that follows it. You might experiment a little and discover this rule (which you have been following all your life), but be careful not to be fooled by the traditional spelling of the words. (Hint: the name "King Kong" also has both types of /k/.)

Speech, then, is the actual behavior, whereas language is the set of rules (categories and plans) which explains the regularities observed in speech. Each person who learns a language (whether he is a two-year-old child or a sixty-year-old linguist) must infer the rules of the language from a sample of actual speech. Fortunately, man's brain is constructed to search for patterns in great quantities of perceptual data. But some regularities in speech behaviors can only be understood by going outside the language system itself to a careful examination of the social context and its influence upon speech. The new field of *sociolinguistics* is concerned with the interaction between language and society. It deals with such topics as speech variation due to social class, bilingualism, attitudes towards language, switching from one dialect to another, and the social context of linguistic change. More and more variation in speech behavior has been shown to be conditioned by sociolinguistic factors; but much free variation will always remain in speech behavior, if only because man is not just a talking machine.

GRAMMAR

We turn now from the study of sound systems, or phonology, to the topic of *grammar*. Few subjects can be duller than the study of the grammar of one's own language when it is poorly taught (and this has certainly been the rule rather than the exception). But grammar can be fascinating if it is taught in such a way as to make us conscious of the categories and plans which have been unconsciously shaping our own speech behavior for years. We will not be able to explore English grammar in any detail; rather, we will give an overview of the way in which grammars "work" and of the ways in which grammatical systems differ from one another.

Grammar is generally divided into two related parts. The first of these, *morphology*, deals with the construction of words. The second, *syntax*, deals with the construction of phrases, clauses, sentences, and other types of structures larger than words. These are not absolute divisions, but they are convenient for our purposes.

Morphology

A little thought will demonstrate that not all English words are of the same type. A word such as "bad" is a single unit and can be divided only into its three meaningless phonemes: /b/, /æ/, /d/. But a word such as "unthinkingly" has four distinct parts, known as *morphemes*; each of these parts is found in many other words and each carries a particular meaning, so that even if you had never heard the word "unthinkingly" before, you could form a pretty good idea of its meaning from the respective meanings of {un-}, {think}, {-ing}, and {-ly}. (The braces indicate morphemes.) Furthermore, the parts of a word are not simply thrown together, for other combinations of these same parts such as "lythinkuning" or "ingthinklyun" are unacceptable (ungrammatical) in the judgment of all English speakers.

Morphology, then, is concerned with the smallest meaningful parts of a language, the morphemes, and with the ways in which these simple morphemes may be combined to form complex words. (It is possible to think of each morpheme as a category whose defining attributes are a number of phonemes in a standard arrangement and which is associated with a definite meaning. The plans connected with such morpheme categories have to do with the ways in which these units may be combined into larger structures.)[3] The number of morphemes in any given language is finite

3. Roger W. Brown, "Language and Categories," in J. S. Bruner *et al.*, *A Study of Thinking* (New York: Science Editions, 1962), pp. 247–312.

but still large enough to make vocabulary learning a real job. As we have seen, morphemes are composed of one or more phonemes *in a conventional order* (/pæt/, /tæp/, and /æpt/ are not the same, and /ptæ/ is not even an English morpheme). Since the association between sound and meaning is also conventional, the primary way of learning the morphemes and their meanings is by memorizing them. However, the plans for putting morphemes together are much more general and, once learned, can be applied to many groups of morphemes to produce words.

One way to study the morphemes of a language is to divide them into *roots* and *affixes.* The root is that part of a word which carries the basic meaning, while the affixes modify this meaning in various ways. For example, the comparative and superlative degrees of English are usually formed by adding to an adjective root the affixes *-er* or *-est.* Since these affixes follow the root, they are called *suffixes.* Affixes that precede the root, such as English *non-,* are known as *prefixes.* In the example above, "think" is clearly the root, while the three affixes must be added in the correct position and even in a specific sequence (that is, we can say "thinking" but not "unthink").

Another type of affix which is seldom used in English is common in the morphology of some other languages (especially the Semitic languages, such as Hebrew and Arabic). This type of affix comes in the middle of the root and is called appropriately an *infix.* The closest thing we have to it in English is a few verbs that form their past tense by changing their root vowel, for example, "swim" to "swam" and "run" to "ran."

One way in which the morphologies of languages differ, then, is in the kinds of affixes they utilize. Most Arabic roots are made up of three consonants and require one or more vowel infixes to complete them: for example, the root *ḳ-l-b* may be completed by infixes such as *-a-* to yield *kalb,* "heart," or *u-uu* to yield *ḳuluub,* "hearts." Other languages, such as Turkish, make extensive use of suffixes (as many as ten affixes may *follow* a Turkish verb root) but make little or no use of prefixes or infixes. English makes much use of suffixes and limited use of prefixes.

Languages may differ in the extent to which they permit *compounding*—that is, the combining of two or more *roots* into a single word. English allows some (for example, "blackbird," "blockhead"), and German is famous for its long compounds which may contain half a dozen different roots (for example, *das Lebensversicherungsgesellschaftsfräulein,* "the insurance-company receptionist"), but some languages never use this type of plan for word-building.

Languages also differ in the amount and kinds of information that can (or must) be carried by a single word. Take, for example, the *grammatical categories* of number and gender. In English, with only a few exceptions (for example, "sheep"), it is impossible to use a noun without indicating whether it is singular or plural. On the other hand, though some English words are inherently masculine or feminine ("cow," "king") and though third person singular pronouns indicate gender ("he," "she," "him," "her," "his"), most English words do not indicate gender, and gender is lost in the third person plural pronouns ("they," "them," "their"). We are so used to this arrangement that it seems quite natural to us; only comparison with the morphology of other languages can show how arbitrary the English system really is. Thus, in French, every noun is inherently either masculine or feminine; but in spoken French the gender can be detected only by the sound of the words (articles, adjectives) that accompany the noun and that must agree with it in gender and number. As in English, much of this information is lost in the plural forms, though the French third person plural pronouns do distinguish between "they (masc.)," *ils,* and "they (fem.)," *elles.*

In Spanish, however, the number and gender of most nouns must be indicated twice: first in the article which agrees with the noun, and again in a suffix added to the noun root which indicates whether it is singular or plural, masculine or feminine; for example, *los gatos,* "the (masc. plural) cats (masc. plural)." Furthermore, since the grammatical category of person in Spanish is clearly indicated by the verb, subject pronouns are rarely used: *Salió sin sombrero,* "[He, she, or it] went out (third person subject) without [a] hat (masc. sing.)." At the same time, object pronouns are often incorporated into the verb as suffixes: *Están escribiéndosela,* "[They] are (plural subject) writing-to-him/her-it."

These last examples have been taken from languages that are related to English and which the reader may himself have studied. When we turn to non–Indo-European languages, the differences are still more striking. Some languages, such as Chinese, allow no modification of a root, so that each word consists of a single morpheme. Others, like Turkish, string a great many affixes onto a root, but all of these parts of the word remain quite distinct. In some languages (including many American Indian tongues), the word is immensely complex: roots and affixes have a variety of different forms; when the parts of a word are put together, they modify one another so that sounds are changed in quality or completely lost; subtle nuances of meaning are expressed in a bewildering variety of ways; and single words carry meanings that English speakers would have to express in quite lengthy phrases. For example, in Navajo there is a single word, *baadeeshʔááł,* which we must translate as "I will give him one (solid) object (which is roundish in shape)." The root of this Navajo word is

ʔáát, meaning something like "to handle a single roundish solid object."

In analyzing and describing the morphology of a language, the linguist attempts to discover and clearly set forth some of the rules that govern speech behavior. From the apparently chaotic variability of a spoken language, he infers both categories of morphemes and plans for word-building. Since the morphology of every language, whether simple or complex, is systematic, he is able, little by little, to demonstrate regularities and describe rules.

Take a relatively simple example with which all English speakers are familiar: the formation of the plural of English nouns. How is this accomplished? If you are still dominated by the written form of language, you will probably respond: By adding an *s.* But think a moment. Of course, there are exceptions: "ox : oxen," "child : children," "deer : deer," and so on. But these are few and can simply be listed. Now listen carefully to your pronunciation of the following forms: "hats," "bags," "taps," "lads," "racks," "roses." If you go on experimenting, you will find that most English nouns form their plurals by adding one of three different sounds, *-s, -z,* or *-əz,* and that there is a simple rule (depending upon the final sound of the singular noun root) that tells you which of these sounds to add. The interesting point is that you have been following this rule all your life without being consciously aware of it.

Creating plural forms by suffixation seems to us the most natural thing in the world; again, only comparison can show how much a matter of convention this particular morphological device is. Hebrew creates most plurals by adding the suffixes *-im* or *-ot,* but which of these is chosen depends upon the inherent gender of the root, not its final sound. Many languages get along very nicely without any plural affix, and their speakers think it rather silly of us to insist on saying "two books" when the idea of plurality is carried by the numeral and "two book" would presumably do as well. Other languages may designate plurality (or singularity) by prefixes or by change of tone or of vowels (as we do in "man : men"), while still others, such as Homeric Greek, distinguish other types of number, for example, singular, dual (two), and plural (more than two). Is one of these systems "better" than the others? No. All of them communicate quite clearly in their own terms. Each morphological system *selects* from the possible ways of combining morphemes and *limits* the ways in which various concepts may be expressed in speech.

Morphemes are contrasted with one another in two general ways. As formal categories, they may be contrasted in terms of their formal attributes—that is, the phonemes of which they are composed. Thus the phoneme sequences /big/ and /pig/ represent different morphemes, and the difference is manifested in the phonemic distinction between /p/ and /b/. But morphemes may also be contrasted in terms of their distributional attributes—that is, the plans that govern their occurrence with other morphemes. For example, "pig" and "big" also differ in that, given the frame "The —— is ——," we know that English syntax permits us to insert "pig" into the first blank and "big" into the second; but "*The big is pig" is ungrammatical. (An asterisk before a linguistic form indicates that it is not used in normal speech or that it represents a reconstructed form.)

The concept of *distribution* is difficult to grasp, but it is important both in linguistics and in the general theory underlying this text. The *distribution of a morpheme* means, most simply, the *contexts* in which it is expected to occur—the other categories of morphemes with which it is found. For example, the plural morpheme only occurs following the category of morphemes called *nouns.* Conversely, if a given word "takes" the plural morpheme (in any of its alternate forms), that word is a noun. Similarly, the past tense morpheme {-ed} occurs as a suffix with *verbs,* and a word that "takes" this suffix belongs in the category of verbs.

Syntax

A fuller understanding of the importance of distribution will require some discussion of the next higher level of language structure, *syntax.* The study of syntax involves the discovery and statement of the rules (plans) according to which the speakers of a language combine words into larger grammatical structures: phrases, clauses, and sentences. There is considerable controversy among linguists at present about the nature of these rules, but some facts are clear. It has been demonstrated that although the number of morphemes is finite, the number of possible grammatical sentences is infinite.[4] This fact has several important implications: it means that we do *not* simply memorize a large number of sentences in learning a language; rather, we learn patterns or plans for speaking. These plans enable us to combine categories of morphemes in such a way that we can understand (and be understood) even if the particular sentence has never before been produced by a speaker of English.

The syntactic rules of human languages are just as conventional and vary just as much as the morphological or phonological rules. For example, in English we rely quite heavily upon *word*

4. N. Chomsky, *Syntactic Structures* (The Hague: Mouton, 1957).

order to tell us who did what to whom. In the sentence "The girl hit the boy," we know that the aggressor is female and the victim male because "girl" precedes the verb; the meaning is clearly different from "The boy hit the girl." But in many languages the *grammatical relations* of subject and object are indicated by affixes, so that word order is less relevant to syntactic meaning. In Latin, for example, the relations of subject and object are indicated by suffixes, so that the order in which they are mentioned makes little difference.

Syntactic rules govern *agreement* among the parts of a sentence. We know that the English verb must agree in person and number with its subject (for example, I am, you are, he is, they are). In Hebrew, the verb must also agree in *gender* with its subject, so there would be different verb forms for "he says" and "she says." But in Navajo, there must be agreement between the verb and the *shape of its object*: a different verb stem must be selected if one is talking about long and thin or flat or round objects. For example, ʔał means 'to lose or toss something,' but only if the something is a flat, flexible object; if it is round or bulky, one must use the verb stem *niił*. Finally, in French both articles and adjectives must agree with the gender (and number) of the noun they modify: thus, since "book" is considered a masculine noun and "table" a feminine one, one must say *un livre blanc,* 'a (masc.) book white (masc.),' and *une table blanche,* 'a (fem.) table white (fem.).'

Syntax also provides patterns for changing verbs into nouns ("hit" to "the hitter"; or "burn" to "the burning"), and for making questions out of statements and negatives out of positives. Such rules may be simple or complex. For example, in Spanish most negatives are formed by simply putting the word *no* in front of a positive statement, and questions have the same word order as non-questions. But in English we must often rearrange the wording of a statement to make it into a question or a negative: "*He went* to the game" becomes "*Did he go* to the game?" or "*He didn't go* to the game." To form a negative in the Micmac Indian language, one must use both a negative word *(mo)* before the verb and one of several negative suffixes after the verb root, as if we were to say: "No, he went-not."

With a great deal of hard, careful work, it is possible to work out a set of syntactic rules which will account for the regularities in a long list of English (or Spanish, or Navajo) sentences. But most linguists today have an even more difficult goal than this: they would like to discover rules which would represent the *knowledge* of a native speaker, including his ability to produce and interpret sentences he has never heard before. Such a "generative grammar" would do for the sentences of a language what Whorf's formula does for the syllables of English: it would predict all the grammatical sentences of a language. This goal is important because it calls attention to the most remarkable property of human languages: their productivity. *Productivity* refers to the fact that, given a few dozen phonemes, a few thousand morphemes, and a set of morphological and syntactic rules, *an infinite number of grammatical sentences* can be constructed, and people who share this abstract language will be able to correctly interpret all of these sentences, including those which they have never heard before.

The problem of how linguistic productivity can be best represented by syntactic rules is a highly complicated one which need not concern us here.[5] But we must recognize that this problem is similar to other important problems in ethnography and social anthropology. Much of human behavior (aside from speech) is governed by conventional rules; this does not mean, however, that we endlessly repeat the same actions. Social rules are also productive. We are constantly engaged in interpreting the (novel) actions of our fellows and judging them as socially appropriate or inappropriate, just as we understand novel utterances and judge them as grammatical or ungrammatical. Productivity is a property of all cultural systems, for in language, technology, or social structure, the rules that limit behavior also provide patterns for new responses (see Epilogue: Culture and Freedom).

SEMANTICS

No survey of the nature of human language would be complete without some reference to the field of *semantics*. Semantics deals with all of the questions that are implicit in the phrase "Morphemes carry meaning." What is meaning? What does it mean to say something carries meaning? How can meaning be described, except by using morphemes whose meaning is already known? And how can we best describe and understand changes in the meaning of a morpheme? These and many other semantic questions are among the most difficult problems of modern linguistics.

The anthropologists must constantly deal with "semantic questions," both in trying to understand the meaning of words and actions in an alien culture and in trying to communicate what he has learned to other scientists. This is a process of translation,

5. See P. Postal, "Constituent Structure: A Study of Contemporary Models of Syntactic Description," *International Journal of American Linguistics*, Vol. 30, No. 1, Part III (1964), pp. 1–122.

and it calls for a sensitive appreciation of *both* languages and cultures. Even when the language is English, there are ample opportunities for misunderstanding. For example, most Americans use the term "breakfast" to refer to a light meal eaten early in the morning. On the island of Jamaica, however, this term is used with several different meanings. Middle-class Jamaicans eat "breakfast" in the morning, but it is a much more substantial meal than in the United States; their lightest meal (called "supper") is eaten in the late evening—sometimes after ten. Poor Jamaicans (estate laborers or peasant farmers) eat their lightest meal early in the morning, but they call it "tea"; for them, "breakfast" is a medium-to-heavy meal eaten at midday!

When even familiar words may have so many different meanings, how can the anthropologist or linguist get at the meanings of words in an unfamiliar language and culture? The basic answer to this is that they learn in the same general way as the little child who must learn how to speak not only grammatically but also *appropriately.* The sentences "That is my dog" and "That is my father" are both grammatical, but normally only one will be appropriate to a given situation. Children learn the correct use (the meanings) of words by observing the speech acts in their social environments, by trying to understand and make themselves understood, and by being corrected (or ignored) when they speak incorrectly.

Words that refer to concrete objects are probably the easiest to learn, and the young child does show a great fascination with the names of things—to the point of driving his parents crazy. The anthropologist, too, can ask, "What's this?" or "What's that?" as soon as he learns how to ask questions; but it is much more difficult to ask the right questions about objects or events that are not physically present: also, many words do not refer to anything concrete (consider the many meanings of the word "on" in English phrases such as "on time," "on the air," "put on," "on the table," and "on your own"). Fortunately, in all languages words fall into classes (categories) which share certain meanings (plans for use), and the learner can try to discover the systematic contrasts within and between these classes.

Words may be classified in a number of different ways. A classification based upon *form* might lump together all words starting with a given vowel or ending in some cluster of consonants, while a classification based upon *distribution* would yield classes, say, of active verbs or of noun suffixes. Semantic classes, on the other hand, consist of words (or morphemes) that have similar *meanings*; such classes are sometimes called *domains,* and linguists speak of the "domain of kinship term" ("father," "brother," "aunt," and so on) or of the "domain of animal names." Some of the most interesting work in anthropological semantics has been done in the domain of color terminology.

Every known language has a group of semantically related words dealing with color. These words divide up the visible spectrum into a limited number of categories; but since the color spectrum is continuous, any division of it into discrete parts must be partly conventional. (According to the Optical Society of America, under laboratory conditions, human beings are able to distinguish as many as ten million different "colors," so the need for *some* sort of classification is apparent.)

One method developed for studying the domain of color terms is to present a speaker of Language X with a large number of standard "color chips," and to ask him to *sort* them into piles of the same color. He is then asked, "What do you call this color (category) in Language X?" Finally, for each color term he is asked to pick the one color chip that is most characteristic of that color (the "focus" of the term).[6]

Application of this method to dozens of languages from all over the world has revealed several surprising points. First of all, the number of *basic color terms* (such as our "red," "green," and "blue," but not "scarlet" or "lavender") ranges from two to eleven. In languages with only two terms, one term labels the whole range of "light" colors and the other term the "dark" colors. (There may be additional specific color terms, but these always refer to limited types of objects, for example, "red soil.") The boundaries of the two color terms may vary from language to language, as do the words used to label the categories, but the *focus* of each term is always the same—respectively, "white" and "black." This last statement may be generalized to more complex systems of terms: for systems with *n* color categories, the boundaries between categories may vary considerably, and the words associated with each category are conventional, but the focus of each of the corresponding categories will be very similar (if not identical).

Furthermore, if we arrange these systems in order of increasing complexity, it turns out that each additional category appears in a *regular order.* That is, a three-term system always adds "red" to the light/dark contrast; four-term systems have the first three plus either "yellow" or "green," and five-term systems include all of these. In sixth place comes a "blue" term, which distinguishes a range of colors that five-term systems include in their "green" and "dark" ranges, while the seventh term added is

6. B. Berlin and P. Kay, *Basic Color Terms* (Berkeley: University of California Press, 1969).

always some variety of "brown." Except for the varying order of appearance of yellow and green, this sequence seems to be *universal.* That is, any language which has a term for "blue" will also have terms for (at least) the five earlier colors. (Beyond seven terms, the order of appearance of basic terms for gray, pink, orange, or purple appears to be quite irregular.)

Let us look at one specific terminological system—that of the Hanunóo, a tribal people of the Philippines, whose culture has been carefully described by Harold C. Conklin.[7] The Hanunóo are a horticultural people who make extensive use of the plants in their tropical environment. They have dozens of specific color terms, but each of these fits into one of the categories labeled by four basic color terms (Figure 2.6):

Clearly this is a system of color categories very different from our own. Conklin was able to show that their system is based on a number of distinctive attributes which are very important to the Hanunóo. For example, the contrast between *marara?* and *malatuy* is of particular significance in terms of the plants upon which these people depend for most of their food: *malatuy* means not only greenness but also something like succulence, and to a Hanunóo it is opposed to *marara?* not only as a range of colors, but also as indicating freshness as opposed to dried-up, mature, or desiccated organic material.

Color Term	*Translation*	*Range of Colors in English*
1. mabi: ru	relative darkness, blackness	black, violet, indigo, blue, dark green, dark gray, and deep shades of other colors and mixtures
2. malagti?	relative lightness, whiteness	white and very light tints of other colors and mixtures
3. marara?	relative presence of red, redness	maroon, red, orange, yellow, and mixtures in which these colors are seen to predominate
4. malatuy	relative presence of light greenness, greenness	light green and mixtures of green, yellow, and light brown

***Figure* 2.6 Hanunóo Color Categories (after Conklin)**

7. H. C. Conklin, "Hanunóo Color Categories," *Southwestern Journal of Anthropology*, Vol. 11 (1955), pp. 339–344.

This brings us to the last general point of this chapter. Just as some kinds of persons in our own society—for example, artists and interior decorators—have a more extensive color vocabulary than does the average citizen, *the kinds of semantic distinctions made by a language system reflect the interests and concerns of the people using that system.* This point is often graphically phrased as "the Eskimo have four different words for snow." But it is equally enlightening to note that English speakers get along with a single term for the kinds of snow that the Eskimo conventionally label with separate morphemes. If an English speaker had to survive in the Arctic with the technology available to an Eskimo, he would doubtless find it necessary to distinguish many of these kinds of snow, and he might end up inventing (or borrowing from the Eskimo) terms to help him keep the differences in mind. (People who ski or who are involved in winter sports as a business usually have an extensive "snow vocabulary." It would be a good exercise in semantic analysis to investigate these terms and their contrasting meanings.)

In conclusion, we have seen that by learning a language, man acquires ways of categorizing sounds, and plans for putting these categories together into more and more complex structures: morphemes, words, phrases, sentences, poems, stories, and so on. Associated with these complex structures is something we call meaning, so that as a person learns a language, he also receives a traditional way of perceiving and dealing with the world. Language aids him in making discriminations and in formulating complicated plans which would probably be impossible in its absence. Through the medium of language, man learns the traditions of his society, including what is expected of him in circumstances he has not yet met. He learns of past events (which may or may not have taken place) and of supernatural forces (which may or may not exist). Alfred Korzybski called man "the time-binding animal," pointing out that through language, man (and only man) gains an awareness of his history and the possibilities of his future.[8] (To get some notion of what men would be like without these capabilities, reread the description of institutionalized idiots in the Introduction to Part Two.)

But language is only one part of culture, and a child is affected by the traditions of his group both before he is born and for some time before he begins to understand or to speak its language, in the next chapter we shall discuss the ways in which culture may influence behavior prior to the acquisition of language.

---

8. A. Korzybski, *Science and Sanity* (Lancaster, Pa.: Institute of General Semantics, 1933).

RECOMMENDED READING

Burling, R., *Man's Many Voices.* New York: Holt, Rinehart and Winston, 1970. A brief survey of many of the most recent developments in anthropological linguistics and sociolinguistics.

Fishman, J., *Sociolinguistics: A Brief Introduction.* Rowley, Mass.: Newbury House, 1971. A survey of basic concepts of sociolinguistics by one of the founders of the field.

Greenberg, J. H., *Anthropological Linguistics.* New York: Knopf, 1968. A thoughtful discussion of linguistic science in relation to anthropological problems.

Hall, R. A., Jr., *Linguistics and Your Language.* New York: Anchor Books, 1960. A clear and amusing introduction to the basic concepts of descriptive linguistics.

Hill, Thomas E., *The Concept of Meaning.* New York: Humanities Press, 1971. A clear exposition by a philosopher of the various competing theories of semantics, the "meaning of meaning."

Hymes, D. H., ed., *Language in Culture and Society.* New York: Harper and Row, 1964. A large and well-chosen selection of articles by outstanding authors on various aspects of language in relation to society and culture, with an outstanding bibliography.

CHAPTER 3
The Process of Enculturation

Each growing child learns the language(s) of his community by *imitation* and *instruction,* and by *inference* from the verbal behavior of others. Language is a highly structured system and language acquisition is largely an unconscious process, so that most children are able to speak with great skill by about six years of age. But each individual continues to add to his linguistic competence and skills throughout life: he learns new vocabulary (technical terms or slang), masters different dialects, and develops a personal style of speech which expresses his individuality at the same time it indicates his social position.

Learning a language, then, parallels the more general process of learning a culture. *Enculturation* is a lifelong process in which imitation, verbal instruction, and inference all play a part. Probably no individual ever knows all the elements that make up his culture; but by the time he is fully grown he has usually learned the common core of beliefs shared by most members of his society (see Chapter 10, especially p. 324), and he has learned the culturally prescribed ways of organizing his knowledge and of adding to it.

The ability of human beings to develop and transmit complex cultural patterns is clearly dependent upon language. Verbal labels facilitate the learning of categories, and by means of language one may learn how to behave in circumstances that one has not yet encountered. The development of writing vastly extended man's ability to communicate and to store his ideas. But a great deal of learning also takes place before a child begins to understand the language of his group. This chapter is concerned with the various kinds of prelinguistic and extralinguistic learning and with the ways in which what is learned in the early and later stages of enculturation differs from society to society.

EARLY STAGES OF ENCULTURATION

The traditions of a society begin to affect a child before he is born. Recent research indicates that the unborn child is not the passive parasite that he has long been thought to be; rather, the child in the womb is aware of light and darkness, hears and responds to loud noises, feels and reacts to pain, sucks his thumb, and actually drinks the amniotic fluid.[1] All societies have beliefs about unborn children and interpret the various signs of pregnancy in traditional ways. Pregnant women are expected to behave in special ways: to exercise, rest, sleep in certain positions, eat (or refrain from eating) certain foods, avoid unpleasant sights or upsetting experiences, or (commonly) abstain from sexual relations for a period of time. Relatively little is known about the long-term consequences of such stimuli upon the developing child, but it seems highly likely that the behavior (and particularly the diet) of a pregnant woman has some effects on the fetus. Some kinds of maternal behavior clearly affect the unborn child. Inadequate nutrition for the mother greatly increases the likelihood of spontaneous abortion or of stillbirth. Venereal disease is transmitted to the unborn child; children have been born addicted to various narcotics, while the effects of synthetic drugs such as thalidomide upon the developing fetus can be most serious.

Contemporary American culture includes a wide variety of beliefs about how an expectant mother should behave. Some of these beliefs have a sound scientific basis and (when they are followed) can be shown to benefit both the mother and her unborn child. For example, it is generally believed that a woman expecting a baby should drink cow's milk during the latter part of her pregnancy; medical experiments have shown the importance of milk (or some other good source of protein and calcium) to the baby's development.

Other common American beliefs seem to make sense, but their scientific validity is still unproved, and contrasting beliefs in

---

1. M. Liley and B. Day, "New Discoveries about an Old Miracle," *McCalls* (August 1965), pp. 92–93, 134–136.

other cultural systems should make us suspend judgment about effects. For example, in the United States (and in most European countries), a woman close to her time of delivery is expected to avoid strenuous tasks: she will usually quit her job a few weeks before the baby is due, rest a good deal, avoid traveling or lifting heavy objects, and so forth. But in many other societies, a woman is expected to keep working at her usual tasks up to the last minute; some anthropological reports tell of women who "turn aside from the path" to bear their children, catching up with their companions soon after. (In some of these societies, the child's *father* then takes to bed to recover from the childbirth experience —a custom known as the *couvade.*)[2]

Finally, there are a number of current American beliefs which are very likely "mere" superstitions, although both similar and contrasting beliefs can be found in other cultures. For example, most Americans are at least familiar with the notion that one can tell the sex of a baby from its position in the womb or from its degree of activity (boys are thought to kick more); and many people feel that it is bad luck to buy or to send gifts of baby clothes before the child is born. Such beliefs are of dubious scientific validity, but they are nevertheless of great interest to the anthropologist, for they indirectly reveal facets of the culture which may not be consciously expressed—expectations about sex differences in behavior or anxieties about childbirth.

Even in the case of sensible or well-founded beliefs, however, there are several kinds of *variations in behavior* that are to be expected. To understand these, we must first ask just what we mean by the statement that certain beliefs or customs are "part of American culture." For the material discussed above, what we are saying is that American culture recognizes a *category of persons,* "women in late pregnancy," and associates with this category certain conventional *plans for action,* such as "drinking milk" and "avoiding strenuous tasks." Furthermore, most, if not all, adult Americans are aware of this category (though they may have different labels for it). They are also familiar with these plans for action, and the conventional association between the category and the plans—to the point where a comedian can get laughs by presenting himself in a sketch as drinking milk and not wanting to lift something "too heavy for his condition."

It is the thesis of this book that the categories and plans which compose a culture *influence* but do not determine the

2. See the comprehensive article on the couvade by John Whiting, Ruth Munroe, and Lee Munroe in the first issue of the new Journal *Ethos,* 1973.

behavior of the members of a society (see Introduction to Part Three). That is, the presence of a custom or the currency of a belief of any kind does not produce automatic compliance. Real behavior is always variable; the scientist looks for patterns and regularities, but he does this in part by analyzing the causes of variation in the behavior of his subjects.

The first source of behavioral variation is what we shall call *individual variability.* This kind of variability arises from the fact that since each individual has a different genetic make-up and a unique set of life experiences, he (or she) will respond to the expectations of his group in a way slightly different from any other person. One American woman might dislike or be allergic to cow's milk, and prefer to take calcium pills or drink an absolute minimum in a disguised form. Another might claim that she never feels more energetic than in the last weeks of pregnancy, and go on working or scrubbing floors until it is time to leave for the hospital.

A second source of behavioral variation is called *subcultural variability.* That is, within a society which "has" a certain belief or custom, there may be various subgroups with different or even completely opposed expectations. These subgroups may be social classes, ethnic groups, communities, age-groups, or even families (see Chapter 5, "Kinds of Groups"). To the extent that an individual values his membership in such subgroups, he will be influenced by their conventions. Thus, lower-class women may work longer into their pregnancy and drink less cow's milk than do middle-class women because the expectations of their friends and family are different; Chinese-American women may have learned from their parents the traditional Chinese distaste for cow's milk. But their behavior is not automatic, and awareness of subcultural variability may increase a person's options.

Finally, we should be aware of *temporal variability*: all cultures change over time, so behavior that is completely acceptable in one generation might have been unexpected or strongly condemned in an earlier generation, and vice versa. The value of drinking milk during pregnancy was once unrecognized in Western culture, just as doctors systematically killed thousands of young mothers by carrying the germs of puerperal fever from one childbed to the next, until Joseph Lister convinced them that it might help occasionally to wash their hands. Similarly, American customs regarding childbirth have recently undergone radical changes, such as the movement back to natural childbirth (including techniques long used in many simpler societies). The mere passage of time does not, of course, *explain* cultural change; but awareness of the fact of temporal variability should warn us against a static conception of culture.

Taking as examples several societies other than our own, let us briefly examine the different ways in which a child may be treated immediately after birth. The circumstances surrounding the process of birth itself differ greatly from place to place. The birth may be private and almost mysterious, with only the mother and a few female relatives in attendance, or it may be quite public with children and male relatives wandering in and out. There may be skilled midwives in attendance, or only a woman who has had "many children." The mother may have to do everything for herself or she may be subjected to a variety of manipulations and herbal concoctions to ease the birth and the passage of the placenta.

Among the Dinka of the Sudan (North Africa), children and men are excluded from the special hut in which delivery takes place. This is partly due to their distaste for witnessing the birth, but also because if the mother is having a difficult delivery, she will be encouraged to confess the names of her lovers. The Dinka believe that a difficult birth is usually a divine punishment for illicit sex; but they have alternative explanations available if the woman's reputation is "above reproach." In Dinka culture, birth establishes a spiritual tie between the child and the midwife who helps deliver it: this woman is called *geem,* meaning 'receiver, accepter,' that is, one who accepts God's gift to man (the child). According to Francis Deng, "As soon as the baby is born, the midwife sucks out the mucus from its nostrils to enable it to breathe. Because this necessity is so repulsive, it dramatizes the midwife's intense . . . devotion to the child and justifies her spiritual power over it."[3]

Immediately after birth, the infant may be subjected to a wide variety of experiences. He may be nursed or otherwise fed immediately, or he may be left without food for hours or days. He may be isolated or kept close to his mother continuously. He may be prayed over, anointed, admired, or perhaps killed. The custom of *infanticide* (child killing) is found in many societies. One need not approve of this custom to be an anthropologist, but it is necessary to suspend moral judgment while investigating such a practice and its consequences. In areas where economic resources are strictly limited, as on a small Pacific island, infanticide is perhaps best understood as a crude but effective method of population control. In such settings, it is usually accompanied by a belief that a child does not become fully human until it has received a

3. F. Deng, *The Dinka of the Sudan* (New York: Holt, Rinehart and Winston, 1972), p. 39. The author of this fine ethnography is himself a Dinka and a son of the former paramount chief.

name or had some other ritual performed for it; thus, infanticide may be regrettable, but it is not murder. (Compare the debates in contemporary American society on the moral and legal status of abortion at various stages of fetal development.) Other types of infanticide relate more to supernatural beliefs. In a few African societies, twins were considered so unlucky for the group as a whole that one or both of them would always be killed. On the other hand, the Dahomeans of West Africa felt that a birth of twins was the ideal, and that a child born alone had somehow "missed" his twin.

The newborn child may simply be wiped off with a leaf or a piece of fabric, but in most societies he soon receives a bath. American culture explicitly prescribes that the temperature of the bath water be close to the baby's body temperature to avoid a shock to his system, but other societies believe quite differently. In many places, children a few hours or days old are plunged into ice-cold water as a matter of course. Whether this "hardens" the child to discomfort or simply eliminates those who cannot endure it is unclear; but one recent study came to the surprising conclusion that in societies where such cold baths are administered, the average height of adults is considerably above what would be expected by chance. The shock to the system seems to be related to increased growth (at least for those who survive).

At the other extreme is the Dinka custom of administering extremely hot baths to infants. Every morning and evening the Dinka child receives a hot bath, even in the most scorching weather. This "bathing period" continues throughout the child's first year of life. The procedure is quite elaborate. A huge pot of water is boiled, and the mother or some other woman of the household sits on a wooden stool, holding a gourd which she uses to dip out the water and cool it to the correct temperature. "As the mother pours the water onto the baby . . . she turns it from side to side, massaging and exercising its arms, buttocks, genitals, thighs, legs, and even its toes. During all this, the baby continues to cry in terror, but that is expected and bothers no one." The purpose of this bath is not cleanliness, which the Dinka recognize could be achieved with milder water, but rather to increase the child's circulation and to help it adapt to postnatal life. It is also considered essential to the proper development of the child: "It helps the baby to grow up healthy, well-built, and well-poised. A child who grows up crooked, or clumsy in build or poise, is believed to be—at least in part—the product of improper bathing. This is why there is such emphasis on the techniques of massaging and exercising during the bath."[4]

4. *Ibid.*, pp. 41–42.

By now we have seen that the question "What does a newborn baby need?" is answered, not by any innate "parental instincts," but rather by the cultural traditions of the community into which the baby is born. Society, in the person of those adults responsible for the well-being of the infant, soon begins to help satisfy his most urgent (or at least most obvious) needs, but only as these needs are defined by the culture and only according to conventional plans for their satisfaction.

Let us consider the cultural aspects of infant nutrition. Every society recognizes that infants cannot feed themselves and that they need assistance from adults in satisfying their need for nourishment. But since human beings lack built-in or instinctive feeding patterns, the what, how, where, and when of infant nourishment are left up to the beliefs of the responsible adults; and these beliefs are part of the group culture. As Dorothy Lee has observed:

> The first experience of solid food will differ according to the culture. If he is a Tikopia, he will get premasticated food, warmed with the mother's body warmth and partly digested through her salivary juices; his mother will put it directly into his mouth with her lips. If he is in our society, he will get this food with a hard metal spoon, introduced into a mouth which has never experienced anything so solid or hard, into which not even teeth have yet erupted. In all this, the culture enters into the food experiences, shaping, emphasizing, even choosing the significant factors for defining the experience.[5]

Some of the constraints upon infant feeding are the result of situational factors. It has been unlikely until recently that Eskimo babies would be raised on mashed bananas or that Arabian nomads would give their children hunks of whale blubber. But aside from such obvious restrictions, the context and content of infant feeding depend upon learned ideas, and thus vary from culture to culture. For there is no such thing as satisfying a child's hunger with food in the abstract: some particular substance must be provided, by some particular person(s), at a given place and time, and in a particular manner. (Do babies need to have their milk heated? Until a few years ago, the answer provided by our social traditions was "absolutely"; but now that it has been shown that most babies thrive on ice-cold milk, doctors are not so sure.)

Gardner Murphy has suggested the term *canalization* to denote the psychological process whereby "needs tend to become more specific in consequence of being satisfied in spe-

---

5. D. Lee, "Cultural Factors in Dietary Choice," *Freedom and Culture* (Englewood Cliffs, N.J.: Spectrum Books, 1959), pp. 154–155.

cific ways."[6] That is, as the child's need for nourishment is satisfied with a particular substance and in a particular manner, he becomes used to these things. Cultural convention becomes "second nature," and we say that the child's need has been canalized. The infant who needed liquid becomes a child who wants a Coke.

But the child learns a number of other things in the process of having his needs satisfied. As his perceptions of the world become clearer, he comes to associate the satisfaction of his needs with the person (usually his mother) or persons who feed and comfort him. Gradually, out of a mass of confusing feelings and perceptions, he comes to distinguish his *self* from other objects. Murphy points out that the sense of selfhood, of being a distinct individual, is something *attained* rather than given; it is the product of long and complex interaction between the child and his environment.[7]

As a result of repeated interactions with persons and objects, the child begins to form more and more stable notions of what his world is like. He learns, in a vague, wordless way, what he can expect from the people around him. He learns how to control and coordinate the parts of his body, and he learns that when he acts in certain ways he can expect to evoke certain regular responses from others. When he cries, he is picked up or nursed or punished or rocked; when he reaches for a shiny object, he is helped or encouraged or slapped or scolded. Equally important is the *emotional tone* of his interactions with adults, for a child is very quick to feel whether in their dealings with him, his parents are relaxed and self-assured or are tense, anxious, and uncertain. This emotional quality may be as important as the actual content of child-training customs in affecting the child's sense of selfhood.

To summarize, culture first influences a child's behavior by the ways in which his needs are met (or ignored). By responding to his needs for food, affection, sleep, activity, sexual stimulation, or elimination in *culturally patterned ways,* the significant adults in his environment shape his behavior in accordance with the expectations of his society. He learns where and when he is expected to eat, sleep, or empty his bowels, and in what ways he can satisfy his cravings for muscular activity and exploration, or for protection and warmth. As the late William Caudill once said, "By three to four months of age, babies are very much cultural beings."

A good way to illustrate these generalizations about the

---

6. G. Murphy, *Personality* (New York: Harper, 1947), pp. 161–191.
7. *Ibid.*, pp. 479–522.

effects of culture upon child development will be to discuss some important research done by Caudill and Helen Weinstein: a comparison of mother-child interaction in America and in Japan. The thirty families selected for study in each country were urban, middle class, and intact; in each case, the parents had only one child, between three and four months of age. Suitable statistical controls were used to ensure that the differences found could be attributed to culture, but these will not be discussed here. Observations of mother-child interaction were done in the homes of the families by trained observers who recorded what took place during 800 one-second "time samples." Significant differences were found between children and between mothers of the two cultural groups; Caudill and Weinstein report that

> the Japanese baby seems passive, and he lies quietly with occasional unhappy vocalizations, while his mother . . . does more lulling, carrying, and rocking of her baby. She seems to try to soothe and quiet the child, and to communicate with him physically rather than verbally. On the other hand, the American infant is more active, happily vocal, and exploring of his environment, and his mother in her care does more looking at and chatting to her baby. She seems to stimulate the baby to activity and to vocal response. It is as if the American mother wanted to have a vocal, active baby, and the Japanese mother wanted to have a quiet, contented baby . . . they seem to get what they apparently want.[8]

The authors point out that these patterns of behavior which are learned so early by the child "are in line with the differing expectations for later behavior in the two cultures as the child grows to be an adult." This is particularly true in the areas of family life and general interpersonal relations where, according to many studies, Japanese tend to be more group-oriented, more passive, and more sensitive to nonverbal forms of communication than are Americans, who tend to be relatively individual-oriented, assertive, and reliant upon verbal communication in a context of physical separateness. These differences are expressed in differing cultural conceptions of what an infant needs:

> In Japan, the infant is seen more as a separate biological organism who from the beginning, in order to develop, needs to be drawn into increasingly interdependent relations with others. In America, the infant is seen more as a dependent biological organism who, in order to develop, needs to be made increasingly independent of others.[9]

It is exactly this kind of unspoken assumption about the relation between individuals and society which can be potently

---

8. W. Caudill and H. Weinstein, "Maternal and Infant Behavior in Japan and America," *Psychiatry*, Vol. 32 (1969), p. 31.
9. *Ibid.*, p. 15.

The Japanese child learns patterns unique to his culture. ***René Burri/Magnum***

communicated to the child during the early stages of enculturation. As Ruth Benedict pointed out many years ago, Japanese attitudes toward nursing make the infant's early experiences with food leisurely and pleasant; their way of carrying children encourages passivity and develops the capacity to sleep anywhere; and traditional procedures of toilet training also emphasize the passivity of the infant:

> When the baby is three or four months old, the mother . . . anticipates his needs, holding him in her hands outside the door. She waits for him, usually whistling low and monotonously and the child learns to know the purpose of this auditory stimulus. Everyone agrees that a baby in Japan . . . is trained very early [and] what the baby learns from the implacable training prepares him to accept in adulthood the subtler compulsions of Japanese culture.[10]

The point here is *not* that a certain technique of toilet training or of child care automatically produces a certain personality type, but rather that fundamental social values, patterns of child care,

10. R. Benedict, *The Chrysanthemum and the Sword* (Boston: Houghton Mifflin, 1946), pp. 257–259.

and the ideal adult personality all fit together in a meaningful way. Early studies of *culture and personality* (such as Benedict's *The Chrysanthemum and the Sword,* quoted above) often neglected problems of sampling and of individual or subcultural variability, producing oversimplified pictures of child-training practices and their consequences. But detailed observational studies (such as that by Caudill and Weinstein) show that cultural differences are real and potent influences early in life, partly confirming Benedict's hypotheses about the consistency between child-training practices and the requirements of the adult culture.

The Social Functions of Child-Care Customs

It is precisely because human infants are so helpless *and* because adults have few (if any) parental instincts that each culture must provide conventional plans for dealing with young children. These child-care customs let adults know what they are expected to do and thus—to the extent that they are followed—serve to provide patterned stimulation for each child born into the society. A society that *lacked* such customs could not survive for long; its youngest generation would starve, fall into the fire, or be consumed by predators. Anthropologists use the term *social function* to refer to the *contribution that a custom makes to the working and survival of the society in which it is found.* In general, child-care customs have two kinds of social functions: they ensure the physical survival of the young by satisfying their basic biological needs, and they help to produce the kinds of persons (personality types) who will fit into the society and maintain its values.

Some system of child-care customs is found in every society: it is a *cultural universal* which satisfies a clear set of social functions. But as we have seen, there can be great variation in *how* a child is cared for. Even the question "Who should care for the young?" may be answered very differently in different parts of the world. Let us consider some of the major possibilities:

1. Mother and/or Father: There are several obvious biological reasons for assigning care of infants to the female parent, but cultures differ in the extent to which they make the mother solely responsible for various aspects of child care. At one extreme we find the type of household in which the male parent is frequently (or always) absent; less common is the other extreme type in which, due to the mother's absence, the father has complete responsibility for the children. Most societies fall between these extremes, but few strike such an even balance as do the Mountain Arapesh of New Guinea. According to Margaret Mead, the Arapesh

In Kenya, a child learns a social role with the help of an adult. ***John Moss/ Photo Researchers***

> regard both men and women as inherently gentle, responsive, and cooperative, able and willing to subordinate the self to the needs of those who are younger or weaker, and to derive a major satisfaction from doing so. They have surrounded with delight that part of parenthood which we consider to be specially maternal. . . . Their dominant conception of men and women may be said to be that of regarding men, even as we regard women, as gentle, carefully parental in their aims.[11]

During the Depression of the 1930s, many American fathers found themselves out of a job and in charge of children and household while their wives worked. Most of these men felt their masculinity threatened by the enforced maternal tasks, but such feelings would be incomprehensible to an Arapesh father. Thus does culture mold our behavior and attitudes.

2. Parents and/or Other Relatives: In modern-day, mobile American society, it is unusual for several generations of the same family to live close together or for adult *siblings* (brothers and sisters) to maintain close ties. The American household generally consists of the husband, his wife, and their young offspring. In more settled societies, however, the household often includes members of several generations and/or siblings of one or both parents, any or all of whom may customarily care for the young. Many groups rely heavily upon the child's elder siblings to provide care. Margaret Mead has commented that in Samoa, for example, "no mother will ever exert herself to discipline a younger child if an older one can be made responsible."[12] Samoan girls of six or seven are generally entrusted with the care of their younger siblings, carrying them about the village all day. Mead remarks:

> Relatives in other households also play a role in the children's lives. Any older relative has a right to demand personal service from younger relatives, a right to criticize their conduct and to interfere in their affairs. . . . So closely is the daily life bound up with this universal servitude and so numerous are the acknowledged relationships in the name of which service can be exacted, that for the children an hour's escape from surveillance is almost impossible.

At the same time, however:

> This loose but demanding relationship group has its compensations. . . . Within it a child of three can wander safely and come to no harm, can be sure of finding food and drink, a sheet to wrap herself up in for a nap, a kind hand to dry casual tears and bind up her wounds.[13]

---

11. M. Mead, *Sex and Temperament in Three Primitive Societies* (New York: William Morrow and Company, 1935), p. 100.
12. M. Mead, *Coming of Age in Samoa* (New York: Mentor Books, 1949), p. 25.
13. *Ibid.*, p. 35.

3. Relatives and/or Nonrelatives: In most societies, children are cared for by their relatives (though we shall see in Part Three that culture is as important as biology in the determination of who is a relative and who is not). It is customary, however, among the wealthier classes of many societies to employ unrelated persons, usually of inferior status, to care for the young, while working

Nonrelatives care for children. A Headstart day-care center in the United States. ***Charles Harbutt/Magnum***

parents in our own society often rely on a series of baby-sitters or child-care centers during a child's preschool years.

4. Individuals and/or Group: In most societies, primary responsibility for a child's welfare rests upon a few individuals; but the social group also takes an interest in this matter and, through the force of public opinion or through legal action, may intervene if its expectations are not met. In some societies, the community or the state may even take primary responsibility for child welfare. For example, in the Israeli kibbutz (a kind of communal farming community), children are raised from birth through adolescence in community-run nurseries, dormitories, and schools. They visit their "real" parents for several hours each week. In such a society, the parent-child relationship is quite different from what we may think of as natural, but there certainly are some advantages, especially the relative absence of family conflict.[14]

Like all cultural patterns, the possible answers outlined above are *conventional,* in that none of them can be predicted from knowledge of human biology alone. But this does not mean that they are unrelated to other aspects of the cultures in which they occur. The pattern described for the Israeli kibbutz was deliberately developed as part of a conscious attempt to equalize the status of men and women by freeing most of the women in the community from child care. Care performed by unrelated baby-sitters or by the unemployed parent is clearly linked to the economic structure of the society (which shows individual, subcultural, and temporal variability), while the Samoan and Arapesh systems of child care are intimately connected with the major values of their societies. To say that a cultural pattern is conventional means only that it *could be otherwise* under different circumstances, not that it is random or that it bears no relationship to human biology or to the rest of the culture.

In this section we have surveyed the kinds of learning that take place early in a child's life as the traditions of his group begin to mold his behavior and his character. Several concepts have been introduced which will continue to be used throughout this book. These include: the concept of canalization; the three kinds of cultural variability; the notion of social function; and the conventional nature of cultural patterns. In the rest of the chapter we shall consider some of the kinds of learning that take place as the child progressively enters into the life of his society and begins to shape for himself, with the guidance of his elders and his peers, a social career which he will follow for the rest of his life.

14. For a fine synthesis of materials on child-rearing in the Israeli kibbutz, see R. Endleman, *Personality and Social Life* (New York: Random House, 1967), pp. 127–178.

LATER STAGES OF ENCULTURATION

As the child grows older, his range of experience broadens. This broadening depends upon his increased bodily control and his acquisition of language. When he can be relied upon to behave in minimally acceptable ways, he is "taken into society," and as he comes into contact with persons outside his immediate family, the pressures upon him to conform to the expectations of the community are increased. As an infant, he could be more or less self-centered. Now he must learn to communicate with others and must become aware that different kinds of persons and situations call for different behavior on his part. He must begin to learn the categories of social life and the plans (both verbal and nonverbal) which are associated with these categories.

Social Function of Language Learning

Parents often lose patience with children who are going through what we call the "why stage." Their constant questioning can be quite annoying (and sometimes it may be continued deliberately to annoy the parents). But if we pay attention to the child's questions, they provide excellent evidence for the conventionality of culture. For the child has so much to learn: the ideas and relationships, categories and plans which adults take for granted are all new to him, and language is a marvelous key which can help him unlock the mysteries.

Cultures differ in the amount of emphasis they put on formal education as opposed to informal learning, and on verbal instruction as opposed to observation or imitation. In some American Indian societies, people are embarrassed to ask how to do a job. Among the Maya of Guatemala, even complex tasks such as operating factory machines or driving a car are learned by observation and imitation: the learner simply watches until he feels he is ready to try on his own; he then takes over, often with surprising success.[15] On the other hand, the people of Guadalcanal rely heavily upon "direct verbal instruction"; in most situations children are subjected to a steady stream of verbal admonitions from responsible adults, telling them what to do and inculcating the primary values of generosity and respect for property.[16] In most nonliterate societies, informal education is supplied by watching and questioning one's elders, while the more abstract traditions of the group are transmitted through legends, myths,

15. M. Nash, *Machine Age Maya*, Memoir 87 (American Anthropological Association, 1958), pp. 26–27.
16. I. Hogbin, *A Guadalcanal Society: The Kaoka Speakers* (New York: Holt, Rinehart and Winston, 1964), p. 33.

and songs. Formal educational institutions appear in only the more complex societies, but they are always supplemented by informal education within the family and peer group. (See Chapter 5.)

Sooner or later, each normal person learns to behave in fairly appropriate ways in the various situations which are characteristic of his society. This includes learning to use language in ways which others consider appropriate. In the words of J. R. Firth:

> Every one of us starts life with the two simple roles of sleeping and feeding; but from the time we begin to be socially active, we gradually accumulate social roles. Throughout the period of growth we are progressively incorporated into our social organization, and the chief condition and means of that incorporation is learning to say what the other fellow expects us to say under the given circumstances.[17]

In many societies a special vocabulary is used toward (and by) very young children. Charles Ferguson has made a comparative study of such baby talk in a number of societies.[18] His investigations reveal, among other things, a striking similarity in the phonology and morphology of different kinds of baby talk, such as the repetition (reduplication) of syllables, for example, "bye-bye," "pee-pee." Contrary to what you might expect, the kinds of pronunciation considered appropriate for children are *not* always easier than the adult pronunciations for which they substitute.

In his study of Comanche baby language, Joseph Casagrande suggests that the anthropologist or psychologist interested in personality development in different societies should study children's speech and baby words, for the vocabulary used by young children indicates a good deal about the child's world. For example, Casagrande cites the Comanche baby word *ʔáʔh,* which carries the meanings "something nasty or dirty; feces, urine, penis, a smell; warning to get away from something dirty; I have wet, dirtied myself; command for baby to defecate." He comments:

> Discipline and attitude are reflected . . . in Comanche where feces, urine, and the genitalia and feeling of disgust are equated, and where there are words used to frighten the child, admonish it, and control its movements. It seems likely that conscious speech training might be correlated with later educational procedures and attitudes towards children.[19]

---

17. J. R. Firth, "On Sociological Linguistics," in D. Hymes, ed., *Language in Culture and Society* (New York: Harper and Row, 1964), p. 67.
18. C. Ferguson, "Baby Talk in Six Languages," *American Anthropologist*, Vol. 66 (1964), pp. 103–114.
19. J. B. Casagrande, "Comanche Baby Language," in D. Hymes, *op. cit.*, pp. 247–248.

To fully appreciate the social functions of language, we must recall that *words are labels for categories of experience.* They enable us to group quite diverse events and sensations under a single heading and to discriminate them from other events and sensations. Recent psychological experiments have shown that having verbal labels for different classes of stimuli makes it much easier for subjects to respond to them in distinctive ways (for example, by pushing a specific button when a certain type of stimulus is presented).[20] Categories that are named by different words also tend to have different plans for the actions associated with them. For example, in certain situations the color categories that we call "red" and "green" also carry the plans "stop" and "go." To call a clear liquid "nitroglycerin" and an animal a "rattlesnake" is also to call forth certain modes of behavior toward them.

Benjamin Lee Whorf was the first linguist to emphasize the close relationship between a person's plans for action and the categories he uses. Whorf had also worked as an insurance adjuster, and he was struck by the number of accidental explosions which took place as a result of carelessness with objects thought of as *empty gasoline barrels.* Now, an empty gasoline barrel is much more dangerous than a full one, because the residual gasoline fumes mixed with air are highly explosive. But the English categories "full/empty" do not normally take air or other gases into account (compare the phrase "an empty room," which certainly does not mean the walls enclose a vacuum). Also, the category "empty" carries the connotative meaning "void, inert, or harmless," and calls forth no special kind of defensive response.[21] Think of how you would react to the shouted warning, "Careful, it's empty."

The grammatical and semantic systems of a language thus imply a way of looking at the world—a way of dividing up continuous or variable phenomena into stable and discrete categories to which we learn to attach different kinds of responses. A beginner in biology must learn the scientific names of hundreds of species, classes, and phyla. In the same way, a beginner in a culture—whether a child or an anthropologist—must learn the names of thousands of categories of phenomena and also the kinds of responses to those categories which his society considers appropriate. In the words of Clyde Kluckhohn: "The human response is, overwhelmingly, to the stimulus or stimulus-situation

---

20. For example, H. C. Ellis and D. G. Muller, "Transfer in Perceptual Learning Following Stimulus Predifferentiation," *Journal of Experimental Psychology*, Vol. 68 (1964), pp. 388–395.

21. B. L. Whorf, "The Relation of Habitual Thought and Behavior to Language," in J. Carroll, ed., *Language, Thought, and Reality* (Cambridge: The M.I.T. Press, 1956), pp. 134–159. See also B. Berlin *et al.*, "Covert Categories and Folk Taxonomies," *American Anthropologist*, Vol. 70 (1968), pp. 290–299.

as defined and interpreted in accord with man-made patterns . . . [and] the *vocabularies* of different languages both reflect and perpetuate habitual and distinctive ways of categorizing experience or modes of thought."[22]

Social Careers

Within his social world, the maturing individual enters upon a social career. He learns that his society values certain kinds of behavior, and that his family and peers expect him to become a certain kind of person. In most cases, he strives to fulfill their expectations. Exactly what he will strive for depends primarily upon the values of his culture. He may seek to accumulate material goods of a certain kind, or he may spend his life earning spiritual merit by a life of prayer or by philanthropy. He may seek intellectual attainments, mystical experiences, or the glories of war. He may hope to father many children or remain celibate. But once he has entered upon a social career, there are many social and psychological forces which operate upon him to maintain his conformity to group expectations. As Everett Hughes has written:

> However one's ambitions and accomplishments turn, they involve some sequence of relations to organized life. In a highly and rigidly structured society, a career consists, objectively, of a series of status[es]. . . . In a freer one, the individual has more latitude for creating his own position or choosing from a number of existing ones; he has also less certainty of achieving any given position. There are more adventurers and more failures; but unless complete disorder reigns, there will be typical sequences of position, achievement, responsibility, and even of adventure. The social order will set limits upon the individual's orientation of his life, both as to direction of effort and as to interpretation of its meaning.[23]

It is characteristic of the simpler societies that only a few careers are available to a person. In some of the so-called primitive societies, only two kinds of careers are available, one for men and one for women. This is related to a *universal* feature of culture, the *sexual division of labor*—that is, in every known society, men and women are assigned different kinds of tasks. This universal feature has a biological basis, for adult males tend to be larger than females, and they are not periodically incapacitated by childbearing; but on top of this biological foundation,

22. C. Kluckhohn, "Culture and Behavior," in G. Lindzey, ed., *Handbook of Social Psychology*, Vol. II (Cambridge: Addison-Wesley, 1954), pp. 921, 938.
23. E. C. Hughes, *Men and Their Work* (New York: Free Press, 1958), p. 63.

each culture erects an arbitrary superstructure, often including quite erroneous or at least scientifically unfounded beliefs about the relative abilities of the sexes. Very different plans may be attached to the categories "male" and "female." For example, the Arapesh believe women should carry heavy loads because "their heads are stronger."

In a society where *only* the sexual division of labor was found, every man would learn to expect a career like that of every other man, and every woman like every other woman. There would, of course, be individual differences, but these would be reducible to matters of emphasis within the general pattern. Thus, for example, every man would expect to hunt and fish in order to provide meat for his family, to make the tools he needed, to construct shelters, and to defend the group. Because of personal preference or particular abilities, some men might specialize or take the lead in one of these activities, but they would still participate in all the others. Similarly, all women would expect to lead lives of the same general kind: caring for children, gathering plant food, preparing food and clothing, perhaps making baskets, and so forth. The activities expected of persons would naturally be different at different times during their careers, but this too would be part of the pattern.

Actually, even the simplest known societies provide some alternatives besides the standard sexual careers. Nearly everywhere are found part-time religious specialists—men or women who take the lead in ceremonies involving religion, magic, and/or curing. Such a person (a *shaman*) is recognized by his fellows as being different, even though he may perform the usual tasks expected of his sex at other times. Some societies have a separate career for men who cannot fit into the usual pattern. Among the Crow Indians, a male who was unsuited for the usual career as a hunter and warrior was able to become a *berdache.* According to Robert Lowie, such "men-women" wore female clothing and performed the usual female tasks, often excelling in them.[24]

In more complex societies, the division of labor is much more elaborate, and a number of different careers may be available to each individual. The development of full-time specializations within a society depends primarily upon the degree of technological development of the society, particularly the production of an economic surplus. When people exist at a bare subsistence level, there is little room for specialization beyond the sexual division of labor. However, in areas of unusual natural abundance or, more generally, in societies that have mastered the techniques of food production, the existence of a surplus

24. R. H. Lowie, *The Crow Indians* (New York: Holt, Rinehart and Winston, 1956), p. 48.

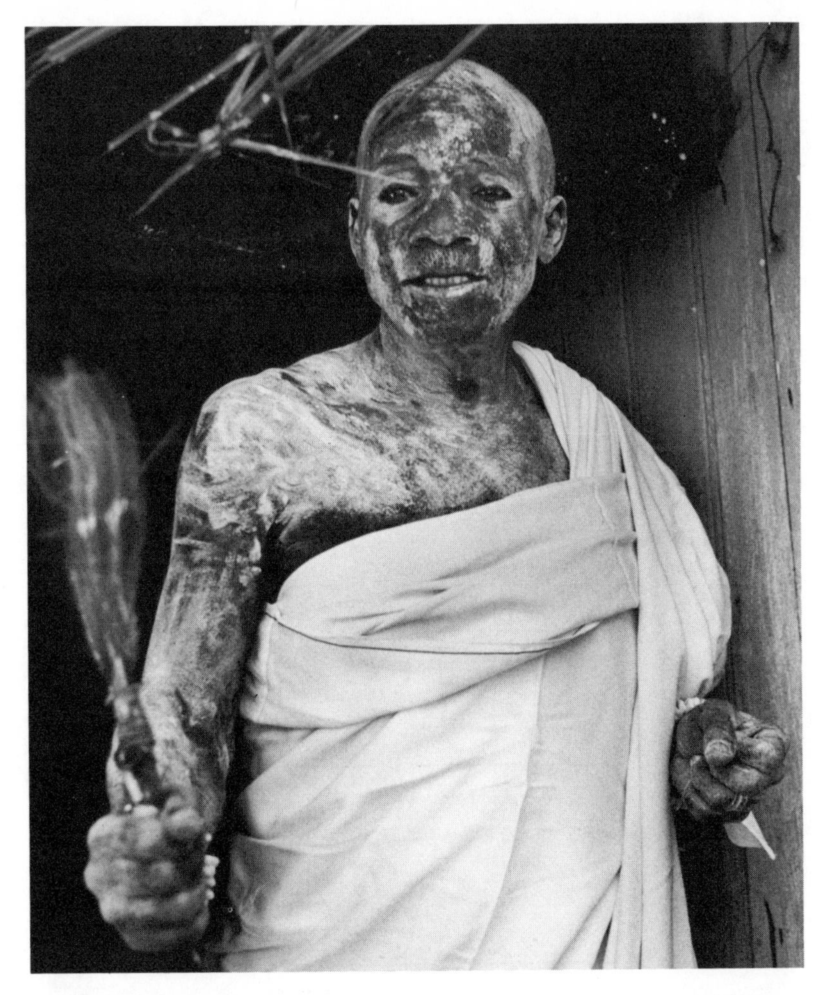

A ritual specialist. In northeast Ghana, a witch doctor painted white to symbolize purity carrying a ceremonial fly whisk. ***Marc & Evelyne Bernheim/ Woodfin Camp***

makes it possible to release some members of the population from subsistence activities. Such persons may then devote much of their time to the production of specialized goods and services, which they then exchange for necessities.

Typical careers found in societies with an assured food surplus include:

1. *Ritual specialists*—priests, diviners, and curers
2. *Technical specialists*—warriors, traders, and craftsmen such as potters, weavers, or metalworkers
3. *Political specialists*—chiefs, judges, tax collectors

These careers may not be equally open to all members of the society, but the existence of such alternatives and the interactions among persons pursuing different careers makes for increased social and cultural complexity. Figure 3.1 diagrams the division of work in both simple and complex societies.

One important effect of the division of labor upon society is the *creation of interdependence* among its members. It was the French sociologist Emile Durkheim who emphasized this social function of the division of labor: if men and women perform different but complementary tasks, this will tend to bind the two sexes more closely together.[25] Similarly, the craftsman and his customers, the curer and his patients, the industrialist and his suppliers—all are bound into a social fabric in which each depends upon the other for goods and services which he cannot himself supply.

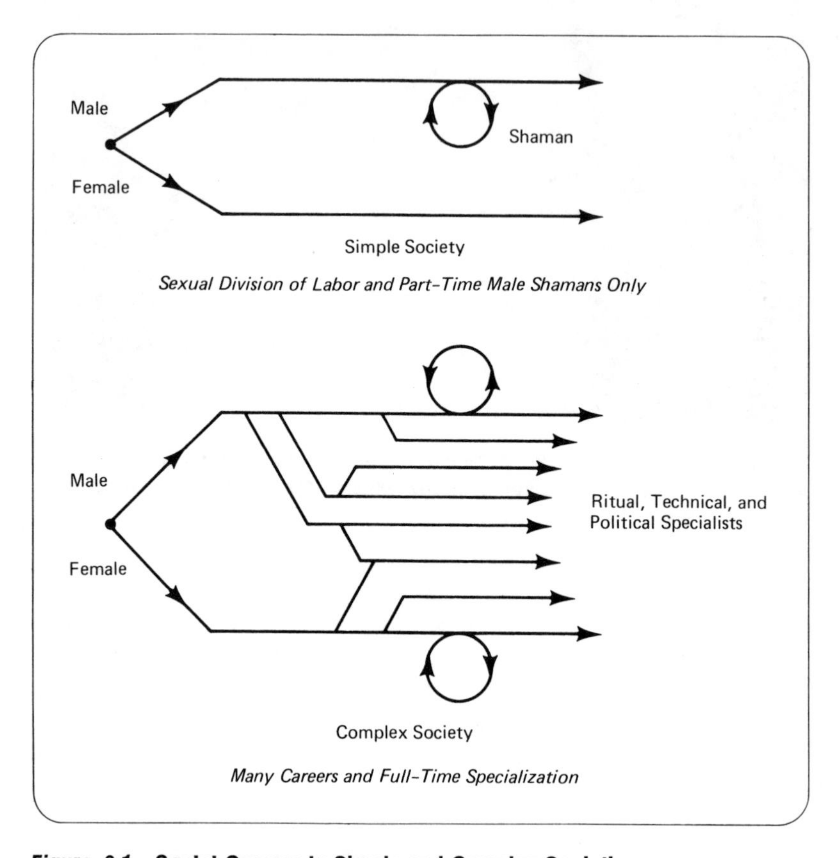

Figure 3.1 **Social Careers in Simple and Complex Societies**

25. E. Durkheim, *The Division of Labor in Society* (New York: Free Press, 1947).

The multiplication of careers calls for a variety of forms of enculturation. Even in societies where the number of careers is small, particular persons or groups must be made responsible for the continuing education of the young. Most often, this social function is fulfilled by the parent of the same sex as the child. The mother will instruct her daughters in the womanly duties, and the father will be responsible for seeing that his sons know what they need to know and behave as they should. But other relatives may supplement or replace the parents as teachers of certain topics. Thus, among the Apache, the mother's brother is the one whom a boy must strive to excel in hunting, running, and general behavior, while among the Dakota the uncle is the chief instructor for everything except "respectability," which is taught by the father and grandfather. A special relationship is also often found between a child and his father's sister. Among the Hopi Indians, this relative names the child; a girl goes to her father's sister for the important corn-grinding ceremony, while a boy is sponsored by her when he enters the warrior society.

A child's behavior reflects back upon his parents and other kinsmen. People everywhere are concerned about what the neighbors will say, and this concern provides an important motive for educating and disciplining the young. The forms of social control are very different in various cultures, but they are always present. This point is stressed because of a widely accepted fallacy concerning primitive peoples: it is sometimes claimed that primitive man adheres to the customs of his group and obeys its laws instinctively and without thought. But primitive peoples no more have law-abiding instincts than they have inborn senses of direction. It is true that in small, isolated societies, people do tend to have greater respect for tradition per se, but in every society, the content of the traditions must be *learned,* and the native (if not the visitor or the ethnographer) is aware of the various social forces which constrain his behavior as well as the punishments which follow misbehavior.

The force of *public opinion* is very great in all small-scale societies (whether in Africa or Arkansas). It is really only in large urban centers that the individual can to some extent attain anonymity and relative freedom from group pressures. But in a little community where everyone knows everyone else and where daily interaction and interdependence are to be expected, one does not violate custom lightly. In such societies, the threat of gossip or of the informal withdrawal of approval and cooperation is sufficient to keep most people in line.

At the same time, the very intimacy of social life makes it difficult for one individual to discipline another directly. Many observers have commented on the relative absence of physical punishment administered by "primitive parents." There are many exceptions to this generalization, but at least among the North American Indians, it is unusual for a parent to use force toward a child. The mother's brother or an eminent tribal elder might be called upon to admonish a youngster and to instruct him concerning his duties, but tribal peoples are often shocked at the "brutality" of "civilized parents."

In some cases, the elders of a community take joint action against a young person whose behavior is disrupting the group. C. W. M. Hart and A. Pilling have described the very interesting institution of the Tiwi "duel." The Tiwi are an isolated group of Australian aborigines. In Tiwi society some of the elderly men accumulate large numbers of young wives, while many men are unable to marry at all until about the age of thirty. Under these circumstances it is understandable that accusations of adultery are frequently made against young bachelors. Such accusations often result in a "duel" in which the unarmed bachelor publicly defends himself against the verbal abuse and thrown spears of the offended husband by jumping and dodging, but must finally allow himself to be wounded to appease the old man's anger. Since the other elders also have a stake in the marriage system, they will gang up on any bachelor who refuses to go through the ordeal. In this way, punishment is administered and others are warned of the penalty for violation. The social function of the "duel," as Hart and Pilling point out, is to reassert the validity of the traditional marriage system:

> When the blood gushed from such a wound the crowd yelled approval and the duel was over. The young man had behaved admirably, the old man had vindicated his honor, the sanctity of marriage and the Tiwi constitution had been upheld, and everybody went home satisfied and full of moral rectitude. Seduction did not pay.[26]

Another effective way of controlling behavior in many societies is through the *threat of supernatural punishment.* Stories of a mysterious owl who "pecks out the eyes of naughty children" or of giants and cannibal spirits who may carry off offenders are widespread means of obtaining obedience. The occasional appearance of such bogymen (in the person of a disguised stranger) contributes to the effectiveness of these beliefs. Among

26. C. W. M. Hart and A. Pilling, *The Tiwi of North Australia* (New York: Holt, Rinehart and Winston, 1964), p. 82.

Social control exercised through impressive ceremonies. Urama taboo-spirits prepare for a performance. *American Museum of Natural History*

the Pueblo Indians, the various gods (or *kachinas*) are impersonated in elaborate and impressive ceremonies; some of these rituals include beating the boys with special whips. In this way, the parents are relieved of the odious task of direct discipline.

Beliefs in supernatural punishment, whether in this or another life, are particularly effective means of social control since they may deter violations which would otherwise go undetected and unpunished. The belief in *reincarnation*—where, as in Hindu India, one's future position is thought to depend upon proper behavior and merit earned in one's present life—is a strong force for conformity and performance of social obligations. Similarly, the belief in *taboo,* or automatic punishment following some offense to the spirits, is also a deterrent to misbehavior: no reasonable man would steal a tabooed object if he believed that such an action would result in an illness or some other retribution.

All such beliefs have the additional advantage of being *self-validating.* If a person is born into a low social position, it is because of his sins in a previous life; who can disprove it? If the sinner is punished, it is because he violated a taboo. If the innocent man suffers, he must have unknowingly offended some spirit or perhaps a human sorcerer. If someone behaves in an unconventional manner, this may be evidence that he is practicing witchcraft: accusation (or even the threat of accusation) may bring confession and conformity. Such an incident reinforces the belief in witchcraft, and even the innocent accused person may be impressed, for many groups believe that one can become a witch without knowing it.

In many societies, the strongest source of social control is the *peer group* of an individual. In our own society we recognize the high degree of conformity to codes of dress, speech, and behavior found in many teen-age gangs; David Reisman (in *The Lonely Crowd*) has suggested that this "other-directedness" is a general feature of American middle-class culture. But peer-group influence is by no means limited to American society. For example, among the Red Xhosa, a traditionally militaristic tribe of South Africa, neighborhood groups of young men meet together regularly for parties and for "cudgel games" (fighting with sticks). As Philip and Iona Mayer have shown, these meetings—which provide opportunities for sexual encounters, fights, and the development of intense local loyalties—are also the means by which Xhosa boys learn to canalize their sexual and aggressive drives into the restrained forms approved of by the youth group.

> These groups also provide a forum where male youth acquire politico-judicial skills and develop a concern with "law"—both highly valued in Red Xhosa culture. In these groups, too, social contacts with peers are progressively widened, in a way that makes for eventual self-identification as a Xhosa, over and above kinship and community identifications.[27]

In every society, then, conformity is brought about by means of education and social control. Ultimately, conformity is maintained by physical force (including such things as prison or the firing squad); but such means of coercion are normally used as a

27. P. Mayer and I. Mayer, "Socialization by Peers: The Red Xhosa Youth Organization," in P. Mayer, ed., *Socialization: The Approach from Social Anthropology* (London: Tavistock, 1970), p. 160.

last resort. The primary controls on behavior are built into the individual in the early and later stages of enculturation, and they are maintained by informal pressure from family, peers, and local authorities.

Formal education in primitive society seldom involves going to a school. More often, elaborate instruction is given as part of a personal relationship between tutor and student or between a master craftsman and his apprentices. In societies where the only truly specialized career is that of shaman, a long and arduous preparation may be necessary before the novice is allowed to practice his new skills. Among the Tapirapé, an Indian tribe of central Brazil, the shamans have many important functions and very high prestige. But as described by Charles Wagley, the "road to shamanism" is difficult and often frightening. Tapirapé shamans exercise their powers primarily by *dreaming*, at which time they are believed to visit the spirit world. Young people of either sex may be recognized as future shamans because of their tendency to dream a great deal. However, persons who wish to become shamans but are unable to dream easily may solicit dreams in the following manner:

> A novice sits upon the ground near . . . his mentor [an established shaman], and swallows smoke from his mentor's pipe until violent vomiting occurs. . . . Generally the neophytes fall backwards unconscious and ill from the smoke; during this state they may dream. . . . The process may be repeated several times over a period of two or three hours.

The apprentice shaman may not bathe, indulge in sexual intercourse, or eat certain foods. Many novices do not continue after the first few nights, but

> other novices, more successful and more persistent, do dream. At first they see smoky forms of ghosts and sometimes forest demons; they as yet do not know how to talk with such spirits. . . . After several seasons the novice may see dangerous forest demons in his unconscious state and he may talk with ghosts. . . . The mere fact that the young shaman has several dangerous dreams does not make him a proved shaman. He must take part in the "fight" against the beings of Thunder, and by the side of his mentor he may attempt cures. If successful, he may be called now and again by people for cures. With a reputation for several cures and with continual dreaming, during which he has supernatural encounters, he builds up his reputation as a shaman over a period of many years.[28]

28. C. Wagley, "Tapirapé Shamanism," in M. Fried, ed., *Readings in Anthropology:* Vol. II, *Cultural Anthropology* (New York: Thomas Y. Crowell, 1959), pp. 421–422.

A good deal of the formal education found in primitive societies has to do with esoteric matters: curing, ritual, tribal mythology, and so forth. In the absence of writing—and this is one of the few characteristics shared by all primitive societies—complex traditions must be communicated orally and stored in the memory. The detailed memory cultivated by shamans and storytellers is indeed astounding. For example, among the Navajo Indians, the "singers" (one type of curer) must memorize and perform complex rituals sometimes lasting for several days and nights, and which must be note- and letter-perfect in order to be effective. These Navajo rites (which also include complicated gestures, manipulation of ritual objects, and construction of sand paintings) have been estimated to require as much effort to memorize as would be needed to commit to memory the entire score of a Wagnerian opera. Such comparisons are difficult to validate, but the memory displayed by the Navajo singers, particularly in the absence of any written model, is most impressive.

In other societies the transmission of ritual and practical knowledge may be made the responsibility of particular groups, often secret societies. Thus, among the Pueblo Indians, a person who has been cured by members of one of the curing societies is required to join that group and participate in its activities. Other such groups carry on activities in connection with warfare or with agriculture, just as experts in various fields of knowledge in our own society (military men, agronomists, doctors, and so on) are made responsible for the practice and transmission of their own specialized skills and knowledge.

In many parts of Africa and India, the blacksmiths form a distinct and usually hereditary group. To an outsider, there is something uncanny and mysterious about their ability to bend and shape metals, while within the group the skills are often surrounded with legendary and magical associations. Thus, although blacksmiths may be considered to be very low in the social hierarchy, they are also accorded a special kind of respect due to their reputation for sorcery. A similar attitude was found in eastern Europe toward the gypsies—another group having metalworking and, allegedly, magical skills.

Initiation Ceremonies

Aside from the relatively formal training of craftsmen and ritual specialists in some primitive societies, there is one fairly widespread custom that in many societies constitutes the most significant educational experience which the individual undergoes. This is the initiation ceremony, and the remainder of this chapter

Preparing a young Masai woman for marriage, a rite of passage. *American Museum of Natural History*

will be devoted to a discussion of its place in the process of enculturation.

The initiation ceremony is one of a number of ceremonies to which Arnold van Gennep gave the name *rites of passage.* Other rites of passage include ceremonies connected with pregnancy and childbirth, betrothal and marriage, death and funerals, and even journeys. The important thing about all of these ceremonies is that they have to do with the movement of individuals from one social position (or status) to another. The change may involve physical locality, group affiliation, or progression within a social career (for example, from childhood to adulthood, maidenhood to marriage, life to death), but in each case the ceremonies contain three ordered stages which dramatize the change of status. Van Gennep called these stages (1) separation, (2) transition, and (3) incorporation; he said:

> Their positions may vary, depending upon whether the occasion is birth or death, initiation or marriage, but the differences lie only in matters of detail. The underlying arrangement is always the same. Beneath a multiplicity of forms, either consciously expressed or merely implied, a typical pattern always recurs: *the pattern of the rites of passage.*[29]

Thus, when moving from one social status to another, the individual is first physically or symbolically separated from his present position; then passes through a transitional state; and finally is reincorporated into society, but in a different status. It is as if the individual cannot go directly from Status A to Status B, but must proceed indirectly, as shown in Figure 3.2. The symbolic enactment of death and rebirth, which plays such an important part in Christian theology and ritual, is an extremely common form of the rite of passage.

Anthropologists have placed emphasis on different parts of this process. For example, in his studies of male puberty rites, John Whiting has emphasized the violent separation of adolescent boys from maternal influence (the cutting of the apron strings) and their incorporation into the world of adult males. His work indicates that in societies where young boys are particularly close to their mothers (to the point of sleeping for years in the same bed), the initiation rites at puberty will be particularly traumatic, often involving circumcision or other genital mutilations.[30]

In many parts of the world, initiation rites have an obvious educational function, and this is our main concern here. That is, during the stage of transition, the initiate must learn the behavior appropriate to his new status and/or demonstrate that he has

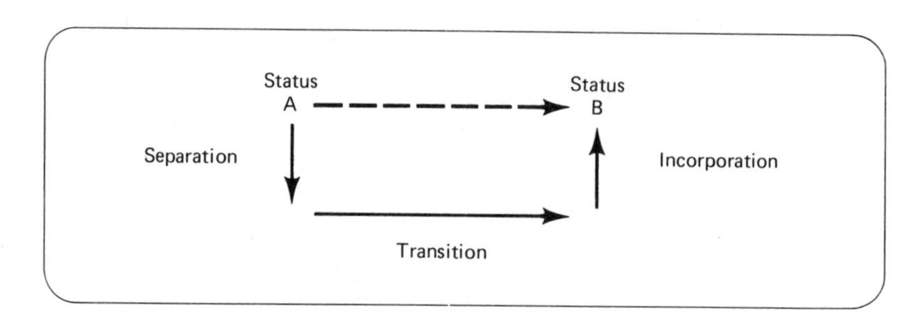

Figure 3.2 **A Rite of Passage**

29. A. Van Gennep, *The Rites of Passage* (Chicago: Phoenix Books, 1960), p. 191.
30. J. W. M. Whiting, *et al.*, "The Function of Male Initiation Ceremonies at Puberty," in R. Endleman, *op. cit.*, pp. 294–309, followed by Endleman's excellent summary of alternative interpretations, pp. 309–330.

mastered the necessary knowledge and skills. This process has many resemblances to basic training in the military: the initiate or recruit is torn away from his family and familiar surroundings; is forced to undergo exhausting, intensive, and often humiliating experiences, during which he must demonstrate his courage and stamina; and generally learns a new (esoteric) vocabulary and mythology as well as ways of behaving which will be appropriate to his new status. When he successfully completes the initiation, he returns to society as a new kind of person, a real "man," or perhaps a Marine.

Initiation rites may last from a few hours up to several years, and the emphasis may be placed upon any or all of the educational elements described above. In some areas, technical skills may be communicated (including some very practical sex education), while in others the emphasis is on learning songs and legends. This is also the time when distinctive tribal marks may be tattooed upon or cut into the body; the latter practice is known as *scarification.* Among the aborigines of Australia, initiation was a long and extremely important ceremony, often involving circumcision, scarification, knocking out of teeth, and intensive training in group traditions and legends.

The division into practical as against religious matters is one made by the ethnographer rather than the native, for these kinds of education may be combined in various ways. Thus, among the Tiwi:

> Small boys picked up the techniques of making spears and throwing sticks by spending time with older boys who in turn improved their skill both in making and using hunting weapons by spending time with the local men.
>
> Although much of this learning was fairly random, other instruction was not. During his initiation period a youth spent long intervals isolated in the bush with a couple of older teachers from whom he received training in religious and ritual matters. At the same time, of course, it was inevitable that the novice absorb some of the older men's experience in bushcraft. There was no corresponding initiation period for girls. What they learned, they learned first from the older women of their childhood household and later from the older women of the husband's household into which they moved as child-brides after puberty.[31]

Tiwi initiations were climaxed by the *kolema* phase, held during the wet season, when the *kolema* yam provided abundant food. This was an annual two-week-long ceremony which always attracted a large attendance. It was quite a contrast with the initiates' isolation in the bush (separation and transition), as well

31. Hart and Pilling, *op. cit.*, p. 49.

as with the usual conditions of Tiwi life, since for most of the year the Tiwi (like most food-gathering peoples) lived in small, nomadic groups composed of a few families. Aside from funerals of important elders, the *kolema* ceremonial was the main religious event of the year, "full of dancing, singing, wailing, and excitement. The excitement was the psychological result of so many people being together at the same time, a rare experience in the life of any Tiwi."[32]

The various rites of passage play an important part in the social life of every group. They provide standardized ways of dealing with the life crises which occur in every society and dramatize (for both the individual and the group) a person's progression within his social career. Such ceremonies serve important psychological and social functions. When they are absent, people often feel unsure about their social position, while the group does not know what it can expect of them. Indeed, there is some experimental evidence from social psychology which indicates that the more painful a rite of passage, the more a person values his new status.[33]

Although the emphasis in this chapter has been upon conformity and the ways a society ensures obedience to tradition, it should not be thought that enculturation is primarily a punishing or restricting process. For one thing, the child actively seeks to master the culture of his group: he wants to speak and to be understood, to be accepted, and to become a real man or woman. The learning of useful skills and the assumption of adult responsibilities are rewarding in and of themselves. There is pleasure to be had in learning how to relate to the world in increasingly complex ways. And most societies try to help the individual through his life crises, recognizing and rewarding his new-found abilities —perhaps by a feast in honor of the first deer or enemy warrior he kills, by a story in the newspaper when he passes his bar examination, or simply by encouragement and approval when he does well. As Ernest G. Schachtel has written:

> Being born and growing up in a concrete society and culture drastically narrows the patterns of relatedness to the world offered to the growing child. On the other hand, it makes it possible for him not to get lost in the infinite possibilities of his world-openness, but to find, within the framework of his culture and tradition, his particular structure of relatedness to the world.[34]

We shall return to this important topic in the Epilogue of this book.

---

32. *Ibid.*, p. 40.
33. E. Aronson and J. Mills, "The Effect of Severity of Initiation on Liking for a Group," *Journal of Abnormal and Social Psychology*, Vol. 59 (1959), pp. 177–181.
34. E. G. Schachtel, *Metamorphosis* (New York: Basic Books, 1959), p. 71.

In conclusion, I shall present an extended ethnographic description of the major initiation ceremony of the Nacirema. The Nacirema live in the general area between the Cree of central Canada and the Tarahumara of northern Mexico. Some of their customs have been described by Ralph Linton, Horace Miner, and Thomas Gladwin.[35] The following description is based upon several years of my personal observation.

During the late spring, large gatherings are held in all of the *setats* to celebrate the passage of the members of an age-grade into the status of adulthood. Initiation begins for members of both sexes at an early age and continues on and off for twelve or more years, until the elders are satisfied that a young man or woman has acquired the necessary amount of esoteric and exoteric knowledge to permit him to compete in the prestige system. Persons who do not complete at least this basic initiation are known as /drábawts/ and are condemned, at least in theory, to menial occupations and low-status marriages; many of them become warriors and attempt to acquire status and property in this way.

A striking fact about the preparation for initiation is that, although division of labor by sex is strongly marked for the adults, persons of both sexes receive (with a few exceptions) the same basic types of instruction—primarily dealing with tribal mythology, folk science, and the manipulation of esoteric symbols. Females sometimes receive training in sewing or cooking and males in woodcraft, but this takes little time compared to the many hours spent in repetitious rote learning of ideology, magical number combinations, and the representation of words by arbitrary conjunctions of signs. The Nacirema feel very strongly about the need for accuracy in using the archaic representations of words, particularly when these bear no phonetic resemblance to the sounds; a single error in a message is enough to discredit the sender. It is not surprising that some successful men who have never been able to master the system employ pretty young scribes to ensure the ritual accuracy of their messages.

In the final initiation ceremony the young initiates are generally grouped together on some high place to which they have marched, while still younger persons blow and beat upon musical instruments. Kinsmen of the initiates watch with pride, sometimes calling encouraging remarks to their offspring. The initiates are

35. R. Linton, *The Study of Man* (New York: Appleton-Century, 1936), pp. 326–327; H. Miner, "Body Ritual among the Nacirema," *American Anthropologist*, Vol. 58 (1956), pp. 503–507; T. Gladwin, "Latency and the Equine Subconscious," *American Anthropologist*, Vol. 64 (1962), pp. 1292–1296.

doubtlessly uncomfortable, but smile bravely, for their ordeal is finally coming to an end. Often, just before the final ceremony, they have been accorded certain adult privileges such as the face-scraping rite (for males) described by Linton, the head-baking rite (for females) alluded to by Miner, and other minor prerogatives for both sexes. Males often have their hair cut shortly before the ceremony. Both sexes are dressed in their finest clothes, but these are covered by black robelike garments, which indicate the sacred nature of the ceremony. On their heads they wear a peculiar black headdress, designed solely with regard for its symbolic value rather than the need for keeping it on top of the head.

Standing with the initiates are the leaders of the initiation school, who were responsible for discipline during the last four years of training, and generally some chiefs of the territorial or local areas. When all have assembled, a leader of some local cult invokes the blessing of the gods upon the initiates and the main part of the ceremony begins. This consists, first, of a number of orations by the leaders, the visiting chiefs, and certain members of the group being initiated. The latter are the most amusing for someone familiar with the culture. The chosen initiates are expected to praise their instructors exorbitantly and to thank them for the great benefits conferred upon them and for allowing them to be initiated; this despite the fact that the restless Nacirema youth have complained unceasingly about the constraints and discipline of the instructors during their preparation. The longest oration is delivered by the highest-status chief present just before the climax of the ceremony. It is notable for its lack of relevance.

The climax of the ceremony is reached when each of the initiates is called forward to receive the blessing of the leaders and the mark of adulthood. Until this point, the initiates have been treated as a group, but at last their individuality is recognized. The classic pattern of a rite of passage is enacted. The initiate leaves his age-group (separation). He humbly approaches the leader, who touches his right hand while presenting him with a magical scroll upon which his name is inscribed in archaic script (transition). He then returns to the group of initiates, having adjusted his headdress to indicate his new status (incorporation). Another blessing is recited, this time by the leader of a rival local cult, and the initiates march off to the sound of drums and horns, soon thereafter to join their families and friends.

The values expressed in the orations and by the ceremony itself relate to the perpetuation of the initiation system and its relation to the form of the adult society. Some parents have been known to take up residence in particular villages so that their children will be initiated by respected leaders and instructors. Initiates who show particular promise are encouraged to go through further ceremonies, acquire esoteric knowledge available only at special cult centers, and become instructors themselves. Although the financial sacrifices in adopting such a life are considerable, many young people (presumably those who are most tradition-oriented) do this and perpetuate the very system against which they had rebelled. Thus does the weighty hand of tradition press down upon each succeeding generation, molding its members to the ideals and expectations of the society. Here, as elsewhere, Nacirema culture shows itself to be ingeniously adapted to the functional requirements of enculturation, though the degree to which these patterns are relevant to the needs of the young people must be seriously questioned.

RECOMMENDED READING

Brown, Roger, *Social Psychology.* New York: Free Press, 1965. Especially Part III, "The Socialization of the Child." A comprehensive and highly readable account of research on a wide range of topics.

Castaneda, Carlos, *The Teachings of Don Juan.* New York: Ballantine Books, 1968. A fascinating account of how a young anthropologist almost becomes a Yaqui shaman.

Endleman, Robert, *Personality and Social Life.* New York: Random House, 1967. Especially Chapter 2, "Socialization: the family and its alternatives," which contains excellent essays on child-rearing in the Israel kibbutz and in three Puerto Rican communities. Also, Chapter 4, "Transitions: *rites de passage,*" contains an interesting variety of materials and interpretations.

Erikson, Erik, *Childhood and Society.* New York: Norton, 1950. Provocative essays on psychosexual development and national character, as well as the author's "colleague" relationship with a Yurok shaman.

Goffman, Erving, *Relations in Public.* New York: Basic Books, 1971. Essays on how the "self" is created and altered in everyday interactions. Chapter 2, "The Territories of the Self," and Chapter 6, "Normal Appearances," are particularly relevant to an understanding of social control, and the concept of "Remedial Interchanges" in Chapter 4 is immensely helpful in understanding, for example, why we smile.

Mayer, Philip, ed., *Socialization: The Approach from Social Anthropology.* London: Tavistock, 1970. Essays by various authors on current approaches to socialization (enculturation).

In Chapter 2, the distinction was drawn between an abstract *language system* and the concrete *speech behavior* which "manifests" that system: that is, between the language conceived of as learned categories and plans for speaking, and the actual movements of vocal organs together with the resultant sound waves. In the following chapters, this distinction—between observable behavior and the systematic rules which may be formulated to account for regularities in that behavior—will be expanded and applied to other parts of culture.

We will look first at the *social system*—that part of a culture which primarily influences the interactions among members of a society. A social system is described by stating the *rules* which best account for observed regularities of interpersonal behavior. For example, if you observe the behavior of uniformed men on a military base, you will soon notice that saluting takes place under a number of circumstances; you may also learn that there are quite explicit rules as to how, where, and when different kinds of persons are expected to salute one another. Much of human behavior is governed by rules, though the rules are seldom as explicit or precise in their details as are those of the military subculture.

We say that a social system *influences* interpersonal behavior because individuals in every society usually behave *as if* they were governed by rules. The social system both influences and is inferred from the actions of specific individuals (see below). That is, we can observe that Private Smith and Private Jones both salute Captain Black (but not one another), while Captain Black salutes Major Brown, who in turn salutes General Green (as do all of the others). The behavior of these individuals toward one another is regular enough for us to assume that it is influenced by some kind of social rule.

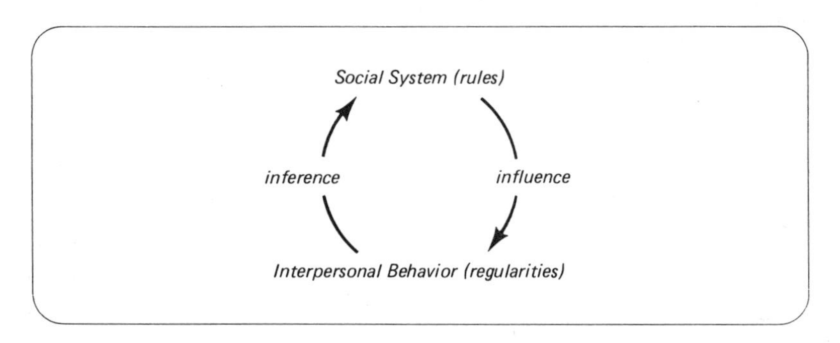

Relations Between a Cultural System and Behavior

Marc & Evelyne Bernheim/Woodfin C.

PART III
Social Systems

We infer the rule from what these people actually do in many concrete instances (and from what they tell us about what they do). But when we come to state the saluting rule as part of the military social system, we do not mention Private Smith or Captain Black as individuals; rather, we state the rule in terms of the categories "privates," "captains," "majors," and so forth. *The rules of a social system apply, not to single individuals, but to categories or "kinds of persons."*

Some social rules may be represented or described by abstract formulas. For example, if we represent "rendering a salute" by the symbol $<$, so that "$a<b$" indicates that "persons of rank *a* render salutes to persons of rank *b*," we may further state that "if $a<b$, and if $b<c$, then $a<c$." This is a familiar rule; it is identical with a theorem of the theory of real numbers in which *a*, *b*, and *c* are real numbers and the symbol $<$ means "is less than." But though the two rules look alike, there is a fundamental difference between them. The mathematical theorem follows logically from certain axioms of inequality. It can be proved: if you accept the axioms, the theorem is necessarily true. No matter how poor your arithmetic may be, four will always be less than eight.

Social rules, on the other hand, are statements of customary or expected behaviors, inferred from observations of actual behavior. Thus a more accurate statement of the saluting rule ($a<b$) would read: "Persons of rank *a* are *expected to salute* persons of rank *b* (and unless there are extenuating circumstances, they will normally be punished for failure to conform)." The saluting rule, then, has two major parts: the *categories of persons* to whom it applies (*a* and *b*), and the *plan for interaction* associated with their approaching one another ($<$).

Social rules may be *violated* for any number of reasons. Ignorance of the law is sometimes a very good excuse, at least for children and for strangers to a society. A violation may result from *confusion of categories*. In the military subculture this is unlikely because uniforms and insignia are designed to make an individual's rank immediately obvious to others in the subculture, and thus to avoid any confusion of categories. But in other situations, one cannot always be so sure of what "kind of person" he is dealing with. (Most people have had the experience of approaching a "salesperson" in a store only to discover that he is really a fellow shopper.)

Even when the category is correctly identified, there may be confusion as to the *appropriate plan* of action, or conflict among *alternative plans.* Young married persons in our society are often confused about what to call their new in-laws. Our culture provides no clear-cut rules for this situation. "Mr. Brown" seems too formal, and "father-in-law" is not generally used in direct address. There may be considerable discomfort on both sides until they are able to settle upon "father

Brown," "Dad," or perhaps "Charlie."

On the whole, however, social life proceeds pretty smoothly. When anthropologists speak of a highly *integrated* social system, they mean one in which the confusions and conflicts have been reduced to a minimum through common understandings and explicit social rules. This is always a matter of degree, for no society is completely integrated. But neither can a social group exist without considerable sharing among its members of common (or at least equivalent) categories and plans for action.

Because social and linguistic rules can be violated, we prefer to speak of culture *influencing* behavior rather than determining it. Some kinds of violations are rapidly and severely punished; but there is nothing which can prevent those violations from sometimes occurring. If I choose to say "an dog," to drive on the left side of the road (in the United States), or to omit saluting my commanding officer, I am "free" to do so, for these rules are conventional. Some kinds of violations rarely occur because we are not aware of the cultural patterns which are influencing our behavior in these areas, and it is hard to break a rule that you do not know you have been obeying. For example, of the three violations noted above, the linguistic one is the least likely to occur (even though its consequences would be the mildest). This is true because very few English speakers are consciously aware of the grammatical patterns which they regularly follow.

Culture, then, influences behavior in regular ways because people who have been enculturated in the same society share (consciously and unconsciously) many beliefs and expectations. Their behavior is predictable to the extent that they live up to one another's expectations. Of course, a culture cannot provide precise rules for every possible occurrence. A social system, like a language system, must be *productive*: from a limited number of categories and plans, a very large, and possibly infinite, number of socially appropriate actions may follow. As we shall see, this involves the application of quite general principles to novel problems and situations.

We shall return to many of these issues in the following chapters where they will be illustrated with concrete examples. For the present, it is sufficient for you to see that understanding how social systems work is a genuine scientific problem. In every society, people learn, store, and utilize a limited number of conventional rules which enable them to act appropriately and to judge behavior (their own and that of others) as either acceptable or unacceptable. The discovery of these rules and of the ways in which they may be productively combined is one task of the ethnographer.

A Note on Plans

An automobile driver in the United States must pay close attention to many features of his environment, but as he approaches an intersection the presence of a traffic light becomes particularly important. Out of his whole field of vision, he must selectively attend to a small lighted disk; judge whether it is red, yellow, or green; and respond appropriately. These three *color categories* (each of which includes a wide range of hues) are conventionally associated with standardized *plans for driving*—in this case, respectively, stopping, slowing, or passing through the intersection. There is nothing "natural" about either the colors (blue would serve as well as green) or their association with particular plans (red could be used to indicate "go"). But here let us consider briefly the nature of the plans themselves.

The best technical treatment of the concept of a plan is given in *Plans and the Structure of Behavior,* by the psychologists George Miller, Eugene Galanter, and Karl Pribram. They define a *plan* as "*any hierarchical process in the organism that can control the order in which a sequence of operations is to be performed.*" Like certain kinds of computer programs, behavioral plans consist of a series of steps toward a predetermined goal, together with a way of testing whether one step has been properly completed before going on to the next.[1]

Applying this idea to driving behavior, we might speak of a general plan for driving, which begins with sitting in the car and turning on the ignition. This includes a subplan (at a lower level of the hierarchy) giving the sequence of operations to be used when approaching an intersection. This intersection subplan calls for the driver to maintain his position on the road while he checks (tests) for the presence of pedestrians, stop signs, other cars, and/or traffic lights. (Note that both flashing red lights and hexagonal signs are associated with the same plan.) The plan for responding to a steady yellow light may be briefly stated as "anticipate a red light." At a still lower level of the hierarchy (depending on the car, the road, and other circumstances), there are a number of alternative subplans which may control the sequence of operations. The driver may slow by shifting to a lower gear, by braking (with either foot), by simply lifting his foot from the accelerator, or by any combination of these. In fact, under certain conditions of speed, distance, and probability of detection, he may "anticipate a red light" with the opposite type of behavior: accelerating quickly to pass through the intersection before the red light appears.

No two American drivers react to a yellow traffic light with exactly the same combination of muscular responses. What they share is a hierarchy of plans which leaves the

1. G. Miller, E. Galanter, and K. Pribram, *Plans and the Structure of Behavior* (New York: Holt, Rinehart and Winston, 1960), p. 17.

details of execution up to the individual. It is these expectations—not the behaviors—which are learned in the process of enculturation. Similarly, in performing our parts in the drama of social life we are not taught—aside from ritual—what our exact "lines" should be. Rather, we learn something in the nature of an outline which each person fills in, with greater or lesser skill. Erving Goffman has defined such a "part" or "routine" as a "pre-established pattern of action which is unfolded during a performance and which may be presented or played through on other occasions." And he suggests that we are really quite good at acting out new parts which we may have formerly only observed:

> Socialization may not so much involve a learning of the many specific details of a single concrete part—often there could not be enough time or energy for this. What does seem to be required of the individual is that he learn enough pieces of expression to be able to "fill in" and manage . . . any part that he is likely to be given. . . . The individual will already have a fair idea of what modesty, deference, or righteous indignation looks like, and can make a pass at playing these bits when necessary. He may even be able to play out the part of a hypnotic subject or commit a "compulsive" crime on the basis of models for these activities that he is already familiar with.[2]

Goffman's book, *The Presentation of Self in Everyday Life*, is—among other things—a useful account of how we translate the bare outlines of standardized routines (for example, "show respect," "take charge," or "look busy") into fairly impressive performances. This process of dramatic realization will be discussed further under the heading of "social organization." We begin, however, with the abstract categories and plans which compose the social structure.

2. E. Goffman, *The Presentation of Self in Everyday Life* (Garden City, N.Y.: Anchor Books, 1959), pp. 16, 73.

CHAPTER 4

Kinds of Persons

In describing social systems, we have seen that we must deal with categories rather than individuals and with general plans for action rather than specific acts. This is true even when the categories are normally represented by only one individual at a time. For example, the President of the United States is an important part of the American social system. In describing that system, we are concerned with the "kind of person" a President is expected to be, his general powers and limitations, and not with Abraham Lincoln or Rutherford B. Hayes (except insofar as their behavior provides evidence for the description). That is to say, we are interested primarily in social roles rather than the individuals who perform the roles.

SOCIAL ROLES

We may define a *social role* as any category of persons which, in a given society, is associated with a conventional plan for interaction with at least one other category of person. When we focus on the role as a category, we are interested in how one role *contrasts* with another: How is a President different from a Vice-President of from an appointed Cabinet member? When we focus upon the role as a plan for interaction, we are interested in the total *content* of the role: What kinds of behavior are appropriate to a President? What are his rights and obligations? These two aspects of a social role are closely related. (You may recall that in the Introduction to Part One it was stated that both contrast and content are needed for a complete definition of man. This statement also holds for "kinds of men.")

The role of President of the United States has many complex plans associated with it. Some of these expected actions are explicitly stated in the Constitution (for example, commanding the armed forces, appointing officials, signing or vetoing bills), while others have developed and changed as the American social system has grown (for example, delivery of a State of the Union address). We shall use the term *role attribute* to designate each of the different *kinds of behavior expected of a person who performs a given social role.* Thus the role of President consists of hundreds of attributes. Most of these are also found as attributes of other roles, but some of them are unique to the Presidency. It is the particular combination of attributes which makes one role contrast with all others, just as it is the selection and arrangement of phonemes which makes one morpheme different from another.

Most social roles have among their attributes one particular kind of attribute called the *role label.* Role labels, together with distinctive uniforms and other types of insignia, help both the members of a society and ethnographers to recognize which roles are being performed. The label is a word or phrase used by members of a society to address or refer to a particular kind of person. Unfortunately for the ethnographer, some roles do not have labels, some have several different labels, and some labels are associated with a number of different roles. Some familiar examples are the sequence "janitor-custodian-sanitary superintendent," or the many possible meanings of the label "doctor." A label may be used, then, as *evidence* for the existence of a distinct role, but only with the greatest caution. (This is similar to the way in which a linguist uses the traditional spelling of a written language in determining its phonomes. See the beginning of Chapter 2.)

Each social role also has one or more criteria for *recruitment* to the role. Recruitment is the process by which individuals become entitled to perform social roles. Recruitment criteria are the prerequisities for legitimate performance of a role: for example, to become President, a person must be a natural-born citizen of the United States, at least thirty-five years of age, receive a majority of the electoral votes in a national election, and so forth. Individuals who perform roles (such as "medical doctor") without possessing the associated recruitment criteria are guilty of *fraud*: they represent themselves as being kinds of persons with rights to which they are not entitled. Considerable light is thrown on the nature of social systems by the study of such frauds. In our society, there are even a number of role labels which are applied to persons who specialize in fraudulent performances: "quack," "impostor," "con man," "bigamist."

Ralph Linton introduced the concept of social role into anthropology in *The Study of Man.*[1] He distinguished two general types of recruitment: recruitment that takes place by *achievement*—that is, one must do something in order to legitimately perform the role (be elected, be ordained, receive a commission or a degree, and so on)—and recruitment that takes place by *ascription*—that is, a role is ascribed to an individual with little or no deliberate effort on his part (for example, one is born into a family, a caste, or a nationality, and one attains legal majority). The distinction between ascribed and achieved roles is not always easy to apply, and many roles require a combination of both types of recruitment: one must be born into the right family or class but also demonstrate achievements and meet requirements.

Each type of recruitment has its advantages and disadvantages. Since a person's ascribed roles are usually determined at birth, those who are going to perform them can begin their training early. Each individual knows what kind of person he will be, whether a king, a warrior, or a shoemaker; and since his future career is determined by forces beyond his control, he has little choice but to prepare for it as best he can. Achieved roles require a different kind of effort on the part of those who wish to perform them, and where there is competition for a limited number of positions, many aspirants may inevitably be frustrated.

Social systems may emphasize one or the other of these types of recruitment. The caste system of ancient India was one in which most roles were filled by ascription. Such systems do have the advantages of stability and individual security. Americans, however, tend to think of ascription as being undemocratic. We believe that encouraging individual achievement is the proper (and ultimately the most efficient) way to ensure good performance, and we offer incentives for people to try to better their positions in society. Unfortunately, recruitment by achievement does not automatically guarantee the "best man for the best job," and it may sometimes reward the most unscrupulous. When there are a limited number of opportunities, some frustration of ambitions is inevitable. This leaves many persons angry, insecure, and without acceptable rationalizations for their failure to succeed.

With these general ideas about the nature of social roles and role attributes in mind, we now turn to a survey of the types of roles that are found in different societies.

1. R. Linton, *The Study of Man* (New York: Appleton-Century, 1936), pp. 113–131. Actually, Linton used the term "role" to designate only the plan aspect of a social role (as defined above); he used the term "status" to refer to the category or social position aspect of a social role. I follow S. F. Nadel in eliminating the term "status" from descriptions of social structure. See S. F. Nadel, *The Theory of Social Structure* (New York: Free Press, 1957).

KINSHIP ROLES

In every known society, at least some persons consider themselves kin of at least some other persons, living and dead. The way in which kinship is expressed and the kinds of behavior which follow from the recognition of this relationship vary from culture to culture. Kinship usually involves some recognition of *organic community,* expressed in phrases like "We are of the same blood (or womb, or bone)." And in every society with which I am familiar, a degree of *mutual obligation* automatically exists among kinsmen which is only conditionally extended to nonkinsmen. But such generalizations are quite risky, for they deal with the content of kin relationships. In this section we shall be concerned with the abstract analysis of kinship roles. The study of kinship-based groups will be left for the next chapter.

Modern genetic theory is only a hundred years old, but culture has provided man with theories of kinship for tens of thousands of years. Although kinship is generally based upon biology, it is biology *as interpreted by culture.* Even today in our society, paternity is assigned with some uncertainty in a large proportion of births. This fact, together with the custom of adoption, means that we must distinguish among three kinds of fathers, even though they are usually the same individual: (1) the true *physiological father,* whose sperm fertilized the ovum from which the child in question developed; (2) the *genitor,* who is believed by members of his community (according to their culturally derived theory of reproduction) to have impregnated the child's mother; and (3) the *pater,* or socially recognized father, through whom the child may claim linkage with other kin.

The facts of mammalian biology make it possible to identify the maternal parent, though even here questions do occasionally arise. For example, until quite recently, a high court official was required to be present at each royal birth in England; and babies are probably mixed up in hospital nurseries more frequently than we should like to believe. Nevertheless, it is useful to distinguish between the *genetrix,* or woman who (it is generally believed) gave birth to the child, and the *mater,* the socially recognized mother through whom the child may claim kinship with other members of the society.

To be considered legitimate in most societies, a child must have both a mater and a pater through whom he derives his social position (in terms of kinship). A person lacking one of these relatives (usually the pater) at birth is generally placed at a social disadvantage (even though his genitor may be known or suspected). Although the genitor and the pater are usually the same individual, the widespread custom of adoption regularly disrupts this connection, and in a number of societies alternative arrangements are fairly common, as will be shown in the following examples.

1. *Toda polyandry:* Among the Toda of southern India it was customary for a woman to marry several brothers; the socially recognized pater of her children was the one who performed a certain ritual before the birth of her first child. Any of the brothers might be the genitor, but the one who performed this ritual was the pater even if he died before the conception of subsequent children.[2]

2. *Nuer ghost fathers:* Among the Nuer of East Africa, if a man died before having offspring, his brother might marry his widow (or some other woman) and father children in the name of the deceased; the pater of these children was considered to be the ghost of the first brother.[3]

3. *Female fathers:* In certain African societies, usually where wealth can be transmitted only from father to child, a noble woman who has accumulated considerable wealth may marry a female slave; the slave then has children by an authorized lover, and these children may inherit wealth and social position from their socially recognized pater (the noble woman).[4]

Other examples can easily be found to illustrate the point that a *kinship system* consists of a number of social roles, resting on a biological basis, but elaborated by the culture in a conventional way. In the words of Robert Lowie, "Biological relationships merely serve as a starting point for the development of sociological conceptions of kinship."[5]

---

2. C. Lévi-Strauss, "The Family," in H. L. Shapiro, ed., *Man, Culture, and Society* (New York: Oxford University Press, 1960), p. 265.
3. E. E. Evans-Pritchard, *Kinship and Marriage among the Nuer* (London: Oxford University Press, 1951), pp. 109–110.
4. Lévi-Strauss, *op. cit.*, pp. 273–274.
5. R. H. Lowie, *Social Organization* (New York: Holt, Rinehart and Winston, 1948), p. 57.

Analyzing Kinship Roles

A few symbols will be useful and sufficient for the analysis of kinship roles:

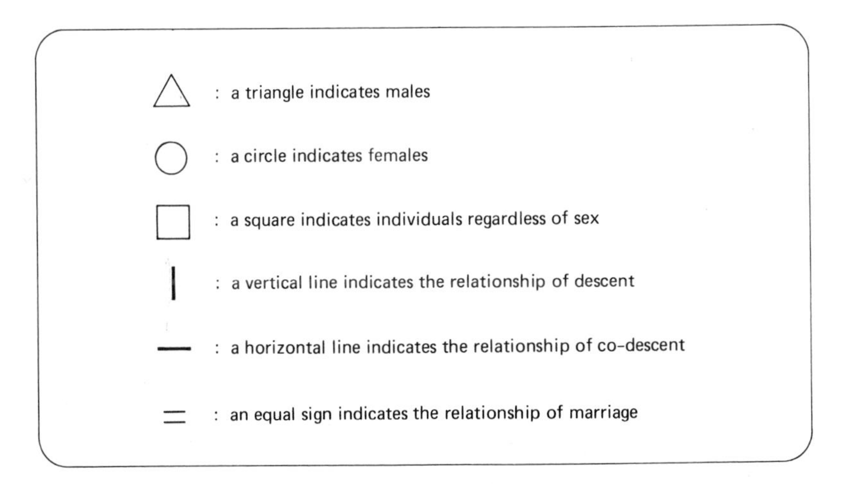

The following symbol cluster designates a parent/child relationship, ignoring the sex of the individuals:
When the sex of the related persons is considered, there are four logical possibilities:

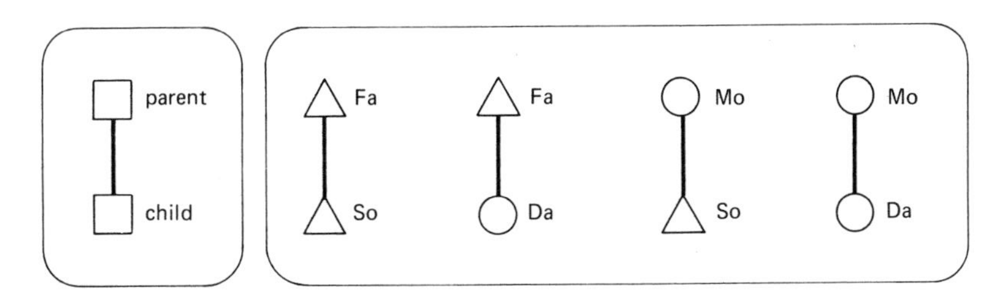

Individuals descended from the same mater or pater (co-descent) are known as siblings. Without consideration of the sex of the individuals, this relationship is represented:

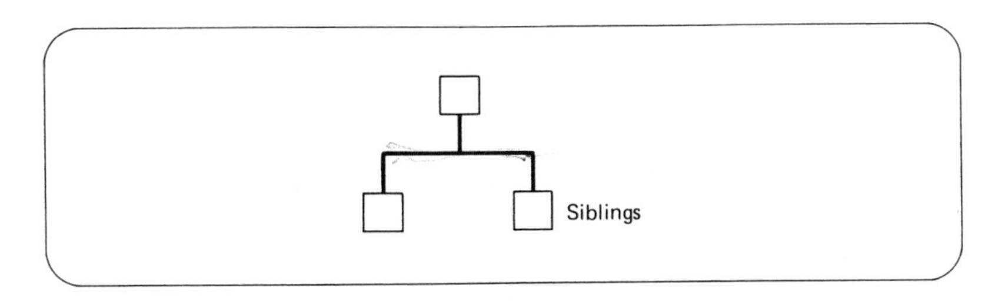

When the sex of any two siblings is considered, there are three logical possibilities:

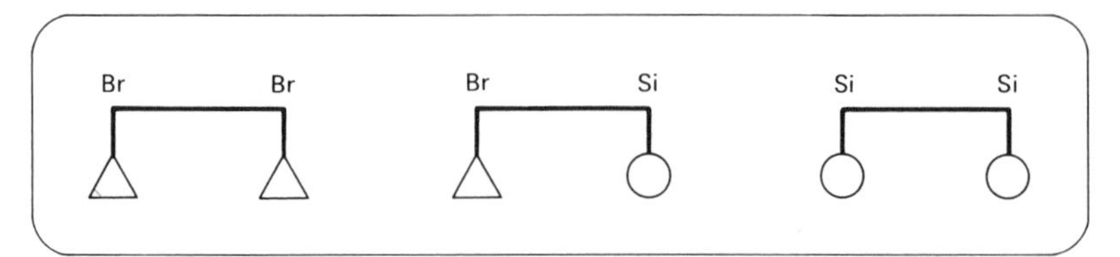

Persons whose linkage to one another (within a kinship system) may be traced through ties of descent or co-descent *only* are known as *consanguineal kin.* Anthropologists use the name "ego" for the person from whose point of view a relationship is regarded, and "alter" for the person to whom he is related. Thus the next diagram shows the linkage (by four ties of descent and one of co-descent) between ego and a distant consanguineal kinsman, his father's mother's father's sister's son:

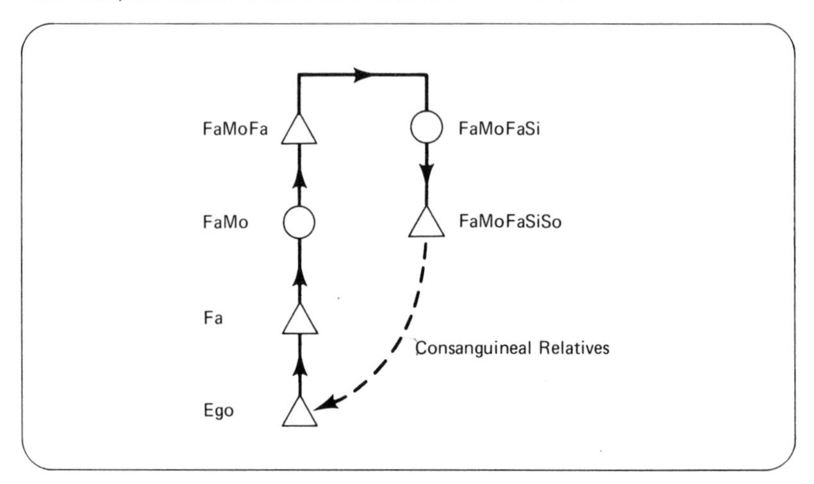

One more relationship will complete those necessary for an abstract analysis of kinship—the relationship of marriage. A married pair with their joint offspring shown as descendants of this relationship is symbolized by the cluster:

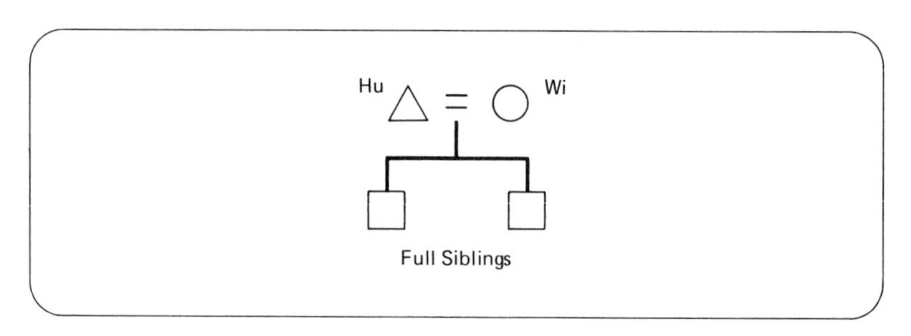

Where more than one spouse is permitted to a person, the relationship of co-marriage becomes possible; the most common form of this is known as polygyny and may be symbolized as:

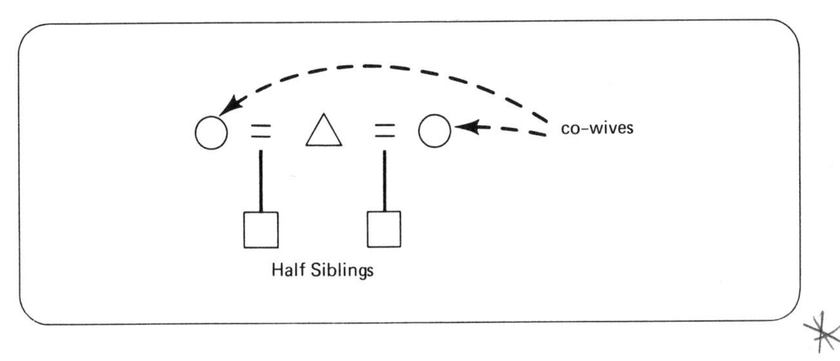

Persons who are linked to one another by ties of marriage rather than (or in addition to) ties of descent are known as *affinal kin.* Thus ego's affinal kin includes his wife and in-laws as well as the spouses and in-laws of all his consanguineal kin. As shown in the next diagram, ego is an affinal kinsman of his brother's son's wife, being linked to her through three kinds of relationships: co-descent, descent, and marriage:

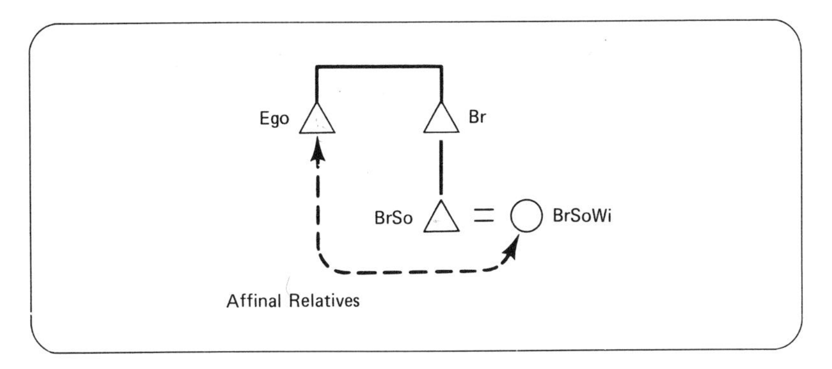

By use of the concepts and symbols defined above, it is possible to describe quite precisely the relationship between ego and any one of his consanguineal or affinal relatives, living or dead, in ascending or descending generations. However, a little calculation will show that one may distinguish several hundred different kinds of relatives going only three generations in each direction from ego. No kinship system can provide a different role label for each of these kinds of relatives (for example, FaMoFaSiSo versus FaMoMoBrSo). Some kind of organization of kinsmen into categories is essential. Here we come to the important topic of kinship terminology.

Kinship Terminology

It was the American lawyer and ethnologist Lewis H. Morgan who first recognized the importance to anthropological theory of kinship terms (the role labels used in different societies to classify kinsmen). In his monumental work, *Systems of Consanguinity and Affinity of the Human Family,*[6] Morgan compiled and compared hundreds of sets of kinship terms from many parts of the world. He found many similarities in the ways relatives were classified in widely separated groups speaking different languages. In keeping with the dominant anthropological theories of his day, Morgan tried to demonstrate an evolution of kinship systems from the primitive classificatory type to the more advanced descriptive type. A *classificatory kinship terminology* was one which lumped together certain relatives under a single term, so that, for example, ego would apply the same kin term to both Fa and FaBr or to both Mo and MoSi. This was contrasted with the *descriptive kinship terminology,* which provided separate terms for such relatives and which theoretically referred to more distant relatives by combinations of the primary terms.

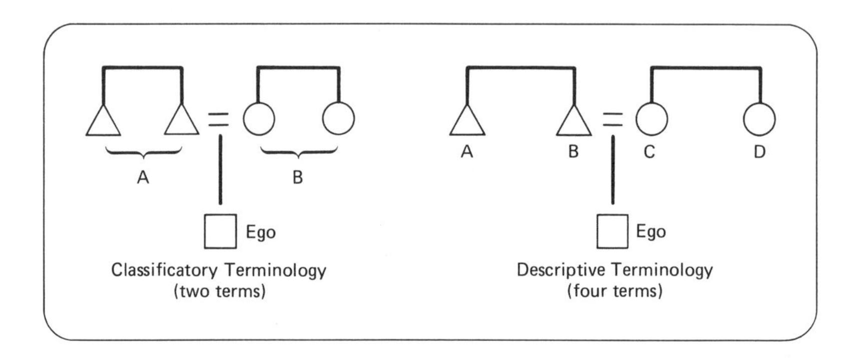

Morgan's distinction between classificatory and descriptive systems breaks down under close examination. It has already been noted that a purely descriptive system would have to provide separate terms for each of several hundred different kinsmen. However, all kinship systems known to anthropology have fewer than fifty different terms. This means that *every* system of kinship terminology is classificatory to some degree. The English system distinguishes between father and father's brother; but the term

6. L. H. Morgan, *Systems of Consanguinity and Affinity of the Human Family* (Washington: Smithsonian Contributions to Knowledge, Number 17, 1871).

applied to the latter relative (uncle) lumps him together with the mother's brother, and is to this extent classificatory. From the point of view of a society in which mother's brother and father's brother are labeled by different terms—and there are many of these—our term "uncle" classifies together two different kinds of relatives.

A more fruitful approach to kinship terminology was first suggested by A. L. Kroeber.[7] In a brilliant paper, which began with a criticism of Morgan's typology, Kroeber outlined an approach to the analysis of kin terms which was picked up and elaborated forty years later by G. P. Murdock in his book *Social Structure*.[8] The Kroeber-Murdock approach suggests that in each society a limited number of criteria are used to define contrasting categories of relatives. For example, when the criterion of *relative age* is applied to all of ego's kinsmen, it sorts them into two classes: those older than ego and those younger. Kinship systems differ in which criteria they utilize and how extensively each criterion is applied. Thus, in analyzing a set of kinship terms, we ask the following for each of the terms: "When ego uses a term to label a class of kinsmen and to contrast them with all other relatives, which criteria are being utilized and which are being ignored?" Let us see how this works out.

Generation

The first criterion, as defined by Murdock, is that of *generation*. The question to be asked is whether a given term indicates the generation of the person to whom it is applied (relative to ego). Thus the English terms "mother" and "grandson" indicate persons who must be respectively one generation above and two generations below ego. In fact, with the exception of our "cousin" term, all English kinship terms do utilize this criterion. A system of kin terms which recognized *only* the criterion of generation would require only as many terms as there were generations: ego could use one term for all members of his own generation (siblings and cousins, regardless of sex), another term for all members of his parents' generation, and so on. No such kinship systems are actually known, but the criterion of generation is very widely utilized in all kinship systems. The so-called "Hawaiian type" kinship of terminology classes cousins of ego's generation together with his siblings. The "Crow type" and "Omaha type," however,

7. A. L. Kroeber, "Classificatory Systems of Relationships," *Journal of the Royal Anthropological Institute*, Vol. 39 (1909), pp. 77–84.
8. G. P. Murdock, *Social Structure* (New York: Macmillan, 1949). The criterion of polarity has been omitted here.

both *ignore* the criterion of generation in some cases, grouping certain relatives in ego's generation together with relatives in higher or lower generations under a single term.

Sex

The criterion of *sex* is another which is generally utilized in kinship terminologies; the only English term which ignores this criterion is (again) "cousin." In many systems of kinship terms, the criterion of sex is ignored in alternate generations: that is, a single term may be used by ego for, say, his father's father and his father's mother, while these persons may also use a single term for both (male) ego and his sister. Although the English system includes terms with these meanings (grandparent and grandchild), the *usual* terms do express the sex of the relative. Similarly, we can refer to female cousin or aunt's daughter, but the usual term (cousin) does not indicate this relative's sex. Every language has ways of indicating some particular relative by a descriptive combination of terms, but in the study of kinship terminology, we are concerned with the categories of relatives designated by the simple role labels usually employed in address or in reference.

Affinity

The criterion of *affinity* is utilized when a kinship term is applied to either consanguineal relatives or affinal relatives (in-laws), but not to both. It is ignored when a term lumps together both types of relatives, as does the English term "aunt," which may designate both a parent's sister and a parent's brother's spouse. As Murdock points out, terms which ignore this criterion are often found in societies which encourage or insist upon marriage with a particular type of relative. For example, where ego is *expected* to marry his father's sister's daughter, he may use a single term for this relative and for "wife," while the term for father's sister may resemble or be the same as that for "mother-in-law." Compare the Micmac terms: *nsugwis,* "parent's sister," and *nsugwijič,* "wife's mother," where the suffix *-jič* is an affectionate diminutive.

Collaterality

The criterion of *collaterality* is often difficult for English speakers to understand simply because it is utilized in all of our consanguineal kinship terms. This criterion involves a distinction among three kinds of consanguineal relatives. Ego's *lineal* relatives are those with whom he is linked solely by direct ties of descent (not by co-descent). Ego's parent, his parent's parent (and so on up), his child, his child's child (and so on down)—all are his lineal relatives; but his parents' siblings or their offspring are *collateral* relatives. Ego's own siblings are classed as *colineal* relatives. Kinship terms which ignore the criterion of collaterality lump together lineal or colineal with collateral relatives, as in the earlier example of a single term applied to both father (lineal) and father's brother (collateral), or to both mother and mother's sister. Such lumping of lineal and nonlineal kin is technically known as *merging.* A common type of merging within ego's own generation involves the labeling of siblings and certain cousins with the same term.

Bifurcation

The criterion of *bifurcation* (forking) is unfamiliar to English speakers, although most societies use it in classifying at least some relatives. When bifurcation is recognized, ego uses different terms for relatives depending upon the sex of the linking relative. This is the distinction which we make in a roundabout way when we speak of a relative "on my mother's side" or "on my father's side." English terms usually lump together analogous relatives from both sides of the family (for example, an "uncle" may be either a father's brother *or* a mother's brother), thus ignoring the criterion of bifurcation. Many societies, however, which merge the father and father's brother (ignoring the criterion of collaterality) carefully separate the father's brother from the mother's brother (utilizing the criterion of bifurcation).

Figure 4.1 illustrates some of the logically possible combinations of these first five criteria.

In general, kinship systems make *systematic* use of the criteria which they utilize. If, for example, collaterality is recognized in the labeling of one pair of relatives, so that father and father's brother are called by different terms, it is likely that this criterion will be used to distinguish other pairs of relatives (for example, son and brother's son). In this respect, kinship systems are similar to phonemic systems in which, as we have seen, a limited number of qualitative criteria (voicing, tongue position, and so on) are systematically utilized to classify sounds into a few significant categories (the phonemes of a language). In language systems and in kinship systems we find a selection of and an emphasis on certain attributes of sounds or of persons, and a systematic tendency to ignore other attributes and the categories which could be based on them.

The criteria discussed above (generation, sex, affinity, collaterality, and bifurcation) constitute Murdock's "major criteria"

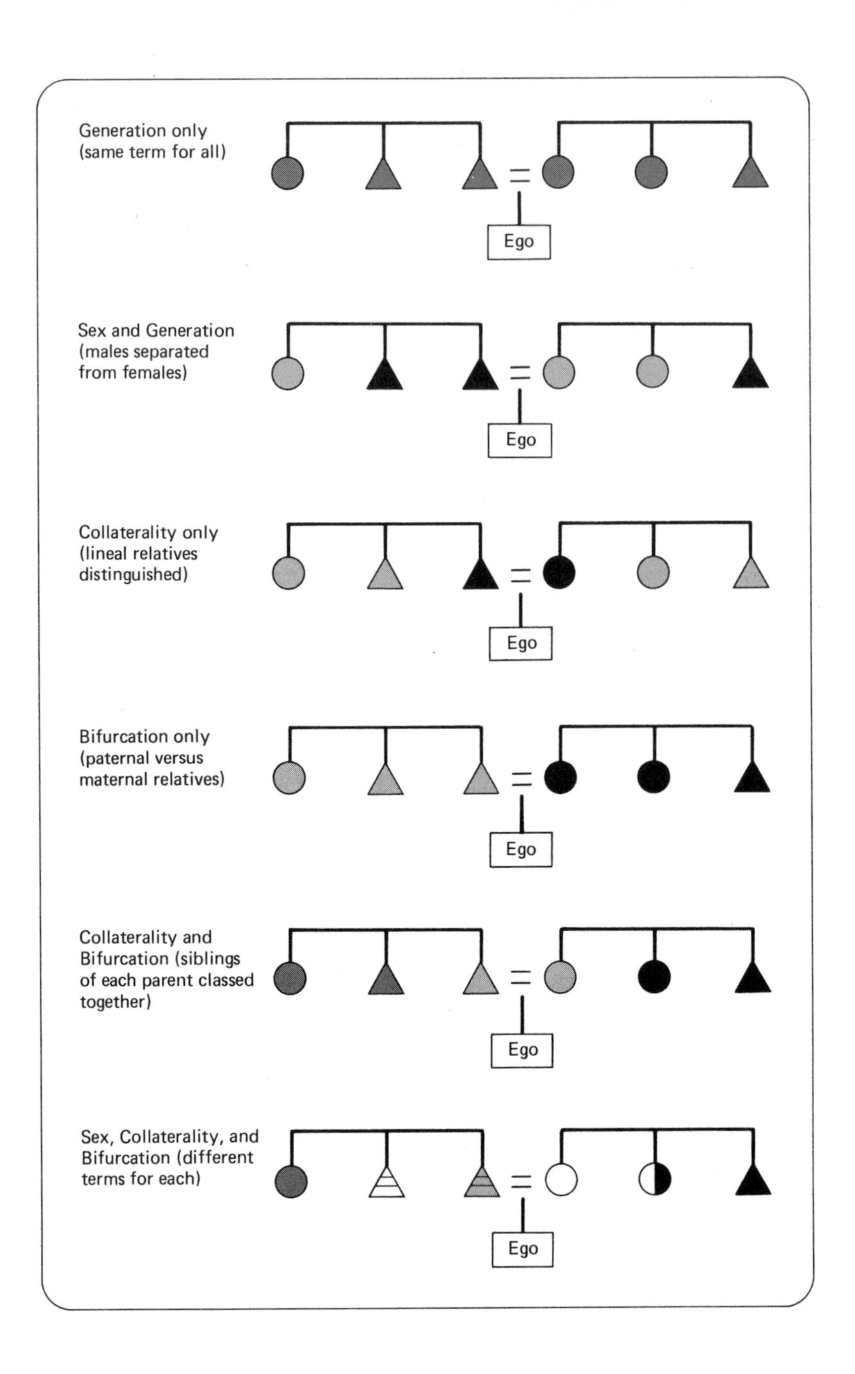

Figure 4.1 **Classification of Relatives with Recognition of Various Combinations of Criteria (same shading indicates use of same term)**

of kinship. They are supplemented by three "minor criteria" which, when they are utilized at all, tend to be restricted to only a few relationships.

Relative Age

In kinship systems where this criterion is recognized, ego may use different terms for elder versus younger siblings, both his own and those of his parents. Relative-age terminology is generally found in societies where a person's seniority gives him some privilege or authority over his kin.

Speaker's Sex

In general, ego and his siblings all use the same kinship term for each type of relative. But when the speaker's sex is recognized, ego and his sister must use different terms. For example, among the Haida Indians (of the Queen Charlotte Islands), a boy and his sister refer to their male parent by different terms; from the Haida point of view, the English term "father" is a classificatory term, covering two quite distinct relationships.

Decedence

Murdock's final criterion, decedence, is recognized when a kinship term used by ego changes upon the death of a connecting relative. It is not too difficult to imagine social customs that would impel ego to use a different kinship term toward, say, his father's brother after his own father's death. Utilization of this criterion, however, is quite rare.

A few other criteria are also used with some regularity in kinship terminologies, but those already considered are sufficient to illustrate this approach to the study of kinship structure. As we shall see in the next section, recognition of these criteria of classification leads to the following questions: How is terminology (categorization) related to expected social behavior (plans)? and Under what circumstances are certain criteria utilized or ignored in terminological systems? There are many other approaches to the study of kinship. Some of these, such as the inductive method called "componential analysis," will be touched on elsewhere in the book.[9] Others are too complex for treatment in an introductory

---

9. For a brief discussion of "componential analysis," see pp. 185–188. For a different approach to American kinship terminology which emphasizes the productivity of our system, see P. K. Bock, "Some Generative Rules for American Kinship Terminology," *Anthropological Linguistics*, Vol. 10, No. 6 (1968), pp. 1–6.

text. But the reader should bear in mind that one reason for our concern with kinship is a practical one, in the kinds of societies traditionally studied by anthropologists, kinship is frequently the key to understanding all kinds of social actions—from marriage to inheritance, and from witchcraft to political power.

Kinship Terminology and Behavior

Anthropological studies have made it abundantly clear that terminology is an important clue to expected behavior. However, we must beware of the fallacy of deducing rules of behavior (past or present) from terminology. Like other kinds of role labels, kinship terms are generally applied to categories of persons toward whom ego is expected to act in the same general way—each kinship category is associated with a set of plans. Thus, if ego uses a single kin term for both his father and his father's brother, it is probable that he is expected to treat them alike in at least some respects and that he has similar expectations of both. This does *not* mean that ego cannot tell the difference between them, or that he cannot state in a roundabout way his specific relationship to each. Nor does it mean, as some would still phrase it, that ego calls his father's brother "father." It does mean that for certain social purposes, the criterion of collaterality which could be used to separate them may be ignored; their common label is best translated as "male relative of the next higher generation on the paternal side." However, since a number of different social arrangements might encourage this type of classification, we must always investigate the actual behavior, as well as the terms.

Among the social customs that affect kinship terminology are the *marriage regulations* of a society. Take a society in which ego is permitted or encouraged to marry a cross-cousin (a daughter of his mother's brother or of his father's sister), but where he is forbidden to marry a parallel cousin (a daughter of his mother's sister or his father's brother). See Figure 4.2. Many societies have such marriage regulations. In one of these societies, it would be highly unlikely that ego would use the same kinship term toward both kinds of cousins, since his anticipated behavior toward them is so different.

Another example of the way in which marriage regulations may influence kinship terminology can be seen in societies where a man, if he takes a second wife, is expected to marry his first wife's sister. This is known as *sororal polygyny* (see Figure 4.3). In such societies, one might expect that ego would use the same kinship term for his mother's sister's daughter as he does for his

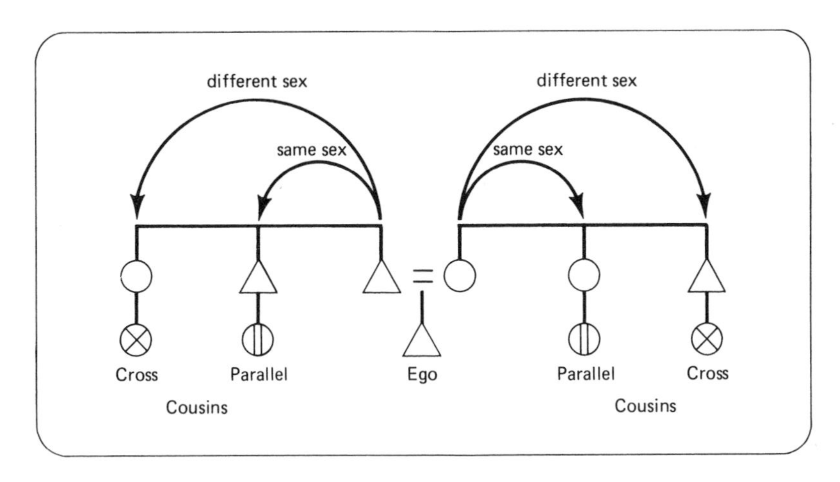

Figure 4.2 **Parallel and Cross Cousins**

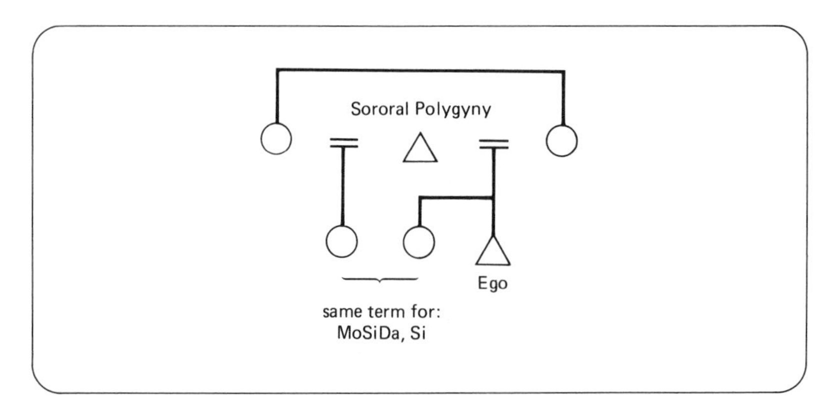

Figure 4.3 **Sororal Polygyny and Terminology**

own sister, since it is probable that his father will be married to his mother's sister.

Murdock found that in sixteen out of eighteen societies practicing sororal polygyny, the same term was in fact applied to both sister and mother's sister's daughter, whether ego's father was actually married to both sisters or not. However, this kind of terminology is also found in some societies which do not permit sororal polygyny. Therefore, although marriage regulations can help us understand certain features of kinship terminology, it would not be valid to infer the existence of a marriage rule simply from the presence of certain types of kinship terms. Kin terms are labels for categories of relatives, but the plans associated with each category must be determined separately for each society.

The major types of marriage regulations found in the world's societies are listed and defined below. Their greatest importance is in connection with the formation of households and other types of social groups and alliances; these are topics which will be treated in the next chapter.

Types of Marriage Regulations

I. monogamy—one spouse at a time
  a. strict—no remarriage
  b. serial—remarriage permitted

II. polygamy—plural spouses permitted
  a. polygyny—plural wives
    i. sororal—wives must be sisters
  b. polyandry—plural husbands
    i. fraternal—husbands must be brothers

III. preferential (or prescriptive) marriage
  a. cross-cousin marriage—should (or must) marry cross cousin
    i. patrilateral—man should marry father's sister's daughter
    ii. matrilateral—man should marry mother's brother's daughter
  b. parallel-cousin marriage—should (or must) marry parallel cousin
    i. patrilateral—man should marry father's brother's daughter
    ii. matrilateral—man should marry mother's sister's daughter (rare)
  c. levirate—man expected to marry widow of his deceased brother
  d. sororate—man expected to marry sister of his deceased wife
  e. mother/daughter marriage—man marries widow and her daughter(s)

IV. group-specific marriage—this includes a variety of rules falling into two major types
  a. exogamy—requiring marriage *outside of* a given social group
  b. endogamy—requiring marriage *within* a given social group
    i. social class or caste
    ii. locality
    iii. kinship group (lineage, clan, moiety, and so on)
    iv. religious group

A question which naturally arises in connection with preferential marriage rules (such as IIIa and IIIb) is this: What if ego simply does not have the right kind of cousin (for example, his father's sister is childless or his mother has no brothers)? The answer to this question brings us back to the significance of kinship terminology. In a society with, say, preferential matrilineal cross-cousin marriage (IIIa-ii), the rule should be stated as follows: ego is expected to marry a woman whom he *calls* "mother's brother's daughter." Since all kinship terminologies are classificatory, ego's own mother's brother's daughter is only one of the females who fall into the category with this label. There will generally be several eligible females called by this term; if not, a compromise or exception can always be made.

Looking at these marriage regulations from another angle, we can see that they define recruitment criteria for the social role "wife." The rules specify that in order to become ego's wife, a woman must qualify as a member of a particular *social category.* In the cases described by some rules of type II or III, the significant social categories are part of the kinship system. But in every society the culture defines certain categories of persons as suitable or unsuitable mates for other categories of persons, and almost every member of a society is influenced by these regulations in his or her choice of a spouse. In American society, the category of suitable mates is based on a combination of racial, religious, ethnic, and social-class factors, and the vast majority of marriages take place between persons who live in the same locality. Thus, before we wonder at kin-based marriage rules, we should realize that in fact, if not in principle, our own range of potential mates is severely limited.

Social Relationships

A final point to be made in connection with kinship roles has to do with the *reciprocal* nature of all types of social roles. That is, a kinship role exists only in relation to a reciprocal role: one can be a mother's brother only in relation to a sister's child, a husband only in relation to a wife. Each such role implies its reciprocal, and the pair of roles taken together compose the *social relationship.* Thus we may say that the "marriage relationship" is composed of the reciprocal roles "husband/wife," the "avuncular relationship" of the roles "parent's brother/sibling's child," and so on.

This is true of nearly all types of roles and relationships: employer/employee, performer/audience, teacher/pupil, doctor/patient, friend/friend, and so on. The reciprocity of social relationships is a basic fact of social structure. Recognition of this fact should help us to see that social roles have an essential *function* to perform: they are cultural devices which make smooth and coordinated interaction among the members of a society possible. They do this by enabling ego to know what to expect of alter (and what alter expects of him) in most situations. By learning and performing those roles to which he is legitimately entitled, each person contributes to the maintenance of his society and of its traditions.

Because the kin roles of any society form a system, and it is very difficult to understand the significance of any one role outside of the total kinship system, we have had little to say in this section about the *content* of kinship roles (the plans associated with various categories of relatives), except for the suitability of marriage. Reading a few ethnographic case studies will give the student a better comprehension of this aspect of kinship than could any number of isolated examples (see Recommended Readings). Nevertheless, we may note that the reciprocal nature of social relationships requires a give-and-take such that each member of a relationship gets something in return for his participation; among the benefits given and received in many kinship relations are food, affection, protection, power, loyalty, labor, pleasure, property, service, and security.

If one member of a relationship continually gives more than he receives, we speak of *exploitation.* Exploitative relationships tend to be unstable, though there are conditions under which they may persist for some time; for example, when the exploiting member has a monopoly of power and/or other benefits. Change within social systems may often be analyzed as the overthrow of the exploiters by the exploited. The Marxist, indeed, applies this formula to the totality of social history. (Other content attributes of social roles will be treated in the following sections and in Chapter 5.)

SEX ROLES AND AGE ROLES

One set of roles found in every human society is the pair *male* and *female.* These are generally lifetime roles, ascribed to an individual at birth (though some kind of intermediate role, such as the Crow berdache or the Cheyenne "half-man, half-woman," may be "achieved" later in life). The two basic sex roles give rise to three possible sexual relationships: male/male, female/female, and male/female. Although most social interaction is governed by much more specific kinds of role attributes, the sex roles provide an ever-present background to social behavior. In an unfamiliar situation, one may have no other clue to the kind of person one is dealing with. In more clearly defined situations, the sex roles of the participants may condition their performances in various ways; for example, a male teacher frequently acts differently from a female teacher.

Two of the most general conclusions of cultural anthropology are that *sex roles are learned* and that the *content* of sexual relationships depends primarily upon culture. This is not to deny for a moment the biological basis of these roles; rather, we wish to emphasize that, as with kinship roles, each culture interprets and elaborates the biological differences in a conventional and partly arbitrary manner. Margaret Mead, who has spent many years studying the relationship of sex to social customs, states that

> the growing child in any society is confronted . . . by individuals—adults and adolescents and children—who are classified by his society into two groups . . . in terms of their most conspicuous primary sex characters, but who actually show great range and variety both in physique and behavior. Because primary sex differences are of such enormous importance . . . most children take maleness or femaleness as their first identification of themselves.
>
> . . .
>
> But it is not enough for a child to decide simply and fully that it belongs to its own sex, is anatomically a male or a female, with a given reproductive role in the world. For growing children are faced with another problem: "*How male*, how female, am I?" He hears men branded as feminine, women condemned as masculine, others extolled as real men, and as true women. He hears types of responsiveness, fastidiousness, sensitivity, guts, stoicism, and endurance voted as belonging to one sex rather than the other.[10]

Each society, then, develops different sex roles which define how a man or a woman is expected to act. The content of these roles is partly arbitrary. Margaret Mead's book *Male and Female* shows that some societies elaborate very little upon the given physiological differences, viewing men and women as pretty much the same, while others emphasize the differences between the sexes in various ways and call forth quite different behavior from each, since people generally learn to behave as their society expects.

The conventionality of the content of sex roles is most easily seen in those attributes which have to do with superficial appearance. In most American Indian tribes it was the men who wore long hair and painted their faces, while among most contemporary Americans these are attributes of the female sex role. Conventional (cultural) standards of beauty and sexual attractiveness have led men and women, in different times and places, to adopt the most outlandish styles of dress and to practice grotesque forms of bodily mutilations. The styles of yesterday generally look pretty silly to people of today, just as the costumes of today will

10. M. Mead, *Male and Female* (New York: Morrow, 1949), pp. 128, 136.

amuse our descendants. Bodily mutilations are by no means restricted to primitive peoples, for alongside scarification, head-flattening, and lip-stretching, we must place foot-binding, ear-piercing, and the bustle. As Miner says of the Nacirema:

> There are ritual fasts to make fat people thin and ceremonial feasts to make thin people fat. Still other rites are used to make women's breasts larger if they are small, and smaller if they are large. General dissatisfaction with breast shape is symbolized by the fact that the ideal form is virtually outside the range of human variation.[11]

Comparative studies have shown that traits thought of as typically masculine in one culture may be considered feminine (or not ascribed to either sex) in another. This is true not only of appearance but also of psychological characteristics (such as aggressiveness or curiosity) and alleged abilities (such as physical endurance or spiritual powers). The division of labor by sex is indeed universal; but *which* tasks will be assigned to *which* sex is largely a matter of arbitrary cultural definition. Thus in some societies only the men perform agricultural tasks, in others only women, and in still others agriculture is the responsibility of both sexes. Similarly, the shamans in one society may be primarily men, and in another, women; just as most medical doctors in the United States are men, while in the U.S.S.R. the vast majority are women. Cultures also contain beliefs which tend to rationalize the existing division of labor—for example, that men or women make better shamans or doctors—but these beliefs are just as conventional as the practices which they justify.

Age roles are also universal, though again the specific age categories and the plans for behavior which are associated with these categories are partly conventional. Aging is a continuous process which begins with conception and ends with death. In between, the various stages of the human career are conventionally established in much the same way as each culture divides up the continuous spectrum into color categories. In traditional Chinese culture, a child was considered one year old at birth, and he advanced to age two at the New Year (when all members of the society added a year to their age), whether that came ten days or ten months after his actual birth. European cultures generally count age for each individual continuously from the moment of birth. In American culture (depending upon the state in which he lives) there are different ages at which a person may vote, marry,

---

11. H. Miner, "Body Ritual among the Nacirema," *American Anthropologist*, Vol. 58 (1956), p. 506.

purchase liquor, drive an automobile, cease attending school, or retire with a pension. These categories, based upon chronological age, operate together to determine a person's *social age* and thus to define his rights and obligations within the social group.

Most preliterate societies do not calculate a person's absolute age in years or months, but they often attach great importance to relative age distinctions (such as older versus younger). And some primitive social systems utilize age to a great extent in organizing group relationships (see p. 159). For example, among the Masai, a warlike people of East Africa, young men in their late teens and twenties lived apart from their families in a special camp for warriors, where they ate, slept, and were visited by their sweethearts. From this camp they departed on offensive or retaliatory raids against neighboring tribes, killing enemies, earning glory, and stealing cattle to bring back to their village. By the time a Masai man had reached his early thirties, the warrior phase of his life would end; he was then an elder, and would be expected to marry and settle down. This was an adjustment as difficult for the Masai to make as is involuntary retirement for the still-active business executive in our society.

Each culture and subculture not only categorizes the "ages of man" in different ways and associates different plans for behavior with these ages, but it also *values* the various age roles differently. In any society we may ask what is considered the best age or the prime of life, and the answer to this question may be very revealing of the basic patterns of the culture. In some societies, childhood, or at least youth, is considered the best time of life; while in others old age is most highly valued, the role of "elder" being a respected and desired one. In still other societies, it is the vigorous young adult who is considered to be at the height of his powers.

The Tarascan Indians of North-Central Mexico associate vitality (*esfuerzo*) with the body heat of an individual, and their division of the life cycle is clear from the following statement:

> a person goes through three "ages" in a lifetime. The first, from birth to puberty, is one of gradually increasing body heat—which spells health—and vigor. The second, from puberty to about 30 years of age, is that of maximum strength and vitality. After 30 a person gradually loses his esfuerzo as his body grows old and cold.[12]

Interpretations of American attitudes toward the ages of man are not in agreement, though all studies show that old age brings

---

12. G. M. Foster, *Tzintzuntzan* (Boston: Little, Brown, 1967), p. 129.

Warriors of the Masai tribe of East Africa. ***Marilyn Silverstone/Magnum***

very little prestige. Some scholars emphasize the youth culture of the United States, pointing out the growing desire of Americans to "think young" as well as to "look young." Others have pointed out that the period thought of as the prime of life comes at a different point in the subculture of each social class. Thus for the lower-class male, whose occupation is likely to involve little education and much manual labor, the prime of life is in the twenties and early thirties. For the upper-middle–class person, these are likely to be years of continuing education and a struggle to get established, with professional and financial success coming later, in the forties and fifties. Such differences between group expectations have far-reaching effects upon the lives of group members and create very different social problems. The conflict between the generations, the bitterness of old maids, and the isolation of elderly people so common to our society take very different forms (and may even be absent) in groups with different ideas about age roles.

OCCUPATIONAL ROLES

As Everett Hughes has pointed out, "Careers in our society are thought of very much in terms of jobs, for these are the characteristic and crucial connections of the individual with the institutional structure."[13] We think of persons other than relatives primarily in terms of their jobs, and a man's social position is largely determined by whether he is a lawyer, a clerk, or a factory worker. In simpler societies, a person is much more likely to be identified with his kinship group or with his locality, for there are no true occupational roles: the division of labor by age and sex, supplemented by a few part-time specialists, is sufficient. But the part-time shaman, trader, or craftsman is the forerunner of the priest, merchant, or artisan. Even in societies where such roles are ascribed to an individual on the basis of kinship, they greatly enrich the social structure by making possible many new kinds of relationships.

In many of the world's societies, recruitment to occupational roles is strictly determined by heredity. Where this is the case, the learning of occupations can take place within a family setting: the son of a blacksmith knows that he too will one day be a blacksmith, and he begins at an early age, as an integral part of his daily life, to acquire the skills and knowledge that he will need later.

13. E. C. Hughes, *Men and Their Work* (New York: Free Press, 1958), p. 64.

In societies where personal preference enters into the choice of occupation, formal training, as an apprentice or in a regular school, is required. The Navajo Indian who wishes to become a ritual singer must persuade an experienced singer to teach him a chant; this involves weeks of concentrated training, for which the teacher receives considerable gifts. The training of the Tapirapé shamans, described in the preceding chapter, requires years of preparation and discipline.

To perform an occupational role, then, a person must claim (explicitly or implicitly) to possess certain *skills* and *knowledge.* He may display these in the material objects he produces or in the services he performs for others. But whatever his task, the performer of a specialized role serves as a repository for some part of his group's total culture—a part which it is impractical or unnecessary for every member of the society to understand. Since they are dependent upon his goods or services, the other members of a society are to some extent at the mercy of the specialist, be he a shaman or a plumber. Members of specialized occupational groups (see Chapter 5) develop their own jargon and attitudes toward the public, while their clients can only hope that the specialist actually possesses and will use the skills and knowledge which he claims—that he is the kind of person he seems to be.

Two dilemmas of social life are illustrated in the specialist/client relationship. The first has to do with the fact that most social relationships have a different meaning for each of the participants. It should be obvious that the obligations of one party to a social relationship are the rights of the other; for example, a worker's right to be paid for his labor implies the employer's obligation to pay him. But beyond this, a person's attitude toward entering into a given relationship depends upon his past experience in the role he must perform. For those specialties known as the "professions," Everett Hughes has summarized this dilemma in a pithy phrase: the client's *crisis* is the professional's *routine.*[14] That is, the critical and unusual situation which brings a person to consult a specialist (be he curer, lawyer, undertaker, or auto mechanic) is exactly the kind of situation with which the specialist deals day after day, from which he makes his livelihood, and toward which he must cultivate a deliberately unemotional attitude. Thus the doctor deals with sick and dying people every day, but each patient (quite understandably) thinks of his own illness as unique.

At the same time, the specialist is faced with a peculiar dilemma of his own that has been analyzed by Erving Goffman.

14. *Ibid.*

Goffman refers to this as the conflict between *action* and *expression.* In order to have clients, the specialist must communicate to them the fact that he is doing something for them; and this requirement for expression often gets in the way of his action. As Goffman comments, if a person wishes to dramatize the character of his role, this may take a good deal of energy. The appearance of casual competence may require long and arduous preparation. The dilemma of action *versus* expression is that "those who have the time and talent to perform a task well may not, because of this, have the time or talent to make it apparent that they are performing well."[15] But it is the *appearance* of competence that inspires confidence, since the fact of competence is usually unmeasurable.

Though most clearly illustrated in the specialist/client relationship, this dilemma is not limited to occupational roles. For example, we are all familiar with the type of student who is so eager to make a good impression upon his professor that he ends up missing the point entirely; he has been tellingly described by Jean Paul Sartre: "The attentive pupil who wishes to *be* attentive, his eyes riveted on the teacher, his ears open wide, so exhausts himself in playing the attentive role that he ends up by no longer hearing anything."[16]

Having learned a role, then, is not enough; one must also translate one's knowledge into action and have one's performance accepted by others as legitimate. Here we can see some further functions of the *rite of passage* (Chapter 3): it *dramatizes* the actor's claim to being a new kind of person, making his change of status clear to the public and to the performer himself.

LEADERSHIP ROLES

By a leadership role we mean a social role involving the legitimate exercise of *authority* over other persons. A person with authority is socially entitled to command the actions of others, and his commands are backed up by *social sanctions:* rewards or punishments.[17] The way in which he exercises this authority varies with the culture and the type of social group. He may drop a casual suggestion or issue a decree, state an opinion or promulgate a new law code; but in any case, when he acts within the limits of his leadership role, his followers can be expected to

15. E. Goffman, *The Presentation of Self in Everyday Life* (Garden City, N.Y.: Anchor Books, 1959), pp. 32–33.
16. J. P. Sartre, *Being and Nothingness,* quoted in *Ibid.,* p. 33.
17. Compare S. F. Nadel, *The Theory of Social Structure* (New York: Free Press, 1957).

obey. Leaders are specialists in decision-making. By virtue of their social position, they are entitled to act for or in behalf of others. The leader/follower relationship may take many forms, but is always characterized by this fundamental *asymmetry* of authority.

Four general types of leadership roles may be distinguished on the basis of the leader's source of authority. The first type is the *hereditary leader.* His claim to authority is based upon his position in a kinship group—for example, as the oldest living male in a royal lineage. Recruitment to such a leadership role is thus of the ascribed type, although when more than one individual has a claim to become leader, certain types of achievement may also enter into the picture. The history of disputed royal successions is filled with poisonings, assassinations, and rebellions, all of which eliminate the careless or trusting person from positions of authority.

Hereditary leaders are socially recognized (their authority is considered legitimate) because of *who they are,* rather than what they can do. This does not mean, however, that their power is unlimited. The Oriental despot is a special and extreme case of the hereditary leader with virtually unlimited power. If we examine alien social systems carefully, however, we often find that the authority of the hereditary leader is limited in many subtle ways. Thus many hereditary African rulers have been referred to as absolute monarchs, but as M. Fortes and E. E. Evans-Pritchard observed:

> The forces that maintain the supremacy of the paramount ruler are opposed by the forces that act as a check on his powers. . . . Institutions like the king's council, sacerdotal officials who have a decisive voice in the king's investiture, queen mothers' courts, and so forth . . . work for the protection of law and custom and the control of centralized power. . . . The balance between central authority and regional autonomy is a very important element in the political structure. If a king abuses his power, subordinate chiefs are liable to secede or to lead a revolt against him.[18]

A second type of leadership role, in which achieved attributes play the largest part in recruitment, is the *bureaucratic leader*. Such leaders attain positions of authority by systematically progressing through positions of lesser authority; their achievements involve *competence* (in a rather narrow sense, often judged by standardized tests) and *seniority* (acquired by a number of years of faithful service). Bureaucracies arise under rather special

18. M. Fortes and E. E. Evans-Pritchard, eds., *African Political Systems* (London: Oxford University Press, 1940), p. 11.

The hereditary leader. A tribal king in Uganda receives visiting dignitaries.
George Rodger/Magnum

social conditions, and they both attract and develop the kind of person who has moderate ambitions and who desires a career filled with routine and security.

A third type of leader, which the great German sociologist Max Weber considered the direct opposite of the bureaucratic type, is the so-called *charismatic leader.* He is a unique person who rises to authority in times of great social crisis; by the force of his personality, he commands enthusiastic followers who may bring about a genuine social revolution:

> Charisma, meaning literally "gift of grace," is used by Weber to characterize self-appointed leaders who are followed by those who are in distress and who . . . believe him to be extraordinarily qualified. The founders of world religions and the prophets as well as military and political heroes are the archetypes of the charismatic leader. Miracles and revelations, heroic feats of valor and baffling success are characteristic marks of their stature. Failure is their ruin.[19]

The upheaval brought about by charismatic leaders is generally followed by what Weber called the "routinization of charisma." Rigid institutions of the bureaucratic type take over and adapt the ideas of the leader, converting what were radical ideas into a dogma that can be taught and followed in a routine manner. In this process, the novel ideas are modified and made acceptable to a large following. This process of routinization may be seen in its most striking form in religion and in politics, but it also occurs in education and the arts. Thus a John Dewey or an Arnold Schoenberg will be followed by a string of more or less competent disciples who work out (and generally dilute) the master's teachings.

The fourth type of leadership role is the *representative leader.* This type of leader may possess attributes of the three other types; he may come from an important family, he may have attained high bureaucratic office, and/or he may possess considerable personal charisma. But these qualities are not the basis of his authority. The representative leader is *chosen by his followers* through general consensus or election. The basis of his authority is the fact that he was chosen by a group of people and is *responsible to them.*

Representative leaders are found in many different types of societies. Whether chosen for a limited or for an indefinite period, they may continue to lead only so long as their followers are willing to obey; also, there are ways of depriving such leaders of authority without overturning the whole social system. For exam-

19. H. Gerth and C. W. Mills, eds., *From Max Weber: Essays in Sociology* (New York: Oxford University Press, 1958), p. 52.

ple, among the Iroquois tribes of New York State, there was an intertribal governing council made up of chiefs and sachems who were chosen by the leading women of certain lineages and who could also be deposed by these women. Among the Plains Indians, a leader was one who had proven himself in warfare, but his authority lasted only so long as he was successful.

In most small hunting and gathering societies (bands), the leader is simply the oldest or the most experienced man in the group. He may decide when and where to move camp, and what hunting techniques should be used; he may attempt to settle intra-band disputes; but beyond these specific functions, he has no power over the members of the band. Marshall D. Sahlins distinguishes "tribal societies" from "chiefdoms" on similar grounds:

> The typical leader in a tribal society is only the glorified counterpart of the influential elder in a hunting and gathering society. Like the latter . . . he builds a following on the basis of personally-established ties. He creates loyalties through generosity; fearful acquiescence through magic; inclination to accept his opinions through demonstration of wisdom, oratorical skill, and the like. Leadership here is a charismatic interpersonal relationship. Since it is based on personal ties and qualities, it is not hereditable. It is not an *office* within a definite group: it is not *chieftainship*.[20]

Authority enters into many role relationships, and since it is always asymmetrical, it is often possible to *rank* a series of roles in terms of this attribute. Bureaucratic organizations such as the military require an elaborate and explicit ranking of roles so that all members of the group may know who is entitled to give orders to whom. Even within the family group, some types of kinsmen (father, mother's brother) will generally exercise authority over ego.

We should not, however, confuse the *ranking* of roles according to relative authority with the *valuation* of roles according to their relative prestige. In some societies, positions of power are treated as necessary evils, and no one will admit to a craving for leadership. The Nuer of northeastern Africa, for example, place so little value on leadership that, in the words of Evans-Pritchard, they "have no government, and their state might be described as an ordered anarchy."[21] Other peoples accord the highest honors to their leaders and are very uncomfortable in the absence of clear-cut authority. In our society, some roles are highly valued but carry little or no authority (for example, concert pianist), while

20. M. D. Sahlins, "The Segmentary Lineage: An Organization of Predatory Expansion," *American Anthropologist*, Vol. 63 (1961), p. 327. See the same author's article "Poor Man, Rich Man, Big-Man, Chief: Political Types in Melanesia and Polynesia," *Comparative Studies in Society and History*, Vol. 5 (1963), pp. 285–303.

others with considerable authority (for example, policeman) are low in prestige. Thus authority and prestige, though they often go together, may also diverge (see pp. 320–328).

THE PERSONAL ROLE AND THE SOCIETAL ROLE

In this last section we shall consider two general types of roles which are found in every society, but which are seldom considered in anthropological studies: the personal role and the societal role. The *personal role* is a social category consisting of a single individual. Its attributes include the specific expectations which members of a group have concerning that individual's "public personality," for it includes all of his unique qualities insofar as these are known to others: the regularities in an individual's social behavior which enable one to say, "Isn't that just like Helen?" or "Who but George would do it that way?" Helen's personal role summarizes the kind of person she is thought to be (hot-tempered, ambitious, artistic); it is equivalent to that unique organization of characteristics which give a distinctive *style* to her performance of each of her social roles.

One important attribute of this type of role is the *personal name.* An individual's name is the role label by means of which he is contrasted with other individuals: John L. Smith is not the same as John P. Smith, even if all of their other roles are identical (for example, if both are twenty-three-year-old male orphans, Baptists, plumbers, and so forth).

The personal name is essential to a person's sense of individuality; when you refuse to use a person's name or when you assign him a number, this indicates that you plan to treat him as a member of a category (official, prisoner, student) rather than as an individual. The whole *process of naming,* including changes of names and nicknames, casts considerable light upon the nature of personal roles in various societies. In Anglo-American society, the last name is inherited in the male line (emphasizing certain consanguineal connections), while the first name is chosen by the child's parents, subject to relatively few social restrictions. In Spanish and Latin American societies, the family name of both parents is used, and the first name should be that of the saint upon whose day the child is born. In American Indian societies, a variety of naming practices are found. The child may be named by some particular kinsman other than a parent, or a name may be chosen from a group of names that are considered the prop-

---

21. E. E. Evans-Pritchard, *The Nuer* (London: Oxford University Press, 1940), pp. 5–6.

erty of the child's kin group. Many American Indian societies give a young child a temporary name; his more permanent name is bestowed later in life in connection with his personal qualities or some specific incident. A person's name might be changed several times during his life. Among the Navajo (and many other peoples), a person's real name was a closely guarded secret which would be known and used only by those people with whom he was most intimate, while a nickname of some kind would be used by others. Nicknames are also quite common in our own society, though we tend to feel that they should be used only by our intimate acquaintances.[22]

Personal names bear the same relationship to the personal role as other types of role labels bear to the roles they designate. Thus there may be many different personal roles which bear the label "John Paul Smith," and a single individual may play a number of different personal roles (he may be one kind of person in the office and quite a different kind of person at home). The use of aliases and professional names also shows that a single individual may quite honestly represent himself as different kinds of persons at different times or to different audiences. Some mentally ill individuals actually believe themselves to be more than one person, and they will answer to different names according to their current state of mind.

The personal role, then, is a social category composed of a single individual. Its attributes include a *label* (the personal name bestowed by some social group) and a set of *plans* (patterns of behavior that define the kinds of actions which that person expects of himself, and which others expect of him). Thus if George acts in an unusual manner we may say that "he is not himself"—he is not playing the personal role which we have come to expect of him, even if identical behavior by another individual would have passed unnoticed. Personal roles are built up out of all the personal and social relationships into which an individual enters. They function to make individual behavior more predictable; at the same time, by interacting with social roles and imparting a personal style to standardized patterns, they also make social life more interesting.[23]

At the other extreme from the personal role is the *societal role.* This is a category which applies to all the members of a society. In a modern national state it is equivalent to the role of "citizen." Attributes of the citizen role include expectations of

---

22. R. Brown, *Social Psychology* (New York: Free Press, 1965), pp. 51–100.
23. Every individual also has a distinctive way of speaking, including his voice quality, habits of pronunciation and preferred vocabulary or sentence structure. These may be regarded as attributes of his personal role. Charles F. Hockett has suggested the term "idiolect" to describe these individual features; see C. F. Hockett, *A Course in Modern Linguistics* (New York: Macmillan, 1958), pp. 321–330.

being loyal to the state, obeying its laws, enjoying the rights of citizenship, speaking the language of the country, and acting in accordance with its unwritten customs. Such expectations apply to all members of the society, regardless of what kinship, occupational, or other roles they may play. The citizen role contrasts primarily with the role of "alien," a kind of person to whom these expectations do not necessarily apply.

The attributes of a societal role are often so subtle that one is quite unaware of them; this is one reason for the vague discomfort that many people feel in visiting foreign countries. Goffman has identified one of the general attributes of the American societal role and contrasted it with the expectations found in the Shetland Islands:

> In middle-class Anglo-American society, when in a public place, one is supposed to keep one's nose out of other people's activity and go about one's own business. It is only when a woman drops a package, or when a fellow motorist gets stalled in the middle of the road, or when a baby left alone in a carriage begins to scream, that middle-class people feel it is all right to break down momentarily the walls which effectively insulate them. In Shetland Isle different rules obtained. If any man happened to find himself in the presence of others who were engaged in a task, it was expected that he would lend a hand, especially if the task was relatively brief and relatively strenuous. Such casual mutual aid was taken as a matter of course and was an expression of nothing closer than fellow-islander status.[24]

In tribal societies, the societal role includes all kinds of customary behavior which is characteristic of *us* as opposed to *them.* This includes speaking the tribal dialect and conforming to local customs. In such groups, the societal role contrasts with the role of "stranger," "outsider," or perhaps "enemy." Quite commonly, the term used by tribal peoples to describe themselves may be translated as "real men," as opposed to inferior outsiders: the Micmac term is *elnu,* "man," while the Navajo call themselves *dene,* "the people." Tribal ways of thinking have also persisted into more complex societies, and a similar conception of the societal role may be studied in those who contrast "red-blooded Americans" with "dirty foreigners."

When we set out to describe a social system, we want to include an inventory of all the social roles found in the group, together with the role labels and as complete a description of the associated plans as possible.[25] In general, our description will be most economical if we begin with the societal role and work down to the more specific social roles because many attributes

24. Goffman, *op. cit.*, p. 230.

of the general roles (societal, sex, age, and so on) carry over to and affect the performance of specific roles.

The concept of social role helps us to understand and predict an individual's behavior by describing the various kinds of expectations which influence him in any given situation. In the following chapters we shall discuss the nature of social groups as well as the temporal, spatial, and organizational factors which are part of any social system. But even after taking into consideration all of these factors which influence an individual's actions—from societal role to personal role and from group membership to social time—there still remains a unique core of individuality and creativity which makes it impossible to predict *exactly* what a person will do. Perhaps this is for the best.

RECOMMENDED READING

General Works on Social Structure

Dahrendorf, Ralf, *Essays in the Theory of Society.* Stanford: Stanford University Press, 1967. Thoughtful essays on the role concept and on contemporary social theory. See especially the essays "Homo Sociologicus" and "Market and Plan."

Goffman, Erving, *Encounters.* Indianapolis: Bobbs-Merrill, 1961. Two studies in the "sociology of interaction" deal with everyday experiences in a way that discloses their unsuspected social basis.

Greer, Germaine, *The Female Eunuch.* New York: Bantam Books, 1972. A comprehensive and lively discussion of sex roles in contemporary society and their historical background.

Rubin, Jerry, *Do It! Scenarios of the Revolution.* New York: Simon and Schuster, 1970. The case for anarchism stated humorously and persuasively. (Yippie!)

Case Studies (Kinship and Leadership Roles)

Firth, R., *We, the Tikopia.* Boston: Beacon Press, 1963. A classic ethnography by a British social anthropologist dealing with the social structure of a Pacific island.

Oliver, D. L., *A Solomon Island Society.* Boston: Beacon Press, 1967. Another classic on a Pacific island; like Firth's study, extremely well written; and demonstrating how different two Pacific islands can be.

Pitt-Rivers, J., *The People of the Sierra.* Chicago: Phoenix Books, 1961. An analysis of the social structure of a Spanish peasant village, written with style and insight, and with valuable material on sex roles, friendship, authority, and social control in a highly egalitarian society.

Radcliffe-Brown, A. R., and D. Forde, eds., *African Systems of Kinship and Marriage.* London: Oxford University Press, 1950. Still the best single source for an overview of African social structures.

---

25. P. K. Bock, "Three Descriptive Models of Social Structure," *Philosophy of Science*, Vol. 34, No. 2 (1967), pp. 168–174.

Wolf, M., *The House of Lim.* New York: Appleton, 1968. A study of a Chinese farm family on Taiwan, written with charm and insight.

A number of brief ethnographic studies are available in the series "Case Studies in Cultural Anthropology" published by Holt, Rinehart and Winston, N.Y., under the general editorship of George and Louise Spindler. Many of these studies contain excellent descriptions of kinship, occupational, and political roles. See particularly: J. Beattie, *Bunyoro: An African Kingdom*; O. Lewis, *Tepoztlán: Village in Mexico*; C. W. M. Hart and A. Pilling, *The Tiwi of North Australia*; E. A. Hoebel, *The Cheyennes: Indians of the Great Plains*; J. Middleton, *The Lugbara of Uganda*; and N. A. Chagnon, *Yanomamö, The Fierce People.*

CHAPTER 5

Kinds of Groups

The preceding chapter surveyed a variety of types of social roles. We saw that societies make use of quite different *criteria* for recruiting and for categorizing kinsmen, age-mates, leaders, and occupational specialists. We also saw that the association of plans for action (attributes) with a given category of persons was largely conventional and thus had to be learned in each generation. Members of a society who share such learned categories and plans are able to enter into *social relationships* in which each party knows (at least roughly) how to behave and what to expect of the other. (A traditional way of phrasing this is to say that the rights of one party to a relationship are the obligations of the other, and vice versa.)

CATEGORIES AND GROUPS

A category of persons can be defined by selecting one or more criteria shared by all members of the category. For example:

People who live in Boise, Idaho
Officers of the Tibetan Merchant Marine
Women with hair longer than fourteen inches
Migrant farm laborers
Students at Reed College in 1974–1975
Women married to Stephen J. Glutz of Cleveland
Living descendants of Thomas Jefferson
The Baltimore Colts

These are all categories of persons, though of clearly different types. One is a "null category"—that is, it has no members since there is no Tibetan merchant marine. Another has but a single member at any given time (unless Mr. Glutz is a bigamist). Still others (which?) are *merely* categories; that is, nothing can be said about their members beyond the fact that they happen to share the defining criteria. However, as Erving Goffman has observed, just about any category "can function to dispose its members to group formation," even though "its total membership does not thereby constitute a group." The League of Red-Headed Men was purely fictional, but there *are* associations of stamp collectors, rose growers, ex-alcoholics, and Lithuanian immigrants, which do constitute true groups.

In this chapter we shall use the term *social group* only if we are dealing with a definite category of persons associated with a plan for "collective action"—its members must display a "stable and embracing pattern of mutual interaction."[1] A group may consist of any number of members, but the two-person (or *dyadic*) group is the limiting case, and is equivalent to a social relationship (see above).

Many different types of groups may be distinguished, as may many different degrees of "groupness." For example, groups may be classified according to the degree of *formality* of their structure. A highly formal group is one with clearly defined rules (a charter, written or unwritten) covering recruitment, division of labor, rights and obligations of members, times and places of meeting, and so forth. An example from our society would be a trade union or a men's lodge such as the Masons. Informal groups, such as cooperative work parties or social gatherings, would lack such explicit rules; the conduct of the members would be regulated only by their personal relationships and the specific task at hand. In between these extremes fall all kinds of semiformal groups which have some but not all of the characteristics of formal groups.

Similarly, we may study such characteristics as *continuity through time* (from relatively permanent through ephemeral), *mode of recruitment* (whether automatic or voluntary, corresponding to ascribed or achieved roles), or *corporacy* (presence or absence of property in which members have joint interest). These characteristics are not independent of one another. For example, a corporate group whose members share in the benefits of some valuable "estate" (for example, land, cattle, or capital equipment) will usually have a relatively formal structure and a high degree of

---

1. E. Goffman, *Stigma* (Englewood Cliffs, N.J.: Spectrum Books, 1963), p. 23.

continuity over time. Semiformal and formal groups also tend to have *names,* and one of the rights of membership may be the right to use the group name or to display its identifying insignia.

Group Integration

Groups also differ in the degree to which their members feel committed to one another and to continued membership in the group. By the degree of *integration* of a group we mean the strength with which the parts of the group stick together. (Two other terms which are used with approximately the same meaning are "cohesiveness" and "solidarity.") It is important to see that the question of why some groups hold together while others fall apart is a meaningful scientific problem. Group integration is a product of many different factors, some of which will be discussed here and some later in this book.

Emile Durkheim first clearly pointed out two different types of group integration; he called them *mechanical solidarity* and *organic solidarity.*[2] Mechanical solidarity is based upon the similarity of the parts (segments) of a social group. That is, the parts of a group may stick together because they are alike: all the persons in the group have similar experiences, ideas, and emotions; they do the same kinds of things, and they understand one another because of this common existence. All groups must possess a certain degree of mechanical solidarity or they could not function as groups. However, as Durkheim pointed out, a group based solely upon mechanical solidarity has a tendency to fall apart precisely because each of its segments is equivalent and thus functionally independent of the others.

Organic solidarity, on the other hand, is based upon *differences* among the parts of a group. It is a consequence of the division of labor, for this makes the segments both unequal and interdependent. Durkheim used the analogy of the organs of the body, each of which has its own task to perform, and each of which cannot function without the others. Organic solidarity requires the constant exchange of *valued* goods and/or services among the segments of the group. No social group can continue without a certain degree of organic solidarity, even if the need for exchange must be artificially established and maintained. As Durkheim noted, much of the sexual division of labor is objectively unnecessary. Men could, after all, learn to cook and sew for themselves. However, by making men and women dependent upon one

2. E. Durkheim, *The Division of Labor in Society* (New York: Free Press, 1947).

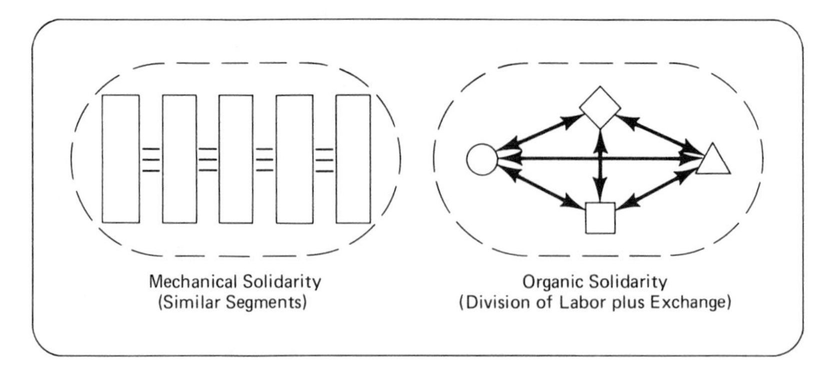

Figure 5.1 **Two Types of Internal Social Integration**

another, the division of labor increases the organic solidarity between the sexes; this furthers the integration of society (see Figure 5.1).

Both kinds of solidarity are essential to group integration. With *only* mechanical ties between its segments, a group is always in danger of falling apart. Organic solidarity is produced by interdependence and difference. But organic solidarity requires a degree of trust and common experience, which can come only from mechanical similarity. Georg Simmel took this paradox a step further when he pointed out that *even social conflict* requires a common basis of understanding and an agreement to abide by certain rules. Conflict and cooperation are both types of social relationships; but total indifference will destroy a relationship, just as its counterpart, apathy, can destroy a group.[3]

In addition to the *internal integration* (solidarity) of a social group, we may also study the degree of its *external integration*—that is, the extent to which it is bound up with other groups in the larger society of which it is a part. The activities of some groups (for example, criminal gangs) are exclusively for the benefit of their own members, whereas other groups perform services for clients and/or for the society as a whole (for example, the Post Office). But the necessity of recruiting new members and maintaining vital services leads even the most exclusive groups into some transactions with the outside world; and the larger society frequently takes an interest in subgroup activities, even when the group is composed of "consenting adults." This leads us to consider the general functions that social groups may perform.

3. G. Simmel, *Conflict* (New York: Free Press, 1955).

Group Functions and Specialization

Social groups serve a wide variety of specific purposes: the plans for collective activity associated with a given category of persons may range from making war to making love, or from producing automobiles to consuming marijuana. Nevertheless, it is useful to consider these purposes as examples of three general social functions. Our intention is not to pigeonhole groups according to which general function they perform, but rather to suggest that any but the most ephemeral social group must to some extent carry out all three of these. Furthermore, the specialization of roles within a group is a consequence of the group's having to perform multiple functions.

The three general functions may be defined as follows:

1. *Task function:* the orientation of the group toward producing objective effects on its physical, biological, or social environment; for example, producing a product, exploiting or protecting a resource, winning a war or a game.
2. *Control function:* the orientation of the group toward maintaining its own internal structure (and growth) through conformity to behavioral and recruitment norms; for example, enculturating and disciplining group members and (when relevant) recruiting qualified new members.
3. *Expressive function:* the orientation of the group toward satisfying the psychological needs of its members, including those needs which result from individual participation in the task and control activities.

Every human group is primarily oriented toward one of these functions, and analysis will generally show that all three functions are present to some degree—if not explicitly, then implicitly. For example, each military unit has a mission (explicit task function), but the leaders of these groups are fully aware of the need to maintain military discipline (implicit control function). At the same time, group morale depends upon the satisfaction of the psychological needs of the men, and a good officer will give this considerable attention (implicit expressive function). Some kinds of activities can perform a number of functions at once; such activities tend to become a regular part of the group schedule.

The task function is usually explicit; however, in some cases it may be implicit as compared with other functions. A classic example is Malinowski's analysis of the *kula* ring of the Trobriand

Islanders. The Trobrianders and their neighbors in the Massim area of Melanesia carry on an extensive interisland trade, using outrigger canoes to carry goods over miles of open sea. From the Trobriand point of view, however, it is not the production of or trade in useful goods which justifies these dangerous expeditions. This task function is satisfied incidentally in the process of exchanging certain valuable but nonutilitarian articles (necklaces and armbands) with one's *kula* partners. These valuables may not be kept for long by any one person, but must be passed along around the circle of islands forming the *kula* ring, the armbands traveling in one direction and the necklaces in the other. As Malinowski described it,

> the acts of exchange of the valuables have to conform to a definite code. . . . The ceremonial attached to the act of giving, the manner of carrying and handling the valuables shows distinctly that this is regarded as something else than mere merchandise. Indeed it is to the native something that confers dignity, that exalts him, and which he therefore treats with veneration and affection.[4]

As a result of the *kula* transactions (which Malinowski likens to a display of the British crown jewels), considerable wealth is created and distributed; but the explicit function of this group effort is to satisfy the psychological needs of the *kula* partners and their associates for prestige.

Many groups find it useful to assign these functions to different individuals or subgroups. The differentiation of task, control, and expressive functions is particularly clear in complex societies. Occupational groups are primarily oriented toward the accomplishment of specific tasks, while the police and the courts specialize in social control. The expressive functions tend to be carried out by part- or full-time specialists in psychotherapy, religion, and the arts. In most societies, however, the family remains unspecialized in function; this is one reason for its universal importance. But even within the family there is some tendency toward specialization of roles, with one parent acting as task leader and the other parent as leader for expressive and control purposes. Experimental studies of small, task-oriented groups have repeatedly shown a tendency for one person to specialize in task direction while another, often more sensitive person becomes the socio-emotional leader.[5] Similarly, groups with primarily expressive functions (such as many communes) eventually encounter difficulties with their environments that call forth specialized task leadership.

---

4. B. Malinowski, *Argonauts of the Western Pacific* (New York: Dutton, 1960), pp. 510–511.
5. Philip E. Slater, "Role Differentiation in Small Groups," in A. P. Hare, E. Borgatta and R. F. Bales, eds., *Small Groups* (New York: Knopf, 1955), p. 512.

The remainder of this chapter will deal with the varieties of social groups which are found in human societies throughout the world. The groups will be classified according to the basis upon which their memberships are recruited (residence, kinship, occupation, and so on). Within each type, concrete examples will be used to illustrate the characteristics of integration, formality, and continuity, and the group functions that were discussed above in general terms.

RESIDENTIAL GROUPS

As is the case with most species of animals, human beings tend to cluster together rather than being distributed at random over the surface of the earth. This clustering is both a cause and a result of group formation. In discussing the origin of the city, Lewis Mumford has suggested the twin metaphor of "the magnet and the container."[6] His idea is that men are first attracted to a place by some desirable quality of the area, and that after they have occupied it for a time, it comes to "contain" both them and their works within more or less permanent structures (walls, temples, granaries).

Certainly, men do become emotionally attached to a place. They learn how to best utilize its resources, and they come to value the alterations which they and their ancestors have made in the environment. These alterations include both material items —paths, cleared fields, irrigation ditches, shrines, or secular buildings—and nonmaterial items—a belief in the presence of benevolent spirits, for example, or a feeling of loyalty to the home of one's ancestors. (See the discussion of place names, p. 175.)

Whatever their original reasons for coming together in a given locality, the sheer fact of proximity makes likely the development of common patterns of experience leading to mechanical solidarity and the division of labor leading to organic solidarity. The *category* of persons initially defined solely on the basis of its spatial boundaries becomes a *residential group* upon the development of a *plan* that specifies appropriate forms of intragroup behavior.

The Household

There are many types of residential groups. In this section, we shall limit ourselves to a brief consideration of the local community and of the subgroups which are typically found within it,

6. L. Mumford, *The City in History* (New York: Harcourt Brace and World, 1961), pp. 3–15.

beginning with the household. Paul Bohannan defines the *household* as "a group of people who live together and form a functioning domestic unit." He cautions that the members of a household "may or may not constitute a family, and if they do so, it may or may not be a simple nuclear family."[7] Even in our society, where the ideal middle-class household is equivalent to the *nuclear family* (a man, his wife, and their children), there are many deviations. In addition to the nuclear family core based upon the marriage tie between husband and wife, other possible members of an American household, often for long periods of time, include grandparents, parents' siblings, children's spouses, and even nonrelatives (friends or servants).

In other societies, the tie between spouses is not so fundamental to the formation of households. For example, among the Hopi Indians of Arizona, the core of each household was a group of sisters together with their daughters (both single and married) and the daughters' children. The husbands of all these women were considered more "guests" than regular household members; a Hopi man was only truly at home in his sisters' household, to which he retired on ritual occasions as well as whenever the tensions in his wife's household became too great. Unmarried males slept in their mother's household only when they were very young; after they were six or seven years old, boys would sleep with brothers and friends at various places in the village.

Still elsewhere, the significant tie on which households are based is that between father and son. For example, among the Tanala of Madagascar, the typical household was composed of a man (the founder) together with his married and unmarried sons and their wives and offspring. Such households are found primarily in societies where the cooperation of persons of one sex is highly valued and economically important. Lest the student think that households of this type are found only in exotic cultures, it should be pointed out that households containing three or more generations of males were not uncommon in rural areas of the United States during the nineteenth century. One of the most usual (though by no means universal) social changes to accompany the growth of cities and of industry in a country is the breakdown of such extended family households and their replacement by more mobile nuclear family groupings.

One society where consanguineal kinship determines residence, completely overriding the marriage tie, is the Ashanti of Ghana, West Africa. Here the typical household consists of an

7. P. Bohannan, *Social Anthropology* (New York: Holt, Rinehart and Winston, 1963), p. 86. For a further clarification of the distinction between household and family see D. R. Bender, "A Refinement of the Concept of Household: Families, Co-residence, and Domestic Functions," *American Anthropologist*, Vol. 69 (1967), pp. 493–504.

old woman, her sons and daughters, and the daughters' children. The spouses of the married adults live in the nearby households of their *own* maternal kin. This is a very logical arrangement, but it does lead to some practical difficulties. For example, children are always running through the streets of an Ashanti village carrying food from their mothers' cooking huts to their fathers' houses, and special arrangements must be made when spouses wish to sleep together!

Among the Tallensi, another tribe in Ghana, the core of the household is a group of men, but here the practice of polygyny gives rise to a complex domestic unit. A typical Tallensi dwelling consists of a number of circular buildings joined together in a circle by a mud wall; the buildings may include one or more cattle sheds; granaries; bedrooms; pantries; and kitchens for the wives of the (male) head of the household; rooms for the wives and young children of his married sons; and frequently a separate sleeping room for adolescent boys. Although personal relationships in such complex households can become most difficult, it is by no means unusual for a woman in a polygynous society to insist that her husband take an additional wife (or wives). The assistance in domestic tasks provided by co-wives may far outweigh any negative aspects of their presence.[8]

There are, then, many possible types of households, and they are built upon different *principles of recruitment.* In Chapter 4, we discussed several ways in which individuals are recruited to fill social roles. Now it should be clear that social groups are formed by means of recruitment rules which specify the kinds of persons who are entitled to membership in the group. In the case of the household, the attributes one should possess in order to take up residence generally have some basis in kinship and/or marriage. Thus among the Tallensi, a young man is entitled and expected to bring his wife into his father's household: he is entitled to membership in this residential group by virtue of his ascribed role as "son," whereas she enters the group as "son's wife," an achieved role.

Anthropologists use a number of technical terms to label the postmarital *residence rules,* which specify where a newly married couple is expected to live. The terms are unsatisfactory because: (1) they do not indicate the actual basis of recruitment to the group; and (2) they have been used to cover either residence *in* an established household or residence *near* the household of a kinsman (where "near" may indicate any distance from next-door to within the same local community). Nevertheless, these terms are widely used for comparative purposes, and a brief discussion

8. M. Fortes, "Primitive Kinship," *Scientific American* (June 1959), pp. 146–158.

A one-family compound of the Kassem tribe in northern Ghana. The round dwellings house the family head and his four wives. ***Marc & Evelyne Bernheim/Woodfin Camp***

should sensitize the student to the variety of possible social arrangements.

Types of Postmarital Residence Rules

I. Unilocal—the couple is expected to live with the kinsmen of *one* sponse
  a. Patrilocal—th couple lives with the family of the groom (Tallensi)
  b. Matrilocal—the couple lives with the family of the bride (Hopi)
  c. Avunculocal—the couple lives with the groom's mother's brother (Trobriand)

II. Duolocal—each continues to live with his own kin (Ashanti)

III. Ambilocal—the couple is expected to live with the kinsmen of either spouse (Norwegian Lapps)

VI. Neolocal—the couple is expected to establish a new residence independent of the family of either spouse (modern U.S.)

Various *combinations* of these rules are also commonly found. For example, in societies which practice "bride service," the couple may first live with the bride's family for a number of years, with the groom under the authority of his wife's father; when the period of service is completed, he and his wife go to live with his family. This is known as "matri-patrilocal residence." In many other societies, the initial period of residence (say, until the birth of their first child) may be with the groom's family, after which the couple may establish an independent residence. This might be labeled "patri-neolocal" residence. It is probably much more common in the United States than is generally recognized.

We have mentioned before that both the patrilocal Tallensi and the matrilocal Hopi have separate sleeping places for young boys. This type of custom (sometimes known as the "extrusion of adolescent males") is found in many parts of the world, and various psychological and sociological explanations have been advanced to account for it. It is most highly developed among certain East African tribes, such as the Nyakyusa: the young boys actually build a separate village with sleeping huts at some distance from their parents, although they continue to eat in their former households and to work in their fathers' fields. The Nyakyusa case is particularly instructive, and will be considered further in the section on age-groups. Elsewhere in Africa the male dormitory or settlement is associated with a *military* orientation of the society, and the young men who live there are often the warriors of the group; their segregation seems intended to keep them free of family ties and ready at all times for raiding or for defense. But the men's house may also have a primarily religious function (as in New Guinea) or be mainly an economic association (as among the Indians of northern California). The point here is that even where residential groups are built upon similar principles of recruitment, the plans associated with these categories of persons may be quite different. Thus, any general explanation of the extrusion of adolescent males which failed to consider both the categories and the plans would necessarily be only partial.

Young men who live apart from the rest of their society are not necessarily deprived of sexual contacts. As noted in Chapter 4, the Masai warriors who lived in a separate camp until about thirty years of age were visited there by their sweethearts. There is an entire book devoted to the men's dormitory (*ghotul*) of the Muria Gond of central India, and it is clear that this institution does *not* function to keep the sexes apart; however, boys and girls who have been lovers are forbidden to marry later in life.[9]

9. V. Elwin, *The Muria and Their Ghotul* (Bombay: Oxford University Press, 1947).

Coeducational dormitories have also been established in many kibbutzim in the modern state of Israel as part of a deliberate attempt to bring about equality of the sexes and to encourage independence of children from their parents.

In the kibbutz described by Melford Spiro, groups of agemates of both sexes are raised together from birth by trained specialists (nurses and teachers), while married couples share rooms in another part of the community and are visited by their children only at certain times. Married women are thus freed from the usual tasks of child care and are able to take an equal role with the men in the economic and political affairs of the community. The psychological effects of this child-raising system have been explored by Spiro in his book *Children of the Kibbutz.*[10] One of his notable findings is that despite the extremely permissive attitudes of the adults toward sexual intimacies, marriage or even sexual intercourse among the individuals who have been raised together in these groups is virtually unknown.

One other type of household which has attracted the attention of anthropologists is the so-called *matrifocal* household—a residential group having as its core a woman and her young offspring. The woman may be married or unmarried, but in any case the man (or men) who fathered her children is not a regular part of the household.[11] Matrifocal households are found in large numbers in many parts of Latin America and also in the United States, primarily in urban areas and among impoverished members of minority groups. Just as the nuclear family household replaces more complex forms in industrial societies, the matrifocal household is produced by an interplay of economic and social forces which are just beginning to be understood. The study of this type of residential group is important for both theoretical and practical reasons: matrifocal households create psychological problems for their members and social problems for the communities of which they are a part; they also present a challenge to all social scientists who are concerned with the structure and functioning of the family.

Anthropologists have become increasingly aware that the structure of households cannot be understood by simply stating the typical residence rule or the average composition (for example, no American family really contains 2.5 children). We now pay greater attention to the "developmental cycle of the domestic group," studying households through time to understand typical *changes* in composition and the socioeconomic factors respon-

---

10. M. Spiro, *Children of the Kibbutz* (Cambridge: Harvard University Press, 1958).
11. R. Fox, *Kinship and Marriage* (Baltimore: Penguin Books, 1967), pp. 1–53.

sible for them.[12] We also try to understand the "plans for household formation" which influence individuals' *decisions* about where to live, and with whom (see Chapter 7).

The Structure of the Local Community

In most societies, the household is integrated into a larger, more inclusive residential grouping, the *local community.* There are a few hunting and gathering societies in which for most of the year the household is isolated and self-sufficient; but even in these cases (for example, the Eskimo), there is usually a period during which several households come together for social and ritual activities. The local community need not be sedentary, and it may have a considerable turnover in its membership. But even if it is nomadic, the local community is almost always associated with a definite range of territory; and despite fluctuations in its membership, the local community maintains its identity over time by recruiting new persons to membership and to leadership roles.

Where economic conditions permit the existence of very large local communities, residential groupings such as the *neighborhood* may come between the household and the local community. These internal divisions of the local community may simply be a matter of convenience, but in primitive societies they often have a kinship basis. A division of the local community into two parts, each of which has functions complementary to the other, is also extremely widespread. Modern American communities tend to subdivide along social class lines (the right and wrong sides of the tracks) with a kind of neutral meeting ground in the downtown area.

All animal populations tend to increase up to the limit set by available resources; however, we may note important differences among human communities in terms of what happens as they grow in size. There seem to be three alternative plans open to a growing community: stabilization, fission, or aggregation. Which of these alternatives is chosen depends upon a complex interplay of natural and cultural forces.

Though human societies differ greatly in their abilities to exploit a given environment, every community eventually experiences the pressure of its numbers upon its food resources, be these wild or domesticated. Where access to further land is strictly limited (as on a Pacific island) the society may choose

12. J. R. Goody, ed., *The Developmental Cycle in Domestic Groups* (New York: Cambridge University Press, 1958).

stabilization: the population is limited by either the natural forces of famine or by cultural practices such as birth control or infanticide.

Fission of the local community means that one or more subgroups migrate to new territory and establish their own communities with access to further resources. Choice of this alternative depends on the availability of free land (and ways to reach and exploit it) or on the power of the fissioning group to take what it needs by conquest.[13] Population growth which results in community fission may cause a kind of chain reaction in which expanding groups put pressure on neighbors who must in turn displace their neighbors. When fission takes place between parts of a descent group (see below), it is usually referred to as "segmentation."

In tribal societies, the newly established communities tend to be small-scale replicas of their parent communities; thus, although both the old and the new communities may be united by the mechanical solidarity of their common origins and experiences, there is no specialization of function to bind them together, and their sense of common identity is eventually lost.

In complex societies, however, the bonds between communities are of a more organic nature. With the development of food production and of effective modes of communication (including transportation of goods), it becomes possible for some local communities to grow to considerable size. When fission does take place (peacefully or by conquest of new lands), the daughter communities remain tied to the parent community through bonds of mutual interest and need. This process may be labeled *aggregation,* and under the right conditions of growth, fission, and integration it may lead to the development of chiefdoms and states.[14]

The local community is the usual focus of ethnological investigations because, at least in tribal societies, it is the smallest unit within which a total culture can be studied by a single anthropologist. As Conrad Arensberg has pointed out, the local community contains all the personnel necessary to carry and transmit the culture of a society. "It is the minimal unit realizing the categories and offices of their social organization. It is the minimal group capable of reenacting in the present and transmitting to the future the cultural and institutional inventory of their distinctive and historic tradition.[15]

13. Compare A. P. Vayda, "Expansion and Warfare among Swidden Agriculturalists," *American Anthropologist*, Vol. 63 (1961), pp. 346–358.
14. Compare M. Fried, *The Evolution of Political Society* (New York: Random House, 1967); R. L. Carneiro, "A Theory of the Origin of the State," *Science,* Vol. 169, No. 3947 (1970), pp. 733–738.
15. C. Arensberg, "American Communities," *American Anthropologist*, Vol. 57 (1955), p. 1143.

In investigating the social structure of a local community, the ethnographer tries carefully to determine the kinds of groups which make up the community, the kinds of persons found in these groups, and the plans which regulate the interaction within and among these categories. Since the household is generally composed of relatives, the plans which regulate domestic behavior are also a part of the system of kinship roles. In many primitive communities, all members of the local group consider themselves to be relatives, and so an understanding of the kinship system is essential to comprehension of the local group. Even where this is the case, however, there will generally be some plans which apply to members of the local community as co-residents, quite aside from their kinship relations. For example, the members of a community often have certain responsibilities for maintaining public order and contributing to community activities; they may also have certain rights over resources within the community's territory —resources such as land, water, and wildlife—which may not be exploited by outsiders without special permission.

For a full understanding of how a society works, the ethnographer must also study the relations *among* communities. This is particularly true where organic solidarity exists among communities which have become specialized within a larger system. For example, a peasant society, as Robert Redfield has defined it, is composed of rural communities which are involved in complex relationships with urban centers. Although the individual peasant community may resemble a tribal farming community, the peasant community also engages in political, economic, and cultural relationships with an urban center—relationships which are unknown in tribal societies. Thus to study a peasant community as an isolated unit would be to miss its most significant characteristics.[16]

To summarize, we have seen that residential groups are categories of persons who are expected to live together, and that the plans associated with both the household and the local community provide for the recruitment of new members, make possible the control of behavior within (and among) groups, and regulate the growth of communities. These plans, it must be emphasized, consist of learned expectations as to what *should* happen; thus, like other cultural rules, they may be violated and/or used by certain individuals to attain their own purposes (see Chapter 7). However, all members of a society must take these rules into account, if only to help them predict the reaction of others to a violation.

16. R. Redfield, *Peasant Society and Culture* (Chicago: University of Chicago Press, 1956). See also P. K. Bock, ed., *Peasants in the Modern World* (Albuquerque: University of New Mexico Press, 1968).

Residence is one of the great principles upon which social groups are organized. The residence rules of a society help people to answer the universal question "Where should I live?" at different times of their lives. The categorical contrast between "resident" and "nonresident" (of any residential group) must be clearly defined if people are to know what is expected of them. On the state level of organization this becomes transformed into the contrast between "citizen" and "alien," and the relationship of these categories to actual physical residence is weakened. Citizens of a state may live and even be born in other countries, where they are considered aliens. Nevertheless, while a state without resident aliens is conceivable, a state without resident citizens is unthinkable.

KINSHIP GROUPS

If residence is the first great principle of group formation, the second is kinship. In both primitive and modern societies, the vast majority of an individual's ascribed social roles and group memberships are limited or determined by *where* he is born and *to whom.* When membership in a group is ascribed on the basis of kinship, we may speak of a *kinship group.* But since each individual may be genealogically related to hundreds of others, most cultures provide *rules of recruitment* into the various kinship groups which compose a society. These rules involve a selection of criteria, recognizing some genealogical attributes and ignoring others.

The most inclusive categories are "relatives" and "nonrelatives." Within the group of relatives, descent rules may define several degrees of closeness. Associated with each group and subgroup are sets of plans for group activity and interaction. These plans often call for economic, religious, or political cooperation among group members, though they need not. In nearly every society, however, kinship groups are concerned with the regulation of marriage, for it is through the marriage relationship that the continuity of a group is ensured. The most common rules of recruitment and the groups to which they give rise are listed in Figure 5.2.

Recruitment Rule	Membership Criteria	Type of Kinship Groups
I. Bilateral (or "cognatic")	Affiliation traced through parents and linking relatives of either sex	Kindreds
a. ego-centered	Traced outward to known limits by each individual; overlapping	personal kindred or "great family"
b. not ego-centered	Traced outward from some prominent person in each generation	stem kindred
II. Unilineal	Affiliation traced from "founder" through linking relatives of one sex only	Descent Groups (lineages, clans, phratries, moieties)
a. patrilineal	Automatic affiliation through father and male linking relatives; bounded	patrilineage, and so on
b. matrilineal	Automatic affiliation through mother and female linking relatives; bounded	matrilineage, and so on
c. duolineal (or "double descent")	Combination of II-a and II-b	each person belongs to *both* a patrilineal and a matrilineal group
III. Ambilineal (or "multilineal")	Nonautomatic: individual has choice of affiliation with the (lineal) group of either parent (or with the group of a spouse's parent)	Nonunilinear Descent Groups (septs or rammages)

Figure 5.2 **Rules of Recruitment and Types of Kinship Groups**

The Kindred

Many students experience difficulty in understanding unilineal descent groups (Type II) because they are alien to our society. American kinship organization leaps from its smallest unit, the nuclear family, to its largest category—the *personal kindred.* Within the personal kindred (which may be defined as "all of ego's known relatives") we do recognize different degrees of "closeness," but this vague criterion never gives rise to clearly bounded groups which act as units. As compared with the majority of kinship systems known to social anthropology, this is a very unusual situation.

Our system is technically described as *bilateral* and *ego-centered* (Type Ia), with collateral extension limited only by ego's knowledge of his genealogical connections. That is, each individual considers himself equally related to kinsmen on both his mother's side and his father's side, regardless of the sex of the connecting relatives through whom the link is traced. A father's brother's child, a father's sister's child, and a mother's sibling's child are all called by the same kinship term and are all considered to be equally close relatives (cousins). However, our plans for interacting with relatives become more vague and less obligatory as their genealogical distance from us increases: many Americans neither know nor feel any obligations toward their third cousins. The American personal kindred may be visualized as a series of concentric circles with ego in the middle, surrounded by his nuclear family, and beyond them, successive circles of kinsmen which ultimately fade out in terms of knowledge and expected behavior (see Figure 5.3).[17]

Although bilateral kinship groups of this type seem right and logical to us, they would have at least two considerable drawbacks if kinship were more important to our total social structure: (1) they are only vaguely bounded, and because "close" and "distant" are relative terms, there is no clear-cut way of *excluding* any consanguine from the group; (2) being ego-centered, the "circles of kin" overlap but do not exactly coincide for most relatives, so that few individuals share the same kindred. Ego shares his total personal kindred only with his siblings and his *double cousins* (persons whose parents are both full siblings of ego's parents and

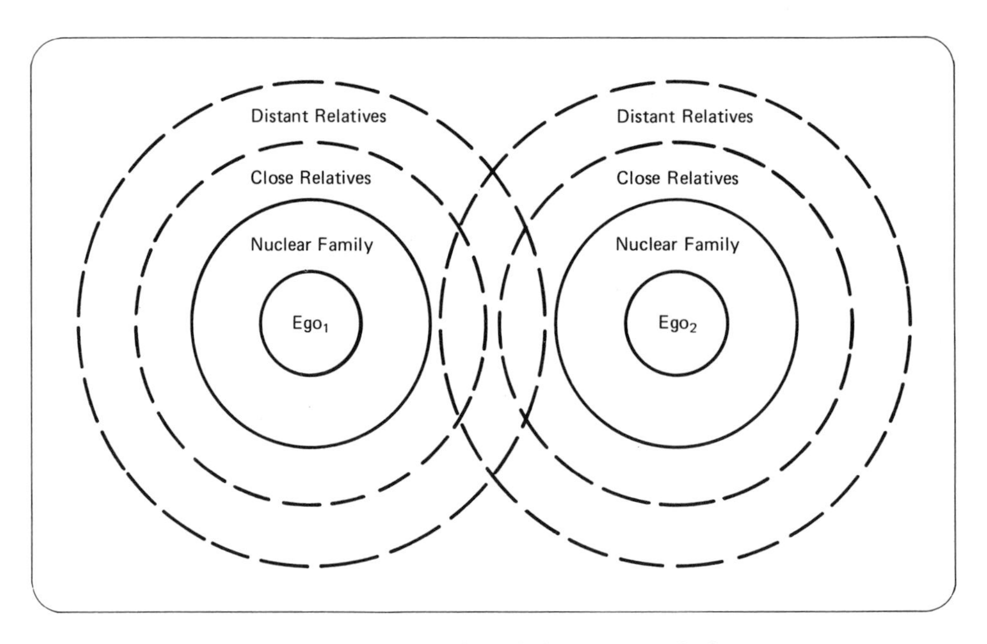

Figure 5.3 **Two Personal Kindreds (showing overlap)**

17. D. Schneider, *American Kinship* (Englewood Cliffs, N. J.: Prentice-Hall, 1968), pp. 23–27.

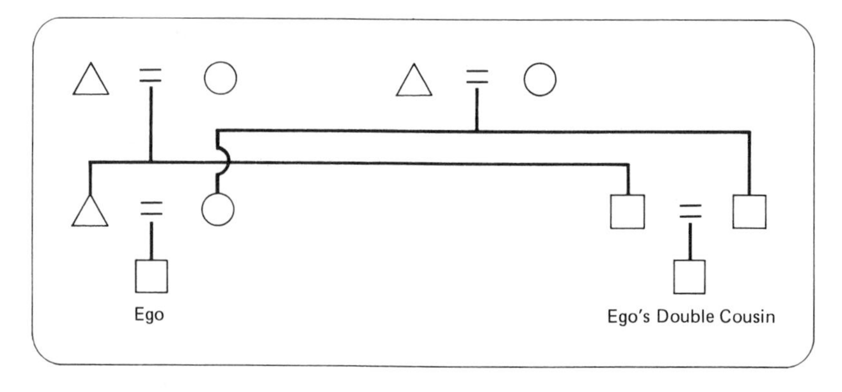

Figure 5.4 **Double Cousins Who, Like Siblings, Would Share the Same Personal Kindred**

who therefore have exactly the same four grandparents; see Figure 5.4). Any other relatives will have different sets of consanguines on at least one side.

These drawbacks of bilateral kinship do not normally trouble us because the American kindred seldom functions as a group. That is, although our bilateral relatives comprise a category and although we possess plans for dyadic interaction with particular kinds of relatives, there are few if any plans which apply to the group as a whole. In some parts of American society it is common for the kindred to gather occasionally for periodic reunions or for life-crisis celebrations (weddings, funerals, or special birthdays). But attendance at these ceremonial occasions is determined as much by proximity in space as by closeness of relationship. The vague boundaries of the kindred become an inconvenience mainly at celebrations such as weddings where the number of guests must be limited—the hurt feelings that can arise out of these situations are proverbial.

When bilateral descent groups do regularly act together, some kind of further structuring is required so that people may know exactly who is included and what is expected of them. In the Anglo-Saxon kindred, this was accomplished by assigning specific responsibilities to different degrees of relationship. For example, first, second, and third cousins were expected to contribute proportionally differing amounts to ego's bride-wealth; and in case ego was murdered, all members of his kindred out through third (but not including fourth) cousins were expected to participate in the blood feud (or to share proportionally in the indemnity paid by the murderer's kindred). Under these circumstances, it is understandable that the Angles and the Saxons were quite adept at calculating their degree of relationship to all other kinsmen. The famous feuds of the southern Appalachian region in the United States and the vendettas of Sicily are probably the most familiar examples of entire kindreds taking responsibility for avenging the murder of a member.

There are other ways of structuring bilateral kinship groups. For example, Robert Pehrson has shown that among the Lapps (nomadic herders of northern Scandinavia) separation into generations and strong emphasis on the sibling group as a point of reference produces fairly clear-cut kin-based groupings.[18] A number of male siblings, their wives, and their children form the core of such a group, and others affiliate with the group by virtue of some bilateral genealogical link with the sibling core. Apparently there is a good deal of shifting between local groups since it is not difficult to find some link to the group leaders, and men sometimes join their wives' groups if there is a need for extra males. These Lapp groups are thus based upon a combination of bilateral kinship and common residence.

Another type of structure is provided by what William Davenport calls the *stem kindred*—the personal kindred of a prominent individual, within a clearly delimited collateral range. Such a group can have clear-cut boundaries (that is, identical personnel for all members). Continuity over time may be given to such a group by the development of a pattern of succession to group leadership, such as primogeniture. An example of this is found in rural Ireland, where title to farm land is passed from a man to his first-born son. The titleholder in each generation has a small personal kindred whose members have definite rights and obligations even if they are not resident on the land.[19]

True Descent Groups

Unilineal kin groups are organized on an entirely different principle of recruitment. If the personal kindred is visualized as a series of concentric circles surrounding ego, the unilineal descent group is best thought of as a line descending from some particular ancestor (the founder) to ego through a number of lineal relatives, all of whom are of the same sex (see Figure 5.5).

In a bilateral kindred, ego traces his relationship to other members through both males and females; but membership in a unilineal descent group is transmitted through linking relatives of *one sex only.* The effect of this difference is quite far-reaching.

18. R. Pehrson, "Bilateral Kin Groupings as a Structural Type," *Journal of East Asiatic Studies*, Vol. 3 (1954), pp. 199–202.
19. W. Davenport, "Nonunilinear Descent and Descent Groups," *American Anthropologist*, Vol. 61 (1959), p. 565.

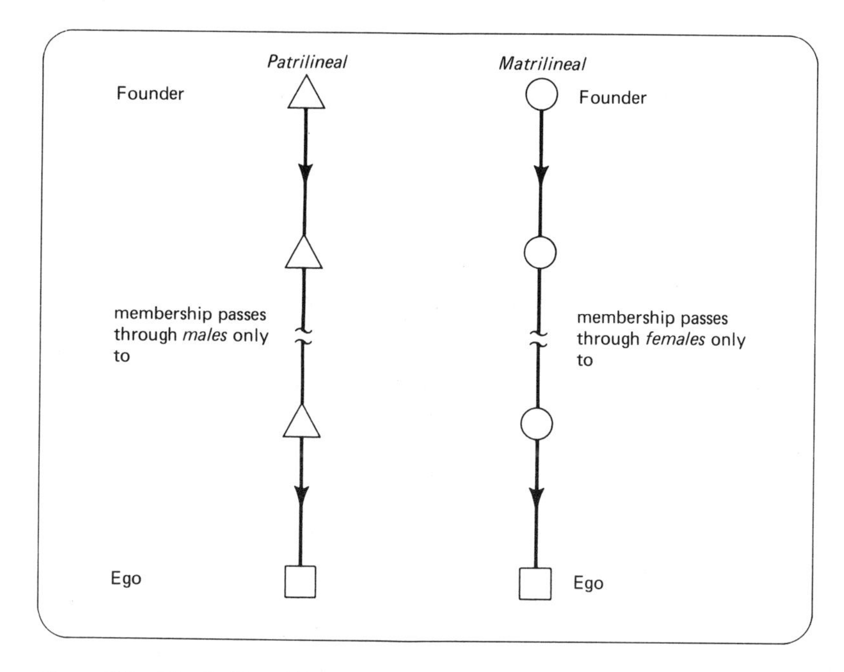

Figure 5.5 **The Unilineal Descent Group**

To begin with, unilineal descent groups are strictly *bounded*: although ego recognizes his kinship with all consanguineal relatives, the unilineal principle *excludes* the majority of his consanguines from his descent group: Because of this consistent exclusion, *the composition of the unilineal descent group is the same for every member of the group.* This is a great advantage when descent groups are to be mobilized for some kind of action, for each person belongs to one and only one such group; furthermore, where *corporate* descent groups are associated with the inheritance or maintenance of an estate, the unilineal principle makes possible greater continuity of management. These advantages may account for the fact that the majority of known societies make some use of the unilineal principle.

The Lineage

A *lineage* is a unilineal descent group all of whose members can trace actual genealogical connections to one another through linking relatives of one sex. For example, Figure 5.6 shows a typical matrilineage: it is composed of the female founder, her children (both male *and* female), the children of her daughters (only), and of *their* daughters. Notice that, while the founder's son (X) is a

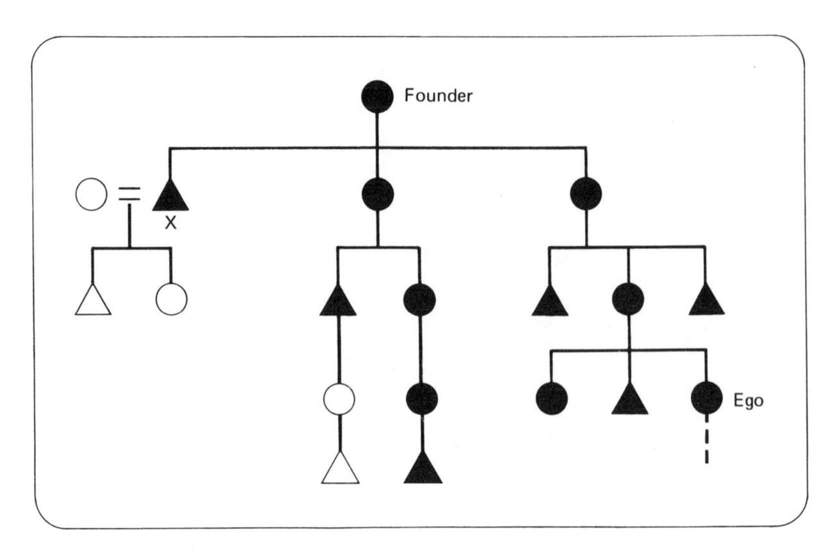

Figure 5.6 **A Typical Matrilineage (black symbols are members)**

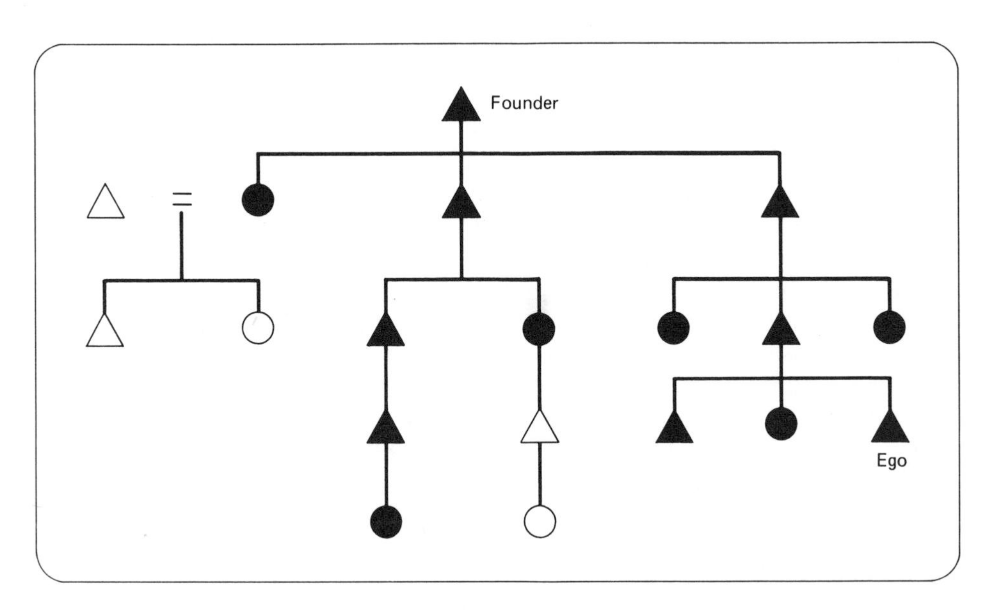

Figure 5.7 **A Typical Patrilineage (black symbols are members)**

member of this lineage, X's wife is *not* a member; nor are their children, for they belong to the lineage of their mother. Note carefully that a matrilineage consists of both males and females, but that membership in the lineage is transmitted through females only. Thus ego's sons and daughters will also be members of this lineage, but the children of her male siblings will not be members.

The patrilineage is the mirror image of the matrilineage in that descent is traced through males only. Figure 5.7 shows a typical patrilineage stemming from a male founder through his sons and their sons. Americans can usually grasp the patrilineal principle if they think of the way in which family names are inherited in our society (although our practice of having a woman change her name at marriage somewhat complicates this). Again we see that both males and females are members of a patrilineage, but that in this case, membership is transmitted only in the male line.

In Figure 5.8 ego's siblings and cousins in his own generation as well as his lineal relatives back three generations are represented. In a bilateral system, *all* kinsmen in this figure would be member's of ego's kindred. Shading has been used to indicate which of these kinsmen are members of ego's matri- and patrilineages. As can be seen, only ego and his siblings are members of *both* of these groups (though his double cousins, if any, would also be members of both). The numerous unshaded figures represent ego's consanguines who are *not members of either lineage;* please note that in ego's own generation all of his cross cousins fall into this category. (Compare Figure 4.2.)

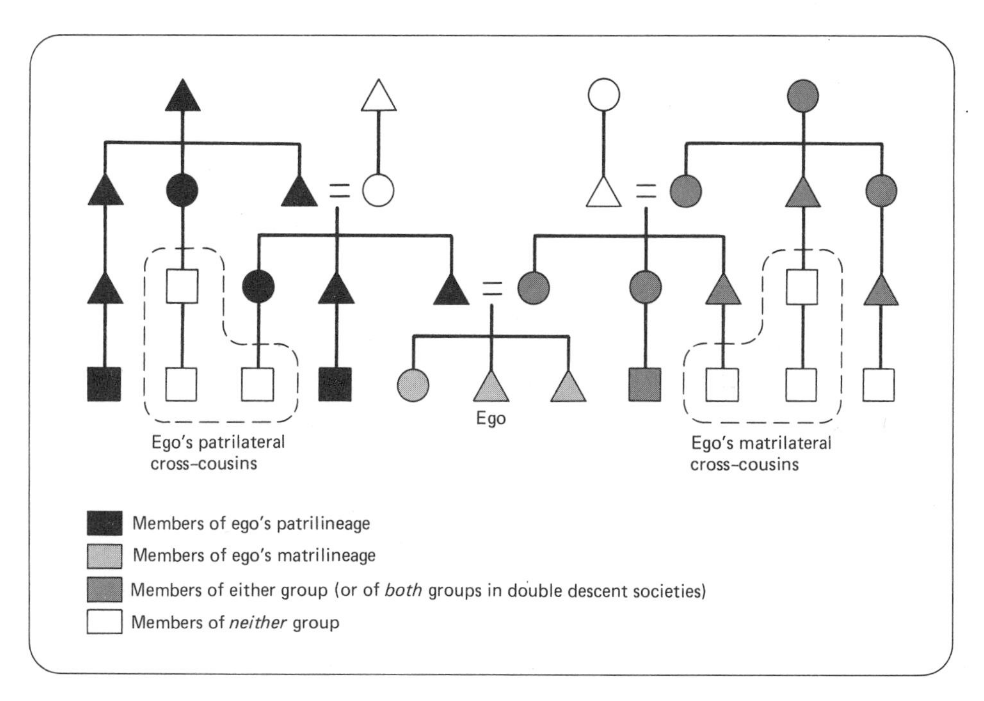

Figure 5.8 **The Unilineal Principle**

Figure 5.8 also makes it possible to illustrate another type of descent group organization. In a double-descent system (Type IIc) both matrilineal and patrilineal descent groups are present (though one may be more important than the other). Thus ego and his full siblings belong simultaneously to two lineages, one through their mother and the other through their father. The last figure shows that this is *not* the same as a bilateral group, for relatives represented by unshaded figures would not belong to either of ego's lineage groups. Even when applied twice, the unilineal principle still forms bounded groups from which some consanguines are excluded.

None of the foregoing statements should be taken to mean that in societies organized on a unilineal principle ego does not consider himself related to kinsmen outside of his lineage. Far from it. Such persons are recognized as relatives; this is why some anthropologists hold that all kinship systems are fundamentally bilateral. We are concerned here with descent groups to which ego may belong—groups of persons who may on occasion act together according to some common plan. By virtue of his membership in a unilineal descent group, ego acquires certain rights and obligations in relation to other members of the group: he is usually able to call upon his fellow members for goods and services, and they upon him, in a way that he cannot do with relatives outside of his group (even if we would consider them equally close under our bilateral principle).

In double-descent systems, the rights and obligations which ego has in his patrilineage are generally quite different from those in his matrilineage. For example, ego may inherit land from his mother, his mother's brother, or some other matrilineal relative, whereas he may inherit cattle from his father or his father's brother. Double-descent systems are not particularly numerous: they are found most frequently in Africa and Oceania, but have also been reported from South Asia and South America. Such systems give ego several structural possibilities for action; they also seem to aid in the integration of societal groups.

Even in societies where only one type of unilineal descent group is found, ego has some rights in relation to descent groups other than his own. For example, in a society with patrilineages, while ego is a *member* only of his father's lineage, he may very well have a standardized relationship with all the members of his mother's patrilineage (for example, her siblings, her father and his siblings, and her father's brother's children). Also, in matrilineal societies, even though ego does not usually inherit from his father, he may be entitled to certain benefits from and have certain obligations toward the members of his father's matrilineage (for example, his father's sister and her children, or his father's brother).

The notion of unilineal descent helps us to understand a form of residence which was passed over without comment in the last section: *avunculocal residence,* in which ego and his bride go to live in the household of ego's mother's brother. Why in the world should a society prefer this type of residence? The answer—at least for the Trobriand Islands, where the practice was reported by Malinowski—is this: in a matrilineal society, it is frequently the case that the mother's brother has considerable authority over his sister's son because the mother's brother is the closest adult male relative who is a member of ego's descent group (see Figure 5.9). Thus ego's father (who belongs to the matrilineage different from ego) has as an heir his own sister's son, and it is this young man (rather than the father's own offspring) who comes to live with him as an adult.[20]

The unilineal principle, combined with the widespread rule against marriage within a lineage, helps to explain the prevalence of cross cousin marriage. As we have seen (Figure 5.8), ego's cross cousins can *never* be members of his unilineal descent group, whether the rule of descent is patrilineal, matrilineal, or duolineal. Thus in a society with unilineal groups, a rule of lineage *exogamy* (out-marrying), and a preference for marriage with some consanguineal relative, the cross cousin is an obvious choice. Where there exists a further preference for marriage with one particular type of cross cousin (usually the mother's brother's daughter), other factors must be taken into consideration.

Although lineages are frequently localized (their living members tend to reside in the same areas), this is not necessarily the case, and it is important to keep separate the principles of descent

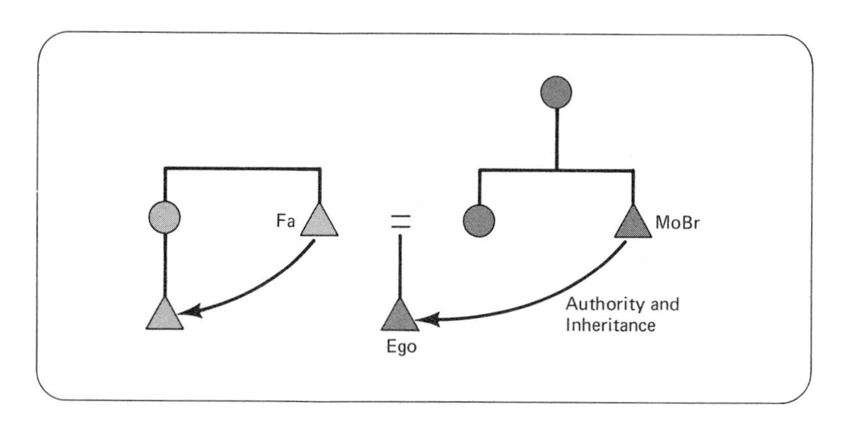

Figure 5.9 **Avuncular Authority in a Matrilineal Society**

20. B. Malinowski, *Sex and Repression in Savage Society* (New York: Meridian Books, 1955).

and residence even when they coincide in a large number of cases. Whether localized or not, lineages do tend to grow and also to decline in size. Thus they are faced with the problem of what to do when they reach a maximum or minimum population level. As with residential groups, lineage groups can combine or undergo fission. Segmentation generally takes place along lines implicit in the lineage itself; for example, the patrilineage represented in Figure 5.7 would most likely split into two parts in terms of descent from one or the other of the founder's two sons.

Clans, Phratries, and Moieties

When fission does take place, the new lineages may either go their separate ways or they may retain ties of one kind or another: this corresponds to the difference between complete fission and fission with aggregation in residential groups. Even in societies where genealogies are carefully kept (or remembered), however, there comes a time when the exact connection between distantly related persons is lost or forgotten. Nevertheless, due to the long-standing relationship between their respective descent groups, such persons may still consider themselves to be relatives. This is a probable origin of the social institution known as the *clan.*

Clans have the following characteristics in most societies where they are found:

1. They are unilineal descent groups, tracing descent in the male or female line from a remote and often mythical ancestor/ancestress.
2. Their members consider themselves to be relatives even though exact genealogical connections cannot be traced and perhaps never existed.
3. They are exogamous (marriage is forbidden among members) and sexual intercourse between members is generally considered incestuous.
4. Unity of the group is generally maintained by a clan name, a clan symbol, and/or ceremonials performed by all component lineages.
5. They may be composed of localized lineages, but the clan itself is not usually localized; rather, it crosscuts other types of residential groups.[21]

---

21. There are many ways of defining the term "clan," and social anthropologists do not agree on definitions or terminology. The five attributes listed here are fairly common characteristics of the groups many anthropologists label as clans, but the student must be careful to discover whether a given author uses the term with a special meaning, for example, in regard to localization, exogamy, naming, or type of descent rule. The term "sib" is used by some anthropologists for what I have called a clan, whereas others contrast sibs (patrilineal descent groups) with clans (matrilineal descent groups). See R. Fox, *op. cit.*

As long as some awareness of membership is maintained, clans can grow to an immense size. In traditional Chinese society, some clans (such as the Wongs) numbered in the tens of millions. Everyone having the same family name considered himself related to everyone else with that name; members of these patrilineal clans were forbidden to marry, and they were obliged to help other clan members even if they were totally unacquainted.

Because clans are not localized, they perform a very important social function: by crosscutting residential groups, they tie together a society which might otherwise break up into numerous geographic subdivisions.

Within the clan there are two major ways in which the component lineages may be related to one another: *equality* and *subordination.* When each of the lineages is considered equal to every other lineage, the clan tends to be relatively formless—a kind of federation of equivalent units with ceremonial or economic functions, and with equal opportunities for members from all lineages to participate. Under certain conditions, however, there may develop a system of ranked or stratified lineages within the clan, and this may have important implications for further social development.[22]

Clans are also frequently grouped into larger units within a society. These associations of clans go by the general name of *phratries;* although a phratry is not itself a unilineal descent group, the members of linked clans commonly cooperate in various ways. A phratry may be named or it may have some other symbol of identity, and it may be involved in the regulation of marriage. That is, in some societies phratries are exogamous (members of the same phratry may not marry), while in others they are endogamous (members of the same phratry are expected to marry so long as they do not belong to the same clan). In some societies phratries in no way control who may marry whom.

When the descent groups within a society are grouped into only two main divisions (whether or not phratries are also present), the two divisions of the society are known as *moieties* (halves). Figure 5.10 is a diagram of a society in which lineages are grouped into fourteen clans, clans are linked into five phratries and the phratries are divided into moieties. This hierarchy of groups binds a society together into an integrated whole in much the same way as does the table of organization of a modern military group. But whereas the military organization is based upon rank and mission, the clan type of social organization is based upon kinship and would clearly be impossible without the unilineal principle to define bounded lineages and clans.

---

22. See Fried, *op. cit.*, pp. 185–226.

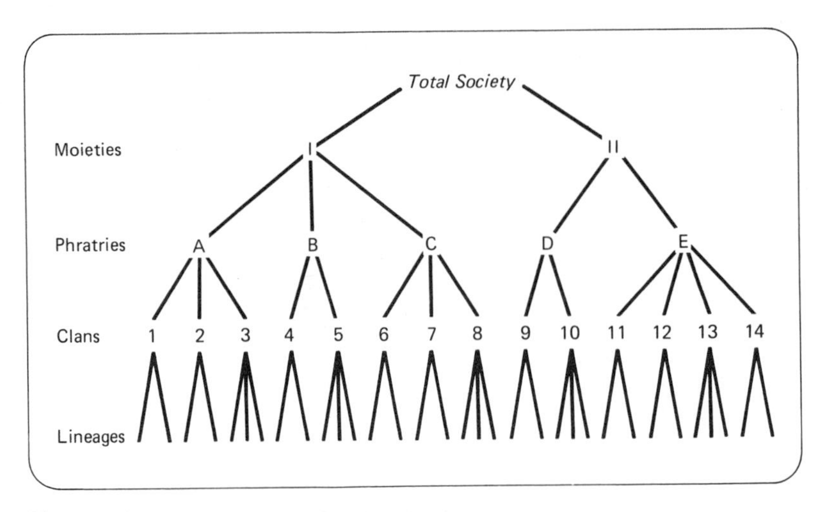

Figure 5.10 **The Structure of a Clan Society**

Descent groups of these types are extremely widespread in tribal societies (particularly in Africa), and they often linger on, though with changed functions, in highly civilized societies. Thus, as mentioned before, clan organization was important in the Chinese Empire, and the ancient Roman Empire as well as the great Aztec kingdom contained unilineal descent groups of some importance. The actual functioning of these groups, however, is easiest to study in living societies. Anthropological investigations have shown the great variety of functions that may be performed by unilineal descent groups; this versatility, together with their power of social integration, accounts for their presence in so many societies. In particular, the clan, whether matrilineal or patrilineal, plays a variety of important roles in the world's societies. That is, given this category of persons defined by the unilineal principle, any number of plans can be associated with it. In some societies (for example, Navajo) the clan is mainly related to the control of marriage; in others (Iroquois, Scotch Highlands, Roman) it has primarily political functions. In some cultures (Pueblo Indian) the control of marriage is mixed with various ceremonial and economic functions; while still elsewhere, the primary functions of the clan seem to be either military, religious, or economic.

Where clans are involved in warfare and feuding, it is quite common for the clan to be viewed as an undifferentiated unit and for vengeance to be taken in what we would consider an indiscriminate manner. "A life for a life" sometimes means just that: if a member of Clan A kills a member of Clan B, *any* member of

Clan A may be slain in reprisal. As can well be imagined, this may lead to a vicious circle of act and counter-act; but it also has the consequence of making the members of a clan feel more responsible for their hot-blooded members. (Interracial and interethnic strife in the United States often have some of these characteristics, and so do, on a somewhat more innocent level, rivalries among schools and colleges.)

Unilineal descent groups may be named or unnamed. It is quite common, though by no means universal, for a clan to be labeled with the name of some species of plant or animal. Among the Iroquois Indians of New York State and Ontario, Canada, the following clan names are still in use: Turtle, Wolf, Beaver, Deer, Ball, Eel, Hawk, Heron, Snipe, and Bear. All of these clans (some of which have several subdivisions) are grouped together into moieties known as Wolf or Turtle. Such clan names help to maintain the unity of a descent group after its members have lost track of their genealogical connections to one another. In some societies, however, clan names (or symbols) have a more far-reaching significance. These are the so-called totemic clans.

A *totemic clan* is a unilineal descent group named after some natural species. The clan members are believed to stand in some special relationship to that species. The relationship is often believed to be one of descent, and all the members of a totemic clan may trace the ultimate origin of their group back to a mythical totem ancestor (who actually was an animal). Whether this belief is held or not, members of a totemic clan commonly share certain responsibilities toward the species for which their group is named; for example, they may be required to carry out certain rituals in connection with it—rituals which are not required of the members of other clans.

Among the aborigines of Australia, totemic clans were extremely important. The food-gathering activities of the natives were a matter of life or death to them, and each clan was responsible for carrying out "increase ceremonies" for its particular totem in order to ensure an adequate supply of food for the entire tribe. The origins of the clans were related in complicated myths, while the lengthy ritual performed at initiations and "increase ceremonies" often involved an acting-out of portions of the myths.

The phenomenon of *totemism* (totemic clans together with their myths and rituals) has long fascinated students of human behavior, including the anthropologist Sir James Frazer, the sociologist Emile Durkheim, and the psychologist Sigmund Freud.[23]

---

23. J. Frazer, *The Golden Bough* (abridged edition; New York: Macmillan, 1953), pp. 799 f.; E. Durkheim, *The Elementary Forms of Religious Life* (New York: Collier Books, 1961); S. Freud, *Totem and Taboo* (New York: Norton, 1952).

Dozens of theories have been advanced to account for the origin of totemic beliefs and practices. Most recent work on totemism, however, emphasizes the categories used in classifying social groups and the relation of these categories to the natural world. For example, Claude Lévi-Strauss has stated that "totemic ideas appear to provide a code enabling man to express isomorphic properties between nature and culture. Obviously, there exists here some kind of similarity with linguistics, since language is also a code which, through oppositions between differences, permits us to convey meanings."[24] His point is that, just as language makes use of selected natural vocal qualities (voiced/voiceless, front/back, and so forth) by systematically organizing them into a conventional code which conveys meanings, a totemic social system makes use of the natural differences among selected species (Turtle/Wolf, Bear/Eagle) to convey notions of social relatedness. When a member of such a society says, "I am a Bear," he is making a statement about the clan to which he belongs, the social (and sometimes psychological or physical) attributes of its members, *and* his relationship as a clan member to members of other groups. (See Chapter 10, Belief Systems.)

Castes

Lévi-Strauss also compares the totemic clan with a type of kinship group that is in some ways similar and in other ways its direct opposite—the *caste*. Castes are best known from the subcontinent of India. They are large unilineal descent groups (usually patrilineal) and differ from clans in that (1) they are endogamous and (2) they are associated with and named for traditional occupations, rather than natural species. Two further characteristics of caste societies include: (3) the *ranking* of castes relative to one another and (4) the *interdependence* of caste groups, brought about by strict occupational specialization within a complex division of labor.

The *endogamy* (required in-marriage) of Hindu castes means that these groups must be fairly large, for in most of India, marriage with close relatives and also within the local community is forbidden. Although a woman who marries into a lower-ranking caste brings disgrace upon herself and her group, the custom of *hypergamy* allows a man to take a wife from a lower-ranking group without prejudice: their children belong to the father's caste. For this reason, Indian castes may be considered patrilineal descent

24. C. Lévi-Strauss, "The Bear and the Barber," *Journal of the Royal Anthropological Institute*, Vol. 93 (1963), p. 2. See also C. Levi-Strauss, *Totemism* (Boston: Beacon Press, 1963).

groups. Unlike clan societies, where integration is achieved through the marriage system ("exchange of women"), organic solidarity in a caste society must come from functional specialization ("exchange of goods and services").

In many parts of modern India the association between caste and occupation is breaking down. In the traditional system, however, there were such castes as the Brahmins (priests), the Merchants, the Farmers, the Weavers, the Barbers, the Potters, and the Sweepers; each had its own role to play in the community, and each jealously guarded its rights. The caste system, with its complex interdependence of parts, so permeated Hindu society that even members of other religions (Christians and Muslims) were incorporated into it. Special relationships were set up between individual members of these castes so that, for example, a farmer would receive the services of a particular priest or barber throughout the year and then, at harvest time, he would present him with sizable "gifts" of grain.

The strict ranking of castes gave a distinct flavor to the traditional Indian social system. This ranking, based upon "ritual purity" and justified by scriptures and legends, created a hierarchy of groups within which each kind of person had his place, his privileges, and his duties. At the top of the hierarchy were the Brahmins, below them the Warriors, Merchants, Farmers, and most craftsmen; at the bottom of the hierarchy were the "outcastes," groups whose impure occupations (such as working leather or otherwise handling dead animals) made them unworthy of consideration. This hierarchy was maintained by a complex series of prohibitions on social contact among members of different castes, and it was morally justified by a theology in which the idea of reincarnation of good men in a higher caste was central. An individual's caste was fixed (ascribed) once and for all by his birth; but it was possible for entire castes to raise their relative position within the hierarchy by adopting a more worthy (less polluting) mode of life. This process took much effort and several generations to complete; but though it was rare, it provided the caste system with some flexibility.

In summary, descent groups are arbitrarily limited categories of kinsmen which have associated with them culturally patterned plans for common action. These plans may regulate only a few activities (marriage, access to land, or economic cooperation); or, as in the case of Hindu castes, they may affect every area of a person's life (religious, economic, and social), leaving the individual with a complete absence of opportunities to alter his position. The descent groups that are dominant in a society generally try to justify their relative positions and privileges by myths and legends which tell of the origin of the group and explain its right to its present position. However, since actual relationships among social groups change with time and circumstance, it is not surprising that the myths which serve to validate the present state of affairs undergo constant alterations to bring them into line with changing situations. This process is as common within primitive groups as it is within civilized societies: it is not just in *1984* that history is constantly rewritten. (See Chapter 10, "Concepts of Authority.")

PEER GROUPS AND ASSOCIATIONS

Although residence and kinship play an important role in group formation in every society, there are other principles of recruitment which may be operative. People who share some interests or social characteristics other than those based on common residence or descent may be called peers. The term *peer group* will be used to designate a category of individuals who share such interests and/or characteristics, and who have also developed a sense of solidarity together with shared expectations about behavior appropriate to members of their group.

Age and Sex Groups

The division of labor by sex is a universal in human society, and all peoples recognize that individuals' abilities vary with age. These two facts, culturally elaborated, give rise to the differing social careers of men and women. In the simpler societies, age and sex are the primary characteristics determining peer group membership. And although they are supplemented by a variety of other career-based criteria, they remain important in more complex societies.

Every society has some age/sex categories with associated plans that prescribe different behavior for, say, old men as opposed to little girls. Here, however, we are concerned not with sex roles but with the formation of groups which act as units under certain circumstances, and which may acquire corporate functions. One example of this type of group is the age-set.

An *age-set* is a group of persons of one sex (usually male) who are members by virtue of their having been born or initiated during the same period of time. True age-sets are most commonly found in Africa, though they are also known from North America. For example, among the Nandi, a pastoral tribe of Kenya, every male belongs to an age-set from birth. The age-sets are bounded groups of males who are circumcised at the same time. G. W. B. Huntingford reports that there are

> seven sets, and at any given time one of these is that of the warriors, two are those of boys, and four are sets of old men. The warrior set is referred to as "the set in power," because during its period of office it is responsible for all military operations, and has in addition certain privileges; it is in power for a period of about fifteen years, at the end of which it retires, and the set next below it, which during this period has been circumcised, takes its place . . . the retiring warriors becoming elders. . . . At the same time the set of the oldest men, who by that time are all dead, passes out of existence as an old men's set and its name is transferred to the set of the small boys, the most junior set. The sets thus work in a recurring cycle, and the names appear again and again.[25]

The Nandi age-sets move through a series of *age-grades*—social categories of "small boys," "initiates," "warriors," and "elders." The age-sets have military and political functions, and their operations cut across all aspects of tribal life. Nandi women have no age-sets, but they go through the grades of *tipik* (girls) and *osotik* (married women), the transition from one grade to the other taking place at marriage (see Figure 5.11). Another type of age association with mainly "control" functions—that of the Red Xhosa—was described in Chapter 3 (p. 76).

Throughout most of East Africa, age-sets cut across the local divisions of tribal societies and function to tie together segments that would otherwise lack integration. Among the Nyakyusa of Tanzania, however, age is made the basis of territorial divisions, giving rise to groups called *age-villages.* Up to the age of ten or eleven, boys live with their parents and herd their fathers' cattle; but as they approach puberty, "they leave the herding of cows to their younger brothers, and themselves begin the business of hoeing the fields which will occupy them until they die; secondly, they no longer sleep in the houses of their fathers but join an age-village of boys."

At first, several young boys will sleep together in a crudely made hut, but later, as the age-village grows, they build more substantial, individual houses to which they will eventually bring their wives. The personal bonds forged during these early years are very important, for Nyakyusa men value above all the "good company" of their contemporaries—that is, eating and talking together with other men of their own age group. After a certain period of time, political authority is officially transferred to the younger generation and permanent village leaders (headmen) are chosen: "Eight or ten years after the young men of the senior

---

25. G. W. B. Huntingford, "Nandi Age-Sets," in S. and P. Ottenberg, eds., *Cultures and Societies of Africa* (New York: Random House, 1960), p. 215. The relationship of age-sets to age-grades is analogous to that between the Class of '76 and the grades "Freshman, Sophomore, Junior, Senior," through which the members of the class pass. That is, the set is an actual group of persons, the grades are a sequence of social positions.

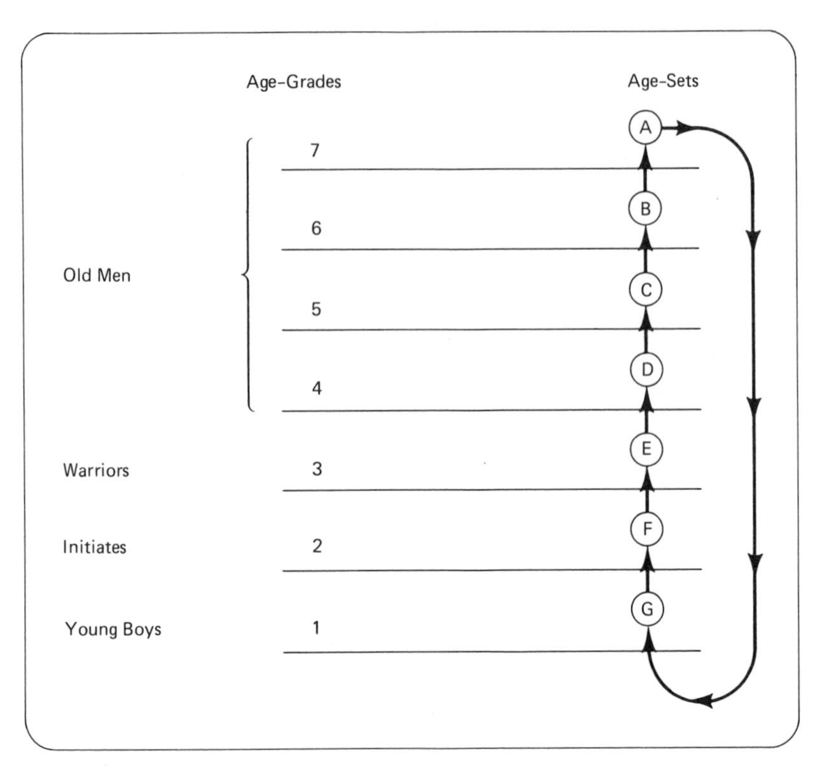

Figure 5.11 **Nandi Age-Sets and Age-Grades**

boys' village of the chiefdom have begun to marry, their fathers hand over the government of the country to them. This transfer of authority is effected in an elaborate ceremony called the 'coming out' (*ubukosa*)."

Fission into two equal parts is the fundamental mechanism of social growth and change in Nyakyusa society. At the time of the coming out, ideally the chiefdom is split into two sides under the rule of the old chief's two eldest sons. At the same time, two age-villages of men are established in each side under the leadership of appointed headmen (who must be commoners), and soon thereafter there develop two boys' villages attached to each village of men. Among the Nyakyusa, "age and locality coincide, while kinship cuts across local groupings, fathers and sons, and very often brothers, being in different villages. But kinsmen tend to be established in the same side of a country, and so to remain within one chiefdom."[26]

In contemporary American society, age and sex are used as

26. M. Wilson, *Good Company* (Boston: Beacon Press, 1963), pp. 19, 22, 33.

criteria for recruitment to a wide variety of roles: educational, occupational, and political. The feminist movement has made us aware of just how extensively (and irrationally) the criterion of sex is used, and it has also given us instances of the "mere category" female becoming the basis for genuine social groups. But although age is used together with other criteria for recruitment to various groups, it is seldom the primary basis of group formation. There are, of course, some exceptions. Voluntary organizations of senior citizens and groups composed of young, unmarried persons (twenty-thirty clubs) have common age as their main qualification for membership. But the closest thing to a true age-set in American society is probably the neighborhood gang and its formal equivalent, the college fraternity or sorority.

The neighborhood gang is a small, homogeneous group whose members find companionship and self-expression in conformity with the local variety of the American youth culture, and frequently in opposition to the adult world. Americans are highly sensitive to the opinions of their social peers, and in the gang the pressures toward conformity are especially strong. But unlike the Red Xhosa group organization, where peers teach one another the traditional values of the larger society, the culture of gangs is frequently opposed to "adult expectations and discipline," being more oriented to athletic competition and sexual conquest, fast cars, drugs, and excitement.[27] Prestige in the gang is often achieved by means that the outside world considers irresponsible or illegal. Indeed, this particular type of youth culture may be seen as a reaction against the dominant cultural patterns of American society in which adult responsibility is stressed and the individual's place in society is determined by his competence in a rather narrow occupational area. In the gang, one is much more of a whole person than on the job. Furthermore, the adult attitude toward this youth culture is an ambivalent combination of hostility ("those darn kids") and imitation ("for those who think young").

Occupational Groups and Associations

In primitive societies there are few, if any, full-time occupational specialities, and the kinds that do exist usually do not give rise to associations. It is only in civilized societies (and particularly in industrial ones) that organizations of men practicing the same trade become important. Craft guilds, business and professional

27. T. Parsons, "Age and Sex in the Social Structure," in *Essays in Sociological Theory Pure and Applied* (New York: Free Press, 1949), p. 221.

associations, and labor unions are examples of *occupational groups* which may be based upon such a criterion. While the functions of such groups are primarily economic, they may also take on social or political functions to the extent made possible by their members' common interests and solidarity.

In the small-scale societies studied by anthropologists, we often find groups of men or women cooperating on some common task, but such groups are better treated as voluntary associations, since the composition of these groups changes as new members join and others leave. By a *voluntary association* is meant any group of persons who act together by choice to attain a particular end. Voluntary groups may be classified in two ways: (1) by their *degree of continuity*—transient or semipermanent; and (2) by the major *explicit function of the group*—task-performance, social control, or expressivity.

The typical transient, task-oriented group is the work party, which in different societies may be devoted to nearly any type of task: hunting, fishing, gathering of resources, preparation of food, transport of heavy or bulky objects, warfare, defense, and so on. Such groups are formed in response to particular short-term social needs and, in many societies, constitute the most highly organized groups present. For example, in the Great Basin area, scattered Indian families would come together annually for a communal hunt of rabbits or antelope; but when this small surplus was exhausted, the families would have to disperse to their respective gathering territories.

In every society, transient work groups are formed at various times. We say that membership in such a group is voluntary, but close analysis often shows that affiliation is based upon the activation of preexistent ties—perhaps of kinship, locality, age group, or some other common interest. Leadership of such groups is usually quite informal if the work to be done benefits all the members of the group equally; but if the benefits are unequally distributed, some kind of task leadership will have to be exercised. Thus, cooperative groups may join in harvesting one another's crops with little overt direction, but if a work party comes to the assistance of one person with particularly large holdings, he will generally have to feast the members of the work party or reward them in some other way.

The explicit function of a work party may be incidental to a more important implicit function. For example, among the Siuai of the Solomon Islands, the slit-gong (a musical instrument used in men's ceremonials) is hollowed out of the trunk of a certain tree. A local leader who wants to increase his own prestige will hire a slit-gong maker to fashion one at some distance from the village. When it is ready, the leader will call together a work party

A work group in Kenya building a community center. ***Marc & Evelyne Bernheim/Woodfin Camp***

to transport the heavy instrument to the men's ceremonial house. The larger the work party, the more prestige the leader receives when he generously feasts them upon completion of the task. Thereafter, whenever the slit-gong is sounded, people remember the feast and speak of the gong as "sounding the renown" of the leader.[28]

Task-oriented voluntary groups become important when continuing social demands cannot be met by any of the regular groupings in a society. This happens particularly in situations of rapid cultural change, where the family or the local community is unable to adapt to new requirements. For example, when a society which has been producing food on a subsistence basis becomes involved in the production of a cash crop for a national or world market, voluntary associations of growers are often formed which cut across kinship and local groups. When tribal peoples migrate into urban centers (as in West Africa), voluntary organizations are often formed to help newcomers adapt to unfamiliar conditions. Such associations facilitate adjustment to urban life "by substituting for the extended group of kinsmen a grouping based upon common interest which is capable of serving many of the same needs as the traditional family or lineage."[29] These organizations are the functional equivalent of the immigrant societies formed by various ethnic groups during the major periods of immigration in the United States; their aims were to aid new arrivals to learn English, get jobs, and otherwise adapt to American culture.

Some voluntary groups have the explicit function of giving their members opportunities for display, activity, or other forms of self-expression. These range from transient play groups through more structured gatherings to fairly permanent organized athletic or artistic associations. To say that such expressive groups are voluntary does not mean that no other relationships exist among the participants. The author studied a Canadian Indian reserve where, on one occasion, the entire membership of the baseball team was drawn from the personal kindred of the team manager. But the members of a voluntary group *need not* have such ties, and they may constitute a selection from some larger group on the basis of common interests.

Expressive groups may also serve other functions. In American society it is standard practice for political activities to be carried on in the context of a cocktail party. Anthropologists have not always considered the formation and structure of voluntary expressive groups to be important, and the careful reporting of

---

28. D. Oliver, *A Solomon Island Society* (Cambridge: Harvard University Press, 1955), pp. 379–386.
29. K. L. Little, "The Role of Voluntary Associations in West African Urbanization," *American Anthropologist*, Vol. 59 (1957), p. 593.

such information is a fairly recent development. A good example of what can be learned about such groups is Charles Frake's work with the Philippine Subanun. There are two types of Subanun gatherings, the festive and the informal, in both of which the drinking of native beer plays an important part. By careful analysis, Frake was able to show standard stages of interaction involved in beer-drinking and to demonstrate that "the Subanun drinking encounter . . . provides a structured setting within which one's social relationships beyond his everyday associates can be extended, defined, and manipulated through the use of speech." Legal disputes are often resolved in such informal gatherings.[30]

Social control and education are often implicit functions, but some voluntary groups have these as primary aims. For example, the cooperative ethnic groups formed by American immigrants were described above as task-oriented; after their tasks had been accomplished, however, many of them lingered on as recreational groups with the explicit aim of preserving ethnic customs or languages, trying to give the American-born generations a sense of their cultural heritage. In primitive societies the closest thing to a voluntary control-oriented group is the secret society (discussed earlier in Chapter 3). Secret societies perform their control and educational functions by indoctrinating new members (teaching them certain esoteric parts of their culture) and by presenting periodic ritual performances in which the myths and values of the group are symbolically enacted. An example is the Buswezi, a widespread secret society of Tanzania. The activities of this group include ritual, spirit possession, dancing, and curing; members are obligated to keep the group secrets and to assist one another. Today, anyone who can pay the fees and who is sponsored by a member can join; after several years, he is eligible for initiation into the inner circle, where more esoteric doctrine is learned.

> The Buswezi is a rare example of a society, consisting of numerous small units which are independent of each other, which flourishes without any organization but the acknowledgment of authority based on erudition and efficiency in spheres connected with the ideological purpose of the society. The organization is strong because it takes no cognizance of the rank or ability of members in any field outside the society.[31]

Secret societies and fraternal organizations of all kinds also flourish in modern American communities. Groups such as the Masons or the Elks may carry on civic programs or extensive rec-

30. C. Frake, "How to Ask for a Drink in Subanun," *American Anthropologist*, Vol. 66, No. 6, Part 2 (1964), p. 131.
31. H. Cory, "The Buswezi," *American Anthropologist*, Vol. 57 (1955), p. 925. See also K. L. Little, "The Role of the Secret Society in Cultural Specialization," *American Anthropologist*, Vol. 51 (1949), pp. 199–212.

reational activities, and they may utilize occupational or totemic names, but the primary function of all such groups has to do with social integration. The taking over of task, control, and expressive functions by public and voluntary organizations seems to be a general pattern of change in American culture. It is related, above all, to the decline of the family as a multifunctional group.

RACIAL AND ETHNIC GROUPS

Within a complex society, racial and subcultural differences may also give rise to organized social groups. These differences can usually be understood as consequences of the varied histories of subgroups, but whether they are biological, cultural, or a mixture of the two, the important anthropological question is: How do these differences *function* within the larger society, keeping some people apart and binding others together? For the functions of racial and cultural differences are not automatic; they depend upon conventional ways of classifying people and traditional attitudes toward the categories. In the United States, persons with one or more Negro ancestors are generally classified as "Negro," but in Haiti, persons with one or more White ancestors are classified as "White." On the other hand, in Brazil there are dozens of terms referring to different "racial categories," but most of these are overlapping and are used in highly ambiguous ways. Each of these sets of categories and plans can be understood in terms of the cultural context in which they function, but none of them makes much sense in purely biological terms.

We have already noted that people who have recently migrated to an urban center or to a new country often form voluntary associations to assist one another in coping with new problems. It makes a big difference, of course, whether one's migration was voluntary or forced, and whether members of one's racial or ethnic groups are admired, ignored, or despised in the new setting. But even if they do not develop formal groups, people who speak the same language (dialect) and practice the same customs will, when placed among strangers, become aware of their "ethnic identity."

Anthropologists frequently study minority ethnic groups, such as American Indians or Australian aborigines, which are the remnants of a once large and diverse aboriginal population. The ancestors of these surviving groups were victims of European expansion and colonial empires from the sixteenth century to the present. Defeated by the superior military power of Spain, England, or the United States, they were often enslaved or confined to "reservations" where they could no longer practice their traditional culture. This is not the place to review the evils of imperialism, the greed of entrepreneurs, or the unhappy consequences of most missionary efforts. What is truly remarkable is the survival of some of these groups despite centuries of war, plague, confinement, and exploitation. Furthermore, the mid-twentieth century has seen a reawakening of racial pride and a sense of ethnic identity among many oppressed peoples—in the United States, from Black Power to the Pan-Indian Movement, and elsewhere, from African nationalism to the state of Israel.

Of course, many ethnic groups have been completely destroyed—their languages no longer spoken, their cultures preserved only in museums. It would be a mistake, however, to assume that the world is inevitably moving in the direction of greater cultural homogeneity, or that groups which insist on their ethnic distinctiveness are being irrationally stubborn. Anthropologists are often accused of being "romantics" or of wanting to preserve tribal peoples as "living museums." But more important is our awareness of the *positive value of cultural diversity.* Just as biological adaptation is always relative to the particular environmental situation, cultural adaptation is also a relative matter: a society (or a species) that becomes overspecialized is in serious danger when the environmental conditions change. Diversity in ethnic groups can be an important source of innovation and creativity for the total society.

Anthropologists have only recently begun to understand the major factors involved in the development, maintenance, or loss of ethnic identity. These include: (1) the presence or absence of differing ecological adaptations; (2) the nature of contact situations and exchange relations among ethnic groups; and (3) the ways in which ethnic identity affects political participation and recruitment to valued social roles. Studies of ethnic groups are particularly important to our understanding of the dynamics of social change and of the relations between individuals and the groups they "belong to." As more and more anthropologists come to work in urban centers and complex civilizations, the importance of ethnic studies can be expected to increase.[32]

Social Classes

Finally, we may note that complex societies tend to become stratified into a number of *social classes,* horizontal divisions of

32. F. Barth, *Ethnic Groups and Boundaries* (Boston: Little, Brown, 1969). The literature on ethnic and minority groups is immense. A good historical survey is F. Fellows, *A Mosaic of America's Ethnic Minorities* (New York: John Wiley, 1972).

the total society whose members differ in their prestige due to differential access to valued resources and positions of power. Social classes are more like categories than true groups in that they share certain attributes but seldom act together—that is, their members do not always share plans for action. Much of Marxist theory deals with the conditions under which the members of a social class become conscious of their joint interests and act accordingly.

Complex systems of social classes were found in the ancient empires of the Old and New Worlds and have continued through the feudal period in the West down to modern industrial civilization. These classes are based on an interplay of the factors of descent, occupation, ethnic identity, wealth, and formal education. Social classes tend to be quite stable, although by definition some movement of individuals from one class to another is possible; otherwise we would speak of a caste system. Social classes develop their own subcultures and are perhaps best characterized by their differing "styles of life" within the larger social system of which they are parts.[33] Further treatment of ranking and class systems will be found in Chapter 6.

SOCIETAL GROUPS AND FORMAL INSTITUTIONS

In this chapter we have described many different kinds of groups. It is now time to ask, what is a society? To begin with, a society is a group. It has members. It is composed of people, and its size can be determined with reasonable accuracy. This point is stressed to clarify the difference between society and culture, for a culture is *not* a group. It has no members. Culture is composed of shared categories and plans. Whether these are shared by two persons or two hundred persons makes little difference to the culture. Furthermore, separate societies may have highly similar cultures, while within one (large) society there may be found a great deal of subcultural variability.

When we attempt to describe a *societal group* (a total society), one way to start is by describing the subgroups of which it is composed: kinship groups, residential groups, social classes and other peer groups, and so on. We want to know the nature, size, and composition of these groups, as well as the plans with which they are associated and how the groups behave toward one another. These groups are the carriers of the culture of the societal group, for the division of labor involves the members of

33. See Fried, *op. cit.*, pp. 101–151; also, T. Bottomore, *Classes in Modern Society* (New York: Vintage, 1966).

different groups in a society in both doing and learning different things. The theory of relativity is a part of American culture only by virtue of the existence of a rather small group of theoretical physicists who are expected to master it and transmit their understanding to others. The same is true of the recipe for crêpe suzettes and the formula for Coca-Cola.

There are, however, some things that every member of a society is expected to know—the attributes of the *societal role* (see the last section of Chapter 4). When you ask a person who he is, he may answer on any of a number of levels: his personal name, his family or descent group affiliation, his peer group, and so forth, depending on the context in which the question is asked. But the most inclusive category with which he identifies himself will generally be that of the societal group to which he belongs ("I am an American," or "I am a Turk"), and this identification will influence his behavior in regular and important ways.

Just how much the societal role influences a person's behavior depends upon the homogeneity and degree of integration of his society. When the societal group is small and relatively isolated—what Robert Redfield called a "folk society"—all members of the group share much of their culture, so many regularities in their behavior can be attributed to the societal role: "He acts like that because he is a Turk." But when the societal group is large, complex, and open to cultural influences from many sources—typical characteristics of an "urban society"—it is harder to define the attributes of the societal role. In all societies, however, this role includes conventional understandings concerning legitimate political leadership of the total group, which involve acceptance of shared plans for settling disputes, making decisions, and coordinating activities.

The folk/urban distinction provides one way of classifying societies in order to compare their cultural characteristics. It raises (but does not answer) the question: In what general ways do the cultures of small, isolated societies differ from the cultures of large, open societies? This is an ethnological question and can be answered only by intensive comparative studies. On the basis of his work in several Mexican communities, Redfield suggested three general kinds of differences. As compared with the typical folk society, he found urban societies to be more secularized, more individualized, and more disorganized. Other scholars have taken issue with one or more of these points, but Redfield's ideas have provided a valuable framework for the investigation of social and cultural change.[34]

---

34. R. Redfield, *The Folk Culture of Yucatan* (Chicago: University of Chicago Press, 1941). A valuable collection of articles on this subject is J. Potter, M. Diaz and G. Foster, eds., *Peasant Society: A Reader* (Boston: Little, Brown, 1967). See also Bock, *op. cit.*, pp. 1–7.

Institutions

One general characteristic of complex societies is the development of a number of *institutions*—relatively self-contained social groups within which a number of different social careers are organized into a system. The term "institution" is used in many senses in the social sciences. Here it refers to actual social groups (such as governments, churches, and military organizations) which play important parts in the structure of large-scale societies. Institutions in this sense tend to be at least semipermanent; they are quite formally organized, often in a hierarchical manner. Within the institution is found a large variety of social roles which are linked into careers and authority relationships.

The modern business corporation is an institution which, no matter what its size, must contain certain types of roles (stockholders, officers, managers, employees). In the small, private corporation, these roles may be played by as few as two persons who hold all the stock, fill the company offices, and constitute the sole employees, while in such industrial giants as AT&T or General Motors there may be thousands of persons in each type of position. In either case, however, the corporation is chartered by a state with certain privileges and with the expectation that it will have some degree of permanent control over an estate. Different individuals may come and go, but the corporation maintains its identity.

Some kinds of institutions, such as prisons, mental hospitals, army barracks, and monasteries, have special characteristics which make them useful objects of study. Erving Goffman has called this type of establishment a *total institution,* defined as "a place of residence and work where a large number of like-situated individuals, cut off from the wider society for an appreciable period of time, together lead an enclosed, formally administered round of life."[35] These relatively isolated social systems provide another type of laboratory for the ethnographer. He may study them for their own sake, seeking to understand their structure and function; but he may also study them in order to compare the subcultures of these total institutions with the culture of the larger society, throwing light on the categories and plans which we take for granted.

The number and size of the major institutions found in a given society provide evidence for the dominant interests and values of the members of that society. At various times in the history of Western civilization, religious, military, political, or commercial institutions have risen to positions of dominance within

35. E. Goffman, *Asylums* (Garden City: Anchor Books, 1961), p. xiii.

particular societies; at other times, two or more types of major institutions have arrived at a balance of power. In Classical times, political and military institutions struggled for power. During the Middle Ages, the Church attained a position of dominance, partly because of the fragmentation of political institutions under feudalism. During the Renaissance, national states and commercial institutions rose hand in hand, with the overthrow of feudal institutions coming at different times in different nations. Today, in most countries we see a balance between military, political, and commercial institutions; this is complicated by the alignment of many states with vast power blocs representing opposing ideologies. For the future, some notable scholars such as Pitirim A. Sorokin and Arnold Toynbee predict an eventual return to dominance by religious institutions.[36] This text offers no prophecies, but suggests that our imaginative writers and poets have often anticipated future trends with far greater wit and accuracy than most social scientists.

We have now surveyed the major kinds of groups found in human societies. The emphasis has been upon kinship and residential groups because these account for much of the structure of primitive societies while they continue to be important in complex societies. We have also discussed the major types of peer groups, associations, and institutions which provide alternative types of structure in societies with economies above the subsistence level.

To summarize: a social group is a category of persons, defined by culturally selected criteria, associated with plans for activity and for interaction with other groups. The problems facing all social groups are similar: adaptation to the demands of the environment, recruitment and enculturation of personnel, and maintenance of conformity to the group norms. The functions of a social group may be viewed as responses to these problems; in every group, the functions of task-performance, expression, and social control (integration) are present, implicitly or explicitly, to some degree. The anthropological study of social systems involves description and analysis of the groups which make up a society and of the ways in which they function.[37]

Man is by nature a social animal. But the social groups in which he lives are culturally as well as naturally determined. Every societal group constitutes a subdivision of the human species on the basis of partly arbitrary factors—linguistic, geographic, his-

36. P. A. Sorokin, *The Crisis of Our Age* (New York: Dutton, 1942); A. Toynbee, *A Study of History* (London: Oxford University Press, 1934 *et seq.*).

37. G. Homans, *The Human Group* (New York: Harcourt Brace, 1950); this work provides a very general framework for the analysis of group structure, interaction, and functions. See also A. P. Hare *et al.*, *Small Groups* (New York: Knopf, 1955), and G. Lienhardt, *Social Anthropology* (London: Oxford University Press, 1964).

torical, and religious. And within a society, separate subgroups are formed by emphasizing some attributes of kinship, locality, or common interest and by ignoring others. The principles of group formation, then, *limit* the range of human interaction and understanding by assigning each person to a specific community, family, clan, caste, or peer group, while setting these off from other such groups. It is only through the selective limitation of possible kinds of behavior that man is able to communicate at all or to know what is expected of him. Once again we face the basic *paradox of human culture:* without selectivity there can be no language and no social system; but this same selectivity means that men will live in different groups and speak different languages. Translation of every human language into every other human language is possible because of the basic similarities among all men. It is on this same common humanity that we must pin our hopes for peace and understanding among human groups.

RECOMMENDED READING

Bottomore, T. B., *Classes in Modern Society.* New York: Vintage Books, 1966. A good summary of knowledge and theories about the nature and future of social classes.

Dumont, L., *Homo hierarchicus.* Chicago: University of Chicago Press, 1970. A unique study of caste in India and the general problem of human inequality.

Fox, J. R., *Kinship and Marriage.* Baltimore: Penguin Books, 1967. A brief and clearly written introduction to the complexities of kinship.

Graburn, N., ed., *Readings in Kinship and Social Structure.* New York: Harper and Row, 1971. An excellent selection of classic and modern papers on a wide variety of societies and structural types.

Lienhardt, G., *Social Anthropology.* London: Oxford University Press, 1964. The British approach to kinship, religion, and political structure, presented with wit and elegance by an eminent Africanist.

Redfield, R., *The Little Community.* Chicago: Phoenix Books, 1956. Thoughtful essays on the variety of ways in which anthropologists approach the study of small communities.

Service, E. R., *Primitive Social Organization: An Evolutionary Perspective*, second edition. New York: Random House, 1971. An approach to many topics treated in the preceding chapter from a point of view which emphasizes ecological relations and regular processes of change.

CHAPTER 6
Social Space and Social Time

Consider the following English words:

adolescence	infancy
adulthood	nation
childhood	neighborhood
city	old age
county	state

Anyone familiar with American culture can immediately group these terms into two sets and organize the terms in each set into a series. He will also recognize that the series are of different types: one set of terms is spatial and the other set is temporal; in one case the relationship among the terms in the series is one of inclusion (a city is in a county which is in a state), and in the other case the relationship is one of order (adulthood follows adolescence, which follows childhood). But temporal terms may also be related by inclusion (second, minute, hour) and spatial terms may stand in an ordered relationship to one another (gate, courtyard, entrance). Various types of order and inclusion may also be identified, as we shall see.

The point of this chapter is simply that every culture includes a set of time and space categories together with plans for organizing these categories into complex units. Members of a society utilize these shared plans and categories to coordinate their activities. We refer to these phenomena as *social space* and *social time* because each society (and to some extent, every social group) has its own system of categories and plans which can be understood only as part of its total culture. Shared expectations and understandings concerning the structure of space and time enable the members of a society to anticipate where and when various types of events will occur and to regulate their behavior accordingly.[1] Thus one function of social space and time is to ensure smooth interaction; but these conceptions also help individuals to orient themselves within a culturally created world which, unlike the universe, is organized on a human scale.

THE STRUCTURE OF SOCIAL SPACE

The comedian Myron Cohen tells the story of a suspicious husband who came home early one day in order to check on his wife's fidelity. On opening the hall closet, he found another man crouched behind some clothing. "What are you doing here?" he demanded. The man replied, "Everybody's got to be someplace."

The story is old but the point is true: everyone *must* be located somewhere in space, and any normal individual can give an answer to the question, "Where are you?" As a matter of fact, that question can usually be answered in a number of different ways; this brings us to an important characteristic of social space: it is *multidimensional.* If I wish to describe the location of a person, object, place, or event, I must do so with reference to some other person, object, place, or event; that is, I have a choice of frames of reference, and thus can locate the phenomenon within several different "dimensions." For example, the question "Where is the Restigouche Micmac Indian Reserve?" could be answered in all of the following ways: latitude about 48° north, longitude 67° west; in North America; in the Province of Quebec; in Bonaventure County; on the Gaspé; across from Campbellton, New Brunswick; on the north shore of the Bay of Chaleur; near the confluence of the Restigouche and the Matapedia rivers; or about 350 miles north of Boston. Each of these descriptions would be appropriate in some contexts; and in each case, *the categories and dimensions of space are culturally derived.* This includes the dimensions of latitude and longitude, which were arbitrarily defined at an international conference and which have no reality outside of these conventional understandings.

Place Names and Spatial Orientation

All men have a sense of being located within a social world, and they learn the categories and dimensions of this world along with

1. P. K. Bock, "Social Structure and Language Structure," *Southwestern Journal of Anthropology*, Vol. 20 (1964), pp. 393–403; reprinted in J. Fishman, ed., *Readings in the Sociology of Language* (The Hague: Mouton, 1968), pp. 212–222.

the rest of their culture. As we have seen, it is easier to learn a category if you can associate it with a verbal label; language is an essential part of the spatial orientation of human beings.

Many tribal peoples have exceedingly detailed systems of *place names.* The Micmac Indians of eastern Canada, for example, have different place names for each little hill, island, stream, cape, and bay along the shore near their settlements. Some of these names refer to outstanding geographical features and may be translated, for example, as "little rocky point," or "where the pines stand." Other place names indicate the types of activities customarily carried on in these areas: "where one looks for bark (for canoes)," "where they fish for salmon with torches," "place of eel traps." Still other names indicate historical or legendary associations: "giant's haunts," "where the dwarfs slide down (the mountainside)," or "hostilities."

In learning the place names used by members of his society, an individual also learns how to get around in his environment. This includes both what is usually called *spatial orientation* (knowing where you are) and also the *plans* associated with different parts of that environment—what particular kinds of behavior are appropriate to specific socially recognized places. The system of place names enables the members of a group to communicate shared beliefs and expectations about their geographic setting and to imbue the landscape with social meaning.

Ridiculous stories still circulate to the effect that "savages" have some kind of instinctive sense of direction or of spatial orientation and that they can find their way in the absence of any explicit guideposts. To the outsider, who is completely dependent upon maps, compass, and street signs, there *is* something uncanny about the way the Eskimo travels across trackless wastes or the manner in which the Polynesian sailor navigates his outrigger canoe out of sight of land using no mechanical aids to navigation. But a careful investigation of the cultural system of any one of these groups will show that it has provided an ingenious set of categories and plans which enable the members of that group to take advantage of slight environmental differences to maintain their sense of direction. Taken away from familiar territory, the "savages' " alleged instincts quickly disappear.

A. I. Hallowell has studied the cultural factors in spatial orientation among the Salteaux Indians of central Canada. He found that the Indians' remarkable ability to travel in the open depended upon their intimate knowledge of the terrain in their own locality, and that this was supplemented by the use of place names and native maps, plus keen attention to general topographical features and the changing direction of the wind. He points out that "topographical cues are . . . so important that if [they are] masked by snow an individual may lose his way even on familiar ground," while "if directional orientation by means of the wind fails, there is nothing to do but make camp and wait until weather conditions change and the usual cues can be picked up again."[2]

So much for directional instinct. But Hallowell goes on to make an even more important point:

> Perhaps the most striking feature of man's spatialization of his world is the fact that it never appears to be exclusively limited to the pragmatic level of action and perceptual experience. Places and objects of various classes are conceptualized as having a real existence in distant regions. Even though the individual never experiences any direct perceptual knowledge of them . . . such regions are, nevertheless, an integral part of the total spatial world to which he is oriented by his culture. For man everywhere has cosmic concepts; he is oriented in a universe that has spatial dimensions.[3]

Every culture, then, provides those who acquire it with beliefs about the world around them. If we wish to understand, much less predict, human behavior, we must recognize the importance of these culturally derived and transmitted images of the world.[4] For the ways in which men act are *influenced* by these images, whether or not the images correspond to any empirical reality. Consider the enormous effect upon human behavior of beliefs in the existence of the following "places": Heaven and Hell, the Cities of Gold, the Edge of the World, a Northwest Passage, Atlantis, or the Promised Land. Place names are *labels* for categories of space, real or imaginary.

Until quite recently, only a small proportion of any population traveled far from familiar territory. Even today, an individual's knowledge of what the world is like is derived primarily from his cultural tradition and not from his personal experience. How many readers of this book have ever seen the city of Warsaw? Most of us accept the fact of its existence as part of our cultural tradition, and from this tradition we may learn about its location, its form, and its history. If we were raised in another society, our culture might tell us nothing about Warsaw, but it might teach us in great detail about the Land of the Dead, or the Home of the Water Dragon. And chances are that we would accept the existence of these "places" and orient our behavior accordingly.

---

2. A. I. Hallowell, "Cultural Factors in Spatial Orientation," *Culture and Experience* (Philadelphia: University of Pennsylvania Press, 1955), p. 197.
3. *Ibid.*, p. 187.
4. K. L. Boulding, *The Image* (Ann Arbor: University of Michigan Press, 1956). Also, Kevin Lynch, *The Image of the City* (Cambridge: M.I.T. Press, 1960).

Territories

Social space involves much more, however, than the knowledge of geography (real and imaginary) of a society. To begin with, areas of social space are generally associated with particular social groups, and this is what we mean by the *territory* of a tribe or a nation. A territory is that part of the earth's surface within which a social group exercises certain rights. These rights may relate to traveling, hunting, cultivating, trading, or simply residing within the territorial boundaries. The relationship between a group and its territory may be extremely complex and imbued with emotion. The Arunta of central Australia spend most of each year in small, nomadic family groups. Each of these families feels itself to be part of a larger whole, called by anthropologists the local group or "horde." The members of these groups consider themselves to be the descendants of a particular kind of plant or animal, the *totem.* Somewhere in the territory of each local group is a totem center where the ancestral spirits reside. When a woman who has married into the horde becomes pregnant, it is thought that a spirit from the totem center has entered her body. "Thus a child born into a local group is tied to that locality forever because it is the residing place of his progenitor, the ancestral spirit."[5]

Beliefs of this type are not uncommon in primitive society, and even in complex civilizations the links between a group and its territory are varied and strong. Attempts to relocate Indian tribes, Pacific islanders, or slum dwellers often run into strong emotional opposition which engineers and urban planners are at a loss to understand since the disrupted groups are offered land that is objectively "just as good." Strangely enough, it is often people with a strong love-it-or-leave-it attitude toward their own territory who cannot understand why other groups refuse to leave their homes and the graves of their ancestors to make way for a dam, a freeway, or a strip mine.

Within the territory associated with a societal group there may be many subdivisions of social space associated with other types of groups, ranging from the lineage village to the clubhouse of a voluntary association, and from a college campus to the city of Chicago. The *boundaries* between these social areas are *always* a matter of cultural convention, even when natural boundaries such as a river or a cliff are involved, for their social significance must be recognized by the groups involved.

It is precisely at the boundaries between social areas that

5. E. Service, *Profiles in Ethnology* (New York: Harper and Row, 1963), p. 17.

one becomes aware of the association between territory and group and of the special rights that group members possess within their own territory. For example, the societal role of "United States citizen" is probably brought most keenly into awareness when one attempts to leave or reenter the country. Similarly, when one attempts to vote in a U.S. national election he becomes aware that the right to enter a voting booth is restricted on the basis of membership in certain age and residential groups—and in some parts of the country, one must belong to a specific racial group as well. Signs which read "No Trespassing" "Members Only," or "You must be twenty-one to enter" also serve to make us aware of the relationship between group and territory.

The ways in which this relationship is established and the particular rights that group members possess within their territory differ greatly in various societies. For example, the notion of *private property* is far from being universal: in aboriginal North America it was usual for tribal or kinship groups to exercise communal rights to hunting, fishing, or cultivation within a certain territory; but the idea that an individual could obtain exclusive rights over a territory larger than needed for subsistence was completely foreign. Many conflicts between the Indians and European colonists originated in misunderstandings about rights over land and who had the authority to dispose of those rights. (See Chapter 10.)

In Africa, the colonial powers constantly imposed European notions of ownership of land, and this had most unfortunate consequences. Many African peoples believed in a special relationship between their chiefs and the land, but this relationship was one of ritual responsibility for fertility and not of ownership in the absolute sense. By assuming that the chiefs had title to the land, colonial governments often caused severe dislocations of the native economy when the chief disposed of "his" land as he saw fit.

Each societal group develops its own notions of social space, subdividing its territory in any number of ways. It is extremely difficult to generalize about social space, since each group handles it so differently. One of the ethnographer's tasks is to discover and report what kinds of persons are expected or allowed to come together in what kinds of places and how they are expected to behave. For example, in the United States, it is expected that the two sexes will eat together but bathe separately; in Japan, common bathing facilities for the two sexes are considered quite proper; while among the Nyakyusa in East Africa, it was considered highly improper for men and women to eat together. Hundreds of such examples could be found to illustrate the differential use of space by sex, age, occupational, or kinship groups.

Space, Status, and Stratification

Perhaps the only safe generalization about social space is that access to certain areas of social space is used in every society as a mark of a person's status (for example, high or low, sacred or profane) within the group. For example, in much of New Guinea, boys must not enter the men's house until they have been initiated, and girls and women may never do so. In Polynesia, it was generally the rule that the chief's head had to be higher than that

The secret men's society clubhouse in New Guinea, which women and uninitiated boys are forbidden to enter. *American Museum of Natural History*

of anyone in his presence. And in virtually every society, we find there is a specific spot designated as a place of honor within the home or at the table, or a position of honor in processions. The conventional nature of these notions of social space is demonstrated by the fact that what is honorable in one society—the right side, or the front—may be quite the opposite in another society, where the left or the back may be most valued.

This general use of concrete spatial relations to mark relative status is our justification for a more abstract use of the notion of social space. Many American communities have their "right" and "wrong side of the tracks," and concrete social groups display their relative status by residing on one or the other of these sides. This arrangement may be viewed as a consequence of shared conceptions of relative social position: people live where they do in part because they "know their place." Whenever members of a society can be ordered in terms of their relative social value, this ordering defines another *dimension of social space*—an evaluative dimension that may or may not be reflected in concrete spatial arrangements, but which nevertheless influences the behavior of group members.

Social classes or castes are examples of groups which are ordered in terms of their relative value. In a society where the main divisions are into nobles, commoners, and slaves, there is no problem in arranging these groups along the evaluative dimension of power or prestige. Given this arrangement, we may then inquire into the size of each of the groups, and we may investigate the possibility of individuals moving from one of these groups into another: the phenomenon of *social mobility*. In Figure 6.1, the broken line between commoners and slaves is intended to show the possibility of mobility between these two groups, while the solid line indicates the absence of mobility into the highest ranking group.[6]

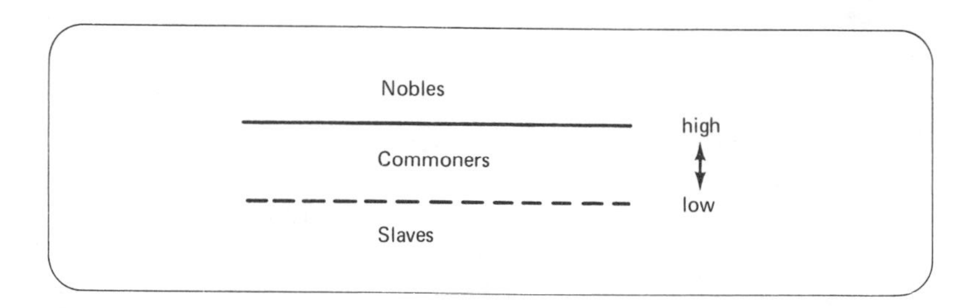

Figure 6.1 **Three Social Classes**

6. P. A. Sorokin, *Social and Cultural Mobility* (New York: Free Press, 1959).

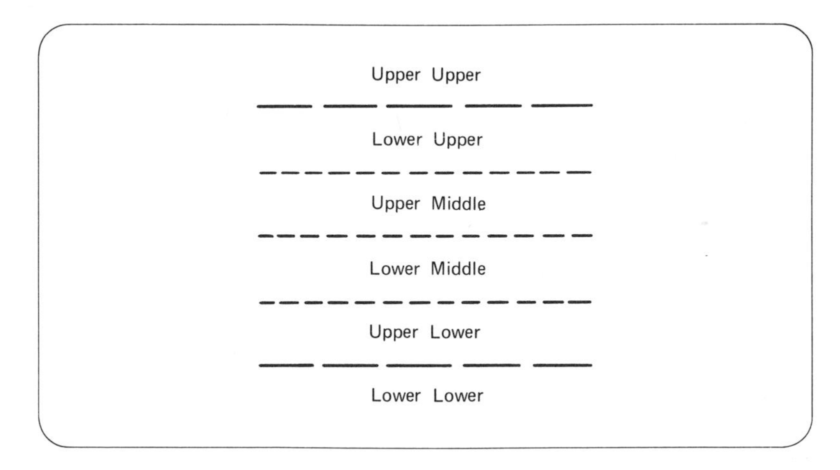

Figure 6.2 **The American Social Class System (breaks in the dividing lines represent opportunities for mobility between adjacent classes)**

The American social class system is difficult to describe, partly because it varies considerably in different regions of the country, but mainly because class membership is based upon a *combination* of social, economic, and cultural factors. There seems to be general agreement that in most parts of the country at least six divisions can be found (see Figure 6.2). Students of the American class system also seem to agree on the following points:

1. There is much less mobility between classes than is generally believed, particularly into the highest and out of the lowest strata.
2. Families tend to be classed together, and the most sensitive indicator of a nuclear family's rank is the occupation of the male family head.
3. The most important channel for social mobility today is the system of formal education.
4. Members of racial and ethnic minorities have much lower chances for mobility than do others.

Within a given society, occupational roles may be ranked in several ways. Sociologists have shown that there is considerable public agreement as to the relative prestige of common occupations, but—at least in American society—the relationship between prestige and salary is not exact. Most Americans consider the occupation of schoolteacher to carry more prestige than, say, plumber, despite the fact that teachers may make considerably less money. This kind of discrepancy shows us that the ordering of cultural units in one dimension of social space need not agree with their ordering along another dimension.

Some dimensions of social space (such as geographic location or cash income) admit of a direct measurement and quantification of positions; but for most dimensions we can state only the relative position of social units in terms of an arbitrary index. Thus in a military system, a major has more authority than a lieutenant and a lieutenant more than a private, but it is an open question as to how the amount of authority should be measured. Nevertheless, the *relative* positions of units within a societal or institutional group can generally be determined with some accuracy.

Thus far we have spoken of two general kinds of social space: (1) a *horizontal* space involving the division of the culturally conceived universe into territories and areas associated with various groups and activities, and (2) a *vertical* space of many dimensions along which cultural units are ordered according to their relative social value. There are two other types of social space which will be discussed in this section: (3) personal space and (4) semantic space.

Personal Space

By *personal space* we mean the way in which individuals in different cultures make use of the area immediately surrounding them and separating them from other persons (and groups). The anthropologist Edward T. Hall has long been concerned with the misunderstandings which may arise between members of different societies because of their culturally derived ideas about how space should be utilized. One of Hall's jobs in the State Department was to try to make Americans aware of their own cultural conventions regarding personal space so that they would be able to operate effectively overseas. He taught that the use of space was part of a "silent language" that, like spoken language, had to be learned.

> The flow and shift of distance between people as they interact with each other is part and parcel of the communication process. The normal conversational distance between strangers illustrates how important are the dynamics of space interaction. If a person gets too close, the reaction is instantaneous and automatic—the other person backs up. And if he gets too close again, back we go again. I have observed an American backing up the entire length of a long corridor while a foreigner whom he considers pushy tries to catch up with him.[7]

7. E. T. Hall, *The Silent Language* (Garden City: Doubleday, 1959), pp. 204–205.

Do these Japanese subway riders feel a violation of personal space? *Paolo Koch/Rapho Guillumette*

What is the *right* distance for a personal conversation? By now you should be aware that there is no one "right" distance or any other kind of "correct" behavior outside of a particular cultural tradition. Within the limits set by man's biological capacities, culture provides conventional rules in order to make possible communication and smooth interaction among the members of a social group. And it is precisely because these rules are conventional that members of different groups may misunderstand one another, particularly when the same object, event, or action has a different meaning in each cultural pattern.

Personal space in American society has been studied by sociologists such as Robert Sommer and Erving Goffman, but there is very little systematic material available on other cultures.[8]

---

8. R. Sommer, *Personal Space* (Englewood Cliffs, N.J.: Prentice-Hall, 1969); E. Goffman, *Behavior in Public Places* (New York: Free Press, 1963).

Some data can be gleaned from ethnographic descriptions of sleeping arrangements, eating practices, and crowd behavior. But few anthropologists other than Hall have explicitly considered the cultural patterning of personal space. However, one type of data that falls between the study of personal space and semantic space is available; therefore, it is appropriate that we turn to this next.

The human body is a continuous unit; nevertheless, for some purposes it is essential to think of it as divided into parts. Since there are few clear-cut natural divisions, the divisions must be partly arbitrary. Where does the "neck" end and the "head" begin? Each culture has its own way of categorizing the parts of the body and its own plans for appropriate behavior in connection with each category—for example, the parts of a person's body that may be seen or touched by others, and under what circumstances. As every reader must be aware, *standards of modesty* vary greatly from society to society and even within the same society at different times. In nineteenth-century France, for example, it was considered scandalous for a woman to allow the nape of her neck to be seen by a strange man, yet this is the country which in the twentieth century pioneered in the use of bikinis. In any case, anthropologists and linguists have recorded the words used for different body parts in many societies, and these terms may be used to study the categories of body parts.

A familiar example of this would be the Spanish term *espaldas*: there is no single English equivalent for this word which refers to an area of the body including parts of what English speakers would call the shoulders, upper arms, and back. A more exotic example comes from the Kewa of Papua (eastern New Guinea). Among the Kewa, the *kádésaa* or "upper trunk" is divided into three major parts, each with its proper function; these are: the *kou,* "back," which is thought of as "an aid to physical work, such as gardens and roads"; the *káágo,* "chest," which is the "decoration center for shells and beads"; and the *kíi,* "arms, hands," which are for "making things." In Kewa anatomy, the arms are directly linked to the trunk, but the back is attached to the trunk by the *mabémaa,* "nape of the neck," and the chest is linked to the trunk by the *pasaa* or "shoulder."[9]

The point here is that every culture provides a conventional way of categorizing parts of the body, together with plans for the use or display of those body parts. These categories and plans are connected with other cultural conceptions of personal space

9. K. Franklin, "Kewa Ethnolinguistic Concepts of Body Parts," *Southwestern Journal of Anthropology*, Vol. 19 (1963), pp. 58–59.

—for example, the American notion of "elbow room," or the French tête-à-tête, 'private interview or conversation' (literally, 'head to head'). The linguistic terms used to label these body parts also illustrate the meaning of semantic space.

Semantic Space and Componential Analysis

There are two basic approaches to the study of *semantic space.* Both of these approaches involve trying to *locate* a given word (and the category which it labels) within some area or dimension of meaning. In the first approach, the idea is to divide up a given semantic *domain* horizontally into its component parts; this is similar to the way in which a group's territory is divided into subareas, except that we are here concerned with an area of meaning (a domain such as color terms, body parts, kinship terms, or names of plants) and the way in which it is structured. For example, we have seen that the Kewa think of the upper trunk as divided into three parts—the back, chest, and arms—with the nape of the neck and the shoulder thought of as linking areas. We may arrange the Kewa terms spatially to show the *part-whole relationship* of the back, chest, and arms to the upper trunks as in Figure 6.3. Each of the terms in the lower boxes is again subdivided into these parts which are considered subordinate to it; for example, the *kou*, 'back,' *pérali*, 'ribs,' and numerous other parts.

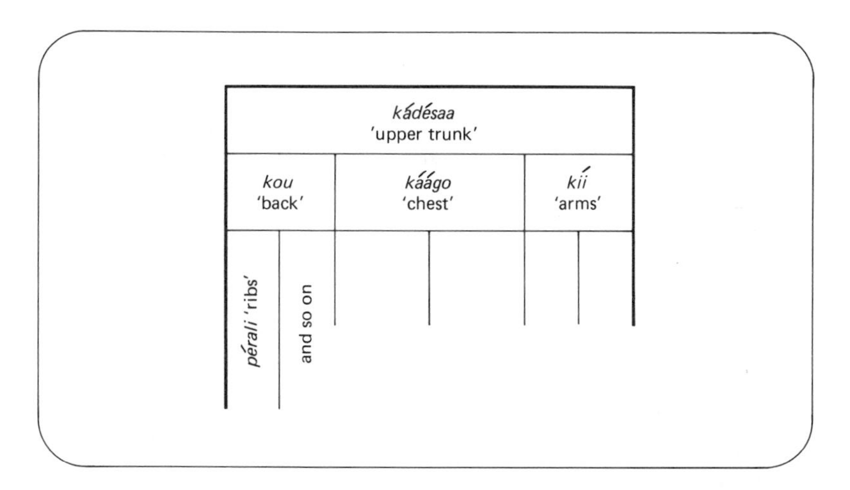

Figure 6.3 **Part-Whole Relationship of Some Kewa Terms for Body Parts**

	Relatives		
	Male	Female	Sex
Collateral	Lineal		Generation
	grandfather	grandmother	+2
uncle	FATHER	mother	+1
cousin	brother	sister	0 (Ego's)
nephew	son	daughter	−1
	grandson	granddaughter	−2

Figure 6.4 **Componential Analysis of Some English Kinship Terms**

The part-whole relationship, in which categories *x, y,* and *z* are considered *parts of* the larger category *A,* is only one of the ways in which a semantic domain may be horizontally structured. Another important type of relationship is that of *species-genus,* in which categories *x, y,* and *z* are considered *kinds of* the larger category *A.* For example, the English terms "elm," "maple," and "cedar" are kinds of trees, while "hammer," "axe," and "pliers" are kinds of tools. These and other types of relationships among terms are used in *componential analysis,* the inductive study of semantic domains.

The object of componential analysis is to understand how a particular area of meaning (semantic domain) is divided into parts and how these parts are related to one another. For example, English kinship terms may be viewed as standing in a species-genus relationship to the category "relative"—that is, a "father" is a "kind of relative." The question, then, is how fathers differ from *other* kinds of relatives. To answer this question one must discover the dimensions of semantic space which separate "father" from the other terms in this domain. To do this, we may use some of the Kroeber-Murdock criteria, as shown in Figure 6.4. The term "father" is separated from "mother" by the criterion of sex, from "uncle" by the criterion of collaterality, and from "grand-father" by that of generation. These are the three major dimensions of the semantic space that define this set of English kinship terms.[10]

Componential analysis has been used mainly in the study of kinship terminologies, but it is also useful in understanding the ways in which plants, animals, colors, tools, and many other kinds of objects or events are categorized in a given culture. In our own society, biologists have developed a complex system of classification for labeling and organizing living and extinct life forms. This system of Latin names (taxonomy) arranged according to species, genus, family, order, and so on up, is essential for a scientific understanding of the evolutionary relationships among the millions of known species. But in every society, no matter how small or simple, we find (instead of or in addition to a scientific classification) a way of classifying life forms that is shared by most members of the society and that enables them to identify and to communicate about the plants and animals which are important to them. Such as system of classification is called a *folk taxonomy.* Some folk taxonomies are extremely complex, while others are rather simple (though few are as simple as that of the city dweller who knew of only two kinds of birds, "sparrows" and "pigeons"; these categories he applied to all small and large birds, respectively). In any case, the important thing about a folk taxonomy is that its categories are closely associated with plans for action. The biologist usually arranges plants in categories according to their evolutionary relationships, but the average man in any society is more interested in what he can or should do with a given kind of plant: whether it is edible or poisonous; whether it can be used to make string, baskets, or cloth; whether it can be utilized as an ingredient in medicine; whether its bark will provide a canoe or a shelter.

Folk taxonomies are much more practically oriented than are scientific taxonomies; they show much greater *elaboration in areas of immediate concern* than they do in other areas. (Recall the many terms that the Eskimo has for different types of snow.) The ethnographer who wishes to fully understand and describe the culture of a strange society must carefully explore these semantic domains; he must try to discover not only the terms themselves, but also the way in which semantic space is structured in each of these areas of meaning. This will frequently lead him into other

10. Compare A. F. C. Wallace and J. Atkins, "The Meaning of Kinship Terms," *American Anthropologist*, Vol. 62 (1960), pp. 58–80. For an alternative analysis, see P. K. Bock, "Some Generative Rules for American Kinship Terminology," *Anthropological Linguistics*, Vol. 10 (1968), pp. 1–6. A bibliography of over 400 articles dealing with folk taxonomies has been compiled by Harold Conklin and is now available from the Department of Anthropology at Yale University. R. M. Keesing has recently published an article appraising the current state of such "ethnosemantic" studies; see his "Paradigms Lost: The New Ethnography and the New Linguistics," *Southwestern Journal of Anthropology*, Vol. 28 (1972), pp. 299–332.

areas of inquiry, as, for example, when Harold C. Conklin did a study of Hanunóo plant classification that eventually led him to analyze their system of color categories (see Chapter 2, Semantics).

The second approach to the study of semantic space involves the *evaluative* or vertical dimensions along which terms may be ordered. In this approach, the relationships among terms that we are interested in include "better than," "stronger than," and "faster than," rather than "part of," or "kind of." A way of measuring these evaluative dimensions, developed by the physiologist Charles Osgood, is known as the *semantic differential.* This technique has been used in a number of different cultures and the results of these experiments have been most unexpected. Intercultural differences are considerable when we examine *which* terms are valued most highly; the *ways* that people evaluate, however, show striking cross-cultural similarities. Thus for samples from eight literate societies in which different languages are spoken, Osgood was able to demonstrate that native terms are evaluated within a semantic space that has three important dimensions. In *all* groups, these dimensions are:

1. Evaluation (good-bad, nice-awful, sweet-sour, and so forth)
2. Potency (powerful-powerless, big-little, strong-weak, and so forth)
3. Activity (fast-slow, noisy-quiet, young-old, and so forth)

That is, despite differences in the languages spoken, members of different societies used very similar *dimensions of meaning* in evaluating words.[11] As a psychologist, Osgood is interested in the biological foundations of this common framework, but he is also intrigued with the possible use of these techniques for cross-cultural comparisons. On the one hand, if these dimensions of meaning are the same in all societies, it may be possible to describe cultural attitudes and values objectively so that they can be systematically compared (see Chapter 11). On the other hand, we may use the semantic differential to investigate the particular adjective scales which define the major dimensions in different societies. For example, in American English the adjective pair "rugged-delicate" is part of the Potency dimension, related to "strong-weak." In Japanese culture, however, the closest equivalent of this pair is part of the Evaluation dimension, with "delicate" indicating "good" and "rugged" expressing "bad." These differences in the connotations of apparently similar terms indicate one source of difficulty in translations.[12]

---

11. C. Osgood *et al., The Measurement of Meaning* (Urbana: University of Illinois Press, 1957).
12. C. Osgood, "Semantic Differential Technique in the Comparative Study of Cultures," *American Anthropologist,* Vol. 66, No. 3, Part 2 (1964), pp. 185, 187.

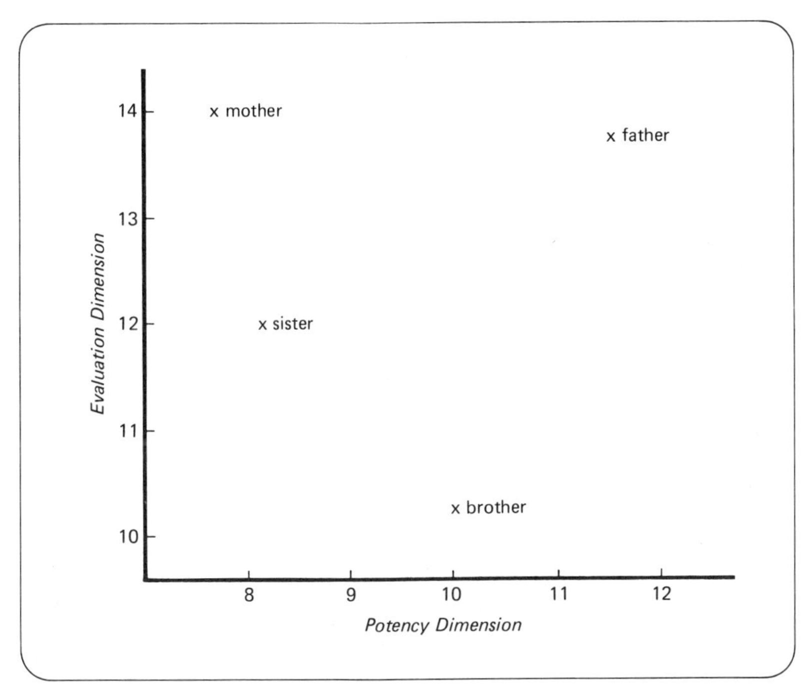

***Figure 6.5* Average Positions of Four Kinship Terms on Two Dimensions of the Semantic Differential (adapted from A. K. Romney and R. G. D'Andrade, "Cognitive Aspects of English Kin Terminology," *American Anthropologist,* Vol. 66 [1964], p. 159)**

A. K. Romney and R. G. D'Andrade have used the semantic differential to locate American kinship terms in semantic space of this second kind. Some of their findings are shown in Figure 6.5. In this figure we see that the term "father" scores very high on both the Evaluation and Potency scales, while "mother" is high on Evaluation but rather low on Potency.[13]

It is clear that this second type of semantic space is quite different from the type represented in the componential analysis of kinship terms (Figure 6.4). Componential analysis displays the *cognitive contrasts* among terms in a semantic domain (the combinations of attributes which distinguish one term from another), whereas the semantic differential attempts to measure the *emotional contents* of given terms. As was stated earlier, both contrast and content are necessary for a complete definition of any cultural

13. A. K. Romney and R. G. D'Andrade, "Cognitive Aspects of English Kin Terms," *American Anthropologist*, Vol. 66, No. 3, Part 2 (1964), pp. 146–170. Romney and D'Andrade use the semantic differential to test the validity of alternative componential analyses of English kinship terms. For a general discussion of semantic approaches to culture, see O. Werner, "Ethnoscience 1972," *Annual Review of Anthropology*; Vol. 1 (1972), pp. 271–308, and, in the same volume, H. Scheffler, "Kinship Semantics," pp. 309–328.

phenomenon. These two approaches, then, are complementary. By studying the systematic relationships among sets of terms, anthropologists hope to gain a greater understanding of the categories for which the terms are labels.

SOCIAL TIME

We have already seen that periods of social time may be related by inclusion (a day is part of a week, a week is part of a month) or by order (Monday, Tuesday, Wednesday). That is, when we analyze temporal relationships we are concerned with notions such as "before," "after," and "during." These relationships among persons, objects, and events pervade our daily lives and are essential to our social plans. As with space, every culture provides a series of temporal categories and relationships in terms of which persons may orient themselves and coordinate their activities. And as with all things cultural, the categories of time found in one society are conventional, differing from those of other societies in significant ways.[14]

Most members of Euro-American societies are partly aware of their temporal categories, but they are *not* aware of how recently some of these categories have developed, or of how culture-bound they are. Our modern sense of time is a very special kind of temporal awareness. In most of the world's preindustrial societies, one rises with the sun and goes to bed when it sets—unless there is a very good reason for keeping a large fire burning after dark. The day has its own rhythm depending upon the tasks to be done, but there is no notion of keeping pace with a clock: time cannot be lost or saved; one may be early or late in coming to an event, but not three minutes late to work or a half-hour early for dinner.

The time categories of Western man are products of the Renaissance and the Industrial Revolution, and many of them have not yet spread to certain European and American rural and ethnic subcultures. But most of us are so used to thinking in terms of minutes and seconds, workdays and lunch hours, it is hard to realize that although the mechanical clock was invented late in the thirteenth century, clocks did not come into general use until the nineteenth, while widespread possession of pocket and wrist watches is a development of the last fifty years.

Above all, it was the Industrial Revolution which brought about

14. P. A. Sorokin, *Sociocultural Causality, Space, Time* (Durham: Duke University Press, 1943). Also, J. T. Fraser, ed., *The Voices of Time* (New York: George Braziller, 1966).

the need for temporal coordination of activities on a large scale and in an exact manner. The Age of Technology required that man measure space in thousandths of an inch; but even more important, it required him to measure time, and learn to value it in monetary terms. The maxim "Time is money" is simply inconceivable in primitive societies, where money is unknown and where there exists no conception of time as a homogeneous and infinitely subdividable continuum. Many books have been written on this subject, some lamenting and some praising this change in the quality of man's temporal awareness. In this section, we shall consider some of the temporal categories of men in other societies, with particular attention to the ways in which their categories are related to plans for action and to other features of their culture.

Varieties of Social Time

In the Introduction to Part Two it was noted that for institutionalized idiots, most interactions seem to take place "without relation either to past or future: in a word, they have the appearance of occurring outside of history." For most men, however, social events are *located* in one or more dimensions of social time: they are repetitions or consequences of what has occurred before and have consequences for what will happen afterward. Like social space, social time is multidimensional; for example, a given event may be temporally located as occurring in 1965, during Lent, on a Wednesday, and/or before the bridge opened, with each of these ways of locating it being relevant in some context, and all of them being true.

There are two fundamental types of temporal dimensions. A *linear dimension* is one in which time period *A* is followed by period *B* which is followed by period *C,* and so on; an example from our own culture is: infancy→childhood→adolescence→adulthood→old age. A *cyclical dimension* is one in which the sequence of periods is repeated a definite or indefinite number of times, as with our days of the week. Clearly, every cyclical dimension includes at least one linear dimension, while some *complex linear dimensions* include one or more cycles[15] (see Figure 6.6).

There are many kinds of cycles in nature which affect man's welfare; therefore, his culture both makes him aware of these cycles and provides him with plans for each part of the cycle. Hunting and gathering peoples are acutely aware of cycles of scarcity and plenty based on the migrations of fish and game or

15. For a further discussion of and notation for social time dimensions, see P. K. Bock, "Social Time and Institutional Conflict," *Human Organization*, Vol. 25 (1966), pp. 96–102.

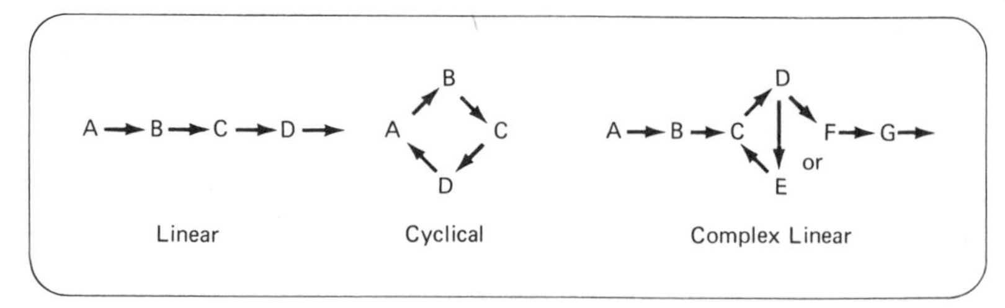

Figure 6.6 **Three Types of Social Time Dimensions**

the availability of various plant foods. Their own migrations and food-gathering techniques show a very nice adaptation to these recurrent conditions (see Chapter 9, Subsistence). But the march of the seasons probably makes its greatest impression upon pastoral and agricultural peoples, for whom the quantity and timing of sunlight and rainfall mean the difference between abundance and famine.

The alternation of wet and dry seasons in tropical and subtropical areas has a major influence on human activities; and many peoples think of time primarily in terms of the *relations between activities.* For example, the Nuer are a pastoral and horticultural people of the Sudan who have a lunar calendar with twelve named months. Yet, according to E. E. Evans-Pritchard, they

> do not to any great extent use the names of the months to indicate the time of an event, but generally refer instead to some outstanding activity in process at the time of its occurrence, e.g., at the time of early camps, at the time of weeding, at the time of harvesting, etc., and it is easily understandable that they do so, since time is to them a relation between activities. During the rains the stages in the growth of millet and the steps taken in its culture are often used as points of reference. Pastoral activities, being largely undifferentiated throughout the months and seasons, do not provide suitable points.

The author concludes that for the Nuer,

> time has not the same value throughout the year. . . . Life in the dry season is generally uneventful, outside routine tasks, and ecological and social relations are more monotonous from month to month than in the rains when there are frequent feasts, dances, and ceremonies. . . . In the drought the daily time-reckoning is more uniform and precise, while lunar reckoning receives less attention. . . . The pace of time may vary accordingly.

Furthermore, the Nuer are able to reckon past time in terms of *relations among groups.* Evans-Pritchard calls this "structural time." He points out that the Nuer can state roughly when events

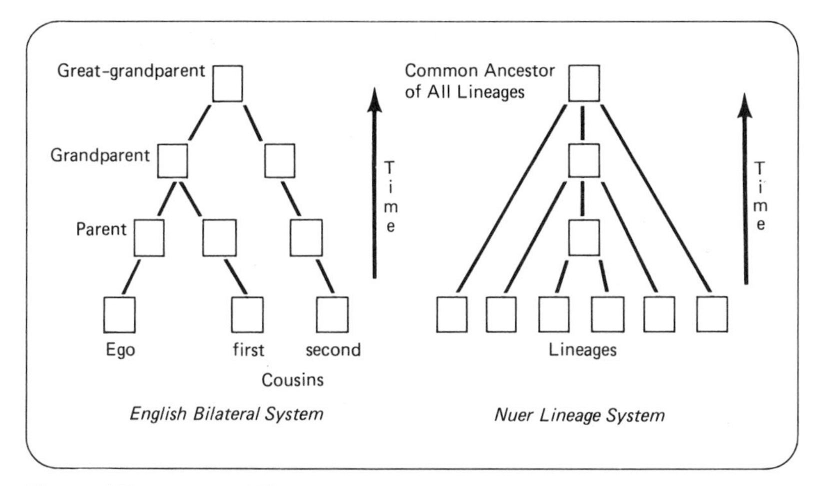

Figure 6.7 **Structural Time**

took place by reference to the appropriate age-set or to the lineage system. For example, a Nuer may say that an event happened after the Thut age-set was born or during the initiation period of the Boiloc age-set without being able to say how many years ago that was. Such reckoning of time is entirely relative to the social structure. Similarly, since any two kinsmen in the lineage system must have a common (patrilineal) ancestor, kinship relations always have a "time connotation couched in structural terms."[16]

An example of structural time from English terminology is found in the temporal connotation of our terms "first cousin" and "second cousin," terms which imply, respectively, the grandparental and great-grandparental generations. For persons to be ego's second cousins they must be able to trace their descent *back through time* to a common great-grandparent, while to be considered first cousins they need only to find a common grandparent. In the Nuer system of patrilineages, the relationships among lineage groups within a clan similarly imply various degrees of time depth (see Figure 6.7).

Time and Society

Each of the major institutions of a society is likely to have its own dimension of social time. In a well-integrated society, all of these dimensions will be coordinated with one another, but there will still be qualitative differences between, say, the structure of the

16. E. E. Evans-Pritchard, *The Nuer* (London: Oxford University Press, 1940), pp. 100–103, 105, 106.

civil year and that of the religious year. The Roman Catholic Church has its own ecclesiastical calendar, which is divided into seasons, weeks, and special days. Persons who play roles within this institution know *what kind of behavior is expected of them* during Lent or Holy Week, on Sunday or Christmas Eve. The same individuals, as members of business or national groups, are influenced by periods such as the fiscal year, inventory week, Independence Day, or Labor Day. Calendars thus make possible the coordination of activities within groups by means of learned associations of time categories with standard plans.

Some kind of *annual cycle* is recognized in all societies, and this "year" is composed of a number of subdivisions which relate to variations in the social life of the societal group. Furthermore, in most societies, the year is thought of as a subdivision of some larger dimension of time. The way in which this larger dimension is conceived is intimately related to the central values of the culture. For example, the Nuer reckon past time in terms of the age-sets and lineages which are central to their social structure, whereas societies with powerful centralized monarchies (such as ancient Rome and Egypt) reckon time in terms of dynasties or individual reigns. In Jewish culture the years are numbered from the traditional date of Creation (somewhat over 5,700 years ago), while the Christian tradition numbers the years in two directions from the assumed date of the birth of Jesus. And Australian aborigines have a still different outlook on the past. According to W. E. H. Stanner, one of their most important categories is "The Dreaming" (*alcheringa* in Arunta):

> A central meaning of The Dreaming is that of a sacred, heroic time long ago when man and nature came to be as they are; but neither "time" nor "history" as we understand them is involved in this meaning. . . . The Dreaming conjures up the notion of . . . the indefinitely remote past, [but] such a time is also, in a sense, still part of the present. One cannot "fix" The Dreaming *in* time: it was, and is, everywhere.[17]

Our *historical sense,* then, as much as our spatial orientation, is a product of culture. Our notions about the origins of the world and of man, of the social groups to which we belong and the cultural devices which make possible our survival—all of these ideas about the order of past events come to us indirectly. Who, after all, has witnessed the death of Caesar or the Boston Tea Party? Yet we accept the occurrence of these events and their consequences just as we accept the existence of Warsaw or of

17. W. E. H. Stanner, "The Dreaming, an Australian World View," in P. Hammond, ed., *Cultural and Social Anthropology: Selected Readings* (New York: Macmillan, 1964), pp. 288–289.

Cultural Group		Most Valued		Less Valued		Least Valued
	Texan	future	=	present		past
	Mormon	future	=	present		past
	Spanish-American	present		future		past
	Navajo	present		past	=	future
	Zuni Indian	present	=	past		future

***Figure 6.8* Time Orientation in Five Social Groups (= indicates nearly equal emphasis)**

Timbuktu. And man in primitive society must also rely upon his culture to orient himself in time.

The Christian tradition views the overall flow of time as fundamentally linear, marked by a number of *unique* historical events which have been and will be of crucial importance to man's salvation. The Asiatic civilizations, on the whole, take a much more cyclical view of history. In the Hindu tradition, this world is only one of many worlds which have been created and destroyed, while man's life is part of an eternal cycle of death and rebirth from which he may try to escape. Such temporal orientations have important consequences for human behavior.

Florence R. Kluckhohn has been concerned with the time orientations of peoples in different societies from a somewhat different point of view. She reasons that each culture must place a distinctive emphasis upon either the past, present, or future, and she has devised a questionnaire to test the varying orientations found in a number of social groups. Thus, for example, in her study of five subcultures in the American Southwest, she came to the conclusions displayed in Figure 6.8. Although each culture placed *some* value upon past, present, and future, which of these time orientations was most valued varied considerably from group to group.[18]

Social careers may also be viewed as dimensions of social time which are defined by an ordered sequence of social roles. We have already spoken of a given lifetime as a social career and

18. F. R. Kluckhohn and F. Strodbeck, *Variations in Value Orientations* (Evanston: Row, Peterson, 1961).

of different cultural definitions and valuations for the various ages of man. More specialized careers often involve standardized sequences of roles which must be passed through in a set order (apprentice, journeyman, master craftsman). In bureaucratic institutions, most careers are organized so that the performance of one role for a certain period is the prerequisite for the performance of the next (more highly valued) role. A description of any society or group must include a discussion of the major social careers open to its members and of the ways in which recruitment to these careers is determined.

Periods of social time, as we have seen, differ from other periods within the same dimension in terms of their *relative order;* but they also contrast with one another on the basis of their *relative value.* (Compare the two types of semantic space.) Some periods of time are considered *more important* than others: the relationship here is not one of "earlier/later" but rather one of "sacred/profane." For example, in describing the Cheyenne ceremony of the Sacred Arrow Renewal, E. A. Hoebel speaks of one period as follows:

> Now . . . not a sound may be heard in the camp, save the murmur of voices of the priests in the Medicine Arrow Lodge, or of the ceremonial drumming and singing that comes through the skins of the lodge. No one is to be seen . . . except the members of a warrior society silently pacing the rounds of the camp. . . . Even the dogs skulk without a sound. Should one so much as growl or yelp, his skull is shattered with a swift blow of a patrolling warrior's club. In the great lodge, the priests have opened the fox-skin bundle in which the four Sacred Arrows are kept. It is the moment of supreme sacredness of the Cheyenne as a people. It is the moment at which the well-being of the tribe as a whole is in the process of renewal.[19]

In every culture we find some categories of time which are most highly valued, and these are invariably connected with plans for great *intensity* of social life. The Cheyenne ceremony mentioned above took place at a time when the entire tribe was gathered together. Initiation ceremonies (such as those of the Nacirema) as well as other rites of passage generally involve the coming together of large numbers of persons and their joint participation in various events. On American college campuses the Homecoming Weekend is probably the most "sacred" period, followed closely by Final Examination Time and Commencement. In Jewish tradition, the weekly Sabbath is regarded as the most sacred period of time, taking precedence over even the annual High Holy Days. In much of rural Latin America, the market day and the

---

19. E. A. Hoebel, *The Cheyennes* (New York: Holt, Rinehart and Winston, 1960), p. 7.

various local fiestas constitute high points in an otherwise uneventful social life.

Individuals learn to handle time very differently in different societies; for example, cultural attitudes toward making and keeping appointments may vary greatly. In *The Silent Language,* Edward Hall gives many examples of the influence of culture on time concepts. His point is that when people are unaware of the cultural nature of their time concepts there is great danger of misunderstanding the behavior of persons from other societies. What Americans might consider an "intolerable and insulting delay" is considered, in many societies, to be only a "normal waiting period." We place great emphasis on promptness and on scheduling events in advance of their expected occurrence; and in comparison with other societies, our time perspective is surprisingly short. As Hall has noted:

> For us a "long time" can be almost anything—ten or twenty years, two or three months, a few weeks, or even a couple of days. The South Asian, however, feels that it is perfectly realistic to think of a "long time" in terms of thousands of years or even an endless period. A colleague once described their conceptualization of time as follows: "Time is like a museum with endless corridors and alcoves. You, the viewer, are walking through the museum in the dark, holding a light to each scene as you pass it. God is the curator of the museum, and only He knows all that is in it. One lifetime represents one alcove." [20]

Time and space are thus parts of the "silent language" of a society, unconsciously understood by all members of a group, and just as essential for an outsider to learn as the spoken language. Here again we can see how culture starts with a continuum (in this case, of time or space) and elaborates upon the natural boundaries and cycles, emphasizing some, ignoring others, to create conventional categories—categories which differ both qualitatively and quantitatively from those of other cultures and which are associated with plans for behavior which make possible smooth interaction among the members of a group.

SOCIAL SITUATIONS

Thus far in this chapter we have considered social time and social space separately. However, in normal human experience, the two are not separated. Although it has a number of nontechnical meanings, I shall reserve the phrase *social situation* to indicate *the intersection of a period of social time with an area of social*

20. Hall, *op. cit.*, p. 30.

***Figure* 6.9 Situation "X"**

space, together with certain social roles which the members of a group expect to be performed in that setting. Space, time, and role are thus the three components of a social situation. In simpler language: every social situation involves shared expectations about who will do what, and where and when. Since a social role is a kind of person who is expected to behave in certain ways, the role component answers the who and what questions. To answer the where and when questions we must also state the space and time components. Put them all together and they add up to a standardized social situation.[21]

If we wish to understand a social situation in any culture, we must have some conception of all three components—space, time, and role (or roles)—because very similar objective situations may have entirely different cultural meanings. Take, for example, the situation depicted in Figure 6.9. Just looking at the picture, try to answer the question: What is happening?

Without some further clues to the nature of this situation, it is virtually impossible to tell what is taking place. Even limiting the setting to our own society, we have no way of knowing whether this is

a burglar preparing to steal something
a housewife setting the table
a priest saying Mass
a salesman in a furniture store

21. P. K. Bock, "Three Descriptive Models of Social Structure," *Philosophy of Science*, Vol. 34 (1967), pp. 168–174.

or any of dozens of other possibilities. Additional information about the time or space components would help to eliminate some of these possibilities—for example, if we knew that the scene was taking place late in the afternoon in a residential dwelling. However, unless we know exactly what role is being performed and what is the *social* significance of the space/time setting, the cultural meaning of the situation will escape us. It follows that, *in observing behavior in our own or an alien culture, we must know (or learn) the categories of space, time, and role in order to understand what is taking place.*

If this analysis is correct, then the social situation is a valid unit of description for the ethnographer who wishes to state the cultural rules which govern the behavior of some group. In any society, there are remarkably few kinds of behavior which occur without any regard for the time and place. Even such a simple act as walking down the street late at night is considered suspicious in many American communities. As Erving Goffman has shown, our public behavior is governed by rules of which we are seldom aware. Take the behavior pattern which he calls "civil inattention":

> In performing this courtesy the eyes of the looker may pass over the eyes of the other, but no "recognition" is typically allowed. Where the courtesy is performed between two persons passing on the street, civil inattention may take the special form of eyeing the other up to approximately eight feet, during which time sides of the street are apportioned by gesture, and then casting the eyes down as the other passes—a kind of dimming of lights. In any case, we have here what is perhaps the slightest of interpersonal rituals, yet one that constantly regulates the social intercourse of persons in our society.
>
> By according civil inattention, the individual implies that he has no reason to fear the others, be hostile to them, or wish to avoid them.[22]

Every reader has performed the ritual Goffman describes thousands of times, probably without being fully aware of its details or its meaning. If you doubt the accuracy of this description, try changing or omitting this behavior on several occasions (if you can) and see what kind of responses you get.

The pattern of civil inattention is associated with that most transient of situations, an encounter between strangers. Behave this way toward a friend and you will soon lose a friend. Use this pattern in a store or restaurant and you will never get waited on. That is, for each of these more structured situations we have learned other, more highly structured, ways of behaving which communicate the kind of person we are claiming to be (at the

22. Goffman, *op. cit.*, p. 84.

moment). And in most cases, the space/time setting in which we perform our social roles serves to *support the performance* by providing various boundaries and props as aids to communication. For example, a doctor is most comfortable in his office, surrounded by the diplomas, books, and medical implements which attest to his claims to special skills and which support his role performance; other persons entering such a setting find it quite easy to take the role of patient and thus to enter into the relationship which is appropriate to the situation.

Social roles, times, and places *fit together* to make up a situation, and each of the components *implies* all of the others. To say that a given room is a courtroom implies that at some definite social time (when the court is in session) the room will be occupied by persons playing the roles of judge, plaintiff, and defendant, and also perhaps of attorney, clerk, witness, bailiff, jury member, and so forth. Similarly, to say that a man is a judge implies that he is entitled to perform that role in a courtroom during some time of trial. In general, the members of any society have a pretty good idea where various kinds of persons can be found at socially defined times and what kinds of persons they can expect to find in various settings. This association between roles and their settings is one of the things that makes possible smooth interaction within a society.

Some kinds of roles do not depend upon any fixed spatial or temporal boundaries but rather carry their settings with them. This presents no special problem of analysis, since even for such highly mobile roles as peddler or troubadour and such general roles as sleeper or drunk, there are some settings in which the performance of these roles is quite likely and other settings from which these performers are expected to be excluded. Nevertheless, the existence of these relatively mobile roles does indicate the relative *primacy* of the expected pattern of behavior as compared with its setting. A setting may create a fairly specific mood, particularly when those present are waiting for a performance to begin; but above all it is the performance of a standardized pattern of behavior (a role) which serves to define a situation. This is why ambiguity or incongruity of behavior can cause such social confusion for those involved in a situation (as when a professor stands on his head in the middle of a lecture).

Human beings *need* to know who they are, where they are, what they can expect of others, and what others expect of them. And it is their culture which answers this need by defining a finite number of kinds of situations and providing them with productive rules which enable them to act appropriately in these situations, even though no two situations (or persons) are exactly alike. This is why Clyde Kluckhohn and William Kelly have stated that "culture is—among other things—a set of ready-made definitions of the situation which each participant only slightly retailors in his own idiomatic way."[23]

RECOMMENDED READING

Evans-Pritchard, E. E., *The Nuer.* London: Oxford University Press, 1940. A classic ethnography of a Sudanic tribe with much fascinating information on time, space, and kinship.

Hall, E. T., Jr., *The Silent Language.* Garden City, N.Y.: Doubleday, 1959. A popular account of anthropological findings on the social relativity of time and space concepts.

Moore, Wilbert E., *Man, Time, and Society.* New York: John Wiley, 1963. A sociological account of how time structures social relations in our own society.

Sommer, R., *Personal Space.* Englewood Cliffs, N.J.: Prentice-Hall, 1969. An interesting book containing much experimental evidence on social concepts of space in our society together with sensible suggestions for "environmental planning."

Sorokin, P. A., *Social and Cultural Mobility.* New York: Free Press, 1959. A complex study by a great sociologist, the first to employ the notion of mobility through social space in the analysis of social change.

23. C. Kluckhohn and W. Kelly, "The Concept of Culture," in R. Linton, ed., *The Science of Man in the World Crisis* (New York: Columbia University Press, 1945), p. 91.

CHAPTER 7
Stability and Change

In the preceding chapters on roles, groups, space, and time, our treatment of social systems has admittedly been rather static. We have emphasized *social structure,* that is, the categories and plans that influence interpersonal behavior in a society, and the ways in which other social structures differ from our own. This approach is useful to make the reader aware of the range and variety of social systems which exist and to demonstrate the degree to which every individual is influenced by the traditions of his society. But the fact is, of course, that people do not just sit around carefully categorizing phenomena and planning what they should do: they act. They put the rules of their culture into operation by making decisions, anticipating the actions of others, developing skills, seeking useful alliances, avoiding unpleasantness, and pursuing positive satisfactions. Although man is far more influenced by his culture than he suspects, he also uses the structures provided by his culture for his own ends. As was observed at the end of the last chapter, a culture is slightly "retailored" by each participant according to his individual needs and experiences.

SOCIAL ORGANIZATION

In this chapter, we will be concerned with how social structures are put into action and with how they change. As the British social anthropologist Raymond Firth has insisted, "to see a social structure in sets of ideals and expectations alone is too aloof. . . . It is equally important . . . to stress the way in which the social standards, the ideal patterns, the sets of expectations, tend to be changed . . . by the acts of individuals in response to other influences." Firth has suggested the term *social organization* to indicate "the systematic ordering of social relations by acts of choice and decision." As we shall see, even the most apparently rigid social structure provides many alternatives and requires that people who use it as a "guide to action" make numerous choices. Thus structure and organization are two *aspects* of every social system: "In the aspect of social structure is to be found the continuity principle of society; in the aspect of organization is to be found the variation or change principle—by allowing evaluation of situations and entry of individual choice."[1]

Once we recognize individual choice as a factor in the operation and change of social systems, we are faced with a dilemma. Some scholars have reasoned that since we cannot predict what choices an individual will make, a scientific understanding of culture change is impossible, though we may study limited, historical problems. Others feel that we can completely disregard the individual and study cultural phenomena on their own level, attempting to establish universal laws of cultural development that will be true of all societies.[2]

The position of this book on the issue of free will versus cultural determinism is an intermediate one. Culture change and, for that matter, cultural stability are here viewed as the result of many thousands of individual choices. In making choices, members of a society take into account the expectations of others and the probable consequences of their own conformity or deviance. Some choices are made almost automatically and unconsciously, while others may require extensive consultation, soul-searching, and emotional upheaval. We may not be able to predict exactly what a specific individual will do in a given situation, but the behavioral sciences are rapidly improving their ability to predict the behavior of groups; and it is the changing pattern of individual choices within a group which in the long run determines the direction of culture change. Furthermore, when we say that man uses his culture for his own ends, we must remember that even the ends that he desires are largely dictated by his culture. Despite individual variation, the *kind* of wealth, prestige, security, or pleasure that a man seeks and the *ways* in which he pursues these valued ends depend upon what his society has taught him to consider valuable and legitimate (see Chapter 12). Thus a careful

---

1. R. Firth, *Elements of Social Organization* (London: Watts, 1951), pp. 31, 40.
2. See L. A. White, *The Science of Culture* (New York: Grove Press, 1949), especially pp. 121–145.

study of social structure and social organization should enable us to understand a good deal about human behavior.

A linguistic example may help to clarify this position. Let us assume that Jack wants to invite Jane to a party. Let us further assume that both of them can speak and understand several languages. In order to issue his invitation, Jack has first to choose which of the available codes he will use. Once he has chosen a particular code, his future behavior is limited by the phonological and grammatical rules of that language's structure. Yet he still has several alternative ways available in which to phrase his request, and he must choose whichever phrasing is best suited to his purpose: formal or informal, serious or joking, and so forth. Once the message has been chosen, Jack still has several alternative channels of communication open to him: he may speak to Jane directly or through a third person; he may write the message, telegraph it, or send it on magnetic tape. The important point is that at each stage of this communication process, Jack's behavior is limited and shaped by the culture he shares with Jane and by each of his prior decisions. It would be foolish of him to choose a language code Jane did not understand, or having settled on a language, to violate its rules in composing the message. Unless he has some ulterior purpose (such as insulting her) his phrasing of the message will be suited to their relationship, and his choice of a channel will depend on other cultural factors—for example, whether Jane can read the chosen language, what the social expectations are about written invitations as opposed to verbal ones, and so on. Each choice that Jack makes limits (or conditions) his subsequent behavior; but without the shared code, no communication would be possible. It appears that we must sacrifice some "freedom" for the sake of social life.

Let us examine one part of this example in finer detail. Assuming that Jack has chosen the English language as his code and direct speech as the channel, he must communicate the invitation to Jane in some concrete situation, taking account of the noise level, his relationships to any others who might be present, and many other factors. Jack must now select and order the words to express his meaning. His choice of channel has already eliminated some possibilities: forms such as "You are invited to a party . . ." can be used in writing, but not normally in speaking. Before Jack begins to speak, he still has thousands of possible ways to word the invitation; but once he has begun, his initial choices influence what he can say next. Some forms are so *standardized* that they are selected pretty much as a unit, for example, "Mary and I are having a few people over Friday night. Would you care to join us?" Others may start out in a number of different ways but terminate in approximately the same manner.

Within the framework of their shared culture, Jack can be as conventional or as creative as he wishes. He can improvise a humorous verbal invitation, compose a poem, or crib a romantic speech from *Cyrano de Bergerac.* But even the most highly conventional verbal invitation will be delivered at a time and in a manner somewhat different from any previous social act. Yet, because they share certain conventional understandings, Jack's behavior cannot be random—it is *not* the case that "anything can happen."

In this example we can see how a person uses the cultural structures which he shares with others in order to achieve a goal (in this case, to communicate information). Jack is, of course, "free" to violate the rules of his language by saying "I are giving a party" or "Can you like to come?" just as he is "free" to use a code or channel which Jane cannot understand. But if his real purpose is to communicate the invitation, he will organize his message in terms of the structures which they share.

Every language (and every social structure) offers many alternatives from which a speaker (or actor) may choose the forms which best suit his purpose. The more alternatives a person is aware of, the more choices are open to him; the greater one's command of a language, the more varied and precise his speech can be. But the availability of many alternatives calls for many decisions, and decisions (as we shall see) require the *evaluation* of alternatives. This can be very exhausting. Thus, one important function of language and social structure is to *limit* the number of possible choices on the basis of prior decisions.

Carried to extremes, this limiting results in persons always doing or saying the most obvious things—conformity of behavior and clichés in speech. But standardized patterns and automatic restrictions on choice are useful in two ways: they facilitate communication, and they relieve individuals of the need for constant evaluation and decision-making. From the anthropologist's point of view, the rules which produce these regularities of behavior constitute the culture which he seeks to describe and understand (see Part Six, The Anthropologist at Work). Speech and social organization are the manifestations of language and social structure, under the direction of human purpose.

ANTICIPATION

When a spider constructs its web or a bird builds its nest, the behavior of these animals and the material products of their behavior anticipate their future needs. Such anticipations, however, are instinctive: the behavior patterns are built into the animals' nervous systems at birth, and they are automatically set off by a combination of internal and environmental factors.

Animals can also be taught to perform various actions by the process of conditioning. If a rat receives an electric shock on one side of his cage a few seconds after a buzzer is sounded, he soon learns to associate the sound with the coming shock; thereafter, whenever the buzzer is sounded, the rat seems to anticipate the shock and moves to the safe side of the cage. There are many ways to interpret this phenomenon, and we need not attribute to the rat any conscious awareness of what is taking place; human beings can be conditioned in similar ways without their consciously knowing what is controlling their behavior. But some kinds of human learning clearly do involve a person's becoming aware of what he should do under a given set of circumstances. Man's culture, particularly his possession of language, makes it possible for him to anticipate and to prepare for many kinds of future events, including some which he has never before personally experienced.

In the chapters on social structure, the term *expectation* was used to indicate the plans for action associated with particular categories of persons. The idea was that persons tend to act in predictable ways because they are influenced by the role expectations held by the other members of their social group and because, consciously or unconsciously, they share these expectations. Here we wish to emphasize the way in which role performances are initiated by different kinds of occurrences and the ways in which the performances may be anticipated.

The conditions which call forth a role performance are of two general types: scheduled and unscheduled. *Scheduled events* are those whose occurrence is fixed and known in advance, usually because they are part of a cyclical time dimension: holidays, mealtimes, work periods, markets. The actual timing of such events may be set by clock and calendar, or in relation to any regular occurrence, such as the flowering of the bush which marks the time of a Nandi initiation or the ripening of the *kolema* yam which signals the onset of the last phase of the Tiwi initiation.

An *unscheduled event* is one which takes place irregularly, and whose occurrence cannot be reliably predicted: a murder or sudden death, an earthquake, an unannounced visit. Each culture provides some plans of action in response to both kinds of events. Indeed, by providing a plan of expected behavior for various crises, culture attempts to convert the unscheduled into the scheduled, allowing the unexpected act to set in motion a chain of events in which each person concerned may anticipate his part. For example, although murder is usually unscheduled, its occurrence influences the subsequent behavior of many categories of persons. Among the Cherokee, when a man was killed, all the other members of his clan were responsible for avenging the murder; at such times the structure of Cherokee society was drastically reorganized until this purpose was accomplished.[3]

Let us now consider the various ways in which events can be anticipated. We are concerned here with *preparations* for scheduled role performances as a part of social organization—seeing how the social structure is put into action in particular cases. Preparation for a role performance may be subdivided according to what is being prepared: personnel, resources, or the setting of the performance. Depending upon the type of performance, each kind of preparation may range from simple to elaborate; but if any performance is to take place, each of these factors will have to receive some consideration.

Preparation of Personnel

To begin with, the personnel who are going to take part in the performance must know their roles. Learning the social roles that one will be expected to play is part of the process of enculturation (Chapter 3). In this sense, a person begins to prepare for future performances from the moment he is born. But in even the simplest societies there are special occasions when instructions for future performances are transmitted, explicitly or implicitly. Preparation for highly specialized roles (such as Tapirapé shaman, Navajo singer, or American doctor) may be lengthy and exhausting. In *The Autobiography of a Winnebago Indian,* Paul Radin's informant tells of his initiation into the Medicine Dance. An important part of this ceremony is the "shooting" and "bringing back to life" of the initiates and other members, and the author of this account was excited about learning this part of his new role:

> The next morning just before day, even while the dance was still going on, the leaders took me out in the wilderness. When we got there we found a place where the ground had been cleared in the outline of the dance lodge. There they preached to me and they told me that the most fearful things imaginable would happen to me if I made public any of this affair. The world would come to an end, they said. . . . I would surely die. After that they showed me how to fall down and lie quivering (on the ground) and how to appear dead. I was very much disappointed for I had had a far more exalted idea of it (the shooting).

3. F. Gearing, "The Structural Poses of 18th Century Cherokee Villages," *American Anthropologist*, Vol. 60 (1958), pp. 1148–1157.

"Why, it amounts to nothing," I thought. "I have been deceived," I thought. . . . However, I kept on and did as I was told to do. . . . As soon as I was proficient in the act (of feigning death), we started back.

They told me that I would become just like them in body, but I did not have the sensation of any change in me. All that I felt was that I had become a deceiver in one of Earthmaker's creations.

During the day, at the regular meeting, I did as I had been taught to do. We were simply deceiving the spectators.[4]

New participants in many roles, both sacred and secular, often feel that they are simply deceiving the spectators, but it is notable that they generally do as they have been taught—that is, act in accordance with the role expectations—no matter how much deception of themselves and others is involved. The tale of "The Emperor's New Clothes" provides a model for much of man's social life.[5]

Among the reasons for the widespread conformity to role expectations is the need for investing a great deal of time, effort, and self-esteem in learning a specialized role. Having gone through a long and often painful learning process and having given up many more immediate satisfactions, it is extremely difficult for an individual to abandon his hard-won role, even if he realizes that it amounts to nothing.

Learning to speak the language of one's group is an essential part of preparing for any social role, and the most specialized roles require the mastery of additional vocabulary (or even of entire languages). Merchants who travel through areas of linguistic diversity must learn a trade language (or several languages), while Hindu and Christian priests must master one or more archaic tongues. Nearly every occupational group has its own jargon. The relationship of "standard speech" to social mobility was the subject of George Bernard Shaw's *Pygmalion,* and this topic is one of the main areas of research for the newly founded discipline of sociolinguistics.

Assuming that a person has learned all the attributes of a future role, he may still require considerable practice before he can perform them skillfully. The *practice* of individuals and the *rehearsals* of groups in anticipation of future performances also come under the heading of social organization, for it is here that we see structural patterns being applied to concrete behavior. The anthropologist can learn a great deal more about the rules governing social action by watching, say, a wedding rehearsal and lis-

4. P. Radin, *The Autobiography of a Winnebago Indian* (New York: Dover, 1963), pp. 20–21.
5. E. Goffman, *The Presentation of Self in Everyday Life* (Garden City, N.Y.: Anchor Books, 1959), pp. 208–255. See also S. Milgram, "Behavioral Study of Obedience," *Journal of Abnormal and Social Psychology,* Vol. 67 (1963), pp. 371–378. [Bobbs-Merrill Reprint P-521.]

tening to the comments, promptings, and advice given than he can by witnessing the actual polished performance of the ceremony.

At a rehearsal, we can see the various roles called for by the social structure being assigned to particular persons. (This corresponds to the division of labor within the society as a whole, with the processes of recruitment and social control brought into sharper focus on this smaller scale.) We can also study the *modifications* which are made as the structure is put into action: how various details of a performance are altered to fit the requirements of a concrete situation—the skills of the different performers, the number of persons involved, the setting in which they are to perform, and so forth. During the summer of 1959, I witnessed three different Sun Dances performed by members of the Southern Ute tribe. (The Southern Ute Sun Dance lasts for three or four days, during which time the dancers remain in the lodge and have nothing to eat or to drink.) Although the basic structure of all three dances was the same, there was considerable variation in details, much of which could be traced to the experience and preparation of the participants. At the third of these dances, the ethnographer had to step out of his role as observer and become a participant because none of the regular singers who knew the "sunrise song" had appeared when it was time for the dancing to begin. On another occasion, the start of the Sun Dance was delayed because someone had neglected to bring the large drum which is beaten by the singers.

Preparation of Resources and Settings

These variations from the "ideal" lead to our next point: performances must be anticipated by the preparation of those resources which will be needed for the event. Take the case of a feast. Throughout the world, people celebrate important social events by consuming large quantities of food. But if the feast is to be successful, the food resources to be consumed must be accumulated and prepared. Thus, although we may focus upon the feast itself as an important part of the social structure, it is the anticipation of this event which affects people's behavior for days or even months beforehand, and this is part of the social organization.

Accumulation of resources may be *direct,* as when the Polynesian mother gathers breadfruit and coconuts for a family meal; but more often it is quite *indirect,* involving many intermediate steps, as when the Bantu laborer works for months or years in the copper mines to accumulate enough money to buy cattle to use as bridewealth in acquiring a wife. Similarly, the fabrication of resources into culturally approved forms may take varying amounts of time or effort. The elaborately carved wooden posts which decorate a Tiwi grave can be made only by those few older men who have sufficient experience and leisure. Their fabrication requires many days of effort; this is one reason that Tiwi funerals are held several months after a death has taken place.

The accumulation and fabrication of resources for a performance cannot always be clearly separated from the preparation of personnel or setting; the preparation of the setting, however, involves the *allocation* of time and space to a particular peformance and the *distribution* of both personnel and resources within the setting. If social interaction is to proceed smoothly, the setting for an event should be chosen to minimize the possibilities of distraction or interruption. Even here, however, there are cultural differences in expectations about what kinds of things should be allowed to take place within the same setting. Latin American businessmen prefer to conduct many different affairs at once, in contrast to the usual North American pattern of one thing at a time. Edward Hall reports the following revealing anecdote:

> An old friend of mine of Spanish cultural heritage used to run his business according to the "Latino" system. This meant that up to fifteen people were in his office at one time. Business which might have been finished in a quarter of an hour sometimes took a whole day. . . . However, if my friend had adhered to the American system he would have destroyed a vital part of his prosperity. People who came to do business with him also came to find out things and to visit each other. . . . To us it is somewhat immoral to have two things going on at the same time. In Latin America it is not uncommon for one man to have a number of simultaneous jobs which he either carries on from one desk or which he moves between, spending a small amount of time on each.[6]

Recent research has shown that in Brazil, the higher a person's social status, the more likely he is to have two or even three jobs at the same time.[7]

The distribution of personnel and resources within the chosen setting moves us from the phase of preparation into the performance itself. At last all is ready: the signal is given and the performance begins. If preparations have been complete the role performers speak and act appropriately, all necessary resources are readily available, and there are no interruptions or distractions. But how often is the social structure so perfectly enacted? Prob-

---

6. E. T. Hall, *The Silent Language* (Garden City: Doubleday, 1959), pp. 29–30.
7. S. Iutaka, "Social Mobility and Occupational Opportunity in Brazil," *Human Organization*, Vol. 25 (1966), pp. 126–130. Also see A. Leeds, "Brazilian Careers and Social Structure," *American Anthropologist*, Vol. 66 (1964), pp. 1321–1347.

ably much less often than we think, for unanticipated intrusions are always possible, and personnel or resources are seldom as well-prepared as they could be. There are many slips between the ideal structure and its concrete manifestation in behavior. How often does a famous speaker have a coughing fit, or a bride not appear for her wedding? We know that too little food is often prepared for a feast and that the Sun Dance drum is occasionally forgotten. But to note these imperfections of social organization is not to deny that there is a social structure behind the variable manifestations. It simply shows that since culture *influences* and does not determine behavior, men must anticipate many factors if a performance is to be a success. As G. P. Murdock once put it:

> Actual social behavior, as it is observed in real life, must be carefully distinguished from culture, which consists of habits or tendencies to act and not of actions themselves. Though largely determined by habits, actual behavior is also affected by the physiological and emotional state of the individual, the intensity of his drives, and the particular external circumstances. Since no two situations are ever exactly alike, actual behavior fluctuates considerably, even when springing from the same habit. A description of a culture is consequently never an account of actual social behavior but is rather a reconstruction of the collective habits which underlie it.[8]

CHOICE AND CHANGE

The preceding discussion of anticipation deliberately omitted the factor of choice. We assumed that for a given initiating event (scheduled or unscheduled) only one kind of behavior would be expected of the players of a given role. Thus if we symbolize the initiating event by *x*, the role under consideration by *R*, and the expected behavior by *a*, we may represent a part of the social structure by the formula

$$\text{If } x, \text{ then } R \rightarrow a$$

where the arrow indicates that any person performing *R* is expected to behave in manner *a*. Within these limitations, anticipation involves the ways in which role players prepare for their perform-

8. G. P. Murdock, "How Culture Changes," in H. Shapiro, ed., *Man, Culture, and Society* (New York: Oxford University Press, 1960), p. 249.

ance of *a* before the occurrence of *x*. For example, a Winnebago Indian being initiated into the Medicine Dance knew that he was supposed to "die" at a certain point in the ceremony; but this role behavior had to be learned and rehearsed so that the performance as a whole would "come off." Similarly, in our society, when a couple becomes formally engaged *(x)*, the fiancé *(R)* is expected (→) to give the woman a diamond ring *(a)*; the role player may anticipate this structural demand in a variety of ways (from saving to theft); at the very least, it is expected that he should find a plausible excuse for not providing the ring.

In reality, social structure generally provides *alternative* ways of behaving in a given situation. This means that each person must constantly choose among the structural possibilities offered to him. Many of these choices are trivial, involving only personal preference and having little effect upon the social system. But it is the thesis of this chapter that in the long run, *patterns of individual choice change the social structure.* That is, the expectations which influence man's social behavior are themselves affected by that behavior. A rule that is continually violated will ultimately disappear from the structure (as did the prohibition amendment from the Constitution), whereas a pattern of behavior which is regularly repeated comes to be expected.

When you order lunch in a restaurant, it makes little difference whether you choose a hamburger or a tuna sandwich. But if no one ever orders the hamburger it will eventually disappear from the menu. On the other hand, if enough people request an item (say, pizza) that is not on the menu, it may eventually be added to the structure. To take a more usual anthropological example, imagine a society in which the residence rule is *ambilocal:* the newly married couple may live with the kin of either the bride or the groom. The social structure provides two equally legitimate alternatives, and the couple decides between them by taking into account various social values (see below). Suppose, however, that for some reason the patrilocal alternative is chosen more and more frequently until matrilocal residence becomes as rare as not living with either set of kin. At some point, the repeated choice of the patrilocal option will affect the expectations of the group as a whole, and patrilocal residence will become the rule. Thereafter, couples who for some reason wish to live with the bride's kin will have to justify their choice in a way that was not formerly necessary, for they will be violating an expectation rather than just choosing an alternative. Such a narrowing of structural possibilities from two alternatives (*a* or *b*) to a single expectation (in this case, *a* or patrilocal postmarital residence) can be expressed as follows:

$$\text{If } x, \text{ then } R \rightarrow \begin{Bmatrix} a \\ b \end{Bmatrix}; \text{ changes to: } \quad \text{If } x, \text{ then } R \rightarrow a.$$

In the same way, new alternatives may become part of a social structure: as a result of repeated violations of shared expectations, the new patterns are finally accepted as legitimate, sometimes replacing the original pattern. The addition of an alternative to a social rule may be diagramed as follows:

$$\text{If } x, \text{ then } R \rightarrow a; \text{ changes to: } \quad \text{If } x, \text{ then R} \rightarrow \begin{Bmatrix} a \\ c \end{Bmatrix}.$$

In the example we have been discussing, this formula might represent the addition of neolocal postmarital residence (*c*) as an accepted structural alternative, rather than as a violation of the patrilocal norm (*a*). Murdock has stated this point most clearly:

> From the point of view of cultural change . . . actual or observed behavior is of primary importance. Whenever social behavior persistently deviates from established cultural habits in any direction, it results in modifications first in social expectations, and then in customs, beliefs, and rules. Gradually, in this way, collective habits are altered and the culture comes to accord better with the new norms of actual behavior.[9]

Decision-Making

We come now to the question of how people decide among the structural alternatives that are open to them. The following discussion of decision-making is based upon two assumptions: (1) that more than one alternative is actually available to a person and (2) that given knowledge of available alternatives and their probable consequences, most people make reasonable choices. This is a *rational model of decision-making*; even though it may not be applicable to many kinds of choices, it can, if properly interpreted, help us to understand social organization as a dynamic process.[10]

An individual faced with the need for making a rational decision begins by consciously or unconsciously *scanning* the available alternatives and *eliminating* those which do not seem objective possibilities. It is obvious that a person's range of

9. *Ibid.*
10. The psychological equivalents of this approach may be found in: G. Kelly, *The Psychology of Personal Constructs*, Vol. I (New York: Norton, 1955); Eric Berne, *Games People Play* (New York: Grove Press, 1964). Formal, mathematical models of decision-making are discussed with admirable clarity in Anatol Rapoport's *Fights, Games, and Debates* (Ann Arbor: University of Michigan Press, 1960).

scanning is limited by his awareness of alternatives, and this is primarily determined by his past experience. As noted above, the greater one's command of a language, the more choices are open to him and the more varied and precise his speech can be.[11] Similarly, the more knowledge one has of the structure of his society, the more alternative ways of acting are available to him. People differ in their awareness of structural possibilities, so that a decision which is obvious to one person may not even be considered by another in the same circumstances.

Even if we disregard this differential *awareness* of alternatives, there remains the factor of differential *access* to alternatives. That is, persons must often eliminate alternatives of which they are aware because they lack certain ascribed qualities, elements of personal preparation, or resources. Take a young male college student who is looking for a summer job. As he reads through the classified ads (scanning), he may eliminate certain possibilities because the positions call for, say, a person who can speak Spanish, or someone who owns a car. Spatial and temporal factors may also eliminate some possibilities, such as a job in a distant city or one for which the application period has already passed.

Again, supposing that our student has objective access to a number of opportunities (he possesses all of the role attributes required for recruitment), still other alternatives will have to be eliminated because of *incompatibilities* between the job requirements and his other commitments. He may have to turn down a perfectly good job because in order to take it, he would have to give up his role as student. That is, the decision-maker tries to avoid or to minimize the probability of *role conflict*—a situation in which different and incompatible expectations would simultaneously influence his behavior.

There are important temporal and spatial factors involved in role conflict. Many of us manage to perform roles which are apparently incompatible by keeping our performances separated in time and/or space. The army officer who moonlights as a jazz musician exemplifies this process when he carefully selects the places where he plays so as to avoid meeting his fellow officers or his subordinates. In a monogamous society, the role of husband is expected to be performed in relation to no more than one woman at a time, but the successful bigamist is able to space out and schedule his role performances so that others are not aware of his double life. Needless to say, in a polygynous society such deceptions are not necessary. Role conflicts and incompatibilities are relative to the social structure of a given group.

11. B. Bernstein, "Aspects of Language and Learning in the Genesis of the Social Process," in D. Hymes, ed., *Language in Culture and Society* (New York: Harper and Row, 1964), pp. 251–263.

Having scanned the possibilities of which he is aware and having eliminated some on the basis of potential access and incompatibility, the decision-maker is faced with the task of *evaluating* the remaining alternatives. A rational evaluation is one which objectively estimates the satisfactions that may be derived from each alternative and chooses that which offers the greatest value and/or the least risk. In economics, this type of choice is considered under the heading of "maximization theories." The usual case is that of the business enterprise which is attempting to maximize its monetary profits. But as Robbins Burling has observed:

> We are "economizing" in everything we do. We are always trying to maximize our satisfactions somehow, and so we are led . . . to the notion that economics deals not with a type but rather with an aspect of behavior. This economic view . . . [becomes] . . . one model for looking at society. It is a model which sees the individuals of a society busily engaged in maximizing their own satisfactions—desire for power, prestige, sex, food, independence, or whatever else they may be, in the context of the opportunities around them, including those offered by their own culture.[12]

Burling also points out that those maximization theories which concern themselves with only one type of satisfaction—be it profit, power, or sex—are unable to explain the complexities of actual social behavior. Human decision-making generally involves a conflict among values. Most decisions represent a compromise between two or more possible types of satisfaction, rather than the all-out pursuit of one type.

Value conflicts are probably unavoidable in human social life, for even if an individual could commit himself exclusively to the maximization of one type of satisfaction, he would eventually meet with conflicting demands from his own body and from the various groups of which he is a member. Indeed, many such conflicts are the product of differing expectations held by the societal group on the one hand and subcultural units (such as the family or the peer group) on the other. Walter Miller's studies of the "delinquent subculture" show how young men, seeking to maximize their prestige within the peer group, inevitably come into conflict with representatives of the larger society.[13] Similarly, numerous sociological studies have shown the conflict between the impersonal bureaucratic ideals of a society and the narrower personal or familial loyalties of its members.

12. R. Burling, "Maximization Theories and the Study of Economic Anthropology," *American Anthropologist*, Vol. 64 (1962), pp. 817–818.
13. W. B. Miller, "Lower Class Culture as a Generating Milieu of Gang Delinquency," *The Journal of Social Issues*, Vol. 14 (1958), pp. 5–19.

Conformity and Alternatives to Conformity

Even after a decision is made, there still remains the social organization of the actions which put it into effect. That is, having decided to comply with a given set of cultural or subcultural expectations, the individuals concerned still have considerable freedom as to the *manner* in which they conform. In most cases, a person can to some degree control both the *timing* and the *intensity* of his performance, and he can use this control for his own purposes. This may be true even when the social structure provides no alternatives. For example, among the Turu (a Bantu tribe of Tanzania), all males are expected to be initiated, but each man chooses the time and place of his own circumcision; initiation is here viewed as a voluntary act, although all men must eventually submit.[14]

The use of timing for personal ends is well illustrated by the Tiwi marriage system.[15] Tiwi girls are betrothed early in life to much older men, but they continue to reside with their parents until after puberty. If a girl's father should die before she goes to join her husband-to-be, the stepfather gains a certain degree of control over her which he can use for his own purposes. For example, although he is not usually able to break the engagement, he is in a position to *delay* her change of residence. By thus holding up the timing of her departure (or by threatening to do so), the stepfather can generally gain some benefits from the aging husband-to-be, who is anxious to acquire his promised bride.

By the intensity of a performance we mean the manner in which an expected but quantitatively variable action is carried out. We have noted that in our society a man is expected to give his fiancée a ring; but the intensity of this performance varies quantitatively with the monetary value of the ring. In many cases, the structure prescribes an action, but leaves the intensity of the act to be determined by the processes of social organization (anticipation and choice).

In total institutions such as prisons and the army one often finds an elaborate vocabulary describing the intensity of a role performance. This is because many members of total institutions are not participating by their own choice. Terms such as "serving time," "gold-bricking," and "gung ho" express the attitudes that may be taken toward a performance much better than any sociological jargon. As Erving Goffman has pointed out, total institutions

14. See Harold K. Schneider, "Turu Esthetic Concepts," *American Anthropologist*, Vol. 68 (1966), pp. 156–160. This article is discussed in Chapter 11.
15. C. W. M. Hart and A. Pilling, *The Tiwi of North Australia* (New York: Holt, Rinehart, and Winston, 1960), pp. 9–30. The politics of Tifi wife bestowal beautifully illustrates the degree of anticipation and choice that are possible within a "primitive" social structure; see pp. 51–78.

are an excellent setting for the study of social organization because their members often develop ways of simulating intense performances without expending much real effort: the most successful goldbrick is he who can *appear* to be gung ho in the presence of superiors.[16]

If a person has chosen to conform with the expectations of a given role, his freedom is pretty much limited to modifying the timing and the intensity of his role performance. His reasons for conformity may be quite different from the stereotyped ones, but so long as his performance remains within acceptable limits, his motives will probably not be questioned. There are, however, at least three types of *alternatives to conformity* with the requirements of a role.

The first possibility we shall call *deception.* That is, one can *appear* to comply with a set of expectations, even simulating a highly intense performance, while one's purposes are actually opposed to those of the role one is playing (or at least greatly at variance with those usually assumed). An extreme case is the secret agent who uses a role such as gardener as his cover. It is essential that he give a credible performance as a gardener, even though his motives for adopting this role have nothing to do with a love of flowers. His apparent conformity to the role requirements is deceptive and will be maintained only so long as it furthers his true purpose of espionage. Deception in less extreme forms is found whenever an individual represents himself as a kind of person which he is not; in this form, it is familiar to all men.

A second possible alternative to conformity we may call *negation*: the refusal of a person to fulfill some or all of the expectations associated with a role. Negation can take many forms, from an outright refusal ("Hell no, we won't go!") to an elaborately reasoned denial that the person is obligated to act in a certain way ("Well, I'm only sixteen, I've got a ruptured spleen . . ."). Most negations are eventually met with sanctions from the group most concerned. But some kinds of negation are built into the social structure itself, and although we do not usually think of them in this way, may be viewed as legitimate alternatives to conformity. In our society, the "sick role" is one of these; by claiming a certain type or intensity of ill-health, a person may be able to negate many of the usual requirements of his occupational, kinship, and other roles. Among the Plains Indians, adoption of The berdache role (see p. 70) allowed some men to escape the usual obligations of being a male. The Cheyenne called such

16. E. Goffman, *Asylums* (Garden City: Anchor Books, 1961), pp. 1–124. See M. S. Fleisher, "The Possible Application of Ethnosemantics to Prison Argot," *Anthropological Linguistics*, Vol. 14 (1972), pp. 213–219, for ways that prison inmates speak of different kinds of time.

individuals "half-men, half-women," implying a reduction and combination of expectations from two standard roles.

Philip L. Newman's analysis of " 'Wild Man' Behavior in a New Guinea Highlands Community" also illustrates a structural alternative to conformity. Among the Gururumba, young men, usually between the ages of twenty-five and thirty-five, will occasionally indulge in public behavior of an extremely bizarre nature. The "wild man" rushes about, shouting and scattering things with an apparent loss of bodily control; he seems to be unable to hear and he speaks only in a kind of pidgin English; he also steals a variety of objects which he destroys before returning to his more normal state. The community responds to his behavior as if they were watching a dramatic performance, despite the fact that "the wild man performs acts which in any other context would engender serious public disapproval and attempts to control the behavior." The consequences of this episode are described as follows:

> There are no recriminations against the wild man after he has gone wild, and no one in his clan or village will mention the episode to him. They do talk about it among themselves, however. It is evident from these conversations . . . [that] they do not think of him as the same kind of person he was formerly thought to be. . . . The Gururumba are aware of the kinds of pressures social life imposes on them. When a man goes wild they also become aware of the fact that this particular individual is not as capable as others of withstanding those pressures. Specifically, there is an observable reduction in the expectation others have of the degree he will participate in exchange transactions and a corresponding reduction in the intensity of demands made on him: He may still have debts, but repayment is not pressed aggressively. . . . The outcome of wild man behavior is thus a reduction of demands made without loss of social support.[17]

Innovation

The last type of alternative to conformity we shall call *innovation.* Under this heading come all kinds of creative responses to situations in which an individual cannot or will not comply with the usual expectations. In one sense, we are always innovating since our behavior never exactly repeats itself in every respect: even repetitions of the same word show some phonetic variation (see Chapter 2). But in addition to this kind of unavoidable free variation, it is possible to place any item of behavior on a continuum from the most to the least conventional. This continuum can be divided into four major parts, as shown in Figure 7.1.

17. Philip L. Newman, " 'Wild Man' Behavior in a New Guinea Highlands Community," *American Anthropologist*, Vol. 66 (1964), pp. 7, 16–17.

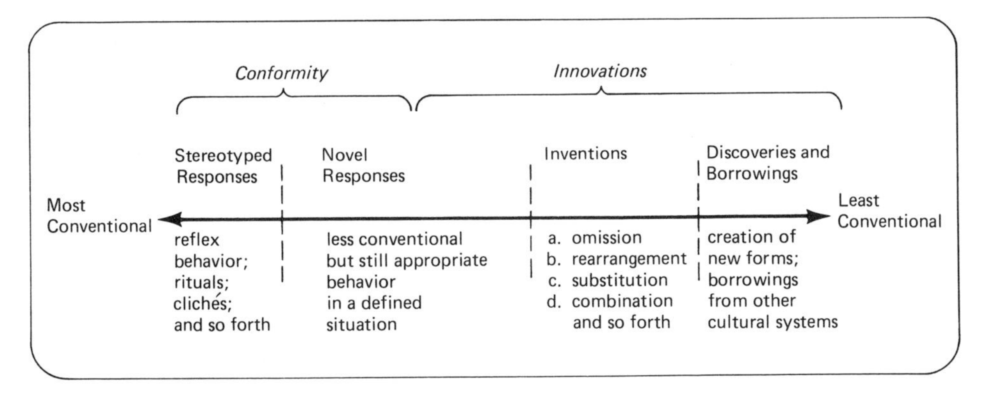

Figure 7.1 **Continuum of Action Probabilities**

Stereotyped responses, such as shaking hands or saying "How are you?" when meeting an acquaintance, are the most conventional actions an individual can perform in a given situation. Religious rituals, such as the Roman Catholic Mass, are also highly stereotyped. There is always a certain amount of free variation; but close conformity to social expectations is itself highly valued in these situations, and the general forms of speech and behavior tend to be highly predictable.

Novel responses, as noted in Figure 7.1, are usually appropriate to the social situation, but they are not entirely predictable. In such instances the individual exercises some degree of choice while remaining within the alternatives offered by the shared structure. Jack's invitation to Jane, discussed at the beginning of this chapter, exemplifies the novel combination of items from a shared code. Most of our daily behavior falls within this range of actions which are acceptable but more or less novel (unpredictable in detail). The least probable of novel utterances would be such deviant but quite grammatical sentences as "Colorless green ideas sleep furiously," or "My pet cobra has three legs."

Inventions often involve the accidental or deliberate *violation* of cultural rules (see Introduction to Part Three). The four types listed in Figure 7.1 do not exhaust the possible kinds of inventions, but are intended to suggest the major ways in which people break social rules. Judging by Homer Barnett's book *Innovation,* most things that we think of as inventions can be analyzed as rearrangements, substitutions of one cultural element for another, or combinations of cultural elements already known to the innovator: that is, *different plans are applied to traditional categories.*[18] Clothing

18. H. Barnett, *Innovation: The Basis of Cultural Change* (New York: McGraw-Hill, 1953).

made out of paper and the electric toothbrush are clear examples of substitution and combination inventions.

Innovations in social structure often involve combination or rearrangement of the attributes of old roles rather than the creation of entirely new roles. The reorganization of a business or a governmental agency usually means the multiplication of vice-presidents or the consolidation of several functions under one supervisor. Within a kinship system, even changes from polygamy to monogamy or from endogamy to exogamy may be viewed as alterations of plans without the creation of any really new categories. In a complex society like ours, each advance in knowledge seems to call forth a new category of persons to master and transmit it. The astronaut and the anesthesiologist are relatively new occupational roles which have developed in response to scientific and technological advances; but though the *content* of these roles is new, their attributes are modeled after familiar military, scientific, and medical roles.

Linguistic inventions involve the violation of rules on the phonological and/or grammatical levels. Sometimes phonological rules are deliberately broken for humorous or artistic purposes (for example, the substitution in "THIMK"), while other inventions involve unconscious omissions or rearrangements.[19] All four major types of inventions can be demonstrated on the grammatical level by the following sentences:

Linguistic Innovations		*Equivalents in Social Structure*
Original: Who is he?		If x, then R → a, b, c
Omission:	Who he?	x, but R → a, c
Rearrangement:	Who he is?	x, but R → a, c, b
Substitution:	Who is him?	x, but R → a, b, j
Combination:	Who is he and she?	x, but R → a, b, c, l, m

Obviously, all kinds of combinations of these violations are possible; for example, "Who him?" or "Is she who?"

The least probable type of innovative behavior is the *discovery*. A discovery need not involve the violation of a cultural rule because many discoveries are so improbable that cultures have no rules concerning them. For example, the discovery of radium or of the planet Neptune, though surprising and unexpected, did not violate any cultural prescriptions such as "You shall not discover radium." Discoveries do often require extensive rearrange-

19. Examples of linguistic inventions can be found in almost any book of modern poetry. See G. Snyder, *The Back County* (New York: New Directions, n.d.); K. Patchen, *Selected Poems* (New York: New Directions, n.d.).

ments of our expectations, for whereas inventions alter the plans associated with known categories, discoveries involve the creation of *new* categories or of *new* plans, or both.

From the point of view of a given cultural system, the *borrowing* of new cultural elements from another system is essentially the same as a discovery made from within the culture. Borrowing is perhaps the most common type of culture change. Like discovery, it introduces new and highly unconventional categories and plans into a culture, and it often has far-reaching consequences for the organization of the society. The borrowing or discovery of a new food plant, weapon, or form of political organization may set in motion a chain of events that will affect every aspect of a culture.[20]

Borrowed elements will usually undergo changes of form and of significance as they become a part of the new cultural system. This is called the *process of reinterpretation.* As M. J. Herskovits has pointed out, reinterpretation goes on between generations as well as among societies: new meanings are assigned to old forms, and borrowed elements are fitted into different categories and associated with different plans.[21] The American-made alarm clock becomes a striking chest ornament in New Guinea; the sacred maize plant of the Maya becomes pig fodder in Nebraska; and the stylish clothes of our parents' youth become, for us, funny costumes or nostalgic "camp." Reinterpretation is a constant and universal process; it accounts for much of the variability of behavior in the realm of social organization.

Because regular patterns of choice gradually alter the social and cultural structure, innovation can be the first step toward structural change. But the innovative behavior of a single performer must be distinguished from the *acceptance* of that innovation by others who perform similar or complementary roles. It is only with the spread of a pattern of behavior or belief through a social group that we may speak of a structural change: that which was highly unconventional must become increasingly conventional and finally expectable. Thus when the cartoonist Robert Osborn invents a new type of caricature by omitting the nose on the faces of his subjects, he is clearly an innovator; but unless other cartoonists adopt this innovation, it will remain an attribute of Osborn's personal role—part of his unique style—and it will not affect the "code" shared by cartoonists and their public. On the other hand, the much more extensive rearrangements of parts of the human face and body employed by Pablo Picasso and other European artists early in this century became expected attributes

20. See the classic case study of this process by L. Sharp, "Steel Axes for Stone-Age Australians," *Human Organization*, Vol. 2 (1952), pp. 17–22.

21. M. J. Herskovits, *Cultural Dynamics* (New York: Knopf, 1964), pp. 190–194.

of the Cubist school of painting and, as such, part of the structure of Western culture.

Acceptance of an innovation, then, requires that a number of people choose to act in the new way, presumably because they have evaluated the alternatives and decided that the innovation offers them certain wanted satisfactions. The innovation may persist as an alternative mode of action, or it may replace the former pattern. On the other hand, it may rapidly disappear (this is what we mean by a fad) or it may gradually lose its novelty and pass into the realm of stereotyped responses and clichés (as with the phrase, "I can't believe I ate the whole thing").

One consequence of this discussion may be stated as follows: *No cultural system is entirely static.* In a primitive society, stereotyped responses are likely to be highly valued for their own sake and to be closely related to other conventional actions; thus it is unlikely that they will be quickly replaced by new patterns. But *innovations are constantly taking place.* Men in every society enjoy some degree of novelty, and most people can alter their expectations very quickly if it is clear to them that it is to their advantage to do so. Structural change is the inevitable result of the process of social organization (anticipation and choice) with innovations providing the new materials from which major structural changes may develop.

ADAPTATION

There are several intentional parallels between the ideas put forward in the last section and the modern synthetic theory of biological evolution. In contemporary evolutionary theory, *mutations* are seen as providing the new materials from which major structural changes may develop. Mutations are alterations in the genetic structure due to omissions, substitutions, rearrangements, and combinations which take place regularly in the course of reproduction. Most of these alterations take place spontaneously, but they can also be induced by physical and chemical agents. By means of a chain of enzyme reactions, mutations bring about changes both in the structure and behavior of organisms in which they occur and in future generations to which they are transmitted. But like social inventions, mutations introduce variations which may or may not be "chosen" (selected for) in a given environment.

The synthetic theory explains biological evolution as the result of *natural selection* acting upon the variability produced by mutation and the reproductive recombination of genetic units. Natural selection is the process which, in the long run, fits a population to its environment by eliminating poorly adapted organisms from the breeding population and enabling the better adapted individuals to survive and reproduce. A genetic mutation which decreases the adaptation of an organism to its environment will be eliminated by selection, while a mutation which increases adaptation will be favored because individuals inheriting this trait have a better chance to reproduce than other members of the group.[22]

Adaptation refers to the ability of a given population to survive in a given environment despite selective forces such as disease, predators, and competition from other populations for limited resources. In order to survive and to meet new challenges, every species must master environmental problems by developing effective structures, behaviors, and forms of social organization. (Familiar examples of each of these would be the quills of porcupines, the hoarding behavior of squirrels, and the "caste system" of bees.) Like other species, man is subject to natural selection: he must adapt to his physical/biological environment if he is to survive and reproduce. Indeed, most of the genetic differences among human races are the result of adaptation to past or present differences in climate, diet, disease, and (in some cases) culture.[23]

But man is also different from all other species. Whereas most animals grow their tools (sharp claws, fur coats, or hard shells) and inherit their essential behavior patterns (fighting, mating, and migrating instincts), *man is a maker of tools and rules:* for millions of years we have relied primarily upon *learned* ways of adapting. A human population can vastly change its way of life in less than a generation, whereas only the slow, opportunistic process of biological evolution alters the structure and behavior of other species.

Natural selection, then, applies as much to man's cultural development as it does to his biological development. Indeed, the two are inseparable, for a new tool, technique, or social innovation cannot persist if it leads to the extinction of any population which accepts it. On the other hand, an innovation which significantly improves the adaptation of a group to its environment will give that group an advantage over other groups which lack the innovation.

---

22. One of the clearest expositions of the theory of evolution including material on the primates is G. G. Simpson, *The Meaning of Evolution* (New Haven: Yale University Press, 1949). For a discussion of the parallels between biological and cultural evolution, see T. W. Gerard, C. Kluckhohn, and A. Rapoport, "Biological and Cultural Evolution," *Behavioral Science*, Vol. 1 (1956), pp. 6–34. Also, A. Alland, *Evolution and Human Behavior* (New York: Natural History Press, 1967).
23. C. L. Brace and M. F. Ashley Montagu, *Man's Evolution* (New York: Macmillan, 1965), pp. 267–326; Y. Cohen, *Man in Adaptation: The Biological Background,* 2nd ed. (Chicago: Aldine, 1974).

From the point of view of adaptation, it makes no difference where the innovations which enter a cultural system come from. They may arise within the society or be borrowed from another group; they may be accidental or deliberate; they may be the product of years of research or of a diseased mind. What does matter is the effect that acceptance of an innovation has in the long run upon the adaptation of the group, including its relationships with other populations (human and nonhuman), for an innovation that leads to the expansion and dominance of one society may mean the decline and even extinction of another.

Not all parts of a culture have equally direct connections with a group's adaptation to its physical/biological environment.[24] Human adaptation is much more complex than that of other animals; it proceeds simultaneously on at least three levels, with different goals, processes, and units on each level. Figure 7.2 summarizes these three levels of adaptation.[25]

Level	*Environment To Be Adapted To*	*Goals*	*Basic Processes*	*Units Involved*
I.	Physical/ biological (nature)	Maximum energy utilization; control of population size; adaptability	Evolution (capture and transformation of *energy*), both biological and cultural	Genetically inherited structures and behavior; culturally transmitted tools and techniques
II.	Social (others)	Social integration; continuity of group	Enculturation (exchange of values: *reciprocity*); social change (acculturation)	Roles, groups; plans for social interaction; conceptions of space and time; situations
III.	Internal (self)	Cultural coherence; personal satisfactions; individual identity	Culture growth (elaboration of *symbolic forms*: art, religion, law)	Ideology; world view; personal construct system; mazeway

Figure 7.2 **Three Levels of Human Adaptation**

24. The indirect effects of a culture trait upon a group's adaptation may, however, be extremely important. See A. Alland, "Medical Anthropology and the Study of Biological and Cultural Adaptation," *American Anthropologist*, Vol. 68 (1966), pp. 40–51.
25. This discussion and figure are based upon ideas found in C. Meighan, *Archaeology: An Introduction* (San Francisco: Chandler, 1966), pp. 1–8.

Adaptation to the physical/biological environment will be dealt with in the chapters on technology, where we will discuss at length the adaptive functions of human tools and techniques as well as the relationship between technology and the social system. Adaptation to the internal environment—the quest for identity—will be one theme of the chapters on ideological systems. For the rest of this chapter, we shall be concerned with adaptation to the *social environment* (Level II). This will be examined in terms of the processes of acculturation, revitalization, exchange, and the norm of reciprocity, for these are crucial to an understanding of how individuals and groups adapt to other individuals and groups. It should be noted, however, that *adaptation on any of the three levels may produce either stability or change.* When adaptation ceases, the result is not stability but death. Let us consider some examples of these generalizations.

Acculturation

When societies which have been relatively isolated come into intense firsthand contact with larger, more powerful, more technologically advanced societies, both groups undergo a process of adaptation which is called *acculturation.* The adaptive changes are most noticeable in the smaller, subordinate group: they range from minor borrowings and modifications to virtual replacement of whole cultural subsystems.

The Micmac Indians first came into contact with Europeans around 1500. Their initial contacts were with sailors who had come to exploit the rich fishing banks off the coast of what is now Nova Scotia. An intermittent trade was set up in which the Indians exchanged fresh food and furs for brandy, metal tools, and trinkets. By 1600 the French had established a flourishing fur trade in their colony of New France (eastern Canada); they built forts and enlisted the Micmac on their side against the British colonies. French missionaries were also successful in converting the Micmac to Roman Catholicism.

The fur trade, the military innovations (especially guns), and the new religion altered Micmac culture in many different ways. Nevertheless, these changes in the social, technological, and ideological systems may be viewed as adaptations which helped to maintain the total culture. For the Micmac could not simply ignore the powerful outsiders: some tribes tried to do this and soon were extinct. They had to modify their way of life if they were to survive as a people under changing social and ecological conditions. But despite (or perhaps because of) adaptive changes in technology and social structure, they clung to the native language and they managed to *reinterpret* (see above, p. 221) the European religious and political doctrines in terms of their aboriginal beliefs and values.

Although much of the native culture has been lost, over four hundred years of acculturation has not destroyed the Micmac sense of identity or their desire to live as Indians. Today, despite disease, warfare, and restriction to tiny, unproductive "reserves," the Micmac number over 6,000 persons—probably more than at the time of first European contact. The men work when they can as fishing guides, in lumbering, and in construction; recently, many young Micmac have gone into "high steel," building bridges and tall buildings in the cities of eastern Canada and New England. While this seems a far cry from the hunting and fishing of their ancestors, we can also see the adoption of these part-time, intensive, outdoor occupations as an adaptive change in one part of the social structure which permits other parts (family and community organization) to maintain themselves. The Micmac have strongly resisted attempts by missionaries and government agents to make them take up agriculture. The choices they have made in the past have certainly produced structural changes, often far beyond what they had anticipated; but these adaptations have also given continuity and stability to Micmac society and culture.[26]

Revitalization

When societies are under intense stress (whether or not this is a result of acculturation), social movements often arise which attempt to relieve the crisis by means which may appear bizarre to outsiders. These movements have been given a variety of names and classified in many different ways. We shall use the term *revitalization movements* for the entire class of phenomena, recognizing only a few subtypes. The important point about these movements is that when they succeed, they often bring about *vast changes* in a whole series of societies in a surprisingly *short time,* whether their explicit goals are radical or conservative, and despite all kinds of apparently irrational elements.

The Cargo Cults of Melanesia are probably the best known of modern revitalization movements. These are directed toward the modernization of societies and, in most cases, they do

26. This summary is based on materials in P. K. Bock, *The Micmac Indians of Restigouche* (Ottawa: National Museum of Canada, Bulletin No. 213, 1966).

achieve notable changes in the social structure and ideology. In the wake of World War II, many native peoples who had been briefly exposed to the military and economic might of the United States attempted to lure precious cargo to their own societies by constructing piers or landing strips and performing magical rituals under the leadership of a prophet who had promised great wealth to all who followed his teachings. Followers often had visions and engaged in frenzied dancing or destruction of property. Although the anticipated cargo did not arrive, these cults generally resulted in major alterations in leadership patterns, division of labor, and ritual practices. In many places, the fantastic programs were also followed by more practical attempts at social reform and economic development.

Paula Brown has suggested that the distinctive features of cargo cults are "the dream or vision of the prophet, the belief in access to supernatural beings, miracles, the swoons, and seizures of individuals and massed dancers." However, she also makes the following, more general point:

> In order for people to join any movement for social change, their wish for a different life must be very strongly held. Their wishes can vary greatly in content. They can wish to return to the golden age of the past (as in the American Indian Ghost Dance); they can wish for a somewhat better standard of living in the present (a labour movement); or they can have millennial dreams of a perfect age and salvation. In its common Melanesian form the wish is for the achievement of European wealth and power. These feelings are often linked with resentment at the native's position. "The white man shall go" is a common, though not universal, element; nationalism is often involved as well.[27]

The American Indian Ghost Dance was a much more conservative (or even reactionary) movement than the Melanesian Cargo Cults. Nonetheless it still comes within the classic definition of a revitalization movement as "a deliberate, organized, conscious effort to construct a more satisfying culture.[28] For the first time in 1870 and again twenty years later, prophets appeared in various Great Basin and Plains Indian tribes, preaching the return of the dead. They organized elaborate ceremonials designed to lead to the magical defeat of the Whites and the return of the buffalo, which had become nearly extinct.

The Ghost Dance was clearly a response to the crisis of White military pressure, colonization, and the deliberate slaughter of the buffalo, which had been the Indians' principal source of

27. P. Brown, "Social Change and Social Movements," in A. P. Vayda, ed., *Peoples and Cultures of the Pacific* (Garden City: Natural History Press, 1968), pp. 484, 474.
28. A. F. C. Wallace, "Revitalization Movements," *American Anthropologist*, Vol. 58 (1956), p. 265.

subsistence. The failure of the 1890 Ghost Dance to produce the desired results led to the virtual collapse of dozens of Indian cultures. But elsewhere, similar movements have had notable success, winning thousands (or millions) of converts to their messages of reform and salvation. The similarities and differences among these movements have been recently explored in a fascinating book by Weston LaBarre, entitled *The Ghost Dance—Origins of Religion.*[29]

EXCHANGE AND RECIPROCITY

Given a social system consisting of several categories of persons together with rules governing their behavior toward one another, the adaptive problem on Level II (see Figure 7.2) is how to keep the system from falling apart. Probably the most important way in which social integration is achieved is through an *exchange of values* among the various parts of a system. This is a major consequence (if not a conscious goal) of the division of labor (as pointed out above, p. 72). But even in the absence of specialization and objective interdependence, the exchange of values is able to create integration because of what appears to be a universal rule of behavior: the *principle of reciprocity.*

The members of a social system have certain definite rights and obligations because of their positions in the social structure—the roles that they play in relation to other members. But according to Alvin Gouldner, "There are certain duties that people owe one another, not . . . as fellow members of a group or even as occupants of social statuses within the group but, rather, because of their prior actions."[30] For example, in describing the social structure of a village in India, anthropologists invariably speak of the solidarity within each caste and of the occupational specialization which makes each caste dependent upon all of the others. But in addition to this characteristic social structure, there are also specific ties between a high-caste patron and the individual workers who provide him with specialized goods and services (the *jajmani* system). The relationships between the patron and his workers are governed by the norm of reciprocity, backed by the mechanical solidarity of the case groups involved.

29. (New York: Delta Books, 1970). See also M. Banton, ed., *Anthropological Approaches to The Study of Religion* (London: Tavistock Publications, A.S.A. Monograph 3, 1966).
30. A. Gouldner, "The Norm of Reciprocity: A Preliminary Statement," *American Sociological Review*, Vol. 25 (1960), pp. 170–171.

> In return for their services, the traditional workers are given biannual payments in grain and are sometimes given the use of a piece of land. The patron-worker tie is a hereditary one: a patron cannot arbitrarily change a traditional worker, and no one other than the hereditary worker will perform the traditional work of a patron under threat of out-casting. Similarly, a traditional worker cannot change a patron without the permission of his caste.[31]

We are dealing here with a principle of social *organization,* not structure, for our concern is with how specific individuals anticipate and choose among the alternative behavior patterns available to them. In every society, men are guided by a general rule that "makes two interrelated, minimal demands: (1) people should help those who have helped them, and (2) people should not injure those who have helped them."[32] This rule (norm of reciprocity) has several important consequences. Because it is so very general and indeterminate, it can regulate behavior in the absence of more specific rules. Even if one does not know what kind of person he is dealing with in a given situation, both persons may still conform to the norm of reciprocity.

> Being indeterminate, the norm can be applied to countless *ad hoc* transactions, thus providing a flexible moral sanction for transactions which might not otherwise be regulated by specific status obligations. The norm, in this respect, is a kind of plastic filler, capable of being poured into the shifting crevices of social structures, and serving as a kind of all-purpose moral cement.[33]

A gift that is given or a service that is performed *does* obligate the recipient, establishing a relationship where there was none or reinforcing social relationships which existed previously. But Gouldner also points out the *temporal* consequences of this norm (see Figure 7.3). The exchange of goods or services creates social integration because the norm of reciprocity requires that a debtor neither break off relations nor launch hostilities against his creditor, while it is obviously inexpedient for a creditor to do so, as long as he expects repayment. The key to this practice lies in the initiation by gift or service of a social *time of obligation:*

> It is a period governed by the norm of reciprocity in a double sense. First, the actor is accumulating, mobilizing, liquidating, or earmarking resources so that he can make a suitable repayment. Second, it is a

31. B. Cohn, "The Changing Status of a Depressed Caste," in M. Marriott, ed., *Village India* (Chicago: University of Chicago Press, 1955), p. 56.
32. Gouldner, *op. cit.*, p. 171.
33. *Ibid.*, p. 175.

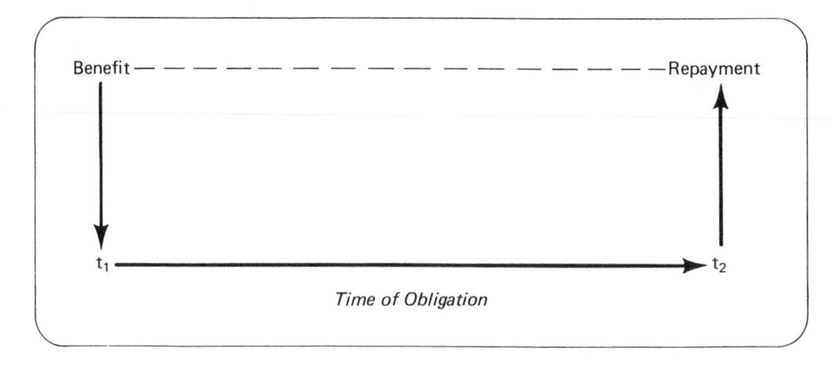

Figure 7.3 **Temporal Consequences of Reciprocity**

> period governed by the rule that you should not do harm to those who have done you a benefit. This is a time, then, when men are morally constrained to manifest their gratitude toward, or at least to maintain peace with, their benefactors.[34]

According to George Foster, in the Mexican village of Tzintzuntzan, each villager attempts to develop a number of exchange relationships (*dyadic contracts*) with his equals and his superiors in order to maximize his security "in the uncertain world in which he lives"; furthermore, this system requires that

> an exactly even balance between two partners never be struck. This would jeopardize the whole relationship, since if all credits and debits somehow could be balanced off at a point in time, the contract would cease to exist. . . . The dyadic contract is effective precisely because partners are never quite sure of their relative position at a given moment. As long as they know that goods and services are flowing both ways in *roughly equal amounts over time*, they know their relationship is solidly based.[35]

The dyadic contract is an aspect of social organization involving both choice and reciprocity, for "the formal social institutions of Tzintzuntzan kinship, neighborhood and godparenthood provide an individual with more potential associates than

34. *Ibid.*, p. 174. Note the resemblance between Figure 7.3, Temporal Consequences of Reciprocity and Figure 3.2, A Rite of Passage. For a different treatment of reciprocity, see M. Sahlins, "On the Sociology of Primitive Exchange," in M. Banton, ed., *The Relevance of Models for Social Anthropology* (London: Tavistock Publications, A.S.A. Monograph 1, 1965).
35. G. Foster, "The Dyadic Contract: A Model for the Social Structure of a Mexican Peasant Village," *American Anthropologist*, Vol. 63 (1961), p. 1185 (italics added).

he can utilize. . . . By means of the dyadic contract, implemented through reciprocity, he patterns his real behavior."[36]

Elsewhere, the emphasis is upon lengthening the period of obligation, so that it is felt to be improper to repay a debt too eagerly. Among the Seneca Indians of New York State, for example, it is felt that a person who wants to repay a gift too quickly with a return gift is an ungrateful person. A similar attitude is found in many American retail businesses: a person who buys on time is felt to be obligated to his creditor and thus likely to purchase more at the same establishment, whereas credit managers refer disparagingly to those who avoid time payments as "cash bums."

An understanding or recognition of the integrative function of reciprocity helps to explain many peculiar customs. For example, in American taverns and coffee shops it is common to see several persons drinking together, and within these groups it is customary for individuals to take turns buying rounds of drinks or paying for the whole group during a given coffee break. The explicit reason for this custom is to simplify the process of payment, and the contributions of all the members are equivalent in the long run. But even this trivial form of reciprocity can produce a degree of social integration: it is my impression that groups which practice this custom have considerably greater continuity over time than those which do not. Similarly, among the Nyakyusa, where the sharing of food and drink is a highly valued activity, men are expected to eat regularly with other men of their age group. Some men's eating groups last a lifetime, but violations of reciprocity can cause a group to break up. As one man put it, "Perhaps one eats at midday and does not summon his friend, but only calls him to the evening meal, then the other, who always calls his friend to the midday meal also, is angry, saying: 'He grudges me food,' and they separate."[37]

Like any other cultural rule, the universal norm of reciprocity *influences* behavior rather than determining it; that is, it can be violated or used by an individual for his own ends. After all, what we call a bribe is only a gift which creates an obligation of which we do not approve; but bribery could not work if the recipient did not feel obligated to reciprocate.

When reciprocity between two persons or two groups breaks down, as in the Nyakyusa example, it is often replaced by hostility. This can happen when one party fails or refuses to repay his obligations. But the norm of reciprocity can also be used to

---

36. *Ibid.*, pp. 1188, 1189.
37. M. Wilson, *Good Company* (Boston: Beacon Press, 1963), p. 68.

humiliate an opponent by presenting him with a gift which he cannot hope to repay (or even to maintain, such as the proverbial white elephant). This practice was developed to a high degree by the Kwakiutl Indians of the Northwest Coast, where high-ranking chiefs accumulated food, blankets, and other valuables to validate their prestige:

> There were two means by which a chief could achieve the victory he sought. One was by shaming his rival by presenting him with more property than he could return with the required interest. The other was by destroying property. In both cases the offering called for return, though in the first case the giver's wealth was augmented, and in the second he stripped himself of goods. . . .
>
> The destruction of goods took many forms. Great potlatch feasts in which quantities of candlefish oil were consumed were reckoned as contests of demolition. The oil was fed lavishly to the guests, and it was also poured upon the fire. Since the guests sat near the fire, the heat of the burning oil caused them intense discomfort, and this also was reckoned as part of the contest.[38]

This is reciprocity with a vengeance.

The consideration of these examples leads us to modify our general principle as follows: *the exchange of goods or services between parts of a system produces social integration only if the parties to the transaction feel that the values exchanged are roughly equivalent.* Exact equality of exchange tends to terminate a relationship, while extremely unequal exchanges tend to produce hostility. In an unequal exchange where *A* gives more to *B* than he receives from *B*, the hostility may be felt by *A* if he thinks he is being exploited; but it may also be felt by *B* if he thinks he is being humiliated.[39]

In conclusion, it should be emphasized that the exchange of equivalent goods or services produces integration among *groups* as well as among individuals. Many authors have pointed to the incest taboo as a source of social integration since women are considered valuable in all societies (though for different reasons) and the incest taboo makes it necessary for men to seek their mates outside of their immediate families. The biological and social consequences of this taboo are so adaptive that it has become universal. Similarly, various rules of exogamy and preferential marriage found throughout the world can be shown to promote social integration by ensuring the regular exchange of women among lineages, clans, or districts.

38. R. Benedict, *Patterns of Culture* (New York: Mentor Books, 1946), pp. 174–179.
39. For an application of similar ideas to problems of foreign aid, see C. Hyman, "The Dysfunctionality of Unrequited Giving," *Human Organization*, Vol. 25 (1966), pp. 42–45.

Claude Lévi-Strauss has pointed out that in a caste society such as India where strict rules of endogamy prevent the exchange of women among major social groups, it is the occupational specialization of the groups which produces social integration by requiring a constant exchange of goods and services.[40] There are many societies in which a number of social units are integrated by what amounts to the exchange of women for other types of valuables. Thus, when two men marry each other's sister, we have an exceedingly *direct* form of such exchange; but a larger number of groups can be integrated by means of an *indirect exchange* in which women travel in one direction while other valuables go in the opposite direction (as shown in Figure 7.4).

At the level of the national state, exchange of goods via foreign trade is an important means of international integration; but we must not underestimate the historical importance of the exchange of women even on this level: royal marriages ensured cooperation just as royal divorces led to hostility (compare the cases of King Henry V and King Henry VIII of England). Also, in many African "feudal" states where the ruler takes a large number of wives, his wives generally come from noble families in different districts of the kingdom; they thus serve, in part, as hostages to guarantee the loyalty of their noble relatives.

Finally, as Lévi-Strauss has made clear, words and other significant symbols are still another type of value, so that the

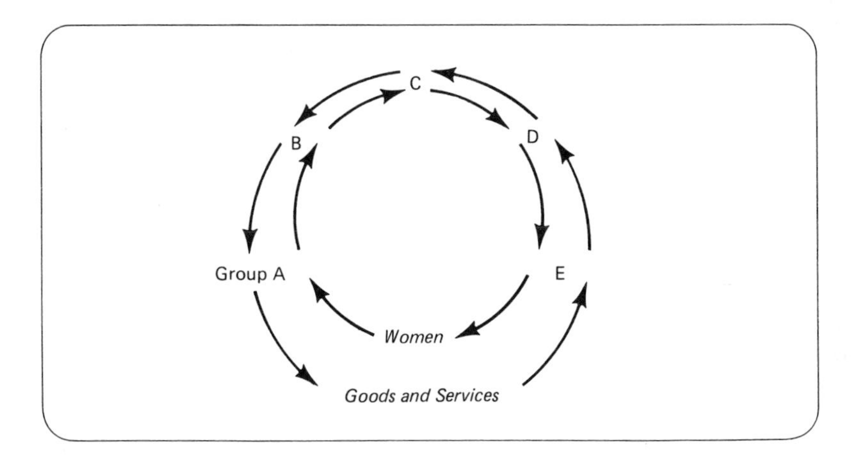

Figure 7.4 **Integration by Exchange**

40. C. Lévi-Strauss, "The Bear and the Barber," *Journal of the Royal Anthropological Institute*, Vol. 93 (1963), pp. 1–11. Compare Cohn, *op. cit.*

exchange of messages plays an essential part in the integration of all kinds of social systems.[41] When we say of two persons that they are not speaking or that they don't talk the same language, the implication is that cooperative activity is difficult or impossible. The free exchange of messages makes possible smooth interaction (though it does not guarantee it) because it is only through the regular flow of information that we can develop reliable expectations about the behavior of others. When communication breaks down between the parts of a system—be it a family, a business, or the nations of the world—the degree of integration of the system is lowered, and hostility is the likely outcome. Ambrose Bierce defined diplomacy as "the patriotic art of lying for one's country," but diplomatic channels of communication are often the only media through which information can flow and thus the only means of stabilizing relations between nations. Dictators have long known what social psychologists have experimentally verified: he who controls the flow of information within a social system, controls the system.

In this chapter we have considered the ways in which individuals put their culture to work for them in order to achieve their purposes and maximize their satisfactions. We have seen that, in all societies, men act within the framework of their social structure, *anticipating* its demands, *choosing* among structural alternatives, *modifying* the manner of their performances, *innovating* more or less novel responses, and *adapting* to their social environment by various means, including exchanges guided by the norm of *reciprocity*. These are the major principles of social organization. They enable us to gain a much more dynamic picture of the operation of social systems than that which comes merely from a description of social structure in terms of roles, groups, situations, and the standard plans for action associated with each of these categories. Regular patterns of choice ultimately change the structure, but we must not lose sight of the fact that *it is the shared structure which makes choice possible and meaningful.*

RECOMMENDED READING

Barnett, H., *Innovation: The Basis of Cultural Change.* New York: McGraw-Hill, 1953. A thoughtful consideration of the how and why of cultural innovation, using principles of Gestalt psychology.

---

41. C. Lévi-Strauss, "Social Structure," in A. L. Kroeber, ed., *Anthropology Today* (Chicago: University of Chicago Press, 1953), pp. 524–553.

Dahrendorf, R., *Essays in the Theory of Society.* Stanford: Stanford University Press, 1968. Many sections of this book, especially the essay called "Homo Sociologicus," can be read as a theoretical justification of the approach taken in this text to the social system.

Firth, R., *Elements of Social Organization.* London: Watts, 1951. The source of the organizing ideas for the present chapter. Also contains interesting observations on primitive art and society.

Murphy, R. F., *The Dialectics of Social Life.* New York: Basic Books, 1971. Delightful and challenging examination of contemporary anthropological theory (especially the work of Lévi-Strauss) with special attention to the dialectical relationship between "norm and action" in social life.

Sisk, J. P., *Person and Institution.* Notre Dame, Indiana: Fides Publishers, 1970. A Roman Catholic layman discusses the relationship between the individual and the Church in a time of change, providing a sensitive account which is equally applicable to all kinds of person/institution interactions.

Wallace, A. F. C., *Culture and Personality* (second edition). New York: Random House, 1970. The best general introduction to problems of the psychology of culture change, with interesting essays on "Culture and Cognition" and cultural evolution.

The part of a culture which enables men to produce objective changes in their physical and biological environment is called the *technological system.* It consists of learned categories and plans for action which are manifested in the tools, techniques, and skills employed by the members of society. The technological system is intimately related to the social system of a group. Because technology does not operate all by itself, changes in technology and in social structure go hand in hand. The techniques and skills which make possible the survival of a human society must be shared and applied by specific categories of persons. Techniques are attributes of social roles and, as such, are expected to be *performed* in culturally defined situations. The technological ability of a population also sets *limits* on its size and on the kind of social structure that the society may have.

Americans and others who live in modern industrial societies that possess complex machine technologies and scientific medicine tend to take these advantages for granted, not realizing how recent such developments are in the history of human culture. The study of primitive technological systems provides a valuable perspective from which we can better appreciate our advantages as well as our debt to the past. As we shall see, the technological systems of primitive peoples are truly remarkable in the way they enable men to adapt to difficult and hazardous environmental conditions, using only the materials immediately at hand. Furthermore, our own complex civilization is largely built upon the achievements of our unknown primitive ancestors. Ina C. Brown has put this point very well:

> We who are citizens of the United States are apt to think of our country not only as self-made but as generous to a fault in giving to the rest of the world. Actually, we are deeply in debt to other peoples. The plants and animals we use for food, our form of writing, the paper and printing presses that bring us the news of the world, the basic inventions that underly our technological civilization, even our ethical values and religious concepts were discovered, invented, developed, or thought out by peoples in other times and places.[1]

In the following chapters, we shall discuss the principal tools, techniques, and skills which have been developed by primitive peoples to help them to survive in various environments. Because environmental modifications often leave traces for the archaeologist to uncover, the history of human technology is relatively well known. We shall take note of several historical sequences of development. The main emphasis of these chapters, however, is upon the kinds of environmental adaptation which specific technologies make possible, and upon the forms of thought and social structure which accompany these adaptations.

1. I. C. Brown, *Understanding Other Cultures* (Englewood Cliffs, N.J.: Prentice-Hall, 1963), p. 136.

Caio Garrubba/Rapho Guillumette

PART IV
Technological Systems

CHAPTER 8
Tools and Human Needs

If the world were arranged entirely for our convenience we should have no need for tools. But it is not. Matter and energy are seldom found in exactly the right forms or quantities to satisfy our needs. The sun rises and sets without regard to our desire for light or heat. Food and water do not appear whenever we are hungry or thirsty. And various obstacles come between us and the objects of our desires.

Furthermore, matter and energy tend to behave in ways that are often contrary to human desires. Some of these "inconvenient tendencies" are described by the physical laws of *inertia* and *entropy.* The law of inertia describes the tendency of an object at rest to remain at rest and of an object in motion to remain in uniform motion unless acted upon by an outside force. The law of entropy has to do with the tendency of physical systems to run down—that is, for the matter and energy within a closed system to change into less and less organized forms and eventually to become randomly distributed. By means of tools, men are able to temporarily overcome these general tendencies in order to arrange the physical world more to their convenience.

An *artifact* is any portion of the material environment that has been deliberately used, or modified for use, by man. Tools are thus a subclass of artifacts. A *tool* is any artifact that is used to augment man's ability to act upon the physical world. This is a very broad definition, but a broad definition is necessary if it is to encompass everything from hand axes to lasers and from clay pots to space capsules, for these are all part of human technology.

Tools are useful to man because (1) he must sometimes

overcome the inertia and entropy of physical systems and (2) his body is not equal to all of these tasks without assistance. In order to understand the adaptive functions of tools, we must bring them into relation with the human needs which they help to satisfy. By *adaptive function* we mean the contribution that a tool makes to the physical survival of the population that uses it.

Not all the artifacts made or used by man are tools. They do not all perform functions on the level of the physical/biological environment. Part of our definition of a tool was that it must "augment man's ability to act upon the physical world." There are many artifacts that have no direct connection with the physical survival of human groups. Works of art, flags, sports equipment, jewelry, and many similar objects promote social integration or cultural coherence, rather than environmental adaptation (see Figure 7.3). Such objects naturally conform to the laws governing the physical world, but they are not tools because their action upon that world is negligible and incidental to their primary function.

All tools, then, bear some relation to human needs. In the following sections of this chapter, we shall discuss three basic human needs and survey some of the tools which have been used to satisfy them in various environments. Our classification will cut across the conventional ethnological categories (shelter, basketry, clothing, and so forth) in order to emphasize the adaptive nature of technology. Also, rather than listing many different tools, a few examples will be discussed in considerable detail.

THE NEED FOR TEMPERATURE REGULATION

Man's body, like those of other animals, can function only within a fairly narrow temperature range. Like the rest of the mammals, we are warm-blooded; that is, we possess a number of physiological mechanisms for regulating our own temperature. But these are not sufficient for survival in many of the environments where humans are found. Man was originally a tropical animal—a primate—and he has been able to inhabit temperate and arctic zones only with the assistance of certain tools. (Cultural devices have also made him more comfortable in tropical and semitropical zones.)

The more familiar physiological mechanisms for maintaining a constant body temperature include sweating, shivering, and the expansion or contraction of peripheral blood vessels in response to various combinations of temperature and humidity. Within limits, such organic controls are extremely adaptive, and

Tool use by the Tasaday, a tribe recently discovered in the Phillipines who live a still primitive existence. ***John Nance/Panamin/Magnum***

via biological evolution, some human populations have developed them to high degrees of efficiency.[1] Our concern, however, is with the environmental controls which man has developed and transmitted via culture.

The development of environmental controls is older than our species, for we know that *Homo erectus* (Pekin Man) controlled fire. More than 50,000 years ago, early members of our own species (the Neanderthals) already lived near the edges of Pleistocene glaciers, surviving under conditions of severe cold (see pp. 11–12). All animals make use of naturally occurring shelters, so it is hardly surprising that early men lived in caves—and that thousands of people still do today. But a cave without fire is an uncomfortable shelter, and it may present more hazards (for example, from dampness and intruding carnivores) than advantages. On the other hand, in the tropics fire is more important for the insect-repelling qualities of its smoke than for the warmth it provides. The mastery of fire, then, was one of the earliest and most important steps that man took in learning to control his environment.

Shelters

Tropical shelters function primarily to protect men from intense solar radiation and from rain. This is accomplished quite ingeniously, using only materials that are available in the immediate vicinity. In tropical regions, the typical shelter is more like a filter than a container. A few examples will demonstrate this point.

Among the Semang, a hunting and gathering people of the Malay Peninsula, small bands of kinsmen pursue a nomadic life within their respective territories. According to C. Daryll Forde:

> A camp is usually made in some small natural clearing in the forest or beneath an overhanging ledge of rock. The shelters of the encampment are abandoned every time a move is made and are improvised again at the next halt, for they are easily built with the large leaves of the many palm trees available in the jungle. . . . In a typical camp group there will be from six to a dozen shelters, generally arranged in a circle or oval. Each shelter is made by the mother for her husband and children. Three or four stout sticks are driven into the ground in a line, sloping over toward the central clearing, and supported by forked struts or held in position by fibre strings pegged in the ground. The outer side of the sloping stakes is then closely thatched horizontally, working from the bottom to the top. Rattan leaves are used, and each is folded on its midrib to give a double thicknes of fronds. This sloping thatch-like wall is adjustable, and its angle is raised or lowered according to the weather. In stormy weather more foliage is heaped on

1. C. L. Brace and M. F. Ashley Montagu, *Man's Evolution* (New York: Macmillan, 1965), pp. 309–315.

> outside and held in position by branches. Beneath it, their heads to the back, raised couches are built to lift their occupants from the damp earth and vegetation.[2]

This lean-to dwelling is one of the simplest known to anthropologists, but it fits the needs of the Semang perfectly. Essentially, it is no more than a roof that deflects the sun's rays and that sheds water with the addition of extra leaves; its position or density is easily adjusted to perform these functions while offering minimal interference to cooling breezes. The leaves used in this single wall have a very low heat retention capacity; they reflect solar radiation rather than absorb it. Finally, the shelters may be quickly constructed from materials that are readily available in all parts of Semang territory—an important feature for these nomadic bands.

Throughout the tropics, extreme heat, humidity, and heavy, intermittent rains are the major climatic problems; in these areas, the dominant element of human shelter is a water-repellent roof. This is often combined with a raised floor and walls of low heat retention capacity, all made of local materials. Woven mats of various kinds are commonly used, for in wet weather the fibers expand to repel water and in dry periods they contract to admit air. One particularly ingenious arrangement has been reported from the plateau area of Nigeria: a dome-shaped mud roof is topped with wooden pegs and a second roof of thatch is set on the pegs. This combines the water-repelling action of the thatch with the heat absorption of the mud roof, plus the insulating property of the air trapped between the two roofs.

In many dry regions we find houses built of stone, mud or mud bricks, finished in light colors, and having small openings for light. Such shelters are extremely functional—provided that the group using them is relatively sedentary, for they take considerable time and effort to construct. They are particularly efficient in hot, arid areas like the American Southwest, where temperatures fall very low at night, even in the summer. Here, the adaptive problem is that of leveling out the extreme temperature differences between day and night. This can be achieved by using high heat retention capacity materials such as mud or stone and adjusting the thickness of walls and roofs according to the intensity of the heat. These shelters absorb solar radiation during the day, and at night they radiate this heat energy to the interior of the house.

Here again we see an environmental problem answered by an ingenious solution which makes use of readily available mate-

---

2. C. D. Forde, *Habitat, Economy and Society* (New York: Dutton, 1963), pp. 13–14.

Constructing a house of mud in Chad, Africa. ***American Museum of Natural History***

rials. Mud cannot be used as the sole construction material in areas where moderate to heavy rainfall occurs, but in desert or semidesert climates its superior insulating properties have long been recognized. The characteristic small windows and light-colored plaster also function to keep the temperature inside the house fairly stable.

Nomadic groups in temperate and subarctic environments often make use of some kind of tent since they cannot count on finding building materials wherever they wish to camp. The tent is what engineers call a tension structure; its design gives a maximum of enclosed space with a minimum of materials—an important advantage for nomads who must carry both frame and covering materials with them. Various kinds of local materials are used for tent covers. The Indians of the Northeast usually used birch bark to cover their conical or hemispherical wigwams, whereas the conical tipi of the Plains Indians was, understandably, covered with buffalo skin. Some pastoral nomads of central Asia make use of felted animal hair (an excellent insulator) as a tent cover. For example, the yurt of the Kalmuk and the Kazak consists of a collapsible willow-rod frame, something like a trellis, which is set up in a circle, topped with an umbrella-like frame over which large sheets of felt are stretched and lashed down with horsehair rope. The floor is covered with felt and a curtain of felt hangs across the door frame.[3] Such easily transported shelters are obviously well adapted to the needs of their nomadic inhabitants.

Probably the most striking example of primitive architecture is the Eskimo snow house, or igloo. The Eskimo lives in a wide range of arctic environments, and different local groups utilize various types of structures, from tents to stone houses. But for those groups engaged in nomadic hunting, the igloo is as perfect a solution to environmental problems as can be imagined. Wood, which is the usual fuel and building material of primitive tribes, is not available to these people. The igloo is made from

> large blocks of snow, cut from a drift of fine-grained, compacted snow with a bone or ivory knife . . . laid spirally and sloping inwards to build up a dome without any scaffolding. Each block is rapidly and skillfully cut out by eye to fit in its place with the right slope and to afford a firm foundation for later courses. The final key block is lowered into position from outside. Any crevices are tightly packed with snow and the main structure is complete. With use during the winter cold its solidity increases, for the meltings on the inner walls are soon frozen again to solid ice. . . .
>
> In some areas the main chamber is lined with skins held in position by sinew cords passing through the walls of the dome and held

3. *Ibid.*, p. 336.

by toggles. A considerable air space is left between the skin ceiling and the snow roof. With such a lining and an air exit hole in the roof a temperature of ten to twenty degrees above freezing can be maintained without serious melting of the igloo, since there is always cool air between it and the interior. While such a house is carefully constructed and takes time to build, *a temporary igloo about two yards in diameter can be built in an hour or so by a single man* or a small party while on a journey and camping for the night.[4]

The igloo has many obvious advantages as a shelter in this environment: it can be constructed quickly out of the only materials immediately available; due to its design it is extremely strong, although the individual blocks of snow are quite light; and the melting and refreezing of the interior surface provides a perfect seal against the wind. Other advantages of this shelter are not so obvious. However, the excellent performance of the igloo is a result of both its form and material.[5] The streamlined hemispherical shape offers the minimum of obstruction to winter gales while exposing the least possible surface to chilling. The dome, as you may recall from solid geometry, encloses the largest volume within the smallest surface; at the same time, it yields that volume which is most effectively heated by a single source of radiant heat (see below). Although dry snow may seem an unlikely material, it is actually one of the best imaginable materials for this environment because of its relatively low heat retention capacity; this means that the walls have excellent insulating properties, and when coated with a glaze of ice, the interior acts as a radiant heat reflector. In short, the igloo is a first-rate shield against icy winds and a nearly ideal container for men and for heat energy.

Nevertheless, the excellent performance of the igloo as a shelter would be impossible without a dependable source of radiant heat, and wood for fuel is simply not available. Thus the Eskimo's adaptation to their environment rests in part upon a simple but essential device: the oil lamp. This is a shallow stone dish with a moss wick which enables the Eskimo to burn oil derived from seal blubber—the only readily available fuel. A single oil lamp, placed near the center of a small igloo, provides all the heat needed to warm the interior.

Clothing

An interior temperature of thirty to forty degrees Fahrenheit probably does not sound comfortable to most people, but the Eskimo

4. *Ibid.*, pp. 117–120 (italics added).
5. J. Fitch and D. Branch, "Primitive Architecture and Climate," *Scientific American*, Vol. 203, No. 6 (1960), pp. 134–144.

are biologically well adapted to cold temperatures and generally sleep naked beneath fur blankets. However, outside the igloo they must carry their shelter with them. The primary adaptive function of clothing in an arctic environment is to shield the body and to assist in the conservation of natural body heat.

Eskimo clothing is admirably suited to its tasks. In most regions it is made from caribou hide, which is lighter, warmer, and more supple than seal skin, and it is carefully shaped:

> Eskimo garments are no shapeless wraps. They are carefully cut out and tailored on established patterns for men and women. For protection against water and damp, waterproof suits of gut are made. Clothing is made by women. It is finely stitched with sinew thread and often beautifully finished with border strips of contrasting colour. To protect their eyes against the continual glare of snow and ice during the spring on the coast the Eskimo wear slit goggles of ivory.[6]

This last passage brings out two important points which should be emphasized. First, although our discussion of shelter and clothing has dealt with their temperature-regulating properties, these cannot be divorced from the other functions they perform, such as shielding from glare, dampness, or insects. The long, flowing robes of Arabian nomads give good protection against the intense solar radiation of the desert, but they also shield their wearers against blowing sand. In many cases, the form of a dwelling or a garment represents a compromise between the need for temperature regulation and other forms of environmental control.

All of these adaptive functions are overlaid (and sometimes contradicted) by notions of modesty and traditional aesthetic values. Ornamentation seldom contributes to the effectiveness of a tool, and standards of propriety and attractiveness (which are both conventional and variable) often diminish the comfort of those who maintain them. Thus in analyzing the technological functions of a tool, we must examine all of its uses in relation to the physical world and as far as possible separate these from its nontool aspects.

The earliest forms of protective clothing were probably animal skins draped about the body, but ornamentation of the body may have preceded this practice by thousands of years. Chimpanzees are said to be indifferent to clothing, although they appreciate a blanket in which to wrap themselves at night.[7] Tailored clothing, fitted to the trunk and limbs, has obvious advan-

6. Forde, *op. cit.*, p. 121.
7. A. L. Kroeber, *Anthropology* (New York: Harcourt, Brace, 1948), pp. 64–65.

Garments of these Turkish women fulfill both a protective and a symbolic function. ***Harry Wilks***

tages in cold environments, but historical records show that this form was not common in Europe until the early Middle Ages, when it was adopted from the "barbarians." Kroeber has pointed out that the basic clothing styles of different regions show remarkable persistence over time. For example:

> Ancient Mediterranean and East Asiatic are each characterized by a distinctive, long-term basic pattern of clothing. . . . Greek and Roman clothing was draped on the body. . . . Sleeves were little developed, trousers lacking, the waist of clothing was not fitted in to follow the body, the general effect accentuated the fall of drapery and the flowing line. . . . Chinese and Japanese dress is . . . cut and tailored, but it is not fitted. It is cut loose, with ample sleeves, or kimono style, to suggest a broad figure. Trousers are ample, so as to have almost a skirt effect. The use of clothing to model or suggest women's bust, waist, and hip contour is wholly outside the Far Eastern pattern. Wit-

ness the Japanese *obi* sash and bow intended to conceal these features, while European women for four centuries or more have worn corsets and girdles to accentuate them.[8]

These examples as well as the rapid changes produced by fashion indicate that the *forms* of clothing are largely determined by nontechnological considerations; but what *materials* are used, at least in primitive societies, is strongly influenced by adaptive requirements. The Indians of the Northwest Coast had clothing which was well adapted to the mild but extremely humid climate of their area and well suited to their seagoing way of life. They wore waterproof hats of finely woven basketry, and some wore garments woven of cedar bark and tightly spun cords. Red-cedar bark was shredded and made into conical, water-repellent rain capes, whereas yellow-cedar bark robes were worn primarily for warmth.[9] Other types of garments were woven of goat or dog hair.

Garments of bark can be used only in highly humid areas because elsewhere they quickly lose their flexibility and deteriorate. In parts of South America and the Pacific Islands, other types of bark cloth are found, worn wrapped about the body (like the Malayan sarong). Grass skirts are also common in these areas, and are worn by both sexes.

The hair of mammals is a natural insulating material and, where the techniques of spinning and weaving or of felting are known, can be used (without killing the mammal from which it was obtained) to replace the hairy covering that man has lost in the course of evolution. These techniques, however, are mainly found among groups with domesticated animals. Similarly, the extensive use of vegetable fibers such as cotton, flax, or hemp tends to be limited to settled societies.[10]

Many other examples could be given to show the adaptive value of clothing and the ingenuity of primitive peoples in devising forms and utilizing local materials. It has been common for the Westerner who looks down on the native forms of clothing when he first enters a tribal area to end up adopting the tribe's garments or footwear because of their comfort or usefulness. But perhaps the most striking example of environmental adaptation comes from our own culture, for in the twentieth century man is moving into entirely new environments: outer space and the depths of the ocean. As the astronauts and deep-sea divers enter these environments, they encounter extremes of heat, cold, pressure, and radiation never before faced by human beings; and as they leave the

8. *Ibid.*, p. 332.
9. P. Drucker, *Cultures of the North Pacific Coast* (San Francisco: Chandler, 1965), p. 35.
10. R. Beals and H. Hoijer, *An Introduction to Anthropology* (second edition; New York: Macmillan, 1959), p. 378.

controlled environment of their capsule-containers, they must wear entirely new types of clothing to protect themselves against these hazards to life. The spacesuit, with its special materials and integral sources of heat and oxygen, represents the first really major advance in human clothing since the bearskin robe.

THE NEED FOR FOOD AND WATER

Man's need for oxygen becomes a problem for technology only at very high altitudes or under water (though if air pollution continues to increase at its present rate, this statement may soon have to be modified). But the human body requires other chemical substances if it is to survive. These include water, carbohydrates, proteins, vitamins, and minerals which the body uses either directly or in the synthesis of the organic compounds required to sustain life. In this section we are not concerned with the details of human nutrition but rather with the tools that are used in the simpler societies to satisfy man's need for food and water.

The amount of water needed to sustain life varies with factors such as a person's size and state of health, his normal activities, and the environment in which he lives. Furthermore, not all water is consumed in pure liquid form: it may be derived from other fluids or from the moisture contained in solid foods. But it must be consumed in some form, or life cannot go on. The main problems facing a group in connection with its water supply are finding a source, getting at the usable portion, and storing or transporting the water.

To find sources of moisture, members of hunting and gathering societies rely principally on their intimate knowledge of their territory and of the characteristics of local plants and animals. Even in extremely arid environments, finding drinking water is more a matter of techniques than of tools; it involves knowing the location of water holes or of moisture-containing plants; it also involves a keen sensitivity to signs that moisture may be present in other places. People who live in arid environments also develop the ability to persist in spite of thirst, and this gives them an advantage over others who tend to give up (and thus die) in the same situations. The only "tool" used to locate water is the widely distributed but totally ineffective divining rod. (Food collectors are generally uninterested in deep underground sources of water; but rural Americans are very interested, and this may account for the discovery that there were at least 25,000 water witches operating in the United States in 1955.)[11]

11. E. Z. Vogt and R. Hyman, *Water Witching U. S. A.* (Chicago: University of Chicago Press, 1959).

Having found a source of moisture, the next step is to get at the drinkable portion: the Eskimo melts some snow in a soapstone bowl; the Bushman inserts his drinking tube (a hollow reed which he carries everywhere) into a crack in a hollow tree. In both these cases, the tools used are simple, but are nevertheless essential.

For nomadic peoples (particularly those in arid environments), storage and transport of water are serious problems. Many hunting peoples use the paunches, bladders, or skins of animals as canteens, and these must be prepared with stone knives and scrapers or sewn with bone or ivory needles. Pottery jars are either unknown or impractical due to their weight and fragility, though they may be employed by nomads who possess beasts of burden. The Bushmen of the Kalahari desert use ostrich eggshells to carry water.[12]

Many peoples who lacked pottery or metal containers solved the problem of how to heat water by the method of "stone-boiling." This method is used with containers made of materials that cannot be placed directly over a fire—made, for example, of basketry, leather, bark, or wood. Stones are heated in a fire and then dropped into the water; in this way, the heat is transferred to the water without burning the container. In the days before European contact, the Micmac Indians used this method to heat water in the large, hollowed-out tree stumps which served them as kettles.

Ensuring an adequate water supply is a serious problem in nearly all societies. Food collectors and small-scale food producers can generally solve this problem with a few simple tools so long as their environment is not too arid. But large, sedentary societies in any environment must somehow bring drinking water to the population centers, often over great distances. Where rainfall is not sufficient for agriculture, large quantities of water must be stored and transported to the fields. Digging wells, building dams, and constructing irrigation systems or aqueducts require both an advanced technology and a social structure which can enforce large-scale cooperative efforts.

Food Gathering

Despite the limitations imposed by their need to be constantly on the move, hunting and gathering people do a remarkable job of exploiting the food resources in their environments. Once again, intimate knowledge of the territory and of its flora and fauna plays

12. For a vivid description of the subsistence technology of the Kalahari Bushmen, see E. M. Thomas, *The Harmless People* (New York: Vintage Books, 1959). Two chapters from this book are reprinted in P. K. Bock, ed., *Culture Shock* (New York: Knopf, 1970).

a major role. Without this knowledge, these people could not survive.

Among food collectors, the gathering of plant food is almost invariably the task of women. This is commonly accomplished with the help of the dibble, or digging stick, which is simply a strong stick that tapers to a point; the point is often hardened by being tempered in a fire to drive out the moisture. The digging stick is a simple, but important, all-purpose tool used as a prod to locate edible roots, as a pick to loosen the soil, and as a lever to extract plants from the ground. According to E. A. Hoebel, the Cheyenne Indians believe that the dibble

> was given by the Great Medicine Spirit and it figures in the ritual paraphernalia of the Sun Dance, for it has its sacred aspects. Cheyenne dibbles are of two types. The short kind has a knob at one end and is pushed under the desired root by pressure against the stomach when the digger is down on both knees. The other kind is long, and used as a crowbar. The sharp ends are fire hardened.[13]

Cheyenne women gather some eight or ten varieties of wild roots, including several kinds of lily bulbs; they also collect more than a dozen different vegetable stalks or buds and sixteen varieties of fruits. Other multipurpose tools are used to process these foods:

> The basic household item of the woman is her stone maul—an oval river stone with pecked-cut grooves on the short sides around which is fixed a supple willow withe firmly fastened with green rawhide. When dried out, the rawhide shrinks and holds the maul within the handle with the grip of a vise. With the maul she breaks up fuel, drives tipi pegs, and crushes large bones to be cooked in soup. With smaller handstones the housewife crushes her chokecherries and pulverizes her dried meat.[14]

From ethnographic accounts such as this one archaeologists can get some idea of the many possible functions of prehistoric tools such as the hand axe and the chopping tool.

The adaptive functions of these tools may be seen when we consider how they give man access to sources of energy which he could not otherwise exploit. For example, the two parts of most plants which contain the greatest proportion of nutritive substances are the roots and the seeds. The digging stick enables food gatherers to get at the starchy roots, and various pulverizing or grinding tools such as the maul and the milling stone enable

13. E. A. Hoebel, *The Cheyennes* (New York: Holt, Rinehart and Winston, 1960), p. 59.
14. *Ibid.*, pp. 61–62.

them to get at the nutritious kernel of seeds, which is usually encased in a hard, inedible shell. The milling stone is essential to an economy based on the gathering of seeds or the cultivation of grains—and these are the most common types of subsistence economies found in the world.

Milling stones appear in the archaeological record of both the Old and the New World about 10,000 years ago. This does not necessarily indicate contact between, say, the eastern Mediterranean and central Mexico at this period, but it does show that following the end of the Ice Age, men in widely separated parts of the world were learning to exploit the food energy found in wild seeds. Such experimentation eventually led to the development of agriculture.

Since the human body is not provided with built-in pouches, the use of seeds, roots, and berries as sources of food also requires strong, lightweight containers for transport and storage. Such containers are less likely to last for 10,000 years than are milling stones, but the arid climate of the American Southwest has preserved a few examples, and ethnographic studies of modern seed gatherers can be used to fill out the prehistoric picture. Burden baskets, woven and utilized by women, were essential tools. Net bags were probably used to carry larger objects. The *tump line,* a rope or strap suspended from the forehead, was used to distribute the weight of a load. Food was processed and stored in baskets, skin bags, covered pits, or, in some cases, pottery jars.

Archaeologists and ethnographers are still debating the origins of sedentarism (permanent settlements), but it is clear that although most food gatherers are nomadic, under special conditions they may become sedentary. For example, among certain California Indian tribes "where large and imperishable food supplies can be accumulated, and still more on the Northwest Coast . . . permanent villages with enduring habitations are occupied year after year."[15]

Another characteristic tool of plant collectors is the seed-beater, a paddle-shaped implement which is used to knock seeds off plants into a container. The Paiute used them in connection with conical baskets when harvesting grass seeds and pine nuts. In the Great Lakes area, many tribes have used similar seed-beaters in harvesting wild rice: one person would slowly guide a canoe through the swampy regions where the rice grew, while the other bent the rice stalks over the canoe and knocked the grains into its bottom.

15. Forde, *op. cit.*, p 374.

A final example of tools used in food processing comes from California, where the Indians developed a number of ingenious means of preparing the acorn. Oak trees are abundant in central California and their annual crop of nuts is quite dependable; the only problem is that most varieties contain a high proportion of tannic acid, which makes them inedible. The devices used to remove this acid are simple, but they made possible the accumulation of "large and imperishable food supplies." For example:

> In aboriginal central California the acorn was a true staple, being eaten in greater quantity than the product of any other genus, animal or vegetable. The acorns were first cracked open with the aid of a small elongated stone for a hammer and a heavy flat slab of stone for an anvil. The nut meats were then ground with a mortar and pestle. . . .
>
> When the meal was ground sufficiently fine, it was taken to the bank of a stream where there was a handy water supply for the leaching process. Most frequently the meal was placed directly on the sand in a shallow depression or basin which had been prepared for the purpose. In southern California, however, the meal was placed in a porous basket. Then water was dipped from the stream and poured over and through the meal in the manner of making drip coffee. Sometimes the water was heated by placing hot stones in a closely woven basket filled with the liquid. Warm water dissolved the tannic acid more readily, but if too hot carried away some of the fat which was a desirable nutritive element. Cold water took longer, but washed away none of the food value. This leaching process was repeated until the bitter taste of the tannic acid was eliminated. The meal was then ready for cooking.[16]

Acorns were also used for food in the Northeastern United States, but here a *chemical process* was used: to neutralize the tannic acid, the whole kernels were boiled in water to which lye (derived from wood ashes) had been added. The whole acorns were then dried or roasted and stored.

Hunting

Acorns and wild rice had been used extensively by the Indians of the Northeast before they learned to grow corn, but because of the great abundance of game animals these vegetable foods had never been very important. Meat is a much more concentrated food than are vegetables; it contains fat and proteins which have already been synthesized from plants by the animal's body. The adaptive problems involved in hunting are similar to those involved

16. H. Driver and W. Massey, "Comparative Studies of North American Indians," *Transactions of the American Philosophical Society*, Vol. 47, Part 2 (1957), p. 235.

in obtaining water and plant food except for the tendency of animals to actively avoid being located or killed. Man's body is too slow and clumsy for him to do much hunting barehanded, but with suitable tools and socially transmitted techniques he has become a skillful and effective hunter.

Clubs and spears are probably the most ancient weapons; certainly every known human group possesses some kind of simple crushing and piercing tool. A fairly ancient improvement upon the spear is the spear-thrower, often called by is Aztec name, *atl-atl.* Found in many different forms, this mechanism serves as an extension of the arm, providing additional leverage and thus multiplying the force which can be applied to the end of a spear. Using a spear-thrower, an average person can learn to hurl his weapon as far as a champion javelin thrower or to throw it with considerable force at close range. The adaptive advantages of this device in hunting or in warfare are obvious. Other improvements on the simple spear include attached points (initially stone, later metal) and detachable heads (as with the Eskimo harpoon).

The bow and arrow, also a characteristic hunting weapon, appears to be much more recent than the spear: the earliest archaeological evidence for the use of the bow comes from rock paintings only 10,000 to 12,000 years old. The earliest arrows were doubtless simple shafts, and the first separate arrowheads may have been only crude chips of stone; but they were rapidly developed into light, thin, finely flaked piercing implements—much lighter and thinner than any spear point. The Semang and the Bushmen use small arrows tipped with a deadly poison; these enable them to hunt quite large mammals.

The simple bow is a mechanism consisting of a single curved piece of wood to which a strong fiber or sinew cord is fastened. When the bow is bent, potential energy is stored in the wood; when released, this is applied (through the medium of the cord) to one end of the arrow. The resiliency of the bow is sometimes improved by fastening strips of sinew to its exterior surface; this is the sinew-backed bow. When wood is lacking or where a powerful small bow is desired, a compound bow can be fashioned from several pieces of bone, wood, or horn. For example, the Eskimo bow is usually made of three sections of wood or caribou antler strips which are bound together in various ways and reinforced with strands of sinew lashed to the outer face.[17] Other bowlike tools are used by the Eskimo for drilling holes in wood or bone and for fire-making.

A weapon preferred by some jungle hunters is the blowgun,

---

17. Forde, *op. cit.*, p. 125.

a long tube through which a dart is guided, propelled by the hunter's breath, and from which it flies to its target. The Sakai, a neighboring tribe to the Malayan Semang, use a bamboo blowgun together with poison-tipped darts to hunt all kinds of small game. Where such suitable materials are not available, the hunter must fashion his weapons with great skill. For example, among the Jivaro Indians of the Amazon basin, the lance and the blowgun were the usual weapons used in hunting, supplemented in modern times by cheap trade guns; but the blowgun is considered the most valuable of these for hunting in the deep forest. The Jivaro are expert blowgun hunters; their blowguns are ten to fifteen feet long and can propel a poisoned dart up to forty-five yards to kill monkeys and birds.[18]

The simplest animal trap is probably the *pitfall:* a hole is dug in the ground and the whole area is covered with leaves or branches both to shield the hole from sight and to allow only fairly heavy animals to fall through into the hole. In some areas sharp stakes are driven into the bottom of the pitfall to impale the falling animal. A variety of *snares* are also constructed by primitive hunters, who set them along paths that the desired animals are known to travel. The snares may be combined with other devices to secure the trapped animal. For example, the noose may be attached to a bent sapling so that when the animal is caught he triggers the release of the sapling and is lifted into the air. The Maori of New Zealand made an unusual type of bird snare consisting of a series of nooses which were set along the limb of a tree on which bait had been placed. In the *deadfall,* a heavy weight is suspended in the air. When an animal triggers this type of mechanism, the weight falls, pinning down or killing the victim.

Cage traps of various kinds are used in Africa and Southeast Asia, particularly where bamboo is readily available. Cage traps for fish and devices known as *weirs* are made of many different materials. A weir is "any sort of fence or barrier sufficient to block a fish yet permit the passage of water."[19] They are usually built in streams, but some are built on tidelands to impound fish stranded by the outgoing tide. Wood is the usual material, but in the Arctic some weirs are constructed of stone.

Spearfishing, angling, and the use of fish rakes were all known in native North America, as was the use of fish poison; but this latter method was most highly developed in South America, where substances from about one hundred species of plants were used to stupefy or to kill fish. Among the Jivaro, for example:

18. E. R. Service, *Profiles in Ethnology* (New York: Harper and Row, 1963), p. 189. Service gives a detailed account of how the Jivaro make their blowguns.

19. Driver and Massey, *op. cit.*, p. 203.

> If the Indians are located on a large stream, they employ several devices for catching fish. Sometimes, if the water is low, a dam is constructed and a poisonous sap from the barbasco shrub distributed above the dam. As the juice permeates the water, the fish rise to the surface in a stupefied condition and are gathered by the assembled villagers. Fish are caught sometimes with rude traps and nets, or speared.[20]

Although much hunting and fishing is carried on by solitary individuals, we must not underestimate the importance of the social organization of these activities. Food collecting is often the concern of organized groups with at least some division of labor. There is archaeological evidence going back to the Upper Paleolithic of cooperative drives, in which herds of gregarious animals were surrounded and driven over cliffs or into the water to be speared by waiting hunters. In the Great Basin, long fences were sometimes constructed and antelope or rabbits were driven into enclosures. On the American Plains, in the days before the horse, fire was used to drive herds of bison into ambushes. The Pygmies of central Africa carry out cooperative hunts in which women and children drive game from over a large area into nets three hundred feet long while the men stand ready with spears.[21] Some Pygmy tribes have even bred a special variety of nonbarking dog (the Basenji, now popular in this country) to assist them in their hunting.

Men have used dogs to supplement their senses since the end of the Pleistocene. The dog was the first domesticated animal, and it functioned as a tool in the struggle for survival. The sheep, goat, and pig were the next animals to be domesticated, but they were used as sources of food and raw materials rather than as tools. Several thousand years had to pass before camels, oxen, and horses were tamed and the tools and techniques developed which made them useful as sources of energy. The role of these animals as means of transportation will be discussed in the following section.

THE NEED FOR COMMUNICATION

Man's need for communication is less obvious than the other needs discussed in this chapter, yet it ultimately derives from the same source. Body temperature must be regulated because, as the second law of thermodynamics indicates, heat tends to flow

20. Service, *op. cit.*, p. 190.
21. C. Turnbull, *The Forest People* (Garden City: Anchor Books, 1962), pp. 97–99.

Pygmy man waits ready with spear for game to be caught in net. ***American Museum of Natural History***

from the warmer to the cooler mass. Our organic controls, though superior to those of the cold-blooded reptiles, are simply not effective enough to ensure survival; therefore man has devised tools such as fire, shelter, and clothing. Similarly, because man's body is a biological system which requires at least a minimum intake of food and water, and because our ancestors relied on their brains as well as their brawn to satisfy these needs, we have in our cultural heritage such things as containers, traps, grinding tools, and weapons. Means of communication are also essential to human survival because matter, energy, and information are not naturally distributed according to man's needs and because their long-run tendency is toward disorganization (increase of entropy).

Transportation: The Transmission of Objects

The oldest and still most common form of transportation is provided by man walking, and the oldest cultural improvements in this process are paths and footwear. A path may be produced intentionally or unintentionally, but once in existence it influences the behavior of those who use it, providing a channel for their activity. Paths are not usually thought of as tools, but they do fall under our definition as portions of the material environment that have been modified for use. The path is a smooth channel through which people and objects can move. It is obvious that the nature of this channel must change with changes in the type of vehicle used: a footpath is not suitable for a ten-ton truck nor is a highway for a railroad engine; but modern-day engineers have often found aboriginal paths useful in planning the routes of new roads, since the natives' intimate knowledge of their territory enabled them to find direct and convenient routes.

Many of the world's people still go barefoot in their daily work, but in some environments footwear is highly adaptive. Sandals woven of vegetable fiber dating back several thousand years have been uncovered in caves in the Southwestern United States and Oregon. The fur-lined boots of the Eskimo and the moccasins of the American Indians provided important protection to their wearers. But perhaps the best example of adaptive footwear is the snowshoe. In many cold areas, men must have been confined to the vicinity of their winter settlements for several months during the periods of high snows until the invention of the snowshoe, "which enabled man to escape from his seasonal bondage, [and] completely changed his winter mode of life."[22] The simplest form of the snowshoe is a slab of wood or bark tied to the bottom of the foot. In the New World, this developed into the netted snowshoe: an oval frame with crosspieces of wood, skin, or rope. The ski was invented in the Old World and, for the most part, took the place of snowshoes. (A ski dated back to 2000 B.C. has been found in Sweden.)

Snowshoes and skis distribute the weight of the person wearing them over a broad area and prevent him from sinking into the snow. The *sled* solves the same adaptive problem for the transportation of material objects. Three types of sleds have been developed by northern peoples: (1) the hollowed-out tree trunk, including the boat-shaped sled, in which the sides of the trunk are extended upward with planks; (2) the plank sled, including the North American toboggan, which "consists of from two to three thin boards which are bound together edge by edge, cut off at the back and swung upward in front in a graceful curve so that they will not dig down into the snow"; and (3) the runner sled, which in its simplest form is only a pair of skilike runners connected by crossbars, but which has also given rise to an improved

22. K. Birket-Smith, *The Paths of Culture* (Madison and Milwaukee: University of Wisconsin Press, 1965), p. 215.

form, "the body of which is raised over the runners by means of uprights or curved crossbars."[23] The first two types of sleds are, like the snowshoe, adaptations to soft snow, while the third type is better adapted to ice. With their usual ingenuity, the Eskimo have developed a complex and admirable form of sled:

> For winter travel on ice and snow and even on smooth mossy tundra in summer the Eskimo use sledge and dog team. The sledge, built of whalebone, or of wood where available, is lashed together with hide thongs through holes made with a rotating stone-tipped bow drill. Guiding handles of antler are often made. The traces and harness are of hide. The runners, from five to fifteen feet long, are made of whale jaw-bone, of wood shod with ivory or whalebone strips, or even of frozen hide. The Arctic snow is often soft and powdery. In it runners will stick as if in sand unless their surfaces are very smooth and friction thereby reduced. Ice provides such a surface, but a layer of ice will not adhere firmly to wood or bone. The runners are therefore shod with a layer of frozen mud, moss, or even seal's blood to which ice does adhere closely. On to this, before setting out on a journey water is squirted from the mouth and smoothed over as it freezes. Each dog pulls on a separate hide trace which is attached above the rump to a harness of hide strips passing under its fore-limbs and round its chest. They fan out in front of the sledge, each dog picking its own way across the irregularities in the snow.[24]

The dry-land equivalent of the sled is the slide-car, known in America as the *travois.* This tool consists of "two separate poles, the back ends of which are pulled across the ground; in other cases the poles are lashed together at the front, so that the whole frame takes on the shape of a long, narrow V." The travois was used by the Plains Indians, with dogs (and later, horses) providing the source of energy, and frequently with tipi poles forming the frame. Kai Birket-Smith feels that slide-cars are ancestral to wheeled carts, pointing out that "Many primitive wagons are simply slide-cars equipped with wheels."[25] In any case, the wheeled cart is only about 6,000 years old; since it requires domesticated draft animals and reasonably good roads for effective use, the wagon is seldom used by really primitive peoples.

Transportation over the water involves the use of vehicles, and we shall use the general term *boat* for all of these. There are four basic types of boats: rafts, canoes, double boats, and plank boats. Each of these four types appears in many forms, depending on the materials used and the purposes for which the boat is designed.

The oldest means of water transport is probably the trunk of a tree. As recently as the nineteenth century, natives of some

---

23. *Ibid.*, p. 217.
24. Forde, *op. cit.*, pp. 121–122.
25. Birket-Smith, *op. cit.*, p. 218.

parts of Australia had no other boats; they would lie on a tree trunk and paddle with their hands. It is only a short step from this to a raft, which is basically a number of trunks lashed together. Rafts are found all over the world, at least as emergency vehicles; but in the absence of sails, which are less widely known, the usefulness of rafts is limited to relatively shallow, quiet waters where they can be propelled and controlled by means of long poles.

The second type of boat is the canoe, of which there are three subtypes: dugouts, bark canoes, and skin boats. A dugout is simply a tree trunk which has been hollowed out—generally with the aid of fire. Like the raft, the dugout is sometimes improved by the addition of planks to raise the sides. Simple dugout canoes, which are extremely unstable and require great skill in handling, are found all over the world and in all sizes, ranging from single-passenger models to huge boats over sixty feet long accommodating dozens of paddlers and many pounds of cargo. The bark canoe is especially useful where long portages must be made because, like the tent, a bark canoe has a large volume relative to its weight. Bark canoes were known in North and South America as well as in Africa and Australia. In northeastern North America, the combination of birch-bark canoes with extensive river systems made possible rapid long-range communication.

The skin boat is often found in regions where suitable trees are not available. A good example is the Eskimo *kayak,* which is used for summer hunting on rivers and lakes. This boat is made of seal skin tightly bound over a frame of wood or whalebone. The top is covered except for an oval hole in which the hunter sits.[26] The kayak is very fast and extremely seaworthy, propelled only by a double-bladed paddle. The Greenland Eskimo often lace their watertight skin coats to the kayak hole; they are able to capsize and right themselves with ease, without getting wet. The Eskimo also have a skin-covered open boat, the *umiak,* which can handle several passengers; it is used for travel and for whaling.

All these light boats are propelled by paddles, though the umiak is sometimes powered by sails. The paddle is fundamentally a lever used to apply force to the water so that the equal and opposite reaction propels the boat in the desired direction. Sails, on the other hand, intercept the force of the wind and transmit it through the mast to the body of the boat. For long-distance ocean travel without mechanical sources of power, sails are essential; but there must also be improvements made to increase the stability of the boat. One way of adding to both the stability and capacity of a boat is to lash two craft together. The double boat

26. Forde, *op. cit.*, p. 123.

Eskimos launch a umiak, a boat covered with walrus skin. ***Dr. George Gerster/Rapho Guillumette***

is simply a pair of canoes joined together by crossbeams on which a platform is constructed. A variant of this is the outrigger canoe, in which a beam of light wood is connected to the canoe so that it rests on the surface of the water parallel to the body of the boat. The Polynesians and other inhabitants of the Pacific Islands made extensive sea voyages with boats of this type.

Although double boats and outrigger canoes are much more stable than the simple dugout, they still have a very limited capacity. The plank boat, however, is capable of nearly unlimited growth; it "unites seaworthiness with increased cargo capacity."[27] With the advent of the plank boat, compound sails, and the rudder, we have most of the elements involved in shipbuilding until the eighteenth century. Then, in a few short years, the development

27. Birket-Smith, *op. cit.*, p. 226.

of the steam engine and its application to ships brought about a revolution in water transportation. These topics, however, are outside the scope of the present chapter.

Communication: The Transmission of Messages

There is a biological basis to the human need for interpersonal communication. From the standpoint of adaptation, it must be obvious that (other things being equal) a species or group that can transmit and store complex messages has a selective advantage over one that cannot. But the need goes even deeper than this: there is ample experimental evidence that infants who are deprived of tactile stimulation (the earliest form of communication being through the sense of touch) deteriorate and eventually die.[28] There is, then, a biological need for social contact. Early in life, the contact (stimulus) must be physical and emotional. A warm, loving mother (or mother substitute) engaged in frequent (mutual) communication with her child is essential to healthy development. But adults too suffer mental and physical disturbances if they are deprived of sensory stimulation for long (as in solitary confinement). Such facts led Eric Berne to say that "a biological chain may be postulated leading from emotional and sensory deprivation through apathy to degenerative changes and death. In this sense, stimulus-hunger has the same relationship to the survival of the human organism as food-hunger."[29]

Through the process of enculturation, the individual is persuaded to give up (or at least compromise with) his desire for the kind of physical intimacy he experienced as an infant. "He learns to do with more subtle, even symbolic, forms of handling, until the merest nod of recognition may serve the purpose to some extent, although *his original craving for physical contact may remain unabated.*"[30] As a psychiatrist, Berne was concerned with the pathological ways in which individuals try to satisfy this persistent need. Our focus, however, will be upon the kinds of tools that men have devised to augment their capacity for social communication.

There are, of course, forms of human communication not based upon speech. We *receive* information through all five senses—perhaps more. But we can *transmit* information about tastes, smells, and tactile sensations only insofar as it can be

28. L. K. Frank, "Tactile Communication," *Genetic Psychology Monographs*, Vol. 56 (1957), pp. 209–255. See also M. F. Ashley Montagu, *The Direction of Human Development* (New York: Harper, 1955).
29. E. Berne, *Games People Play* (New York: Grove Press, 1964), p. 14.
30. *Ibid.* (italics added).

transformed into visual or auditory stimuli. Speech is certainly the principal means of human communication, and in many of its functions, *speech is a tool.* It enables man to transmit information through space, by means of modulated sound waves, in order to produce objective changes in his environment.[31]

From this viewpoint, we can see most other forms of communication as tools for transmitting or storing information in situations where direct speech is not possible. Sign languages, drum signals, smoke signals, semaphore codes, and writing are all devices invented by man as substitutes for speech. The primacy of speech has been eloquently asserted by Robert A. Hall, Jr.:

> Speaking is an activity that we learn in our earliest childhood. . . . Writing, on the other hand, is an activity that we always learn *after* we learn to speak, if we learn it at all. . . . Moreover, writing is a derivative of speech; that is to say, the symbols we use (whether they are hieroglyphs, cuneiform signs or letters) are always based on speech, directly or indirectly, and are a more or less complete and accurate representation of speech. . . . There are other ways of communication, such as Morse telegraphic code or various cyphers, which in their turn are based on writing—and therefore, through writing, ultimately on speech. Even the so-called "gesture language" of the Plains Indians, to say nothing of the "finger language" of deaf-mutes, is ultimately based on speech.[32]

In Africa, Middle and South America, and the Pacific we find a variety of drum, gong, and whistle languages. These forms replace direct speech in certain ritual or interpersonal settings and are also used to transmit messages over considerable distances. They are found particularly (though not exclusively) in groups having tone languages—linguistic systems employing contrastive pitch phonemes. In a true drum or gong language, the player reproduces selected characteristics of the spoken message. In theory (if not in practice) any message could be sent by these systems; this distinguishes them from simple arbitrary codes which signal only a limited number of messages (for example, "When I shoot twice, you set fire to the barn.").

Among the Jabo of eastern Liberia, a variety of instruments are used for signaling specific messages. One of the Jabo's instruments is used in this way:

> *The wooden signal-drum or* "slit drum" consists of a hollowed-out tree-trunk with a longitudinal slit, the lips of which vary in thickness

---

31. The functions of speech are many and complex. This statement applies primarily to speech considered as a part of human technological systems. Compare D. Hymes, "The Ethnography of Speaking," pp. 13–53 in *Anthropology and Human Behavior* (Washington, D.C.: The Anthropological Society of Washington, 1962).

32. R. A. Hall, Jr., *Linguistics and Your Language* (Garden City, N.Y.: Anchor Books, 1960), pp. 32–33.

> between themselves and in different places of the same lip, thus producing a number of points for producing various tones. Two straight sticks are used for beating. . . . The drums are the property of the military and policing organization of the town which includes all males, and which holds periodic assemblies and social gatherings. The drummer, a regular official of this organization, signals to a distance when he summons a member who may be in the fields to come to the village, or when an assembly is called unexpectedly. But the main duty of this drum is to serve somewhat like a chairman's gavel. The drummer regulates the meeting; he calls for order or dismisses the meeting, and so on, with special signals.[33]

Among the musical instruments used in various parts of the world for signaling are whistles, horns, flutes, musical bows, drums, gongs, and xylophones. All of these are used to *transmit messages through space.* But when the problem is to *store information over time,* different kinds of devices must be used.[34] The simplest examples are standardized ways of blazing a trail or indicating which branch has been followed. These shade into simple picture symbols or signs used to communicate a limited number of messages when scratched on rocks, bark, or hide. Tally sticks, used to keep track of the score in a competition or to mark the time until a scheduled event, also fall into this category.

A more complex form of information storage is found in the quipu, or knot record, employed by the Indians of Peru. This was a tool which preserved information (mainly numerical) in the form of knots tied in a series of colored hanging cords. It was used in connection with temple accounts and seems to have been unique to South America.

Prior to the information revolution of the present century, *writing* was the most remarkable tool devised by man for the storage and transmission of information.[35] The basic nature of writing is an encoding of speech into more or less permanent, visual forms. Thus, writing functions as a container for information. A. L. Kroeber speaks of three stages which may be distinguished in the development of writing:

> The first is the use of pictures of things and actions, and, derived from these, pictorial symbols for qualities and abstractions. This is the pictographic and then the picto-ideographic method. In the second stage the representation of sounds begins, but is made through pic-

33. G. Herzog, "Drum-Signaling in a West African Tribe," in D. Hymes, ed., *Language in Culture and Society* (New York: Harper and Row, 1964), p. 313.
34. In the first edition of this book (New York: Knopf, 1969), pp. 223–225, a distinction was made between two basic tool types, the *container* which stores matter, energy, or information over time, and the *medium* which transmits matter, energy, or information through space. The presentation of this basic tool typology has been removed from the second edition but it has been retained as an organizing device, as this paragraph clearly shows.
35. The history of writing and the alphabet are traced in fascinating detail in Kroeber, *op. cit.*, pp. 509–537. This chapter should be required reading for anyone interested in the history of culture.

tures or abbreviations of pictures; and pictures or ideographs as such continue to be used alongside the pictures whose value is phonetic. This may be called the mixed or transitional or rebus stage. Third is the phonetic phase. In this, the symbols used, whatever their origin may have been, no longer denote objects or ideas but are merely signs for sounds—words, syllables, or the elemental letter sounds.[36]

An alphabet is a system of writing of the third type, whose symbols correspond (more or less) to the significant sounds of the spoken language (its phonemes). As was discussed in Chapter 2, the English alphabet is far from being a reliable guide to our sound system, but other alphabets (as, for example, the Russian) employ letters that correspond quite closely to the spoken phonemes. In any case, alphabetical writing makes possible the visual representation of the essential elements of speech in a compact form. Its adaptive significance for complex societies is self-evident, for such societies must store and transmit vast quantities of information.

According to Kroeber, it is notable that "all the alphabetic systems that now prevail in nearly every part of the earth—Roman, Greek, Hebrew, Arabic, Indian, as well as many that have become extinct—can be traced to a single source."[37] This first alphabet was then borrowed, reinterpreted, subjected to all the processes of invention (omission, substitution, combination, and so forth), and borrowed again, to the point that it can serve as a model of cultural diffusion and change.

Modern developments in the communication of goods, persons, and information have made possible, for the first time in man's history, a world-wide network of communication. Since social groups are in part defined by the existence of stable patterns of communication among their members, this development could ultimately shatter the conventional cultural boundaries which divide man from man and nation from nation.[38] A world society is now possible. But this does not mean that such a society will necessarily come into being, for there are also strong social forces opposed to such unification. Not the least of these is the process of enculturation itself, for this process must take place within a relatively small group. Each child must learn a particular set of cultural and linguistic rules in the context of a specific family and local community. This means that his primary social and emotional allegiance is necessarily directed to a small group and its provincial traditions. These local allegiances can, to some extent,

36. *Ibid.*, p. 510.
37. *Ibid.*, p. 514.
38. G. C. Homans, *The Human Group* (New York: Harcourt, Brace, 1950), p. 84. See R. J. Lifton, *Boundaries: Psychological Man in Revolution* (New York: Vintage Books, 1970) for an insightful discussion of what happens when various types of boundaries break down too quickly.

Modern communications system: closed-circuit television instruction in Niger, Africa. ***UN/UNESCO/RACCAH Studio***

be weakened and superseded by wider loyalties later in life; but they are never completely dissolved, and consciously or unconsciously, they continue to shape our behavior. (See Epilogue.)

The mass media and modern methods of rapid transportation are perhaps the most important forces now operating to bind together human groups; they increase both the mutual awareness of men and their interdependence. But whether we are concerned with contemporary society or the culture of "primitives," a careful examination of the means of communication is of the utmost importance. It is only by communicating that men can come to share the categories and plans which make possible smooth interaction and genuinely adaptive behavior. In an age when a single misunderstanding could lead to the destruction of humanity, it is not difficult to see the hot line between Washington and Moscow as a tool essential to the survival of mankind.

RECOMMENDED READING

Birket-Smith, K., *Primitive Man and His Ways.* New York: Mentor Books, 1963. A good, brief introduction to culture history with primary attention to the adaptive functions of technology.

Forde, C. D., *Habitat, Economy and Society.* New York: Dutton, 1963. Standard account of primitive technologies in their geographic and social settings.

Roszak, T., *The Making of a Counter-Culture.* Garden City, N.Y.: Anchor Books, 1969. Exciting examination of current cultural movements in the United States, showing many phenomena to be extreme reactions against a mechanized, "technocratic" society.

Spier, R., *From the Hand of Man: Primitive and Preindustrial Technologies.* Boston: Houghton Mifflin, 1970. A clear explanation of how tools are made and how they work.

Usher, A. P., *A History of Mechanical Inventions.* Cambridge: Harvard University Press, 1954. A careful study of technological innovations in relation to economic history.

CHAPTER 9
Techniques and Skills

In the last chapter we deliberately but artificially separated tools from the techniques and skills employed in making and using them. This is somewhat like the earlier separation of social structure from social organization, because such an approach to tools gives a static view of technology. In the present chapter we shall discuss the relationships among tools, techniques, and skills, showing the place of each within the technological system.

A *technique* is *a set of plans believed to achieve a given end.* Some techniques require the use of tools external to the human body. Thus, if I wish to drive a nail, I must find a hammer, must hold it in a certain way, and must strike the head of the nail with the head of the hammer (taking care to remove my thumb), because the carpentry techniques that I have learned require these actions. The difference between my hammering and that of a professional carpenter is primarily a matter of skill. By a *skill* is meant *the acquired ability to apply a given technique effectively and readily.* One either knows or does not know a technique; but persons who share the same technical knowledge may employ it with varying degrees of skill.

Some techniques do not require the use of any external tools. Swimming, for example, can be performed without any tools, though many devices are now available to augment man's swimming abilities, from rubber flippers to scuba tanks. The adaptive significance of techniques is the same as that of tools: it is easy to see how the technique of swimming would be valuable to human groups in many environments. Indeed, of the two, techniques are more basic than tools since they include knowledge of how to make the tools. In the short run, this may not be apparent: given the need to drive a nail in a hurry, what I want is a real hammer, rather than knowledge of how to make one. But in the long run, techniques are more fundamental, for material objects do not last forever, and a complex tool is of no use to a person who does not know how to operate it. If all of man's tools were to evaporate tomorrow there would be chaos, but civilization could eventually be rebuilt; however, if all techniques were suddenly forgotten, our species would probably become extinct before the techniques could all be rediscovered.

The dependence of human society upon culture (learned techniques) was clearly stated by Benjamin D. Paul:

> If all mankind were suddenly annihilated except for a contemporary Adam and Eve, whole in body and brain but without the benefit of socially-transmitted learning, these two human animals would be quite incapable of regenerating a society remotely resembling any now known to us. Even if they could survive and leave progeny, it would take tedious thousands of human generations to rediscover the ways and wisdom needed to run any human society now in existence.[1]

The skill component, though often neglected in discussion of technological systems, is also of great importance. Clearly, skill can only develop on a foundation of technical knowledge. But consider the case of a linguist who has compiled a grammar and dictionary of some language trying to converse with a native speaker of the language. Though both of them may possess equivalent knowledge of the language system, it will be a long time (if ever) before the linguist achieves the fluency in speech of the native—that is, before he can apply his knowledge effectively and readily. The same holds for any technique, be it woodworking, athletics, or even science:

> Craftsmanship tends to survive in closely circumscribed local traditions. Indeed, the diffusion of crafts from one country to another can often be traced to the migration of groups of craftsmen . . . [and] an art which has fallen into disuse for the period of a generation is altogether lost. . . . These losses are usually irretrievable. It is pathetic to watch the endless efforts—equipped with microscopy and chemistry, with mathematics and electronics—to reproduce a single violin of the kind the half-literate Stradivarius turned out as a matter of routine more than 200 years ago.[2]

---

1. B. D. Paul, "The Cultural Context of Health Education," *Symposium Proceedings* (Pittsburgh: University of Pittsburgh School of Social Work, 1953), p. 31.
2. M. Polanyi, *Personal Knowledge* (New York: Harper Torchbooks, 1964), p. 53.

Most skills involve activities—both muscular and intellectual—of which the performer is largely unaware and which he cannot put into words with any precision. Complex skills can be learned only by long, intimate association with persons who have already mastered them—by apprenticeship. (This is another cause of the local allegiances discussed at the end of the last chapter.) Even when general rules or maxims can be formulated, they are mainly of use to persons who have already acquired a high degree of unspecifiable skill: it is the advanced chess player, not the beginner, who can really benefit from an evening with Bobby Fischer.

By definition, a technique is directed toward some goal, such as keeping warm, getting food, healing a sick person, or building a canoe. People use a technique because they believe it will enable them to achieve the end they desire. Sometimes they are mistaken—the technique may be invalid or inappropriate to the end in view. For example, some people open the doors of their refrigerators in order to cool off their kitchens; this technique is invalid because it is based on a misunderstanding of the nature of heat exchange. The device which cools the interior of the refrigerator also discharges heat into the room, so opening the door only makes this device work harder at heating the room. Similarly, some people fire guns in the air to drive plagues away from their villages; so far as we know, this does not affect the course of epidemics. In other cases, the chosen technique may be valid, but the performers lack the skill necessary to make it effective; it *is possible* to make a fire by rubbing two sticks together, but a person can freeze to death while developing the necessary skill.

It must also be remembered that *all techniques involve a cost* (in time, energy, resources, and so forth). The decision as to whether a given end is worth the cost can only be resolved within a particular social and cultural context and through the processes of social organization. Given two or more techniques that are thought to produce the same results, the choice between them is not always obvious. Even if we assume that people are usually rational, this does not mean that they will always choose the most immediately *efficient* technique.

In the remainder of this chapter, the techniques considered will be grouped according to the general ends toward which they are directed. Members of different societies evaluate *specific ends* differently: one group may think that corn is the ideal food, while another favors acorns or taro or bison meat. But there are some general *kinds of ends* (such as good health and sufficient food) that are sought in every society and for which techniques will always be provided by the culture. The four groupings of techniques which we shall discuss have to do, respectively, with harnessing energy, getting food, healing sickness, and making useful objects.

TECHNIQUES FOR HARNESSING ENERGY

In our discussion of types of tools it was assumed that some *source of energy* was available to operate the tool. However, societies differ vastly in the amounts and kinds of energy which are available to them and in their abilities to convert one form of energy into another, more useful form. In this section we shall survey major sources of energy that have been used by human beings in adapting to their physical environments.

Human muscle power is the most ancient and still the most widespread source of energy available to men. It has been estimated that the average man, if he is adequately nourished, can do work equivalent to one-twentieth of a horsepower (for the source of muscular energy is food intake—see below). Men can apply their muscular energy in a wide variety of ways—pushing, pulling, lifting, carrying, and so forth—and the effectiveness of these actions can be augmented by a variety of tools; but the actual output of energy varies within rather narrow limits.

A man's endurance or the effectiveness of his actions can, of course, be improved by training and practice. These are matters of skill, and though there are considerable individual differences in speed or strength, the development of these abilities is a matter of culture. Thus the four-minute mile, which was once a dream, has become a commonplace. Clearly, in societies where men must track game from morning to night, the endurance of the average individual will far surpass that of a deskbound office worker from another society. But in every population there will be a distinctive range of skills produced by the interaction of innate ability with experience.

The effectiveness of group activities may be improved by the use of *cooperative techniques* which enable group members to coordinate their efforts, either by pulling together or by dividing the labor so that each person does that task for which his abilities best fit him. Learned techniques of tool utilization—how to wield an axe or throw a spear—also contribute to the effective employment of human muscle power. But even with the best possible tools and techniques, a society with no source of energy other than human muscles must be limited in its accomplishments.

Leslie A. White has attempted to show that the cultural development of a society is a function of the amount of energy harnessed and the effectiveness of the tools used. According to White, the "basic law of cultural evolution" is:

> Other factors remaining constant, *culture evolves as the amount of energy harnessed per capita per year is increased, or as the efficiency of the instrumental means of putting the energy to work is increased.* Both factors may increase simultaneously of course. . . . But this does not mean that the tool and energy factors are of equal weight and significance. The energy factor is the primary and basic one; it is the prime mover, the active agent. Tools are merely the means that serve this power. The energy factor may be increased indefinitely; the efficiency of the tool only within limits. . . . When these limits have been reached, no further increases in efficiency can make up for a lack of increase in amount of energy harnessed. . . . And, since increase of energy fosters improvement of tools, one may say that it is energy that, at bottom, carries the culture process onward and upward.[3]

Aside from fire, the earliest energy source used to supplement human muscles was the muscle power of other animals. Once a suitable animal has been domesticated, its muscle power may be applied to certain tools. But this application requires the invention or discovery of still other tools—for example, the harnesses and traces used with the Eskimo dog sled, or the yokes, collars, and reins used with other beasts of burden. Also, new techniques for training and handling the animals must be developed: it was a brave man who first mounted a horse.

Once the mediating technology is developed, however, animal power makes many other developments possible. The speed of transportation may be vastly increased; monotonous and fatiguing tasks (such as pumping water) can be assigned to animals; or the beasts may be used for pulling plows or wagons, trampling grain, or lifting weights. Each of these inventions opens up many possibilities for cultural development, but in each case, the *advantages* of a new technique must be balanced against its *cost*. For example, draft animals or beasts of burden cannot be killed for food; rather, they must be fed. If they are to be useful, they require a regular supply of food and water, as well as considerable attention, time, and protection. Only a group which has a fairly reliable food surplus can make effective use of animal power.

Within our solar system, the sun is the ultimate source of all the kinetic and potential energy that man can use. Kinetic energy is also available in the form of moving fluids (wind or water), but these can be harnessed only with the assistance of tools. The water wheel and the windmill have long been used to capture and convert these forms of energy, as have boats with and without sails.

3. L. A. White, *The Science of Culture* (New York: Grove Press, 1949), pp. 368–369, 375–376.

Electrical energy occurs in nature primarily in the form of lightning, but lightning is too powerful and unpredictable to have been helpful to early men (though occasionally it may have started a fire that they could use). It is only in the last hundred years or so that devices such as hydroelectric generators have been invented to convert other kinds of kinetic energy into electricity. Future developments of this kind will doubtless involve the utilization of nuclear energy and tidal power as well as the direct conversion of solar radiation into electricity. But for the present, as in the past, man is primarily dependent upon the potential energy stored in wood and the fossil fuels.

Plants capture solar energy and, through photosynthesis, convert it into a form that man can burn either within his body (as food) or without (as fuel). The decomposition of ancient plants yields the fossil fuels—coal, oil, and natural gas—while the digestion of food plants produces the animal fats and oils which are used by some groups as fuels. The energy stored in fuels is released by controlled oxidation (usually fire), and fire must be started by the local application of heat (kindling).

A few human groups do not possess any kindling techniques. For example, Allan Holmberg reports:

> Fire making is a lost art among the Siriono [of eastern Bolivia]. I was told by my older informants that fire (*táta*) used to be made by twirling a stick between the hands, but not once did I see it generated in this fashion. Fire is carried from camp to camp in a brand consisting of a spadix of a palm. This spongelike wood holds fire for long periods of time. When the band is traveling, at least one woman from every extended family carries fire along. I have even seen women swimming rivers with a firebrand, holding it above the water in one hand while paddling with the other.[4]

Knowledge of kindling techniques and skill in applying them are obviously of great importance to the survival of man. Only a few peoples are known who do not possess these skills (the Siriono, the Andaman Islanders, and certain African Pygmy groups); but chances are they have only forgotten the techniques. This could happen because all peoples seem to prefer keeping a fire going to kindling it over and over.

The basic kindling techniques are simple but, as noted above, they do require skill. Rubbing two sticks together will produce a fire only if the sticks are dry enough and if they are rubbed in the proper way. A stick may also be twirled rapidly between the palms with its end resting in a hole surrounded with tinder; eventually a

4. A. R. Holmberg, *Nomads of the Long Bow* (Chicago: University of Chicago Press, 1960), p. 11.

flame will be produced. This process is accelerated by using a bowdrill. The fire-plow consists of a grooved board and another, somewhat harder stick which is rubbed back and forth in the groove until the surrounding tinder catches fire. The modern match is really a chemical version of this converter.

Still another ingenious device is the fire-piston, found in Indochina and parts of Indonesia. It consists of a wooden cylinder enclosing a tight-fitting piston; when the piston is sharply struck, it compresses the air in the container, raising its temperature high enough to ignite the tinder at the bottom. Another technique makes use of "two split pieces of bamboo or a single piece of bamboo and a strip of cane, the one of which 'saws' in a cross-groove in the other. It is native to a comparatively limited area extending across parts of India, Indonesia, New Guinea, and Australia."[5] Finally, the strike-a-light is any device that yields by percussion a spark which can be nursed into a flame. Sparking stones were probably discovered accidentally by early tool-

Fire, the earliest energy source. *John Nance/Magnum*

5. K. Birket-Smith, *The Paths of Culture* (Madison and Milwaukee: University of Wisconsin Press, 1965), p. 70.

makers, since flint was one of the materials favored by Paleolithic man. In most areas, the combination of flint and steel has replaced earlier materials; it is found today in the cigarette lighter.

Whatever technique of kindling is used, maintaining a fire requires the recognition and preparation of satisfactory tinder and firewood (or other fuels). Also, if fire is to be useful to a human group, there must be techniques for controlling and applying it as desired. Fire can be used directly for heat, light, and some kinds of cooking (roasting); but supplementary tools and techniques are necessary for other uses of fire. We have already described the technique of stone boiling in some detail (p. 250); Sir Edward Tylor first identified this technique and traced its world-wide distribution.

Baking food in a pit or in an earth-oven also seems to be a very ancient cooking technique. The techniques of drying and smoking are especially useful to hunting and fishing peoples who must preserve a part of their seasonal surplus for harder times. With the invention of fireproof containers (ceramic and metal), the uses to which fire could be put were greatly increased. Techniques for intensifying the heat of a fire were important to the development of metallurgy (see below). Finally, the discovery and use of the fossil fuels made available, in compact form, quantities of potential energy which have made possible our modern industrial society. In the words of Leslie A. White:

> Until the beginning of the Fuel Age, about A.D. 1800, no culture of the Old World surpassed, in any profound and comprehensive way, the highest levels achieved in the Bronze Age. . . . And it is reasonable to suppose that culture never would have exceeded the peaks already achieved by this time had not some way been devised to harness additional amounts of energy. . . . A way was found, however, to do this: energy in the form of coal, and later, oil and gas, was harnessed by means of steam and internal combustion engines. By tapping the vast deposits of coal, oil and natural gas, a tremendous increase in the amount of energy available for culture building was quickly effected. The consequences of the Fuel Revolution were in general much like those of the Agricultural Revolution: an increase in population, larger political units, bigger cities, an accumulation of wealth, a rapid development of the arts and sciences, in short, a rapid and extensive advance of culture as a whole.[6]

Now, in this century, man has succeeded in tapping a new and immensely powerful form of energy in the nucleus of the atom; but whether this will initiate a great new cultural advance or the end of mankind remains to be seen. It seems ominous, however, that the techniques for destructive use of atomic energy

6. White, *op. cit.*, pp. 373–374.

have thus far been developed far more quickly than techniques for its peaceful employment.

This section would not be complete without some discussion of the notion of spiritual energy. By this we mean forms of energy other than those recognized by modern physics. Most human groups have beliefs which we would consider supernatural, though the members of these groups do not necessarily separate these in any consistent manner from the rest of their belief systems (see Introduction to Part Six). Included in many technologies, then, are techniques for harnessing spiritual energy. Such techniques do often have some observable effects on the course of events, but the effects are seldom those expected by the persons employing the techniques.[7]

Techniques for harnessing spiritual power include familiar types of behavior such as prayer, sacrifice, divination, ritual, and the use of amulets or fetishes, as well as those more direct attempts to control the supernatural usually referred to as magic. In every known society we find the belief that *verbal formulas* can affect persons, objects, or future events, provided that the correct formula is spoken or chanted in the proper manner. Many magical procedures simply involve the use of a formula that is believed to produce its effects automatically. But usually there are other features as well. Sir James Frazer distinguished two main types.[8] *Imitative magic* refers to those procedures in which the desired end is depicted or acted out, as when hunters shoot arrows at an image of their prey before setting out on a hunt. *Contagious magic* requires that some portion of a person (such as his hair or nails) or a substance which has been associated with him (food or clothing) be obtained; this material is then subjected to a procedure believed to affect the person in a similar manner—killing him, curing him, or causing him to fall in love. The ingredients in a magical procedure may also be used in the belief that their attributes (potency, speed, beauty, and so forth) will be transferred to the object of the procedure.

In most societies, spiritual and nonspiritual techniques are closely intertwined. As B. Malinowski pointed out, men tend to employ spiritual techniques in addition to their physical efforts whenever the outcome of these efforts is *uncertain*.[9] The gardener does not simply perform his magic and then sit back, waiting for his crop to grow. He knows that he must plant, weed, cultivate, and harvest; but he also knows that the yield of his garden is

---

7. For a fascinating example of the indirect adaptive functions of ritual procedures see Roy A. Rappaport, "Ritual Regulation of Environmental Relations among a New Guinea People," *Ethnology*, Vol. 6 (1967), pp. 17–30.

8. J. Frazer, *The Golden Bough* (abridged edition; New York: Macmillan, 1953), pp. 12–52.

9. B. Malinowski, *Magic, Science and Religion* (Garden City: Anchor Books, 1955), pp. 79–87.

affected by forces beyond his control. Similarly, the Trobriand sailor knows that there are few dangers within the peaceful lagoon. But when he ventures out onto the open sea, he recognizes the limitations of his boat and of his skills, and it is here that fishing spells and canoe and trading magic become important to him.

Wherever uncertainty and anxiety enter into human life, spiritual techniques flourish. From the anthropological point of view, it is more important to understand the role that these techniques play in a society than to criticize their premises as magical or irrational. Certainly, if a group sincerely believes in the existence of spiritual powers, it would be the height of foolishness for its members not to try to establish contact with or control over these powers. In any case, it seems clear that these techniques do something for the groups using them. Whether the effects are psychological (relieving anxiety or increasing individual confidence) or sociological (coordinating group efforts or promoting social integration), the fact remains that all human societies have developed some such beliefs and procedures.

TECHNIQUES FOR GETTING FOOD: SUBSISTENCE

In this section we shall survey the development of techniques for getting food as revealed by the archaeological record and by contemporary ethnographic studies.

Food Collecting: Hunting, Fishing, and Gathering

Only a minute proportion of the world's peoples lives today solely by food collecting. It is important for us to realize that until approximately 10,000 years ago *all* men engaged in this way of life and no other way was known. The total human population at that time was less than that of New York City today. But the fact that the technique of food collecting is ancient does not mean that it is simple. The collection and utilization of wild foods require considerable knowledge and skill. For example, among the Tiwi, early each morning, the women

> scattered in every direction from the camp with baskets and/or babies on their backs, to spend the day gathering food, chiefly vegetable foods, grubs, worms, and anything else edible. Since they had spent their lives doing it, the old women know all about gathering and preparing vegetable foods, and they supervised the younger women. This was one important reason for men marrying widows, and even a man with many young wives was quite likely to remarry an elderly

widow or two nonetheless. A husband with only young wives might have a satisfactory sex life, but he still needed a household manager if he wished to eat well.[10]

Similar patterns of hunting (by men) and gathering of wild vegetable foods (by women) have been noted in hunting and gathering groups throughout the world. Recent studies of surviving groups such as the Bushmen of South Africa indicate that the contribution of the women to the diet of the group is often more important than that of the men, even though the techniques the women use are less dramatic.[11]

The *subsistence techniques* of a hunting and gathering group consist of their *categories of useful plants and animals* and the *plans for locating, capturing, preparing, and consuming each type.*

A family returns from the hunt in Ecuador. ***Cornell Capa/Magnum***

10. C. W. M. Hart and A. Pilling, *The Tiwi of North Australia* (New York: Holt, Rinehart and Winston, 1960), p. 33.
11. R. Lee and I. DeVore, eds., *Man the Hunter* (Chicago: Aldine Publishing Company, 1968). See also E. Service, *The Hunters* (Englewood Cliffs, N.J.: Prentice-Hall, 1968).

Thus, wherever a group is largely dependent on the hunting skills of its men, it is essential that the hunters be familiar with their territory and with the characteristics of local animals. Adequate tools are certainly important to this process, but the knowledge and skill of the hunters are primary.

Among hunters the needs for knowledge of a territory and for highly developed cooperation are important determinants of social structure. Julian H. Steward has suggested that "in most parts of the world subsistence patterns required sufficient regularity of cooperation and leadership to give definite form and stability to multifamily social groups." He has tried to show that the essential features of certain widespread types of social groups have been produced by similar patterns of adaptation to the environment. For example, the *patrilineal band* is characterized by patrilocal residence, exogamy, and communal land ownership. The patrilineal band is found among groups such as the Bushmen, the Pygmies, the Australian aborigines, the Semang, and the Ona Indians of Tierra del Fuego. These groups differ from one another in many ways, but according to Steward, they share a common "cultural core" as a result of their adaptation to similar environments:

> The environments of the patrilineal bands were similar in that, first, they had limited and scattered food resources, which not only restricted population to a low density but which prevented it from assembling in large, permanent aggregates. Second, the principal food resource was game, which unlike wild seeds, may be profitably taken collectively. Third, the game occurred in small, nonmigratory bands rather than in large, migratory herds. This kind of game can support only small aggregates of people, who remain within a restricted territory.[12]

Under other environmental conditions and with different subsistence technologies, different forms of social structure become more likely. Steward has proposed, for example, that where the principal game hunted occurs in large, migratory herds, the *composite band* is often found. This type of social group consists of many unrelated nuclear families which are "integrated to form villages or bands of hunters, fishers, gatherers and simple farmers on the basis of constant association and co-operation rather than of actual or alleged kinship."[13] Steward's ideas about the relationships between subsistence techniques and social organization have been challenged on some points, but his description of the patrilineal band fits well with a considerable body of ethnographic data.

---

12. J. Steward, *Theory of Culture Change* (Urbana: University of Illinois Press, 1955), pp. 122–124. Dr. Steward died in 1972.
13. *Ibid.*, p. 143.

Food collectors are seldom content just to take from nature what they can find. All such groups make attempts to ensure or to augment their food supply by a variety of physical and/or spiritual techniques. For example, the Paiute Indians of Owens Valley had no domesticated plants; nevertheless, they did a certain amount of irrigating to encourage the growth of wild plants. Other gathering groups sometimes fenced off areas where favorite wild foods were growing in an attempt to keep them safe from animals until they could be harvested.

There is a widely held belief among hunting peoples that game is under the control of a supernatural protector who, if offended, will withhold further opportunities from the offending hunters. This animal master is often pictured in folk tales as an exceptionally large member of the species, one who can also take on human form. He may be offended in many ways: by a waste of food, by improper words or deeds, or by mistreatment of the blood or bones of "his" species. Fortunately, in most cases he can also be placated by the performance of appropriate rituals. It is entirely understandable that hunters, whose success depends upon many unpredictable factors, should seek to explain fluctuations in their success as the result of supernatural whim. Certainly, the notion of an animal master is no more incredible than many of the tales told by modern weekend hunters and fishermen to explain their successes or failures. Indeed, the animal master, totemism, and similar beliefs form part of an integrated world view in which men and animals are conceived of as much closer and more equal than most Americans think of them.

Many hunting peoples also participate in *increase rites*—ritual techniques intended to assure a continuing supply of game or other wild foods. Among the Australian aborigines, complicated increase rites are an important part of many tribal ceremonies. Each Arunta totemic group carries out great ceremonials called *mbanbiuma* to promote the increase of its totem species. These ceremonies are usually held

> at the time of year at which the particular totem species produces fruit or seed or gives birth to its young. The ceremonies of each group differ greatly from one another in detail, but in all of them the following features are common:
>
> 1. The heart of the ceremony is the special and very detailed ritual performance which helps increase the numbers of the totem species.
> 2. The inkata [caretaker of the local group's totemic center] must eat a little of the species, as a sort of communion service.
> 3. Then the other members of the group ritually and sparingly eat a little of it.

4. After this, other people who are present (but who have not witnessed the secret ceremony) feast freely on the totem.[14]

The requirement that certain groups avoid touching or consuming a species, item, or substance is known as a *taboo.* In some Australian societies, the totem animal of a person's group is completely taboo to him; he may kill or capture it, but he must never eat it himself lest the entire species perish. Here we find a special type of division of labor, since as a consequence of this rule, members of different totem groups are forced to exchange food with one another, just as the rule of exogamy forces them to exchange women.

In many North American hunting societies, menstrual blood was taboo to the old, the sick, and the hunters; generally, a hunter kept himself and his hunting equipment far away from all menstruating women for fear of losing his luck. For many tribes of the Great Plains, the Sun Dance was an increase rite intended to ensure success in buffalo hunting, and, at least among the Southern Ute, to this day menstruating women are not allowed inside the dance lodge.[15]

In one direction, increase rites shade into the fertility rites of agriculturalists, while in the other they are allied to food taboos observed by members of all societies. For example, there is a widespread taboo in our society against eating oysters during the period from May through August. Most Americans believe that serious illness would result from violating this taboo. Actually, the months without an *r* constitute the period during which oysters are most delicious, and absolutely no harm follows their consumption. This fact is well known to gourmets and to oyster dealers; but the dealers also know that the summer months are the breeding period of these mollusks. Thus, by perpetuating this seasonal taboo, they indirectly ensure the increase of the species upon which their livelihoods depend.

Food Producing: Horticulture, Agriculture, and Pastoralism

Starting about 10,000 years ago, men in several different parts of the world began to cultivate plants and to tame animals. The transition from food collecting to food production was gradual; wild foods remained an important supplement to domesticated types until food production had become highly efficient. This

14. E. R. Service, *Profiles in Ethnology* (New York: Harper and Row, 1963), p. 19.
15. See P. K. Bock, "Love Magic, Menstrual Taboos, and the Facts of Geography," *American Anthropologist,* Vol 69 (1967), pp. 213–217.

transition was less a matter of new tools than of new knowledge: the crude sickles, axes, and grinding stones used by food gatherers were easily adapted to the new economy, while the digging stick served as a hoe, and fire as a tool with many functions. But each new species brought under domestication was a triumph of practical knowledge and came as the result of hundreds of years of experimentation. It is a tribute to our prehistoric ancestors that though the ancient breeds have been much improved by modern technology, *no significant new food crops have been domesticated in the last 2,000 years.*

There are many theories about the origin of cultivation. These need not concern us here except to note that there appear to have been several independent centers of development in both the Old and the New World. For example, a seed-planting tradition based on wheat and barley spread from its Middle Eastern origin into Egypt, Europe, and Southwest Asia. Another seed-planting tradition based on rice spread in all directions from its probable area of origin in Southeast Asia. In the New World, the maize-planting techniques seem to have originated in Middle America. But there was also an apparently independent center of cultivation of root crops in South America; there, the techniques of vegetative reproduction were developed (that is, new plants were started from cuttings rather than from seeds).

The major techniques of hoe cultivation (or *horticulture*) include selection of seed or cuttings, preparation of the soil, planting, cultivation, and harvesting. To these may be added such supplementary techniques as fertilization, irrigation, and transplantation. The specific techniques used vary according to the crops planted and local conditions of soil, topography, and rainfall, but there are several fairly widespread patterns, and we shall describe one of them.

The *slash-and-burn technique* of horticulture is found primarily in tropical areas. It gets its names from the way in which the soil is prepared for planting: overgrowth is cut, dried, and burned right on the field to be planted. In this way, the field is cleared and fertilized at the same time, for the ash from the burned plants provides important minerals, and this often makes it possible to harvest sizable crops several years in a row. Robert Redfield has described the preparation of the *milpa* (cornfield) in the Maya village of Chan Kom as follows:

> The bush is felled with the small steel ax used throughout Yucatan. Everything is cut down except a few of the largest trees; these are left "because a little shade is good for the growing corn in a time of drought, and because too much ash would result if they should be

burned." Small growth is cut at the roots; larger trees a foot or two above the ground. . . .

Most of the felling of the bush for new milpas takes place in the autumn and early winter. At least three months is allowed to elapse before the milpa is burned. This is a critical juncture, and one calling for the exercise of judgment by the agriculturalist. If he fires his milpa too soon, it may still be too green to burn properly; and if he waits too long, the rains may come and make necessary a second clearing of the land before it can be burned. . . . The act of kindling the milpa is partly ceremonial and is accompanied by propitiatory offerings. The firing is usually done on a day when the wind is in the south or east. Two or more men set the dry bush on fire; some run along the east side and some along the south side, pausing at intervals to kindle the field with a torch, and whistling for the winds to come.[16]

Once the rains begin, the cultivator places several grains of maize mixed with bean and squash seeds into three-inch-deep holes approximately one meter apart which are made with a digging stick. Little further care is taken of the field except to clear the second growth with a small hooked knife and to try to protect the ripening plants from marauding animals.

Similar patterns of cultivation, with various modifications and elaborations, are found throughout the world. There is always a mixture of physical and spiritual techniques. As Malinowski says of the Trobriand Islanders, "There is a whole system of garden magic consisting of a series of complex and elaborate rites, each accompanied by a spell. Every gardening activity must be preceded by a proper rite."[17] The principal crop of the Trobrianders is the yam, several species of which are cultivated. These people believe that at the call of a magician, yams can wander around beneath the surface of the ground. (How else account for the different yields of apparently similar gardens?) Therefore, they have numerous spells designed to encourage their yams to become deeply rooted and to stay in place. Also, since the burning of cut and dried scrub is a crucial stage of the gardening, we find that here, as in Chan Kom, the burning is accompanied by spiritual techniques:

Some herbs, previously chanted over, have to be wrapped, with a piece of banana leaf, round the tops of dried coconut leaflets . . . as torches to set fire to the field. In the forenoon . . . the torches were lit quite without ceremony (by means of wax matches, produced by the ethnographer, not without a pang), and then everyone went along the field on the windward side, and the whole was soon ablaze. Some children looked on at the burning, and there was no question of any

16. R. Redfield and A. Villa Rojas, *Chan Kom: A Maya Village* (Chicago: University of Chicago Press, 1962), pp. 43–44.
17. Malinowski, *op. cit.*, p. 192.

taboo [although] in a neighboring village . . . the *towosi* [garden magician] got very angry because some girls looked on at the performance from a fair distance, and I was told that the ceremonies were taboo to women in that village.[18]

Many horticultural peoples are familiar with *techniques of intensive cultivation* such as fertilization, crop rotation, terracing, or irrigation. Wherever sufficient land is available, however, they seem to prefer *extensive* techniques, such as slash and burn, which involves constant shifting from partly exhausted fields to land that has never been cultivated or to land where the brush has had time to grow back. Although the new plots must be cleared and may be at some distance from the old settlement, their high initial productivity and relative ease of preparation make them more attractive than the partly exhausted and weed-filled fields nearer to home. Various mixtures of intensive and extensive techniques are also found. In parts of West Africa, for example, the staple grains (millet or maize) are planted on shifting plots, whereas bananas and plantains are harvested from permanent groves. In any case, given adequate land and the necessary techniques, horticultural systems can be brought to a high level of productivity with simple tools and with human muscles as the only source of energy.

The subsistence pattern known as *pastoralism* was found aboriginally only in the Old World, for the few domesticable animals native to the Americas could not support this specialized way of life. Pastoralists are necessarily nomadic, moving with their herds in search of water and pasture at different seasons, generally over a set route. There are many types of pastoralism, from the reindeer-herders of northern Siberia to the camel-breeders of Arabia. We shall limit our illustration to the important and well-studied cattle complex of East Africa. This is a cultural area in which the great interest attached to cattle provides "a dominating, integrating force" in the culture:

> Cattle determine a man's rank, as where, among the Bahima, chiefs were appointed to rule over a given number of cattle instead of a given region; or among the Zulu, where [rank] is established by the derivation of the cattle that passed on the occasion of one's mother's marriage. Among the Ba-Ila, a man has an ox that he treats like a pet, that sleeps in his hut and is called by his name. When this man dies, the skin of the ox is his shroud; its flesh supplies his funeral feast.
>
> The languages of the area yield significant illustrations of the importance of cattle. Evans-Pritchard, for example, cites forty different words, each of which applies to the color of a particular kind of cow

18. *Ibid.*, pp. 194–195.

Cattle herders in east Kenya. ***Marc & Evelyne Bernheim/Woodfin Camp***

or ox. The imagery in the poetry of the peoples living in this region is replete with references to their cattle.[19]

The Masai are a fairly typical group of this area. Although presently decimated by war and disease, they formerly roamed at will over large areas, raiding other pastoralists for cattle and trading hides or milk products for vegetable foods. This age-graded society was well represented by its tall young warriors. The Masai keep some sheep and goats, but

19. M. J. Herskovits, *Man and His Works* (New York: Knopf, 1949), pp. 195–196.

> cattle are by far the most important live stock of the Masai, and nearly every family formerly had a considerable herd. . . . Most of the male calves are gelded soon after birth and kept to swell the size of the herd and to provide hides and meat for payments, gifts and feasts. . . . Cows are never slaughtered although they may be eaten when they die. They are indeed treated with the greatest care and much affection. Each has its personal name and the herdsman has his favourites among them. . . .
>
> Milk is drunk either fresh or sour; it is boiled only for the sick. Butter is made from cream by laboriously shaking it in a large gourd, but cheese making is unknown. Blood is a favourite and important element in the diet. . . .[20]

Nearly all pastoralists are aware of the techniques of cultivation, and they realize that these techniques make possible a more settled and economically productive mode of life; yet they often cling to their nomadic pattern out of preference. In areas where pastoralists and cultivators are in contact, the pastoralists generally have greater prestige because of their superior military striking power. It was, after all, waves of horseback-riding nomads who conquered the Egyptian, Roman, and Chinese Empires. Throughout East Africa and parts of the Sudan are found stratified societies in which cultivators are ruled by a noble class having a pastoral background. In this area are also found societies with mixed economies in which the men tend herds while the women are solely responsible for cultivation.

The uses to which the animals are put vary with local conditions and knowledge. Where only the meat and hides are utilized, domesticated animals are little more than tame game; many pastoral peoples do not employ any dairying techniques, much less use their animals for their wool, as beasts of burden, or for riding. Such uses, however, would be the most economical, since they do not require that the animal be killed.

When a domesticated animal is put to the plow we have true *agriculture* (as opposed to horticulture). Of all those human subsistence patterns thus far discussed, agriculture is the one that has the greatest productive potential. As Forde has observed:

> Plough cultivation is nearly everywhere associated with much knowledge and considerable equipment, in addition to the use of the plough itself. These include the use of water-lifting devices . . . the regular use of manures . . . crop rotation and an appreciation of the value of pulses as restorers of the nitrogen content of the soil which is depleted by cultivation of cereals. The ripe grain is trodden out by animals or threshed by driving over it wooden sleds. . . . All these

20. C. D. Forde, *Habitat, Economy and Society* (New York: Dutton, 1963), p. 295.

A donkey pulls a plow on a people's commune in central China. ***Marc Riboud/Magnum***

and many other details of agricultural practice are unknown to the lower cultivators.[21]

Because such intensive agricultural techniques can provide a large and continuous yield from fixed fields, the farmer can afford to invest time and labor in constructing strong, permanent facilities: fences, storage buildings, dwellings, and, above all, irrigation systems. With the development of the plow and allied techniques, a fairly dependable crop surplus can be harvested in areas of moderate fertility and rainfall. This surplus makes possible both a denser population and a more extensive division of labor than do any of the other food-getting patterns. In agricultural societies, crafts can be practiced by full-time specialists, with a consequent improvement in both efficiency of technique and quality of product. With the development of metallurgy and its application to agricultural implements, food production becomes still more productive and a considerable proportion of the population (though seldom over 20 percent) can be freed from direct participation in food-getting activities.

Civilization

Agriculture requires extensive cooperation, particularly where irrigation is an essential part of the food-producing pattern. Karl Wittfogel has emphasized that the coordination of effort needed in the building and maintenance of extensive irrigation systems (dams and canals) is intimately related to the rise of civilization in parts of the Old World. This is known as the "irrigation civilization hypothesis," and it points to an important relationship between technology and social structure. For example, it has been suggested that the early rise to dominance of the priestly class in ancient Egypt is associated with the ability of these specialists to predict the time of the annual flooding of the Nile. This knowledge allegedly put the priests in such a crucial position with respect to agricultural activities that they gained extensive control over the entire society. Similarly, in the city-states of ancient Mesopotamia, the temple was clearly at the center of the social structure: here the priests kept accounts, coordinated agricultural work, divided the land, and stored surplus crops against times of famine.

It is hardly surprising that members of agricultural societies are greatly concerned with fertility and the growth process. The

21. *Ibid.*, p. 391.

progression of the seasons is intimately related to their work cycle. In the civilizations of the ancient Near East there developed, in connection with priestly observations of the celestial bodies, a view of the world based upon birth, growth, death, and rebirth. This *cyclical world view* of history was, and is today, exceedingly influential. Many of the ritual techniques and mythological themes of Western civilization have their origin in this era: a time when man's increasing control over plant and animal reproduction merged with his awareness of the orderliness of astronomical phenomena and his desire to understand his place in nature.[22]

Agriculture has been the subsistence base of all the Old World civilizations for thousands of years. But only with the large-scale application of machine technology to food production in the last fifty years have we moved into an era in which the vast majority of the members of a society can be released from food-producing activities and are enabled to congregate in ever-growing urban centers. In the absence of general birth control, the world-wide population explosion will soon produce a tragic, world-wide famine; but hopefully this will be countered by the development of new techniques of food producing such as hydroponics and artificial synthesis. Also, paradoxically, we shall probably return to food-gathering—but this time it will be a mechanized gathering of the vast untapped resources of the oceans.

TECHNIQUES FOR HEALING SICKNESS: MEDICINE

Medicine is an applied science: it consists of practical techniques which are part of a larger body of knowledge and belief about the human body and the causes of disease. Where this knowledge is limited or the beliefs are inaccurate, the derived medical techniques *may or may not work.* For example, where bloodletting is a standard remedy for certain ills, people generally *do* feel better after such a treatment. This is because psychological and physiological processes are interrelated in complex ways; therefore, we must be extremely cautious in dismissing the skills of native curers as mere superstition. Furthermore, the healers in primitive societies frequently make use of many substances which Western medicine has found to be empirically effective and has therefore adopted. (Aspirin and quinine are probably the best known of these.) For this reason, there are several large drug

22. See Joseph Campbell, *The Masks of God*, Vol. I (New York: Viking, 1959). On the "irrigation civilization hypothesis," see Steward, *op. cit.*

companies that spend sizable amounts investigating the techniques of medicine men throughout the world.

The general formula for any healing technique may be stated as follows:

Illness X (category)	calls for	Treatment Y (plan)

This indicates the two major phases of medical action: (1) *diagnosis,* in which the category of illness from which a person is suffering is determined, and (2) *therapy,* in which a plan of action is carried out—a technique with the goal of restoring the sick person to health or at least relieving the symptoms. The treatment is based upon the healer's understanding of the agent and cause of the diagnosed illness: a virus, a parasite, a poison, a psychological trauma, a sorcerer's spell. In general, the healing activities attempt to avoid, remove, or nullify the influence of whatever or whoever is believed to be responsible for the illness.

Diagnosis of disease involves a folk taxonomy consisting of the categories of disease and the attributes by which they may be recognized. In American folk culture, for example, a cold is recognized by symptoms such as stuffiness, aches, slight fever, and so forth; but if the fever is high and accompanied by certain other discomforts, the disease may be categorized as the flu. Charles Frake has given us an excellent analysis of the diagnostic process as carried out by the Subanun of the southern Philippines:

> Subanun diagnosis is the procedure of judging similarities and differences among instances of "being sick," placing new instances into culturally defined and linguistically labelled categories. . . . There are 132 diagnostic categories which possess unique, single-word labels. The Subanun must consequently rote-learn unique and distinctive labels for the vast majority of his diseases [and] all Subanun do, in fact, learn to use such a copious vocabulary of disease . . . terms with great facility.

The disease categories found in any culture are not independent of one another: they are grouped on several contrasting levels within what Frake calls "taxonomic hierarchies." For example, the general category used by the Subanun to indicate "wounds" is *samad*; this contrasts with the general term for "skin diseases," *nuka.* But within the latter category there are several more specific levels. These include such specific disease names as *pugu,* "rash," and *bugais,* "spreading itch," but also such intermediate categories as *beldut,* "sore," which itself includes a number of specific illnesses (see Figure 9.1). Thus the disease terminology of the Subanun is ordered within an area of semantic

samad 'wound'	*nuka* 'skin disease'													
			meŋebag 'inflammation'			*beldut* 'sore'						*buni* 'ringworm'		
						telemaw 'distal ulcer'		*bagaʔ* 'proximal ulcer'						
(many subdivisions)	*pugu* 'rash'	*nuka* 'eruption'	*pagid* 'inflamed quasi bite'	*Bekukaŋ* 'ulcerated inflammation'	*meŋebag* 'inflamed wound'	*telemaw glai* 'shallow distal ulcer'	*telemaw bligun* 'deep distal ulcer'	*bagaʔ* 'shallow proximal ulcer'	*begwak* 'deep proximal ulcer'	*beldut* 'simple sore'	*selimbunut* 'spreading sore'	*buyayag* 'exposed ringworm'	*buni* 'hidden ringworm'	*bugais* 'spreading itch'

Figure 9.1 **Subanun Skin Disease Terminology (from C. O. Frake, "The Diagnosis of Disease among the Subanun of Mindanao,"** ***American Anthropologist,*** **Vol. 63 [1961], p. 118)**

space (kinds of diseases), with each term occupying a part of that space on one or more levels (see Chapter 6, p. 186).

Most types of disease recognized by the Subanun can be diagnosed by observation and verbal description of their symptoms. Some types of disease, however, can only be *fully* diagnosed by other means, particularly if the patient wishes to know how and why he fell sick. Although all Subanun are farmers, some engage in part-time specialties:

> There are religious specialists "mediums" (*belian*), whose job it is to maintain communications with the very important supernatural constituents of the Subanun universe. Mediums hold curing ceremonies, but the gods effect the cure. They make possible verbal communication with the supernaturals, but again the information received comes from the gods. The medium is but a channel for the divine message.[23]

In many cultures, similar kinds of divination (spiritual techniques) are used to diagnose the cause of disease or to indicate the proper therapy. Among the Navajo, for instance, there are several types of diviners; one of these is the hand-trembler. In

23. C. O. Frake, "The Diagnosis of Disease among the Subanun of Mindanao," *American Anthropologist,* Vol. 63 (1961), pp. 114, 115–116, 124–125.

diagnosing an illness, he prays to Gila Monster while sprinkling pollen on his arm and laying out four different kinds of beads; then he begins a song. "As soon as the hand-trembler begins to sing, and sometimes even before, his hand and arm begin to shake violently. The way in which the hand moves as it shakes provides the information sought."[24] In the Navajo case, divination generally reveals which of the many curing chants should be performed for the patient's welfare. Similarly, in the Philippines, diagnosis (by observation of symptoms or through mediums) is an important step "in the selection of *culturally appropriate responses to illness* by the Subanun. It bears directly on the selection of ordinary, botanically-derived, medicinal remedies from 724 recorded alternatives. The results of this selection . . . govern the possible therapeutic need for a variant of one of 61 basic, named types of propitiatory offerings."[25]

There are so many different types of healing techniques that we cannot even begin to survey them. Some of the most common types, however, will be used to illustrate our discussion of two questions: Why is one type of treatment rather than another used in a given society? And what is the reason for the effectiveness of some techniques which, according to modern biological knowledge, should have no organic effect at all?

The first question—why a certain technique is used—can generally be answered with reference to the belief system of the society in question. (See Chapter 10.) For example, most American doctors have been trained in the germ theory of disease: since they believe that certain categories of infectious diseases are caused by bacteria which can be destroyed by penicillin, their plan of treatment is to inject the patient with a suitable amount of penicillin. *The technique is deduced from the belief system*—in this case, the beliefs in bacteria as agents of infection and in penicillin as an effective antibacterial drug. (This does not explain, of course, why thousands of doctors give penicillin injections for virus infections upon which the treatment can have no effect.)

If one's culture includes beliefs in such dangers as witchcraft, viruses, soul-loss, nuclear radiation, or possession by evil spirits, it will probably also include techniques for dealing with these causes of illness; and the techniques will be based upon cultural expectations about how these causes operate. For example, the Navajo Indians believe that violations of taboo or contact with such things as bears, snakes, lightning, or enemy ghosts can bring on illness. The illness, however, is primarily regarded as a *symptom of disharmony* between the sick person and the

24. C. Kluckhohn and D. Leighton, *The Navaho* (Cambridge: Harvard University Press, 1946), p. 148.
25. Frake, *op. cit.*, p. 131 (italics added).

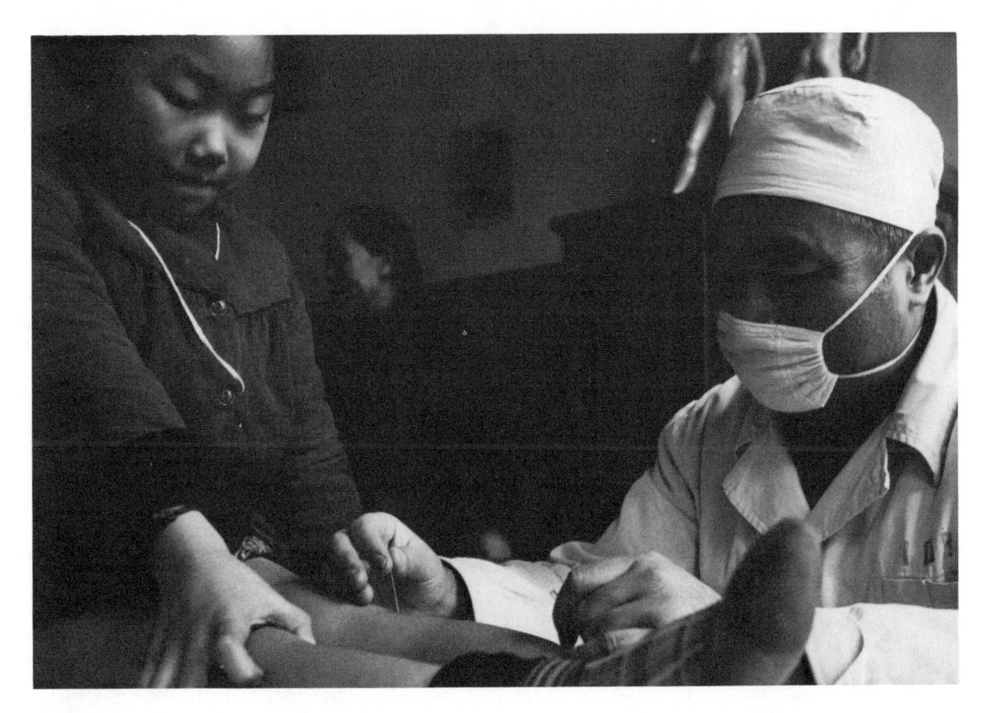

Treatment through the technique of acupuncture, in the Children's Hospital in Peking. ***Marc Riboud/Magnum***

supernatural world. Thus, although the Navajo distinguish between contagious "disease" (*naatniih*) and a more general category of "body ache" (*tah honeesgai*), they also believe that

> all ailments, mental or physical, are of supernatural origin. The notion of locating the cause of a disease in physiological processes is foreign to Navaho thought. The cause of disease, of injury to the body or to one's property, of continued misfortune of any kind, must be traced back to some accidental or deliberate violation of one of the [taboos], or to contact with a ghost, or to witch activity. It follows logically that treatment consists in dealing with these causative factors and not with the illness or injury as such. The supernaturals must be appeased. If a visible sign of attack is present, it must be removed, or the patient must be treated on the general principle that he has been attacked by supernaturals or by supernatural means and that his supernatural relationships need to be restored to normal condition again. The ultimate aim of every curing ceremonial is this restoration.[26]

But this does not explain why "primitive cures" are so often successful. How is it possible for "unscientific" practices to pro-

26. Kluckhohn and Leighton, *op. cit.*, pp. 132–133.

duce cures or, in the case of "black magic," to bring on illness and death? First of all, we must recognize that when a person is sick he wants something done to make him well; in all societies it is nearly as important that *something* be done to give him confidence as that the medically correct thing be done. This phenomenon is known as the *placebo effect.* A placebo is "a pharmacologically inert substance that the doctor administers to a patient to relieve his distress when, for one reason or another, he does not wish to use an active medication." Some common placebos include sugar pills and salt-water injections; however, as Jerome D. Frank points out, until quite recently *most* of the medications that physicians prescribed were "pharmacologically inert" whether the doctors realized it or not. "Despite their inadvertent reliance on placebos, physicians maintained an honored reputation as successful healers, implying that these remedies were generally effective."[27] Recent studies of the placebo effect have confirmed this rather surprising fact: placebos have been shown to be effective in curing such diverse illnesses as peptic ulcer, warts, and mental disturbances.

But how can a placebo produce a cure? To begin with, when a physician in our society prescribes a medication he is doing what is expected of him by the patient—performing his role. This very action seems to raise the patient's hope and allay his anxiety. There is experimental evidence that placebos are most effective for those patients who have a favorable attitude towards medicine and doctors to begin with. As Frank puts it, "It appears that the ability to respond favorably to a placebo is not so much a sign of excessive gullibility, as one of easy acceptance of others in their socially defined roles."[28] At least two factors, then, are involved in these cures: suggestion and social support.

Students of hypnotism have long been aware of the remarkable effects of simple suggestion upon some people. The suggestion that "this (pill, prayer, or amulet) will help you" is an important part of every healer's power—the more so if the patient really wants to believe. The apparent successes of many faith healers can be attributed to this factor. Suggestion can even cause some drugs to have the opposite of their usual effects.[29]

In primitive societies, where the shaman or medicine man has the confidence of his patients and where his powers are bolstered by sleight of hand and confident claims, suggestion probably plays a large part in producing cures. But we must not overlook the factor of social support, for in nearly every society the sick person has a special place in the social structure—the

27. J. D. Frank, *Persuasion and Healing* (New York: Schocken, 1963), p. 66.
28. *Ibid.*, p. 70.
29. *Ibid.*, p. 67.

sick role—and this entitles him to special consideration including release from certain obligations (working, attending classes). Furthermore, a severe illness generally results in the mobilization of a social group to aid and comfort him. Among the Navajo, for instance, when an illness has been diagnosed, the patient becomes the center of attention during a curing ceremonial which may last as long as nine days and nights. During this time, the patient must have his sense of self-esteem raised, for his relatives rally around to pay for and assist in the ceremonial while the Singer—an older man of high prestige and great experience—assures him that he will recover. Indeed, the patient may well have participated in a similar ceremony in which a friend or relative was cured. In any case, he has "the sense of doing something about a misfortune which otherwise might leave him . . . feeling completely helpless."[30]

Finally, we may note that many techniques for curing illness involve considerable pain or at least discomfort for the patient. Western psychologists have come to the conclusion that many psychosomatic illnesses are triggered by an individual's *need for punishment*: his suffering (which is genuine) represents an attempt to atone for unconscious feelings of guilt. It is thus possible for a painful or humiliating treatment to satisfy this need for punishment and indirectly relieve the patient of his symptoms. Perhaps the effectiveness of some primitive techniques rests upon such a psychological mechanism. (It has been suggested that the apparent therapeutic value of psychiatric shock treatments derives from this source.)

The superiority of "scientific" medicine (when it is superior) is due to its more valid beliefs about human physiology and the nature of disease. Western culture has accumulated an extensive body of such knowledge and has also developed elaborate means of recording, evaluating, teaching, and applying this knowledge by means of medical publications, schools, conferences, hospitals, and so forth. But these techniques are expensive, and the costs are not only monetary. There have been losses as well. Part of the primitive curer's effectiveness comes from his intimate personal knowledge of the patient and what is likely to be troubling him—for example, whether his illness is complicated by economic problems or by family conflict. But scientific medicine tends to be impersonal, with patients known to the doctors only as cases or numbers. And our hospitals, excellent as they often are, have become total institutions which all too often cut a patient off from the social support which he needs and render him less open to positive suggestion. Here, anthropology has an important practical

30. Kluckhohn and Leighton, *op. cit.*, pp. 164–165.

role to play: the anthropologist can identify the positive and negative aspects of medical treatment in all societies, including our own, and may help in discovering more effective techniques of healing.

The new subfield of *medical anthropology* studies both the curing techniques of non-Western societies and the institutions of Western society (hospitals, mental asylums, tuberculosis sanitariums, and so forth) to understand how they do or do not help those who need them. Medical anthropologists have also studied such diverse subjects as the training of medical students, nutrition, old people's homes, and resistance to the introduction of scientific medicine in other societies. Such studies have important consequences for the populations studied and also for anthropological theory.

TECHNIQUES FOR MAKING OBJECTS: CRAFTS

Associated with most categories of man-made objects are plans (techniques) for making more such artifacts. These *craft techniques* are often a mixture of practical knowledge and supernatural belief, plus certain acquired skills which, though difficult to describe, are extremely important. Even within our own civilization, many skills and techniques—such as those involved in making fine violins or stained-glass windows—have been lost. In the remainder of this chapter, we shall give a brief survey of the variety of techniques employed by primitive man in weaving, pottery-making, canoe-building, and metallurgy.

Weaving Baskets and Fabrics

Weaving must be a very ancient technique, for some kind of woven objects are found in every primitive society. Even the Siriono, who manage to subsist "with a bare minimum of material apparatus," make two kinds of baskets from palm leaves and spin both bark fibers and cotton to use in making hammocks, baby slings, bow-strings and arrows.[31]

Baskets are widely used as containers by hunting and gathering peoples. The Australian aborigines, for example, wove a few crude types of baskets. In general, basket-making is a female occupation, perhaps because it is closely associated with food-gathering, which is also usually women's work.

31. Holmberg, *op. cit.*, p. 11.

In southern California, only *coiling* was used in basket-making. This technique involves a spiral foundation (the warp) which is bound back upon itself with a more flexible material (the woof) and shaped upward as it grows in diameter. Farther north in California, coiling was combined with various other techniques to produce exceptionally fine baskets. Among northern California tribes such as the Pomo and the Maidu, basket-making reached great heights of perfection. The masters of this craft used dozens of different materials and techniques for weaving and decoration. Furthermore, the very elaboration of the techniques showed an appreciation of the "aesthetic value of technical perfection." As Franz Boas wrote:

> Virtuosity, complete control of technical processes . . . means an automatic regularity of movement. The basketmaker who manufactures a coiled basket, handles the fibres composing the coil in such a way that the greatest evenness of coil diameter results. In making her stitches the automatic control of the left hand that lays down the coil, and of the right that pulls the binding stitches over the coil brings it about that the distances between the stitches and the strength of the pull are absolutely even so that the surface will be smooth and evenly rounded and that the stitches show a perfectly regular pattern. . . . The same observation may be made in twined basketry. In the handiwork of an expert the pull of the woof string will be so even that there is no distortion of the warp strings and the twisted woof will lie in regularly arranged loops. Any lack of automatic control will bring about irregularities of surface pattern.[32]

The craftsman is seldom aware of exactly how his skill is applied. He may be able to state the criteria he uses in choosing and preparing materials for weaving, and the specific techniques of weaving can with some difficulty be communicated through verbal instruction and visual demonstration. But developing the skills is another matter.

Weaving of fabrics is seldom very much developed among food collectors, although the Northwest Coast Indians wove cedar-bark capes and fine blankets of goat hair, while in the Great Basin strips of rabbit fur were "finger-woven" into warm robes. Weaving is often found "among the lower cultivators on the fringes of higher civilization."[33] An example would be the Pueblo Indians of the American Southwest, whose weaving techniques and use of cotton were borrowed from Mexico.

In true weaving, two sets of threads are used, the warp and the woof, crossing each other at right angles. *Simple weaving* involves passing the woof under and over alternate warp threads.

---

32. F. Boas, *Primitive Art* (New York: Dover, 1955), p. 20.
33. Forde, *op. cit.*, p. 383.

More complex forms of weaving (also found in basketry) include *twilling,* in which the woof passes over two or more warp threads, and *twining,* in which alternative woof strands either twist around one another or actually wrap around the warp threads (wrapped twining).

Many other variations of weave, as well as increased speed of production, are made possible by the introduction of the *loom* —a device for holding the warp threads and for storing the completed work. Typical improvements in the loom include use of the *heddle rod,* with thread loops (heddles) which are attached to groups of warp threads to lift them together, and the *shuttle,* which carries the woof across the warp. In Europe, Africa, and parts of Asia the warp threads were suspended vertically in an *upright loom* which had a frame consisting of posts driven into the ground. But in South and Southeast Asia, the *horizontal loom* has long been the major form. In one subtype, the back-strap loom, the horizontal warp threads are held taut by means of a strap passed around the weaver's back. (Such horizontal looms were spread widely through the Pacific islands; the occurrence of the back-strap loom both in Indonesia and in pre-Columbian South America has been pointed to as evidence of trans-Pacific contacts.)

Making Pottery

Pottery-making is a much younger craft than weaving. The earliest known pottery appeared in the Near East somewhat less than 8,000 years ago, but pottery-making techniques spread rapidly in both the Old and the New World. This craft is found everywhere that cultivation is found and among some food-collecting peoples as well. As was noted in the section on transportation (Chapter 8), pottery is not really suitable for nomadic or highly mobile societies; but with settled villages and a food surplus it becomes most useful.

The average modern American would hardly know where to begin if he had to make a piece of pottery. The location and preparation of suitable materials involve a good deal of specialized knowledge. But even if he were provided with a quantity of prepared clay, he would probably attempt to shape the desired form directly with his hands and fingers. This technique, known as *modeling,* can be used to make small figurines or decorations for larger items, but it is not suitable for larger objects. A beginner would be well advised to start with the technique of *coiling.* Coiling is the basic pottery-making technique throughout the New

Pottery-making. ***Arthur Tress/Magnum***

World and in the Old World outside of true agricultural areas. It is similar to the coiling of a basket; as described by Boas:

> Long round strips of clay are laid down spirally beginning at the bottom. By continued turning and gradual laying on of more and more strips in a continued spiral the pot is built up. Complete control of the technique will result in a perfectly round cross section and in smooth curvatures of the sides. Lack of skill will bring about lack of symmetry and of smoothness of curvature. Virtuosity and regularity of surface and form are here also intimately related.[34]

Coiled pottery may be finished in any number of ways: the exterior may be scraped smooth with a shell and polished with a stone; it may be left plain; or it may be decorated by pinching the

34. Boas, *op. cit.*, p. 21.

coils together, by smoothing with a paddle, by stamping or painting with a design, by covering with a slip of thin clay, and so forth.

Since pottery is one of the most varied and durable objects made by man, archaeologists have studied its manufacture in great detail; they use their knowledge of materials, techniques, form, decoration, and firing to identify pottery and pottery fragments (potsherds) with great accuracy in order to establish chronologies, historical distributions, and past culture contacts. (See Chapter 2.)

In the agricultural areas of the Old World there developed a technique for shaping fine pottery in large quantities. This technique was based on the use of the *potter's wheel.* It is striking to note that in most places where the potter's wheel has been introduced the making of pottery has changed from a skill practiced as part of the usual female role to a craft practiced primarily by a few male specialists. The potter's wheel is, of course, derived from the true wheel. In its early forms it is turned by the hands or feet of the potter; only later is it harnessed to other sources of energy. The principal advantage of the wheel is that once the techniques are mastered it makes possible the rapid manufacture of highly symmetrical and standardized pottery.

Aside from decoration, the remaining major techniques of pottery-making relate to *firing* the completed vessel. Before firing, the pots must be carefully dried, because an excess of moisture will cause them to break in the firing. The vessels must be heated to over 400°C (about 750°F.) to transform the clay into pottery and to ensure that it will not revert to clay when wet. Excessive heat, on the other hand, may either melt the clay or make it too fragile for use. There are many techniques and skills involved in firing; in general, "nonliterate peoples bake their clay vessels in open fires, but peoples culturally more advanced use enclosed heating chambers, such as kilns or ovens."[35]

With a process as risky as pottery-making, it is understandable that the potter should take certain ritual precautions at various stages of the procedure—particularly in connection with the firing. In the American Southwest, for example, it is considered dangerous to praise the quality of a potter's work prior to its firing, for the vessels will be sure to crack.

Building a Canoe

Canoe-building is also a highly skilled craft, and since the consequences of a canoe coming apart can be much more drastic than

35. Beals and Hoijer, *op. cit.*, pp. 324–325.

those of a pot breaking, the entire process is often surrounded with ritual. Among the Trobriand Islanders, for example, the seagoing canoe (*masawa*) is closely associated with the dangerous *kula* trade (see p. 131); its construction involves two main stages of work and at least three different systems of magic. In the first stage of the work:

> the component parts are prepared. A big tree is cut, trimmed into a log, then hollowed out and made into the basic dug-out; the planks, poles, and sticks are prepared. . . . This stage generally takes a long time, some two to six months, and is done in fits and starts, as other occupations allow or as the mood comes. The spells and rites which accompany it belong to the *tokway* magic, and to that of the flying canoe cycle. To this first stage also belongs the carving of the decorative prow-boards. This is done sometimes by the builder, sometimes by another expert, if the builder cannot carve.
>
> The second stage is done by means of intense communal labor. As a rule this stage is spread over a short time. . . . The actual labor in which the whole community is energetically engaged takes up only some three to five days. The work consists of the piecing together of the planks and prow-boards . . . and then of the lashing them together. Next comes the piecing and lashing of the outrigger, caulking and painting of the canoe. Sail-making is also done at this time. . . . The second stage of canoe-building is accompanied by Kula magic, and by a series of exorcisms on the canoe. . . . The lashing of the canoe with a specially strong creeper, called *wayugo*, is accompanied by perhaps the most important of the rites and spells belonging to the flying canoe magic.

The *tokway* magic is addressed to the evil spirit who lives in the chosen tree; it is an attempt to expel him from the tree before it is cut down. The flying canoe magic is related to a mythological cycle and is intended to impart great speed to the canoe; it also gives protection from evil spirits, such as the dreaded "flying witches" who are the principal dangers to travelers. The *kula* magic is primarily concerned with ensuring a safe and successful trading voyage, and parts of it are performed in connection with building and decorating the canoe. Magic enters into every phase of the construction, and though some spells may be omitted, others (such as the *tokway* spell and the rites connected with the adze used to hollow out the log and the *wayugo* creeper used to bind the parts) must always be performed. The Trobriand natives do not separate the technical and the magical aspects of the construction; as Malinowski comments, "The magician does not produce the impression of an officiating high priest performing a solemn ceremony, but rather of a specialized workman doing a particularly important piece of work."[36]

---

36. B. Malinowski, *Argonauts of the Western Pacific* (New York: Dutton, 1961), pp. 125–126, 142.

Dugout canoes are found in most parts of the world where suitable trees occur, and their manufacture always involves considerable technical knowledge and skill. In some regions, large vessels were made solely of bark.

> To make one of these simple canoes the Amazonian Indians first set up a complete scaffolding around one of the giant trees of the primeval forest, whereupon they carefully detach the bark so that it does not crack or split. Then the bark is made supple by means of heat, the sides are distended by crossbeams, and the stem and stern are forced upward. [Because they are sometimes not even sewn together at the ends] these canoes are not particularly seaworthy, but are only intended for gently running rivers.[37]

The uncertainty of most seagoing expeditions accounts for the association between canoe-building, sailing, and the supernatural. This association has persisted into modern societies: in most contemporary fishing villages, there is an annual blessing of the boats, and all around the Mediterranean one still finds ships painted with large eyes to ward off evil.

Metallurgy

Metallurgy, like pottery-making, involves a chemical transformation of compounds by means of intense heat. It requires considerable technical knowledge as well as precise control of fire. In man's first attempts to use metals he treated them like malleable stones. This is because nuggets of gold and nodules of native copper (metals which occur in relatively pure forms in nature) could be cold-hammered into useful or decorative shapes. These techniques were known to many peoples who never found a way to extract the metals from their ores (for example, the so-called Copper Eskimo); but in some areas such experience with naturally occurring metals gave rise to true metallurgy.

Copper was the first metal to be extensively used, starting perhaps 6,000 years ago in the Near East. In this region, copper was known in its native form and some of its carbonate ores were used as cosmetics. These ores can be reduced to metal at fairly low temperatures, and it has been conjectured that the technique of reduction may have been discovered by accident—perhaps when some Egyptian matron left her make-up kit too near the fire one windy night. In any case, the techniques of copper-working were first developed in the Near East and spread from there. By

37. Birket-Smith, *op. cit.*, p. 223.

about 3000 B.C., two important new techniques had been developed: *annealing* and *alloying.* When copper is hammered, it becomes quite brittle; but the technique of *annealing* can soften it again. To anneal copper, the metal is heated white hot and plunged into cold water. *Alloying* is the mixing of two or more metals or nonmetals; in this case, copper was mixed with tin to produce bronze—an alloy which is much stronger than either of its component metals alone.

The Bronze Age, which lasted for about 1,500 years in the Near East, was an era of great developments in civilization, though only a few of these were direct results of the progress made in metallurgy. Techniques of working bronze were reflected in the fine craftsmanship displayed in art objects, weapons, personal decorations, and agricultural tools. Among the refined techniques were ways of *casting* bronze, which speeded and standardized the production of practical objects: the molten metal was poured into open molds formed in the shape of the desired object and the rough blanks were finished by hammering and grinding. The Sumerians also developed a specialized casting technique, the *lost wax method*:

> In casting an object by this technique, the craftsman first made a core of clay in the general shape of the object to be cast. When the core was thoroughly dried, he covered it with a layer of wax on which he modeled and incised the details which he wished reproduced in the casting. Lastly, the core and wax layer were enveloped in a clay shell, and the whole fired. The wax melted and ran out, leaving a cavity into which the molten metal could be poured. After the metal had set, the outer shell was broken off and the inner core dug out, leaving a hollow metal casting. This technique has never been improved upon for delicate metal work or for objects only one copy of which was required. It is still used by our own artists in casting small bronze figures.[38]

The Iron Age began at about 1500 B.C. in the Near East and much later elsewhere. At first iron was so rare that it was used only for small, decorative items. The archaeological remains in the tomb of the Egyptian King Tutankhamen (c. 1350 B.C.) demonstrate that "in Egypt iron was a rare metal just beginning to come into use. Nearly all the metal in Tutankhamen's tomb is copper, bronze, gold, or silver. It is clear that iron was too rare and costly to be available to the common man and even royalty possessed little of it." Among the iron objects in the tomb were an iron-bladed dagger, a set of sixteen chisels with small, thin

---

38. R. Linton, *The Tree of Culture* (New York: Knopf, 1955), p. 106. This book gives an excellent summary of world culture history with special attention to the history of technology.

iron parts set in full-sized wooden handles, and an iron eye set in a golden bracelet.[39]

Actually, iron ores are much more plentiful than copper ores, and the metal does occur in a relatively pure state in meteors (thus its ancient Egyptian name, which is translated "star metal"). But the techniques required for smelting iron from its ores are quite different from those that will work for copper. Attempts to transfer copper-working skills directly to iron-working can result in disaster. For example, annealing cast iron can produce a violent explosion; on the other hand, applying this technique to forged iron results not in softening the metal but in hardening it. (This is technically known as *tempering.*)

The basic techniques of iron-working call for two things: patience and a source of intense heat. The heat, which can be provided by a forge with a forced draft, is needed to convert iron ore into the "bloom"—a gray, spongy substance which must be patiently hammered to remove the encased iron droplets. Iron must be worked at a high temperature and repeatedly hammered (forged) to give it a toughness equivalent to bronze. Actually, iron remained inferior to bronze in most respects until techniques of smelting were improved and until the metallurgist learned to produce at least a low-grade *steel.* Steel is iron containing a small amount of carbon which toughens the metal, allowing it to be shaped and sharpened without becoming brittle. Steel-making techniques may have first been developed in southern India. Some groups in this area still use a simple technique in which "filings of relatively pure wrought iron obtained from the local ores are put in sealed clay vessels with grass and the whole heated in charcoal furnaces. The grass is charred to almost pure carbon, which combines with the molten iron to give steel."[40]

The general use of metals in cutting tools and containers is actually quite recent, and even in contemporary American culture, wood, basketry, and ceramics are much more important than we realize. A final point should be emphasized. We think of ourselves as living (technologically) in the Iron Age, and we often read in the mass media about some Melanesian, South American, or African tribe "still living in the Stone Age" and about the difficulties which such "backward" peoples experience in "moving overnight into the twentieth century." But how many of the "civilized" readers of this book know how to recognize or to smelt iron ore? Or how to mix copper with tin in the correct proportion to produce bronze? Or for that matter, how to fashion a decent piece of pottery, basketry, or even flint work?

---

39. C. Meighan, *Archaeology: An Introduction* (San Francisco: Chandler, 1966), p. 103.
40. Linton, *op. cit.*, p. 109.

It is all very well to be proud of the accomplishments of one's culture, but let us recognize that it is our *culture*—socially shared and transmitted knowledge, beliefs, and expectations—which gives us such technological superiority as we may possess. Without the knowledge and skills of our society's metallurgists and blacksmiths, every one of us would be more helpless than a Stone Age man. Luckily, the "primitive" is *not* thousands of years behind us, for the time required to acquire or to lose the most complex culture pattern is *less than a generation.* If this were not true, none of us could know all the things that we do know.

RECOMMENDED READING

Boas, F., *Primitive Art.* New York: Dover Books, 1955. The "father of American anthropology" discusses primitive arts and crafts with special attention to the relationship between technique and design.

Geertz, C., *Agricultural Involution.* Berkeley: University of California Press, 1971. A stimulating discussion of ecological change, agricultural techniques, and social structure and how these interacted over several centuries in Indonesia. Includes an excellent discussion of the slash-and-burn technique.

Lee, R., and I. DeVore, eds., *Man the Hunter.* Chicago: Aldine Publishing Company, 1968. A collection of articles dealing with recent research on hunting and gathering peoples.

Linton, R., *The Tree of Culture.* New York: Knopf, 1955. Human culture history in a readable nutshell. Also available (slighty abridged) in paperback.

White, L., *The Science of Culture.* New York: Grove Press, 1949. Essays by the founder of "culturology" on the evolution of culture and its relation to man's growing control over sources of energy.

The term "ideology" usually refers to a system of explicit beliefs concerning political and economic affairs. In addition, it has a rather negative connotation: one's enemies are said to have an ideology which distorts their view of reality, whereas one's own political or economic views are (of course) based on an unbiased and reasonable appraisal of "the facts."

In the following chapters, however, we shall use this term in both a broader and a more emotionally neutral sense. *Ideology* will denote *any set of more or less systematized beliefs and values shared by the members of a social group.* In particular, we shall discuss those concepts which deal with perennial human concerns such as authority, property, power, morality, and beauty. In this sense, every social group has an ideology, though the degree to which it is made *explicit* or *systematic* varies greatly from person to person and from group to group. Our aim will be to survey the varieties of ideological systems found in nonliterate societies and to note the relationships between ideology and the other aspects of culture.

The definition of ideology given above refers to beliefs *and* values. That is, an ideology includes conceptions of both what *is* and what *should be.* Although we shall separate these kinds of concepts for purposes of analysis, it is well to remember that they are more closely intertwined in human thought than most of us like to realize. Facts and values do not come neatly separated into mutually exclusive compartments. Any real event or person is sufficiently complex that contradictory descriptions can be framed simply by selecting different sets of equally factual points. For example, a Northerner's conception of the Civil War and a Southerner's of the War Between the States may be so different that one must doubt whether they are referring to the same event; yet the factual basis of each of these conceptions may be equally valid. Similarly, the political or religious leader who is a hero to one party may well be a villain to the opposing party. Selection and emphasis can produce vast ideological differences, even when the same phenomena are regarded as facts.

Considerations such as these have made many social scientists reluctant to study ideological systems. Yet ideologies are no more abstract or subjective than are other parts of culture: languages, social systems, and even technologies are all composed of shared ideas which must be *inferred from behavior.* No one has ever *seen* a morpheme, a social role, or a technique. These categories and their associated plans must be *discovered* by painstaking comparison of similar forms, aided by native judgments of rightness (grammaticality, appropriateness, and so forth). In the same way, an ideological system must be inferred from social behavior (including speech), supplemented by explicit native value judgments. (It is true that an in-

PART V
Ideological Systems

formant cannot always give explicit or consistent reasons for his behavior, but this does not mean that an ethnography becomes more objective by ignoring the explanations he does offer.)

Probably the greatest advance in the systematization and explicit transmission of ideology came with the invention of *writing* and the rise of *literate elites* which have had the leisure and the means to "work over" their society's oral traditions—standardizing, elaborating, and codifying them in various ways. This is one of the characteristics of that relatively recent social development we call civilization. In the words of Robert Redfield:

> In a civilization there is a *great tradition* of the reflective few and there is a *little tradition* of the largely unreflective many. The great tradition is cultivated in schools or temples; the little tradition works itself out and keeps itself going in the lives of the unlettered in their village communities. The tradition of the philosopher, theologian, and literary man is a tradition consciously cultivated and handed down; that of the little people is for the most part taken for granted and not submitted to much scrutiny or considered refinement and improvement.[1]

Until the very recent development of tools and techniques for mass communication, the two traditions were usually separated by physical distance as well as by social class. The great tradition took form in urban centers, while the little tradition was rooted in the surrounding rural communities. The two traditions are, however, dependent upon one another: in the village, the great tradition is modified to blend with local practices; but it is also here that it is revitalized by simple faith and vivid imagery.

> Great epics have arisen out of elements of traditional tale-telling by many people, and epics have returned again and again to the peasantry for modification and incorporation into local cultures. The ethics of the Old Testament arose out of tribal peoples and returned to peasant communities after they had been the subject of thought by philosophers and theologians. . . . Great and little tradition can be thought of as two currents of thought and action, distinguishable, yet ever flowing into and out of each other.[2]

Even in the absence of a literate elite, however, a high degree of systematization can take place within an oral tradition. Paul Radin, in his book *Primitive Man as Philosopher,* has suggested that in every society some individuals reflect upon their tradition and try to establish some coherence among its parts; he has gathered many texts which demonstrate the abstract concerns of such primitive "philosophers."[3]

But remarkable as these individual achievements may be, it remains a fact that in all societies, primitive *or* civilized, most people manage to get through life with only the vaguest kind of ideology.

---

1. R. Redfield, *Peasant Society and Culture* (Chicago: University of Chicago Press, 1956), pp. 41–42.
2. *Ibid.,* pp. 42–43. Compare A. Weingrod, "Cultural Traditions in Developing Societies," in P. Bock, ed., *Peasants in the Modern World* (Albuquerque: University of New Mexico Press, 1968), pp. 99–108.
3. P. Radin, *Primitive Man as Philosopher* (enlarged edition; New York: Dover, 1957).

This does not mean that they are without beliefs or values—only that their ideology is implicit in the social roles they play and the institutions they participate in, so that there is normally little need to make their ideas explicit or logically consistent. Indeed, it is mainly in times of *conflict* that systematizations arise, either to defend the status quo or to point out its inconsistencies and call for its overthrow. This is true of even highly intellectual ideologies such as the Western scientific tradition. As Thomas S. Kuhn has pointed out, "normal science" is a great deal like puzzle-solving; during periods of normal science, scientists go about their work with little theoretical discussion, guided by standardized concepts and research procedures which Kuhn calls *paradigms*.[4] It is only when these paradigms begin to produce inconsistent or inexplicable kinds of data that the traditional concepts, procedures, and theories are genuinely questioned and defended.

One of the most important functions of anthropology is to help make us aware of the implicit ideology which governs our lives. In the absence of contrasting examples, each society takes its own ideology as the only possible view of the world. History can show us the *changes* which have taken place in our own tradition, but it often leaves us unaware of the *continuities* (because even the historian takes these for granted). Through intensive comparisons, anthropology, with its greater range in space and time, can teach us what is universal and what is particular, local, or conventional, while helping us to understand how ideology, technology, language, and social structure all interact to produce a living, changing culture.

4. T. Kuhn, *The Structure of Scientific Revolutions* (Chicago: Phoenix Books, 1964), p. 90.

CHAPTER 10
Belief Systems

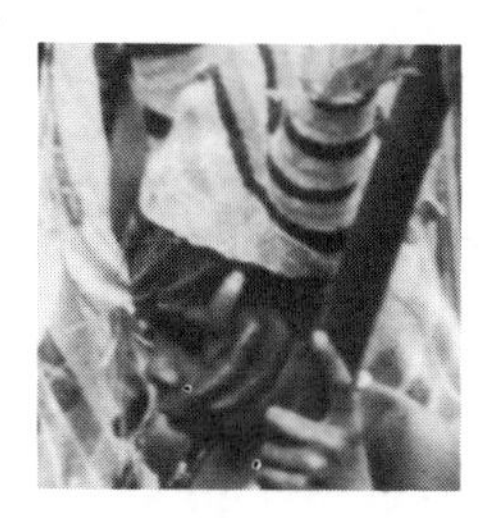

What is the world like?
How did it get that way?
What is man's relationship to the world?

Every culture provides implicit or explicit answers to questions such as these. As we saw in our discussion of social space (Chapter 6), cultures go far beyond what is directly observable in orienting men to a universe of which their firsthand knowledge is necessarily limited. Culture also provides answers for many questions which do not have any objective answers, but which *must* be answered if human society is to function.

Belief systems, then, include all kinds of historically developed and socially transmitted ideas. Some of these ideas are relatively obvious (for example, that the earth is flat and stationary, and that the sun travels across the sky from east to west every day); other conceptions of the world are based on more elaborate inferences from observations (that men evolved from lower forms of life, or that there exist various classes of spiritual beings which are interested in human affairs). Within a given culture, however, the ideas held about the nature of the universe and man's place in it tend to form a relatively coherent system. By definition, a homogeneous and well-integrated culture is one in which all such beliefs are reasonably consistent with one another and mutually reinforcing.

Few if any cultures are actually so well integrated; indeed, a perfectly integrated ideological system would be highly unstable, since a change in any one part would have immediate repercussions throughout the culture. But cultures do exhibit a *tendency toward internal coherence.* We shall discuss the ways in which ideology orients man toward the world and helps him to define his position and potentialities in that world by providing comprehensive systems of beliefs. An essential function of each society's ideology, then, is to help its members answer the very *personal questions*: Who am I? and What must I do? As we shall see, an individual's *sense of identity* is largely constructed out of materials provided by his social tradition.

COSMOLOGY

Cosmology is that part of an ideological system which includes beliefs about the origin, structure, and destiny of the universe. Every society has some such conceptions, and these are transmitted to each generation through the process of enculturation, along with the rest of its traditions. By and large, people accept their society's cosmology as they do its language or technology, without ever being aware of alternative systems. Even where a culture includes competing ideologies, a person's choice of beliefs is more often dictated by his social position (group membership) than by his independent evaluation of the alternatives.

Both striking similarities and tremendous variations exist among the cosmologies found in nonliterate societies. These ideas are often articulated in the form of "creation myths," which seek to account for the present state of the world by relating sequences of past events. One extremely widespread notion is that the earth was once completely covered by water and that specific actions on the part of legendary individuals "caused the dry land to appear." In Asia and North America, this idea is frequently encountered in the "earth-diver" myth, in which "the culture hero has a succession of animals dive into the primeval waters, or flood of waters, to secure bits of mud or sand from which the earth is to be formed. . . . One after another animal fails; the last one succeeds, however, and floats to the surface half dead, with a little sand or dirt in his claws . . . which is then put on the surface of the water and magically expands to become the world of the present time."[1]

Another widespread story describes the *emergence* of human ancestors from some kind of "underworld" by means of a magical "world tree." One such myth is told by the Keresan-speaking Pueblo Indians of New Mexico:

1. E. Wheeler-Voegelin, "Earth-Diver," in M. Leach, ed., *Standard Dictionary of Folklore, Mythology and Legend*, Vol. I (New York: Funk and Wagnalls, 1949), p. 334. For a psychoanalytic interpretation of this myth see A. Dundee, "Earth-Diver: Creation of the Mythopoeic Male," *American Anthropologist*, Vol. 64 (1962), pp. 1032–1051.

The world of the Pueblo Indians was not created in the beginning; it was always there—or here. But it was somewhat different in the beginning than it is now. The earth was square and flat; it had four corners and a middle. Below the surface of the earth there were four horizontal layers; each one was a world. The lowest world was a white one. Above that lay the red world and then the blue one. Above the blue world, and just beneath this world that we are living in today, was the yellow world.

In the beginning the people were living deep down inside the earth, in the white world, with their mother, Iyatiku. Finally it was time for them to come out, to ascend to this world. Iyatiku caused a great evergreen tree . . . to grow so that the people could climb up its trunk and boughs to the next world. . . . The people climbed up into the red world and lived there for four years. Then it was time to climb up into the blue world. Again Iyatiku had a tree reach up to the world above, and . . . she had someone make a hole through the hard layer so the tree and the people could pass through.

At last the people were ready to ascend into this world. Iyatiku had Badger make a hole through the hard crust. . . . Badger looked out. "It is very beautiful up there," he told Iyatiku. "There are rain clouds everywhere." So Iyatiku decided it was all right for the people to complete their ascent and emerge into this world. Iyatiku had created societies of medicine men in the lower worlds and had given them their altars and ceremonies. These societies—the Flint, Fire, Giant, and Kapina medicine men—came out with the people. There were some evil spirits, too, who also came out . . . but no one knew this at that time.

They came out at a place in the north called Shipap. Everything was new and "raw." The earth was too soft for people to walk upon so Iyatiku had the mountain lion use his magic power to harden it. . . . Iyatiku told them they were to migrate toward the south. She said: "I shall not go with you. I am going to return to my home in the white world, but I will be with you always in spirit. You can pray to me and I will always help you." Before she left she appointed a man to take her place. . . . She gave him an ear of corn. "Take this," she told him. "This corn is my heart. This is what you will live on; its milk shall be to you as milk from my breasts."

Iyatiku returned to the lower world and the people began their journey to the south. They stopped at a place and established a pueblo. They called it Kashikatchrutiya or White House. They lived here a long time.[2]

This emergence myth has many interesting features, such as the use of the magical number four and the color symbolism, both of which appear in many Pueblo myths and rituals. But note also that the origin of various cultural features is explained by the story—for example, the various medicine societies, the evil spirits, and the corn plant. Cosmologies often have the dual function of telling what the world is like and of explaining the origins of important social institutions.

2. L. A. White, "The World of the Keresan Pueblo Indians," in S. Diamond, ed., *Culture in History* (New York: Columbia University Press, 1960), pp. 54–55.

Although all peoples have some sort of cosmology, this need not include an emergence or even a creation tale. Among the Ojibwa Indians of the Great Lakes region, for instance, the characters in sacred stories "are regarded as living entities who have existed from time immemorial. While there is genesis through birth and temporary or permanent form-shifting through transformation, there is no outright creation. Whether human or animal in form or name, the major characters in the myths behave like people."[3]

Every cosmology includes ideas about the constitution of the world and about the various *categories of beings* which are believed to inhabit it. Associated with each category are further beliefs about the attributes of its members and their relationship to mankind. In nonliterate societies, such beliefs are codified in and transmitted through the myths and legends of the oral tradition. For example, in the following myth from Dahomey, in West Africa, the creator, *Mawu-Lisa,* gives birth to the major gods and assigns a function to each:

> Since Mawu is both man and woman, she became pregnant. The first to be born were a pair of twins [a man and a woman]. The second birth was So [=Sogbo], who had the form of his parent, man and woman in one. The third birth was also twins, a male, Agbé, and a female, Naété. The fourth to be born was Agé, a male; the fifth, Gu, also male. Gu [the god of iron] is all body. He has no head. Instead of a head, a great sword is found coming out of his neck. His trunk is of stone. The sixth birth was not to a being, but to Djo, air, atmosphere. Air was what was needed to create men. The seventh to be born was Legba. Mawu said Legba [the trickster] was to be her spoiled child, because he was the youngest.
>
> One day Mawu-Lisa assembled all the children in order to divide the kingdoms. To the first twins, she gave all the riches and told them to go and inhabit the earth. She said the earth was for them.
>
> Mawu said to Sogbo he was to remain in the sky, because he was both man and woman like his parent. She told Agbé and Naété to go and inhabit the sea, and command the waters. To Agé she gave command of all the animals and birds, and she told him to live in the bush as a hunter.
>
> To Gu, Mawu said he was her strength, and that was why he was not given a head like the others. Thanks to him, the earth would not always remain wild bush. It was he who would teach men to live happily.
>
> Mawu told Djo to live in space between earth and sky. To him was being entrusted the life-span of man. Thanks to him also, his brothers would be invisible, for he will clothe them. . . .
>
> When Mawu said this to the children, she gave the [first] twins the language which was to be used on earth, and took away their memory of the language of the sky. She gave to [Sogbo] the language he would speak, and took from him the memory of the parent lan-

3. A. I. Hallowell, "Ojibwa Ontology, Behavior, and World View," in Diamond, *op. cit.*, p. 27.

guage. The same was done for Agbé and Naété, for Agé, and for Gu, but to Djo was given the language of men.

Now she said to Legba, "You are my youngest child. . . . I will keep you with me always. Your work shall be to visit all the kingdoms ruled over by your brothers, and to give me an account of what happens." So Legba knows all the languages known to his brothers, and he knows the language Mawu speaks, too. Legba is Mawu's linguist. If one of the brothers wishes to speak, he must give the message to Legba, for none knows any longer how to address himself to Mawu-Lisa. That is why Legba is everywhere.

You will find Legba even before the houses of the *vodun* [priests], because all beings, humans and gods, must address themselves to him before they can approach God.[4]

The oral tradition itself is frequently divided into *categories of tales,* some of which are more important than others. For example, in Dahomey the older men do not tell *heho*, "mere stories"; they concern themselves only with the class of narratives called *hwenoho*, "traditional history." Herskovits subdivides the latter into three subclasses:

1. *Myths,* comprising stories of the gods and the peopling of the earth.
2. *Clan-myth chronicles,* recounting the origin of the great families or clans and including explanations of ritual behavior, food taboos, and so forth.
3. *Verse sequences,* composed by professional verse-makers to aid in the memorization of genealogies and ritual events.

The sacred myths (such as the creation story given above) are narrated primarily by diviners and priests; but the second and third subclasses are different for each clan, and are usually told by clan elders to other males of the group. The family *hwenoho* are recited only to clan members; usually only the adult males attend the councils at which they are told. The *heho* are told only at night, but the *hwenoho* are told during daylight hours. As one experienced storyteller put it, "Tales [*heho*] tell of things which never existed and are inventions of people. History [*hwenoho*] is based on history. But one learns from the tale what one can."[5]

Although one cannot reason directly from a people's cosmology to their behavior in concrete situations, these shared beliefs about the nature of the universe can give important clues to the pervasive attitudes found in a society. Beliefs in protective and/or malignant spirits, in a limitless or a bounded cosmos, in inevitable

4. M. J. Herskovits and F. Herskovits, *Dahomean Narrative: A Cross-cultural Analysis* (Evanston: Northwestern University Press, 1958), pp. 125–126.
5. *Ibid.*, p. 16.

progress or certain calamity—all these produce or reflect varying attitudes toward man's place in the universe. One cannot understand the origins of Christianity without realizing that the Apostles expected the imminent destruction of the world. The patterns of any culture are related to its cosmology. In complex societies, these relationships are often indirect and complicated. Among the Yaruro Indians of southern Venezuela, however, Anthony Leeds discovered a homogeneous world view which clearly corresponded to the basic facts of Yaruro social structure.

The Yaruro are simple horticulturalists who also do a limited amount of hunting and collecting. There is a strong division of labor and of property along sexual lines, but little other social or economic differentiation. Each Yaruro village is composed of several related households; the village has a spokesman, but his authority is slight and there are no larger political units. There is great individual freedom of choice in economic, social, and even religious affairs. Each village constitutes a separate and independent center of relationships with neighboring villages and consequently has its own unique assortment of outside relationships, based partly on choice. This situation, like so many other aspects of the socioeconomic organization, is reflected in the cosmology.

> According to the Yaruro, the cosmos originally lacked not only humans, but even gods. There existed only three, concentric, rigid, blue, celestial domes; below them, a flat, undifferentiated, vast savanna all of sand; and a cold, dark, flat underworld. Beyond these there was, and is, nothing. Thunder, already then, was to be found between the upper celestial domes, while Sun, his wife, Moon, and their children, the stars, were already revolving between the lower two.
>
> Into this cosmos were spontaneously born the primordial gods. The goddess Ku'man, the grandmother of us all, who lives in a land to the west, out of the savanna created the discrete lands of her fellow gods and of the Yaruro. She created the . . . peoples. . . . She instructed the men and the women in their crafts. She ordained the social order.

The Yaruro do not conceive of the different parts of the cosmos as being rigidly separated; rather, there is continuous communication among the various worlds. The gods are believed to be tied to one another and to men by kinship and by visiting, just as the Yaruro households and villages are interrelated:

> The gods and the dead are conceptualized as continuous with those of us on earth. Conceptually they appear to constitute the two highest steps in the age levels: infant, child, young adult, elder, the dead, and the gods. . . . The relations between men and gods, the communication between the hither- and other-worlds, the cosmography itself, all show quite clearly that there is no separation of "natural" and "super-

natural" as discrete classes of events. The cosmos, society, and man are a single system in Yaruro thought.

The principal mode of communication between the two worlds is the night-long religious ceremony known as the *tonghé,* during which a village shaman visits the other-world and the gods, in turn, visit the village through his body. At dusk, surrounded by the entire community, the shaman begins to sing.

> In hundreds of improvised verses and melodies, he describes his journey, and then, after his arrival about midnight, his adventures in the lands of Ku'man and subsequently of the other gods. In each verse, the shaman sings an intonation which the entire community repeats in an identical antiphon. Thus the full experience of the shaman is transmitted to and shared by every member of the community. All is public; there is no secret knowledge. . . .
>
> The directness of contact between man and gods again emphasizes the unity of cosmos, society and man. Within this unity, the sharp division of a male sphere from a female sphere is found. These quite coordinate spheres, in the other-worlds as in the hither-world, in religion as in socio-economic life, are linked through the household.[6]

Every cosmology also contains beliefs about *death,* and most (but not all) include some conception of an afterlife. For the Yaruro the dead are not far away—they continue to help and advise their living kinsmen. During the tonghé, they speak through the shaman's body, exhorting the community to follow its ideals of peace and equality. They do not coerce or punish, nor are they manipulated by the living.

But this is only one of many different kinds of attitudes that primitive societies have developed toward death and the dead. Among the Navajo, for example, the ghosts of the dead are greatly feared, and anything connected with death is carefully avoided. Traditionally, if a death took place inside a Navajo hogan, that dwelling was abandoned or destroyed; Navajo patients have been known to flee from a hospital upon learning that a death has taken place there. The Navajo have no desire to establish contact with the dead; indeed, many of their elaborate ceremonies are designed to drive away ghosts or to cure illnesses which are believed to result from contact with a ghost.

Among the Trobriand Islanders, as Malinowski observed, the attitudes of the people towards the *baloma* (spirits of the dead) are highly ambivalent. On the one hand, it is believed that the baloma will some day be reborn in another body; they are honored by feasts at harvest time when they return to their villages

6. A. Leeds, "The Ideology of the Yaruro Indians in Relation to Socio-Economic Organization," *Antropologica,* Vol. 9 (1960), pp. 1–10.

from Tuma, the island of the dead. On the other hand, there exists a belief that another aspect of a dead man's spirit, called his *kosi,* leads "a short and precarious existence after death near the village and about the usual haunts of the dead man, such as his garden, or the seabeach, or the waterhole." These two sets of beliefs exist side by side, and the Trobrianders do not usually attempt to reconcile them. "People are distinctly afraid of meeting the *kosi,* and are always on the lookout for him, but they are not in really deep terror of him. Nobody has ever been hurt, still less killed by a *kosi.*"[7]

True *ancestor cults* are found in many Oriental and African societies, and anthropologists have demonstrated the relationship of this form of belief to a lineage structure. Each major lineage honors its own set of founding ancestors, and it is often believed that sickness or disasters affecting the members of a lineage are due to neglect of ancestors. In the case of clans, the founding ancestor may be legendary, but the belief in common descent from a founder and participation in the ancestor cult are among the forces that serve to integrate such dispersed groups.

Individual attitudes toward death are strongly influenced by social ideology. The dying person and his kin may be comforted by beliefs about reincarnation or a happy afterlife; but whatever the specific contents of the belief system, it generally provides the survivors with something to *do* in the face of death and thus channels their grief into socially acceptable actions. Ritualized mourning and funeral procedures are found in most societies. In many groups, almost every death is believed to have been caused by witchcraft, and so the response to a death is to find and punish the guilty party. Death in war often calls for retaliation against the group (though not necessarily the individual) held responsible. Among the Crow Indians, for example, grief was generally translated into aggressive action. But there was also a notable development of stoicism among the warriors, and death was not feared by most men. One class of warriors, known as "Crazy-Dogs-Wishing-to-Die," was pledged to such recklessness that its members usually got their wish within a year, although only after doing great damage to the enemy.[8]

Personal bravery and disdain for mere long life were basic ideals in Crow society. One vision-song was translated as follows: "Eternal are the heavens and the earth; old people are poorly off; do not be afraid." Lowie describes the sentiment articulated in this song as "one of the most characteristic of the Crow: mortals

---

7. B. Malinowski, *Magic, Science and Religion* (Garden City: Anchor Books, 1955), pp. 150–151.
8. R. H. Lowie, *The Crow Indians* (New York: Holt, Rinehart and Winston, 1956), p. 330.

Funeral rites practiced by the Small Nambas in New Hebrides. ***Kal Muller/ Woodfin Camp***

cannot expect to live forever like the great phenomena of nature; let them console themselves with the thought that old age is a thing of evil and court death while still young."[9]

These few examples should demonstrate that a great variety of beliefs about and attitudes toward death exists in human societies. Any generalizations that state that primitive man has an irrational fear of death must be taken with a grain of salt. Many of the simpler societies have also been influenced to some extent by great traditions, and in the belief systems of such groups it is quite common to find *syncretisms*—amalgamations of elements from very different cultural sources. Concepts and practices derived from the world religions often exist side by side with aboriginal customs in what may strike the observer as an incongruous fashion. For example, in Central America it is not at all unusual to find Jesus, Mary, and various saints incorporated into a Maya or Aztec pantheon and worshiped alongside native gods, while in parts of India we find many tribal peoples who have added the Hindu concept of reincarnation to their otherwise distinctive religion. Such syncretisms are also found in the "higher" religions, as anyone familiar with the origins of the Christmas tree or the Easter bunny will recognize.

The topic of religion has not been treated in any one place in this book. Religious roles, techniques, and beliefs have been discussed, respectively, in relation to the social, technological, and ideological systems of which they are a part. This is somewhat unconventional, but it has been done to stress the point that in most societies, religion is not a separate category of experience and action. There is, rather, a *religious dimension* to every part of life, and the Western contrast between "natural" and "supernatural" is simply not relevant to the understanding of such societies. In the words of Dorothy Lee:

> The world view of a particular society includes that society's conception of man's own relation to the universe, human and non-human, organic and inorganic, secular and divine, to use our own dualisms. It expresses man's view of his own role in the maintenance of life, and of the forces of nature. His attitude toward responsibility and initiative is inextricable from his conception of nature as deity-controlled, man-controlled, regulated through a balanced cooperation between god and man, or perhaps maintained through some eternal homeostasis, independent of man and perhaps of any deity. The way a man acts, his feeling of guilt and achievement, and his very personality, are affected by the way he envisions his place within the universe.[10]

In the present section we have briefly considered some

9. *Ibid.*, p. 114.
10. D. Lee, *Freedom and Culture* (Englewood Cliffs, N.J.: Prentice-Hall, 1959), p. 170.

"primitive" cosmologies. The examples were not selected for their exotic contents, but rather to demonstrate the ways in which men everywhere attempt to understand and bring order and value into the natural world. In our own cultural tradition, science has taken over much of this task, but the religious dimension is still important enough to us that we can understand how "religious conceptions and symbolism . . . unify the understanding of human experience, by emphasizing certain aspects of it . . . and placing them in a significant order and relationship one with another."[11] We find that the social function of myth and ritual is to create a "coherent pattern of meanings, in terms of which the worshippers understand the order of the world and their relation to it. These go with differentiation of roles of the actors in the sacred play . . . and the evaluation of spaces and objects in the material world according to the position they are assigned in this whole structure of thought and imagination and action."[12]

CONCEPTS OF AUTHORITY

In Chapter 4 we discussed several types of leadership roles: hereditary, bureaucratic, charismatic, and representative. The essential attribute of each of these roles was *authority*—the right to make decisions and to command the actions of others within a socially defined sphere. The four types of leadership roles differ not so much in their content as in their respective modes of *recruitment*—whether they are filled according to birth, competence, personal qualities, and/or by group selection. In this section, our main interest will be in how authority is conceptualized in different ideological systems. We shall examine in particular those beliefs which serve to *legitimate* the authority of leaders.

The problem of social authority can be stated quite simply: Why do "followers" follow? That is, given the fact that some individuals command the actions of others in most societies, what is it that allows them to do so? One obvious answer to this question is that most social systems provide positive and negative *sanctions* (rewards or punishments) which are applied to ensure obedience. Thus, a follower may obey a command out of his expectation of benefits (such as land, money, and prestige) or his fear of punishment. In a military social system, lines of authority are very strictly drawn: the penalties for failure to obey an order are clearly defined, while the benefits which may be conferred for obedience

11. G. Lienhardt, *Social Anthropology* (London: Oxford University Press, 1966), p. 136.
12. *Ibid.*, p. 133. Compare V. Turner, *The Ritual Process* (Chicago: Aldine, 1969).

are also well understood (promotions, passes, medals, and so forth). Within a family system, the distribution of authority may not be spelled out quite so clearly, but in most societies, parents are able to command the actions of children and have certain sanctions at their disposal which can be used to exact obedience.

This is only part of the story, however, for although sanctions (or the threat of sanctions) are important to social control, they are not sufficient to ensure obedience. Throughout history, people have given up benefits, submitted to punishment, and otherwise rebelled against authority for *ideological* reasons, especially when they have ceased to believe in the legitimacy of a leader's claim to authority over them. All social relationships require that both parties live up to the rights and obligations of their respective roles. But as we have seen, the leader/follower relationship always involves some asymmetry of authority, and this is contrary to the norm of reciprocity. Thus, if authority relationships are to exist without constant conflict, the followers must believe in the *right* of the leader to make decisions and command actions.

What would life be like in a society where no man was believed to have legitimate authority over any other man? Political philosophers have tried to imagine such a society, but they disagree about whether anarchy is desirable (or even possible). The ethnographic evidence is also conflicting. The Nuer have been described, for example, as living in a state of "ordered anarchy." Lacking chiefs, courts, or any kind of centralized government, they nevertheless maintain order and ensure cooperation through the balanced opposition of lineage segments. Disputes are often settled through the good offices of certain religious officials (leopard-skin chiefs). But even the Nuer have a greater differentiation of authority than do some of the simpler hunting and gathering groups, such as Yaruro or the Canadian Cree, among whom the ideal of complete equality was very nearly realized. Many of the Indian tribes of the Canadian subarctic are characterized by a pattern of "fierce egalitarianism" which makes large-scale cooperation virtually impossible, since they reject all but the most temporary kinds of authority.[13]

Peter M. Gardner has described a similar pattern of life among the Paliyans of South India.[14] This society represents an extreme of egalitarianism and individualism. The main feature of Paliyan social structure is what Gardner calls *symmetric respect.* This is a conception of ideal social relations according to which

---

13. See P. K. Bock, *The Micmac Indians of Restigouche* (Ottawa: National Museum of Canada, Bulletin 213, 1966), pp. 65–71.
14. P. Gardner, "Symmetric Respect and Memorate Knowledge: The Structure and Ecology of Individualistic Culture," *Southwestern Journal of Anthropology,* Vol. 22 (1966), pp. 389–415.

"one should avoid both aggression (hence competition) and dependence (hence cooperation)." This pattern is manifested in the following areas of Paliyan culture:

1. Socialization

Paliyan children, after an initial period of indulgence, receive a minimum of parental supervision and soon become extremely independent and self-reliant.

2. Noncooperative Behavior

The largest cooperating groups are nuclear families, and even here sharing is minimal; marriages are unstable and many people never marry; village membership is constantly changing. "No corporate functions are associated with village life. . . . There are no formalized ways of uniting, either 'democratically' or under leaders, during times of crisis." *Self-sufficiency* is expected of all persons. "To fail in this regard is to interfere with the rights of others." Paliyans "are hesitant to become emotionally involved with others and equally reluctant to unite toward practical goals."

3. Avoidance of Competition

The Paliyan ideal is nonviolent. "Avoidance of overt aggression is considered to be their first rule." Even competition in games is forbidden. "Social or economic differences must be minimized or denied and Paliyans are self-conscious about receiving anything which sets them off from others." *Disrespect* in any form is strictly prohibited: nothing must be said or done which appears to lower or disparage the status of another; in American slang, the greatest sin is to "put down" another person.

4. Social Control

No individuals or groups are empowered to resolve disputes, but a number of informal techniques are available. To avoid the outbreak of hostility, drinking of alcohol is forbidden and tension is released in fantasy. "When friction does arise, mature individuals frequently step forward and talk to the parties in conflict, joking with them or soothing their feelings. . . . The efforts of the conciliators are acted out without imposition of authority from above, for [they] have no mandate to order, arbitrate, or even suggest more appropriate behavior."

Separation of parties whose conflict cannot be conciliated is a frequently used device, and married couples often separate after their first serious quarrel, resulting in "serial marriages." In serious crises, when decisions must be made, certain individuals become "possessed" and the gods speak through them. Thus necessary authority can be exercised without disrupting the "purely human patterns of symmetric roles and self-reliance."

5. Ideology

Individualism is found even in the sphere of everyday knowledge and beliefs; for example, informants frequently disagreed on the folk taxonomy of common plants, and "lacked either the ability or desire to repeat songs, prayers or rituals." They placed no special value on set or traditional versions: "There were no formalized bodies of knowledge . . . formal teaching did not exist. . . . Paliyans communicate very little at all times and become almost silent by the age of 40. Verbal, communicative persons are regarded as abnormal and often as offensive. Gossip is practically non-existent."

We see here a society in which avoidance of authority is so extreme that even some basic cultural categories are not shared within the group but vary idiosyncratically. Gardner attributes this wide range of individual variation, in part, to the low level of communication within and among Paliyan villages; he comments that, as the Paliyan example shows, "culture is possible in which the cooperation leading to conformity is replaced by individualism . . . and in which formality and taxonomic precision are maximally idiosyncratic and minimally valued."[15]

The high degree of variation within the Paliyan belief system is both a cause and a result of the lack of communication and cooperation in the Paliyan social system. As we have stressed throughout this book, the sharing of common categories and plans is essential to smooth social interaction; but it is also true that such sharing of culture is *produced* by a high level of interaction. When people communicate freely with one another, they come to share common or at least complementary expectations; but when communication within or between groups breaks down, interests and beliefs tend to diverge and cooperation becomes increasingly difficult. This process may be seen in the relations among all kinds of groups, from families to nation states.

Most of the small societies studied by anthropologists show a relatively homogeneous *core* of shared beliefs plus a variable amount of *specialized* or esoteric knowledge which is carried and transmitted by the performers of specialized roles (see Figure

15. *Ibid.*, pp. 390, 393–399. Compare C. Turnbull, *The Mountain People* (Garden City, N.Y.: Doubleday, 1972).

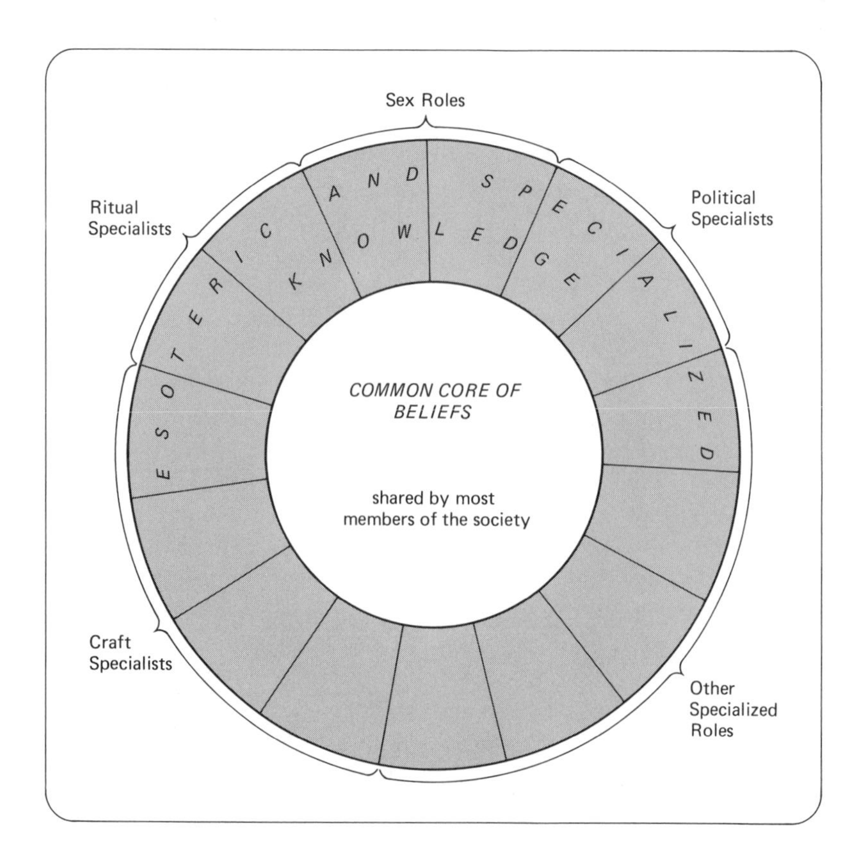

Figure 10.1 **The Structure of Culture in a Typical Folk Society**

10.1). This kind of "cultural structure" is highly adaptive for sedentary, moderately differentiated societies, since it promotes social integration (through sharing and interdependence) while permitting culture growth (through the addition of new specialized roles). Societies differ, however, in exactly what kinds of knowledge they allocate to specialists *and* in the ways in which these specialists are recruited. This is particularly true of political specialists who gain positions of authority or have these positions thrust upon them. Let us examine in detail one society in which charismatic leaders develop their prestige, wealth, and authority by systematic manipulation of the social structure.

The Siuai are a "society of forest-dwelling gardeners and pig-breeders" described by Douglas L. Oliver in his book *A Solomon Island Society.*[16] This fine ethnographic study focuses upon the indigenous leaders known as *mumis.* The role of mumi

16. D. Oliver, *A Solomon Island Society* (Cambridge: Harvard University Press, 1955).

is gained by achievement. Any authority that a mumi possesses has been built up by him as an individual in culturally prescribed ways. He is not an official of a political system. The mumi gains renown (*poku*) and power through personal effort, primarily by acquiring wealth and distributing it generously in fulfillment of his kinship obligations and in competitive feast-giving.

Not all Siuai males aspire to become mumis: they recognize that this takes a certain type of character as well as much hard work and sacrifice. As one native put it, " 'When he sits down he works and thinks about pigs and money; when we [non-leaders] sit down we sleep.' "[17] Wealth alone is not enough to make a man a mumi; it must be translated into symbols of prestige: a large and often frequented clubhouse, many slit-gongs, magical formulas, and feasts that are long remembered. There are no great differences in the everyday living standards of the natives, but the miser who possesses wealth but does not give feasts or who skimps on his funeral contributions is held in contempt and could never become a leader. Every powerful mumi in the course of his career builds a clubhouse and fills it with slit-gongs—or rather, has it built and filled for him. For it is by organizing the men of his community to do his bidding and then by compensating them with a generous feast that his renown grows.

Before the days of the Australian administration of the Solomon Islands, mumis were engaged in warfare; they acted as sponsors and organizers of raids (through the manipulation of property and alliances), rather than as warriors. Today, competitive feast-giving has replaced the outlawed hostilities, and rivals are vanquished by making them guests of honor at great food distributions which they can never hope to repay. (Compare p. 232, on the *potlatch* of the Northwest Coast Indians.)

In the absence of more formal political institutions, the mumi becomes the principal symbol of his community. Indeed, since the Siuai have little in the way of recurrent religious ritual and since kin-based allegiances crosscut the local communities, local solidarity centers on the mumi almost out of necessity. The leader does not possess any supernatural attributes himself, but it is symbolic of his importance to the society that the natives believe he controls a fierce demon (*horomorun*). This demon is thought to inhabit his clubhouse; it helps protect the mumi's property and person. While many natives have spirit-familiars, the horomorun is believed to be the most powerful in his area and must be appeased with many sacrifices and feasts. The more feasts a mumi gives, "the more nourishment is provided for his club-house demon, which waxes in size, in ferocity, and in loyal and protec-

---

17. *Ibid.*, p. 396.

tive adherence to the owner's person as well as property."[18] The respect and fear which the natives display toward this demon is a reflection of their attitudes toward the leader; thus the horomorun provides supernatural sanctions for the authority of the mumi.

In any society, the leader is a source of both continuity and change. He is a decision-maker, a determiner of *social organization.* His choices are constrained by the social structure, but as a unique individual he necessarily introduces personal factors into his decisions which then react upon the social structure, stimulating various activities and ultimately producing structural change. Among the Siuai, the authority exercised by the mumi stimulates the following kinds of activities: agricultural production and pig-raising for feasts; the building of structures and the manufacture of tradable articles; the procurement of shell money; the circulation, accumulation, and consumption of goods; and artistic activities, including music, drama, and various crafts. Thus the "political" leadership in this society has important implications for ritual and economic affairs.

In most tribal societies, it is difficult and artificial to separate the political, economic, and religious functions of leadership. Whatever his title, the leader commands the actions of others for the benefit of the social group as a whole. Where a significant surplus is produced, a leader may accumulate considerable "wealth," but this must either be translated into symbols of prestige (which reflect glory on his residential or kinship group) or be redistributed to the followers whose allegiance supports his authority. A Kwakiutl noble, after all, could personally consume only so much fish oil and use so many blankets; but by giving away or destroying surplus property in potlatches, he was able to legitimate his high status and that of the kin group which supported him. The *redistribution of accumulated wealth* is a common pattern in societies which do not have money economies:

> In non-industrial societies—even where trade plays some part—the redistribution of wealth is primarily a simple, direct transaction between the poorer and the richer. One man's surplus is used to relieve the wants of his kin, his friends, his neighbours, as happens certainly among the poorer sections of the population in the modern industrial world. This sharing of the necessities of life is an insurance against local failures of the food supply and individual misfortunes. Where life is precarious from year to year, and generosity is high among the virtues, it is in the interest of all to give when they can, so that they may receive when they must.[19]

Before turning to the closely related topic of property, let us consider the concepts of authority found in one other society

18. *Ibid.*, p. 379.
19. Lienhardt, *op. cit.*, p. 76.

where recruitment to leadership roles and the exercise of command are both quite different from the preceding examples. In the days before the British colonial administration, the Soga peoples of Uganda were divided into fifteen small kingdom-states, each of which was ruled by a king. According to Lloyd Fallers:

> In each of the kingdom-states there was a royal clan or lineage . . . which was set above commoner groups as having higher rank and an inborn fitness to rule. The ruler's position was hereditary within the royal clan. He was the active head of the kingdom and the overlord of all other holders of authority. He was also the chief priest for, as the ancestors of commoner lineages were thought to both assist and control the behavior of their descendants, so the royal ancestors . . . took a similar interest in the affairs of the nation as a whole. . . . Inherited regalia and a courtly style of living centering around an impressively constructed capital symbolized and enhanced the ruler's power.

Junior members of the royal clan were found throughout the kingdom in control of groups of villages. These princes constituted a threat to the king's authority. Civil war often broke out when the problem of succession arose, for there was no clear-cut rule of seniority within the royal group. An important stabilizing influence in the kingdom, however, was the patron/client relationship. The administrative staff which was responsible to the king was not recruited from the royal clan; rather, the prime minister and territorial chiefs were *commoners* bound to the ruler by personal loyalty. Since they did not share the inherited rank of the princes, these clients had no legitimate claim to the kingship, but they did act as "a check upon the ruler's power, since if he failed to govern within the limits set by custom they might combine in support of a rival prince and drive him from his position."

Traditional Soga society was thus organized in a *hierarchy* not unlike the feudal system of the late Middle Ages in Europe:

> At the top was the hereditary ruler—the paramount holder of authority and the central symbol of the kingdom's unity. At intermediate levels were the princes administering villages or clusters of villages and, counterbalancing them, the ruler's administrative staff of client-chiefs administering other villages or village clusters in the name of the ruler. Forming the broad base of the society were the communities of commoner agriculturalists organized into corporate patrilineal groups. Commoner and royal, kinsman and kinsman, patron and client, were bound together by highly personal rights and obligations. Subordinates owed superiors economic support through the payment of tribute, military support in war, the recognition of judicial and administrative authority, and personal loyalty. Subordinates in turn received paternalistic protection and aid.[20]

20. L. Fallers, "The Predicament of the Modern African Chief: An Instance from Uganda," *American Anthropologist*, Vol. 57 (1955), pp. 296–298.

Thus we can see that recruitment to positions of authority in this African society was determined primarily by birth. The legitimacy of the royal clan's claim to the kingship was supported by myth and popular belief. But there were also ways for ambitious and talented commoners to gain power, for the ruler's clients were often chosen from among ordinary peasants' sons who had been sent to the palace as servants, in hope of social advancement through royal favor.

Fallers describes how this system of recruitment to leadership roles based on kinship and personal loyalty eventually came into conflict with the British colonial administration. After their conquest of Uganda in 1892, the British gradually established a *bureaucratic* civil service (the African Local Government) in which advancement was to be based on *objective competence.* During the 1930s, payment of tribute to chiefs was forbidden; literacy, education, and ability were increasingly made the basis of recruitment to positions of authority. At first, the rulers' and chiefs' sons who monopolized the mission schools had an advantage in gaining positions in the civil service, but with more widespread education, eligibility was extended to others.

Although the transition from hereditary to bureaucratic leadership was made quite smoothly in this society, the traditional ideology did not disappear: it continued to exist alongside the new beliefs and values, causing recurrent conflict. The principal incompatibility is that between the traditional norms of kinship obligations and personal loyalty on the one hand and the bureaucratic norm of disinterested service on the other:

> As a civil servant, one ought to treat everyone alike without regard to particular status considerations. One applies general rules and procedures. One's competence is severely limited to what are called "official matters" and one is enjoined not to become involved in, nor even to know about, the personal lives of those with whom one has relations. . . . The strength of kinship ties is, however, a constant threat to the civil service norm of disinterestedness. The wide extension of kinship bonds means that a chief is frequently put into the position of having to choose between his obligation to favor particular kinsmen and his official duty to act disinterestedly. He may, for example, be asked to favor a kinsman in a legal case or to exempt him from taxation. Again, the institution of clientship survives and leads a *sub rosa* existence within the civil service.[21]

Since both the traditional and the bureaucratic ideologies are accepted by most Soga, and since it is the same individuals who are subjected to their conflicting demands, it is not surprising

---

21. *Ibid.*, pp. 299, 301.

that there is a high "casualty rate" among chiefs. Whichever norm they follow, they necessarily break the other. Fallers feels that in a way, this is preferable to having Soga society split into opposing factions; but the contradictory demands do create a serious predicament for individuals in positions of authority. "There are indications that for chiefs who do contrive to avoid falling afoul of sanctions, and who remain in office, this success is achieved at considerable psychic cost."[22] The conservative and progressive factions found in so many native societies undergoing modernization are symptoms of the same kind of ideological conflict working itself out in different institutional settings.[23]

CONCEPTS OF PROPERTY

Our concern in this section is with beliefs about legitimate rights over property: what these rights are and how they are acquired and maintained in various societies. The *legitimacy* of an individual's or a group's claim to some kind of property is really the crucial point, for unless we are prepared to agree with Proudhon that all "property is theft," we must recognize that every known society allocates to individuals exclusive control over certain resources and benefits, both tangible and intangible. The legitimacy of this control is attested by the existence of socially recognized ways of settling property disputes and of sanctions which can be applied to violators.

Property, then, is a cultural universal; but specific concepts of property vary widely among (and even within) human societies. This variation is found in both the *categories* of property recognized by different peoples and the *plans* for action associated with each category. What is a personal possession in one society may be public property in another, and vice versa. According to M. J. Herskovits, "there is no group who live so precariously that there is not some tool, some weapon, some bit of ornament or clothing that is not regarded as indisputably the possession of its maker, its user, its wearer."[24] Nevertheless, in some societies even highly valuable items may be taken or used without permission by specific categories of kinsmen. For example, in both Polynesia and South Africa, a sister's son is "permitted to take many liberties

22. *Ibid.*, p. 303. Compare J. Beattie, *Bunyoro: An African Kingdom* (New York: Holt, Rinehart and Winston, 1960).
23. See the comparison of European and American Indian concepts of leadership and authority in W. B. Miller, "Two Concepts of Authority," *American Anthropologist*, Vol. 57 (1955), pp. 271–289.
24. M. J. Herskovits, *Economic Anthropology* (New York: Knopf, 1952), p. 327.

with his mother's brother and to take any of his uncle's possessions that he may desire."[25]

The rules governing the control of various categories of property are often quite complex. One important distinction is that between rights of *use* and rights of *disposal.* That is, a society may recognize the exclusive rights of a group or of specific individuals to use some category of property and yet may place limitations on their right to dispose of the property as they see fit. In many nonliterate societies, what looks like ownership of tribal lands on the part of a ruler is actually more like a public trust. We have already discussed how the radical differences between European concepts of land ownership and those of African and American Indian societies led to misunderstandings and tragic conflicts. In much of Africa, the usual pattern was one of symbolic ownership by the ruler, but with constant redistribution and free use of land by members of the group. The idea that rights over land could be sold to an outsider was simply not present in the traditional ideology.

Hunting and gathering groups tend to range freely within their tribal territories, though particular fishing sites, berry bushes, or trees may be controlled by specific bands or families. Individual ownership of tracts is usually found only where trapping fur-bearing animals or gathering a cash crop (such as rubber) comes to supplement or replace subsistence activities. In any case, it is what the land yields rather than the land itself that is important to these groups. Similarly, the herding peoples of Africa and Asia seem to have placed few limitations on land use within the tribal territory, though watering places (especially wells) were often controlled by specific families. As Herskovits has noted:

> Grazing land as such is rarely if ever owned by individuals, and . . . a presumption of group ownership is strong. It also seems probable that the vagueness of the boundary lines where restriction of tenure exists is a result of the seasonal nature of grazing and the large resources of land available to most herding peoples. This in turn must lower any scarcity value it may possess, making it a matter approaching indifference where a given herd grazes, since all herds can be adequately cared for.[26]

It is among horticultural peoples that the greatest variety of land tenure beliefs and practices is found. Where land is plentiful, the general rule is that anyone who can clear and plant a tract is entitled to its yield. But when there exists a *scarcity* of land or

25. A. R. Radcliffe-Brown, *Structure and Function in Primitive Society* (New York: Free Press, 1952), p. 16.
26. Herskovits, *op. cit.*, p. 349.

water or where considerable investment of labor in irrigation or terracing is necessary, notions of tenure are more complex. Under these conditions, each individual must assert his claim to rights over land on the basis of those criteria recognized as legitimate by his society.

In Chapter 5, we defined a *corporate group* as a category of individuals who sometimes act together and who share in a common estate. Such corporate groups as clans, lineages, and local communities often control all of the productive land within a tribal territory; thus an individual can acquire rights of use only through membership in or relationship to some such group. For example, in a society with corporate matrilineages, a man can claim certain rights in the land of his own (that is, his mother's) lineage. But he may also have other claims to land. In many matrilineal societies, a man has some claim to the land controlled by his father's matrilineage even though he himself is not a member of this descent group. Among the Hopi, a married man usually works the fields allocated to his wife's household by her clan. A unilineal group which has more land than it needs may adopt members. Thus, men may acquire rights over land in a variety of ways.

It is not unusual to find several types of land tenure within a single society. Malinowski's data show three different categories of land in the Trobriand Islands, each of which is associated with a different plan for use. The three categories are (1) village sites, (2) uncleared forest, and (3) garden plots. Restrictions are placed on the first and third land categories, while every member of the community has access to the second. The garden land is divided into plots, and an individual or a gardening team works each one.[27] Furthermore, in the Trobriands there are at least *nine* distinct categories of persons who have an *interest* in each plot of garden land and its yield; these include the district chief and village headman (who receive some of the produce as tribute), the garden magician, the head of the local subclan, the village community as a whole (which retains certain rights over all surrounding land), the actual gardener, and finally the *sister* of the gardener (who receives much of the produce in the form of gifts made at the harvest).

Three different kinds of landownership are also found on the island of Uvea in Polynesia. They are: *public land,* where any member of the tribe may gather wood or exploit the lakes; *village land,* which includes public paths and strips of land along the shore, where "patches of taro are worked on land belonging to the whole village, the individual plots being redistributed at intervals

---

27. *Ibid.*, p. 351.

by the village council"; and *lineage land,* the most important category, which is controlled as a unit by the head of each patrilineage. Herskovits states:

> Tenure is assured every member of a lineage as his inherited right, despite the fact that the title to the land he is using rests in the group of which he is a member. In addition to a part of the land possessed by his own—that is, his father's—lineage, each person has also a "subsidiary right" to the land of his mother's line, though the exercise of this latter right is usually regarded as a "resource in case of need." Women as well as men are entitled to lineage land, so that even though a woman's principal means of subsistence is the produce of her husband's garden, she does not by the fact of her marriage forfeit her right to a portion of what is grown on the land of her own lineage.[28]

In many parts of Africa and Asia, this general pattern of landholding by corporate descent or residential groups is supplemented or replaced by a variety of "leasing" arrangements. For example, among the Nupe of Nigeria, there are two basic ways of acquiring land:

> (1) Acquisition in virtue of membership of a group (kinship group or village community), holding "corporate" right to land. (2) Acquisition of land in virtue of a contract between individual landowners—a short-term contract such as the "borrowing" of land, or a long-term, or definite, contract such as is embodied in tenantship and in the granting of land for services rendered.[29]

The landlord/tenant relationship may take a variety of forms depending primarily on the tenant's security of tenure and the amount of return owed to the landlord. In most tribal societies, the individual's right to use the land he has cultivated is fairly secure, and "rent" paid to a landlord is difficult to distinguish from "tribute" offered to a ruler as symbolic owner of the land. True exploitation of tenants by a leisure class of absentee landlords is a development of "civilization."

The rules governing land tenure in a given society provide a structure within which individuals frequently have a number of different options. As we have seen, a man may use his membership in or relationship to one or more corporate groups in claiming rights to land. It is also the case that the *same basic rules* can produce very *different patterns of landholding* in different or changing environments. (Elizabeth Colson has demonstrated this point for a village cluster among the Valley Tonga of Zambia.)[30]

---

28. *Ibid.*, p. 352.
29. S. F. Nadel, *A Black Byzantium* (London: Oxford University Press, 1942), p. 181.
30. E. Colson, "Land Law and Land Holdings among Valley Tonga of Zambia," *Southwestern Journal of Anthropology*, Vol. 22 (1966).

The processes of social organization and the environmental variables *interact* with an abstract social structure to produce concrete behavior.

The rules governing rights to other kinds of property are just as complex as those involved in land tenure.[31] A partial listing of common criteria on which claims to property are based may give some perspective on this problem (see Figure 10.2).

Many of these types of claims may apply to land and to goods other than land, including intangible possessions such as titles, songs, designs, and magical formulas. Among the Nootka Indians of the Northwest Coast, for example, there was a category of "ceremonially recognized property" called *topati,* which included "knowledge of family legends, which are transmitted like other property to the holders' heirs, a ritual for spearing fish . . . names of many kinds that are exclusively held and applicable at the pleasure of the owner, rights to carve certain designs on totem-poles and grave-posts, to sing certain songs, to dance certain dances, and many other rights of a highly specialized ceremonial nature."[32]

Determining the nature of property rights in a given society requires a careful investigation, in native terms, of the various categories of property and of how rights to each category are acquired. Among the Gururumba of highland New Guinea, Philip L. Newman found that an individual's property rights are conditioned by his or her sex role:

I. Membership in Corporate Groups (Descent Groups, Residential Groups, Others)
   A. Membership by birth
   B. Induction—including initiation, adoption, apprenticeship, marriage, and purchase of membership
   C. Indirect claim—based on relationship to group member

II. Claim Based on Personal and/or Social Role of Individual
   A. Individual inheritance
   B. Outright purchase of property
   C. Manufacture—including improvement and original creation
   D. Discovery—including capture of property
   E. Leasing—various forms of tenantship
   F. Status rights—including claims based on age, sex, and social class
   G. Custodianship—temporary control over property

***Figure 10.2* Common Bases of Claims to Property (Tangible and Intangible)**

31. See L. Pospisil, "A Formal Analysis of Substantive Law: Kapauku Papuan Laws of Inheritance," *American Anthropologist*, Vol. 67, No. 6, Part 2 (1965), pp. 166–185. In this article the author describes seventeen categories of property and the different ways in which each category is inherited.
32. Herskovits, *op. cit.*, pp. 390–391.

> Attending court cases and minor disputes makes it clear that men and women have different kinds of rights over various classes of property. Men exercise ultimate control over land and the usable products on it. For example, a woman planted a pandanus nut tree on her husband's land when she first married him and tried to claim the nuts from the tree after she divorced him. She lost the case because, although she had planted and tended the tree for many years, it was on his land. . . . In fact, there is very little property over which a woman can exercise final control except her implements, clothing, ornaments, and a few spells or charms associated with garden magic. She has rights of usufruct over land, dwellings, or patches of forest containing usable plants that are contingent upon her marriage or family affiliation, but she has no rights of alienation over any of these things for that right rests with men—either individually or in groups.[33]

Disputes over ownership probably arise in every human society. Even in those societies where intragroup theft is virtually unknown, the existence of overlapping or competing types of claims to property makes some conflict inevitable. It is one of the functions of a society's legal system to resolve such conflicts. A *legal system* consists of shared beliefs and expectations about how conflicts should be resolved; it includes *categories of disputes* and *plans for dealing with them*—plans which range from self-help and the informal sanctions of public opinion to formal legal institutions such as courts, trials, and prisons. It is sometimes argued that true legal systems are found only in societies with codified laws and clear-cut judicial institutions, but our concern here is with the goals rather than the procedures or mechanisms of conflict resolution.

Although most primitive societies have plans for the *punishment* of serious or repeated offenders, a far greater stress is usually placed upon *conciliation* of the parties to a conflict. Where there are competing claims, a compromise is sought, and where one party has clearly wronged another, the offender is encouraged to make restitution. Working against the common urge to retaliate, many tribal legal systems seek to prevent any widening of the conflict and to restore the social equilibrium through *compensation* of the victims and *rehabilitation* of the offenders. Two examples should make this process clear.

John Beattie has described the settlement of disputes among the Nyoro by means of "neighborhood courts." The basic pattern, he says, is always the same:

> After the parties to the dispute have stated their cases and the witnesses, if there are any, have been heard, the assembled neighbors discuss the issues raised and usually reach a unanimous decision.

33. P. Newman, *Knowing the Gururumba* (New York: Holt, Rinehart and Winston, 1965), pp. 40–41.

> They then direct the person who has been found to be at fault to bring beer and meat to the injured party's house on a specified day and time. If the person charged accepts the tribunal's decision, he does this . . . and there follows a feast, in which both the parties, and the neighbors who adjudicated on the case, take part. After this the dispute is supposed to be finished, and it should not be referred to again. . . . It is plain that the primary aim of these village tribunals is the restoration of good relations, not the punishment of an offender. . . . The beer and meat are not a "fine," for their purpose is to rehabilitate rather than to punish.[34]

Similarly, among the Cheyenne Indians, the greatest possible offense (other than homicide) was for an individual to hunt buffalo before the annual communal hunt. A single hunter "can stampede thousands of bison and spoil the hunt for the whole tribe. To prevent this, the rules are clear, activity is rigidly policed, and violations are summarily and vigorously punished." Yet even after the commission of this terrible offense, the ultimate goal of the tribe members having to deal with the offenders remains rehabilitation. E. A. Hoebel has reported on a typical case when the tribe was moving together, looking for buffalo:

> All the hunters were in a line with the Shield Soldiers to restrain them until the signal was given. . . . Just as the line came over a protecting ridge down wind from the buffalo, two men were seen riding in among the herd. At an order from their chief, the Shield Soldiers charged down on them. . . . The first to reach the spot killed the two hunters' horses. As each soldier reached the criminals, he slashed them with his whip. Their guns were smashed.
>
> The offenders were sons of a Dakota who had been living with the Cheyennes for some time. He said to his sons, "Now you have done wrong. You failed to obey the law of this tribe. You went out alone and you did not give the other people a chance."
>
> The Shield Soldier chiefs took the lecturing. The boys did not try to defend themselves, so the chiefs relented. They called on their men to consider the plight of the two delinquents, without horses or weapons. "What do you men want to do about it?" Two offered to give horses. A third gave them two guns. All the others said, "Good!"[35]

Needless to say, there are many cases in which arguments for restraint and attempts at conciliation are of no avail; but the fact remains that in every human society we find some shared conceptions of legitimate property rights on the basis of which settlements may be reached and social equilibrium restored.

Societies also differ in the extent to which they consider or treat various kinds of *persons* as property. In all societies an

34. J. Beattie, *op. cit.*, pp. 68–69.
35. E. A. Hoebel, *The Cheyennes* (New York: Holt, Rinehart and Winston, 1960), pp. 53–54.

individual has certain exclusive rights over his or her own body and over the "personal space" immediately surrounding him. Thus, except under unusual circumstances, murder and forcible rape are everywhere considered to be crimes; but there are many societies which phrase such crimes as violations of property rights. All corporate groups have a common "interest" in their members. We have already discussed clan vengeance as an instance of this principle (p. 154). But it is also common for such groups to accept *compensation* for the murder or injury of a member. In many parts of Africa the lineage of a murderer may avoid retaliation by paying a certain number of cattle to the victim's lineage, the exact size of the payment being proportional to the social importance of the murdered person. Compensation for damages to an individual's body or self-esteem is also found in many primitive societies. For example, among the Yurok Indians of northern California, an insult, a blow, and especially an injury that drew blood all called for the payment of compensation in shell money or other valuables; similar payments were common among the ancient Vikings.

As was pointed out in Chapter 5, in analyzing intergroup relations it is often useful to consider *women* as "valuables" employed in alliance-producing exchanges. Women are the highest type of valuable that can be exchanged, so "wife-givers" are generally considered superior to "wife-receivers." This is particularly true in patrilineal societies, where each exogamous descent group can perpetuate itself only by acquiring rights to the offspring of women from other descent groups. The payment of bridewealth is often best regarded as the purchase of a woman's reproductive powers (not the woman herself) from her corporate group; this is certainly the case in those societies where bridewealth need not be returned upon divorce so long as the woman's children remain with her husband's group.

Elsewhere, the bridewealth payment serves as an important *stabilizer of marriage,* for once it has been distributed among the members of the bride's corporate group, they all acquire an interest in the marriage (that is, in avoiding repayment). Furthermore, in most societies where bridewealth is given, the legitimacy and the social status of a woman's offspring depend upon the size and type of payment made at her marriage; thus, far from feeling humiliated, many women will brag about the circumstances of their "purchase." If women are property, they are a very special kind of property: part of the "prestige economy," as Herskovits calls it, rather than the subsistence economy. Their value cannot be reduced to a least common denominator, since they are exchanged only for other "prestige items," such as cattle or ritual valuables. And what is purchased is not the person as such, but rather certain limited rights in her reproductive, sexual, and domestic powers.[36] Similarly, it should be remembered that in our own society it is still possible for a husband to sue another man (and receive monetary compensation) for "alienating the affections" of his wife and thus depriving him of the woman's "domestic services."

True slavery is rarely found in the primitive world, and in most cases the "owner" acquires (whether through purchase, indebtedness, or capture) only *limited* rights over the person of the slave. In many areas, the children of a female slave are born free. Among the Lango of East Africa,

> the ownership of slaves is . . . so limited that the lot of the slave is almost indistinguishable from that of a freeman. On the payment of the usual dowry an enslaved girl is given in marriage by her captor, who stands in the place of a parent to her, and her only disability is that in the event of continued conflict with her husband she has no family to summon to her aid. Male slaves are usually adopted by their owners; they marry Lango wives and are in no way discriminated against.[37]

In societies which lack means of producing an economic surplus, slavery cannot be very profitable, and except when there has been an outside market for slaves (in "civilized" nations), their main use is in the households of their masters. Thus, although slaves may have had some prestige value, in most of these groups they produce little more than they consume. Herskovits concludes a brief survey of slavery in nonindustrial societies by remarking that

> whatever the manner of acquisition of slaves, and whatever the work required of them, their status as human beings invaded to a considerable extent their status as property. As a result, some limitations on free use and on unrestricted right of disposal were always present, and in many communities this operated eventually to take slaves out of the category of property, or at least to mark them off from other forms of property.[38]

The analysis of primitive economic systems—the production, distribution, and consumption of goods and services—is a complex subject which we shall touch upon only briefly. As we have seen, property rights, craft specialization, exchange within and among groups, and the ultimate consumption of resources are

---

36. Herskovits, *op. cit.*, pp. 381–384. For a somewhat different interpretation of women as "property" see R. A. Gould, "The Wealth Quest Among the Tolowa Indians of Northwestern California," *Proceedings of the American Philosophical Society*, Vol. 110 (1966), pp. 67–89.
37. Herskovits, *op. cit.*, p. 385.
38. *Ibid.*, p. 387.

all closely linked with other aspects of social life—kinship, leadership, religion, and so forth. Many of the characteristic features of what we think of as an economy—markets, money, banks—appear only sporadically in the primitive world. In the typical primtive society, specialization is limited, production is for personal use, accumulation for redistribution, and exchange for prestige or alliance. Among small-scale agriculturalists, whatever capital goods exist are usually the common property of corporate groups. There is little concentration of the means of production in the hands of an exploiting upper class. Even the accumulation of wealth is difficult due to the perishability of resources and the absence of any portable, durable "repository of value," that is, money.

Furthermore, built into many cultures are *leveling mechanisms* which ensure that "accumulated resources are used for social ends." As summarized by Manning Nash:

> Leveling mechanisms are ways of forcing the expenditure of accumulated resources or capital into channels that are not necessarily economic or productive. Every society has some form of leveling mechanism, but in primitive and peasant economies leveling mechanisms play a crucial role in inhibiting aggrandizement by individuals or by special social groups. Leveling mechanisms may take various forms: forced loans to relatives or co-residents; a large feast following economic success; a rivalry of expenditure like the potlach of the Northwest Coast Indians in which large amounts of valuable goods were destroyed; the ritual levies consequent on holding office in civil and religious hierarchies in Meso-America; or the giveaways of horses and goods of the Plains Indians. Most small-scale economies have a way of scrambling wealth to inhibit reinvestment in technical advance, and this prevents crystallization of class lines on an economic base.[39]

Such practices are often important obstacles to economic development in the Third World, but they cannot be eliminated without producing significant disruptions in native social systems.

In primitive societies, then, it is easier to analyze *economic action* than it is to isolate specifically economic institutions. Many kinds of economic action were discussed in Chapter 7 under the heading of "social organization." There we considered how people anticipate needs, allocate labor and resources, and make decisions in order to maximize some social value or combination of values. The *problems* of economic action are roughly the same in all societies. What differs is the *institutional setting* of the action (including technical knowledge and manpower) and the *social values* toward which the action is directed. In Chapter 11 we shall

39. M. Nash, *Primitive and Peasant Economic Systems* (San Francisco: Chandler, 1966), pp. 35–36.

discuss the nature of value systems and how they influence all kinds of social action. But first let us consider the way in which belief systems are integrated.

EIDOS: INTEGRATING PRINCIPLES OF BELIEF

The term *eidos* was used by Gregory Bateson to designate those general principles which give *coherence* to a system of beliefs.[40] The beliefs which make up an ideology are not a random selection: they fit together into an integrated pattern which makes sense, even if there are numerous loose ends and unresolved contradictions. Their coherence may be described by stating the *premises* (explicit or implicit) which underlie the belief system. For example, in our own culture, hundreds of specific beliefs about legitimate legal procedures are understandable in terms of the premise that "a man is considered innocent until proven guilty." Similar statements can be found which act as premises in other areas of American life. For example, Cora DuBois has suggested that there are four basic premises which underlie much of American middle-class culture; these are the assumptions, shared by most Americans, that: "(1) the universe is mechanistically conceived, (2) man is its master, (3) men are equal, and (4) men are perfectible."[41]

Often, the premises of a belief system are not explicitly stated by those who hold the beliefs, and it is up to the anthropologist to discover them. As Clyde Kluckhohn phrased it, the "implicit philosophy" of a people is, in large part, "an inferential construct based on consistencies in observed thought and action patterns."[42] After many years of ethnographic and linguistic study, Kluckhohn attempted to present the implicit philosophy of the Navajo Indians in terms of its underlying premises, and also the "laws of thought" which he feels characterize Navajo reasoning. Following are a few of the basic premises that Kluckhohn has described:

1. The universe is orderly: all events are caused and interrelated.
   a. Knowledge is power.
   b. The basic quest is for harmony.
   c. Harmony can be restored by orderly procedures.
   d. One price of disorder, in human terms, is illness.

---

40. G. Bateson, *Naven* (second edition; Stanford: Stanford University Press, 1958).
41. C. DuBois, "The Dominant Value Profile of American Culture," *American Anthropologist*, Vol. 57 (1955), p. 1233.
42. C. Kluckhohn, "The Philosophy of the Navaho Indians," in M. Fried, ed., *Readings in Anthropology*, Vol. II (New York: Crowell, 1959), p. 427.

2. The universe tends to be personalized.
   a. Causation is identifiable in personalized terms.
3. The universe is full of dangers.

. . .

7. Human relations are premised upon familistic individualism.
8. Events, not actors or qualities, are primary.

Kluckhohn elaborates each of these points to show its consequences for social action. For example, number 7, the premise of *familistic individualism,* is explained as follows:

> The Navaho, particularly as contrasted with the Pueblo and some other communally oriented groups, is surely an individualist. Ceremonial knowledge is acquired—and paid for—by the individual. Certain animals in the family herd belong to definite persons. Some rites give considerable scope to individual self-expression. Yet this is equally certainly not the romantic individualism of American culture. No unacculturated Navaho feels his independence sufficiently to break from his relatives. . . . In his cognitive picture of his world the Navaho insists that family life is the hub of interpersonal relations. He does not consider himself primarily as a member of a local community, nor of his tribe. . . . One's first loyalty is neither to oneself nor to society in the abstract but rather, in attenuating degrees as one moves outward in the circle of kin, to one's biological and clan relatives.

In addition to these basic premises, Kluckhohn states four general *laws of thought* which he feels the Navajo utilize in drawing conclusions from their premises. These are:

(a) Like produces like (e.g., the eagle flies swiftly so that the runner can well carry a bit of eagle down).
(b) A part can stand for a whole (e.g., witches can work upon hair or nail parings as effectively as upon the victim himself).
(c) *Post hoc ergo propter hoc* (e.g., the grass no longer grows as high as in the old days when taboos were strictly kept; therefore, the decrease in vegetation is caused by carelessness in observing the rules).
(d) Every subjective experience must have its demonstrable correlate in the sense world. (It is not enough for a Navaho to say "I *know* a witch is after me." Witch tracks must be found or dirt must fall mysteriously from the roof of the hut at night. All interpretations must be documented in terms of actual sensory events. . . .)[43]

Statements of this type (describing integrative principles of thought or belief) are useful to the extent that they sum up and make comprehensible a wide range of observations. They may also be *compared* with statements about integrating principles in other societies, for instance, Gardner's description of "sym-

43. *Ibid.*, pp. 428, 434, 435.

metric respect" in Paliyan society (see p. 321). Kluckhohn's description of Navajo familistic individualism may also be fruitfully contrasted with a premise suggested by Edward Banfield to account for the economic and political behavior of a peasant community in southern Italy.

Banfield defines *amoral familism* as the *belief* that one should "MAXIMIZE THE MATERIAL, SHORT-RUN ADVANTAGE OF THE NUCLEAR FAMILY; ASSUME THAT ALL OTHERS WILL DO LIKEWISE."[44] He contends that the people of the village called Montegrano behave *as if* they were following this rule; in this way, the premise of amoral familism is a generalization which makes a large range of behavior intelligible to an outsider, and even predictable. From this premise, Banfield derives a number of logical implications which do indeed correspond to important features of social life in the village. For example, Banfield argues that in a society where people accept the premise of amoral familism, behavior outside of the nuclear family will lack any moral constraints; therefore:

1. No one will further the interest of the group or community except as it is to his private advantage to do so, since the hope of short-run material gain is the only recognized motive for participation in public affairs. Only bureaucratic officials will even concern themselves with public matters, for only they are paid to do so. It is assumed that they will take bribes and otherwise use their positions for private advantage. (This attitude extends also to teachers and other professionals.)
2. Organized activity will be very difficult to achieve and maintain since it requires trust and loyalty, and these sentiments do not extend beyond the nuclear family. This retards economic development and even emigration, for those who have emigrated feel no attachment to their kindred who have remained in Montegrano. There are "no leaders and no followers," for no one will take initiative, and if someone did, the group would refuse to cooperate out of distrust.
3. There is no connection between political ideology (in the usual sense) and actual behavior. Claims of "public spirit" are regarded as fraud, and long-run interest, class interest, or public interest do not affect voting behavior *if* the family's short-run material interest is in any way involved.
4. Law is disregarded when there is no reason to fear punishment: it is assumed that everyone cheats on taxes; minimum wage laws are universally ignored; workers are

44. E. Banfield, *The Moral Basis of a Backward Society* (New York: Free Press, 1958), p. 85.

> paid only at the convenience of their employers. These atitudes even affect land tenure, for as Banfield states, the mutual "distrust between landlord and tenants accounts in part for the number of tiny owner-operated farms in Montegrano." The peasants prefer owning a few acres of land to leasing a much larger quantity.[45]

It is questionable whether all these attitudes and behaviors can be directly deduced from the premise of amoral familism, but they are certainly consistent with it, and to this extent, the general principle is useful in understanding the ideology of these people.

There are a few principles of conceptual integration which appear again and again, in various parts of the world. The cultural *contents* which are organized by these principles differ according to region, but the structural patterns are clearly similar. One of these widespread principles is *dualism*: the division of various conceptual and social realms into two opposed or complementary parts. In South and Southeast Asia, dualism often permeates every part of a belief system in the form of an elaborate symbolism opposing left to right, good to evil, male to female, purity to pollution, and so forth, and connecting all of these pairs into an overall duality. This pattern is frequently found in societies where there is a similar dual organization of social groups into moieties.

One of the African societies with such a pervasive dualistic pattern is Dahomey. Since we have already quoted the Dahomean origin myth at some length (p. 313), let us see how this principle appears in other parts of the culture. As P. Mercier has noted:

> Among the patterns which are to be found in the divine world and in the system of kingship, the most characteristic is the dualistic pattern. At the head of the Dahomean pantheon we have seen the dual divinity, creator or rather demiurge, *Mawu-Lisa*, a pair of twins or according to some, described as twins simply in order to express both their unity and their dual nature. The ideal type of every group in the divine world is a pair of twins of opposite sex or, more rarely, of the same sex . . . among men also the ideal birth is a twin birth. . . . This twin structure of the gods is the rule, even though, in the present stage of its elaboration, not everything has been integrated into this framework; it is typical that in many cases they speak of androgynous beings, to such an extent does the double nature seem entirely reasonable. . . .

The principle of dualism which is evidenced in this elaborate cult of twins in Dahomey is even more clearly seen in the sphere of political organization:

> At the head is the king, and he is two in one. . . . There is only one royal personage, but there are two courts, two bodies of exactly sim-

---

45. *Ibid.*, pp. 86–93.

ilar officials, two series of rituals in honour of the royal ancestors. The reigning king bears two titles: 'king of the city' and 'king of the fields'. . . . Every title and every administrative office is conferred simultaneously on a woman within the palace and a man outside it. . . . Moreover, titles, already dual in themselves, are organized in pairs—one left and one right.[46]

Another widespread integrating principle which may be illustrated in Dahomean culture is the notion of *hierarchy.* The officials controlling Dahomean society are arranged in a hierarchy of offices under the king. Each of the principal chiefs who governs a large region of the kingdom has minor chiefs under his direction who are directly responsible to him. In the same way, each of the children of *Mawu* has a number of minor deities under his control who are responsible to him. As Mercier comments, "There is a remarkable correspondence between the government of the universe and that of human society, between the structure of the world of gods and that of the world of men."[47]

Finally, there is the important figure of Legba, the "spoiled child" of Mawu who transmits messages among the gods and men. Legba has no twin in the origin myth, but during the last two centuries he has become paired with an abstract principle, the conception of *impersonal fate.* This notion, introduced into Dahomey from other African societies, is known as Fa. The concept of Fa has been "inserted into the very heart of Dahomean cosmology."[48] Fa is believed to govern the destiny of groups and of individuals. Each individual is born under a double sign, and it is possible to learn what destiny has decreed for one through various rituals of divination. Nevertheless, the Dahomeans do not believe in an absolute determinism, and this is where Legba enters the picture:

He introduces into destiny the element of chance or accident. Man is not a slave. Though his fate binds him strictly to the structure of the world, it is no more than the guiding line of his life. He is not debarred from all freedom, and *Legba* ensures this in the world of the gods. *Legba* has stratagems and tricks to evade the rigid government of the world. It is clear that the mythology of *Legba* is connected with that of *Fa*, of which it is in some sort the reverse. He is not the power of evil, he may be the bearer of evil or of good, he may protect man but equally he may make his lot harder. *Legba* is universally venerated in all the cult groups and in every home. Each man has a *Legba* as he has a destiny, and he must propitiate him lest his destiny becomes worse.[49]

46. P. Mercier, "The Fon of Dahomey," in C. D. Forde, ed., *African Worlds* (London: Oxford University Press, 1954), pp. 231, 232.
47. *Ibid.*, p. 233.
48. *Ibid.*, p. 215.
49. *Ibid.*, pp. 228–229.

Here we can see how the integrating principle of dualism has operated to bring two originally independent conceptions (Fa and Legba) into a paired relationship. In Dahomean culture, the dualistic and hierarchical *eidos* provides a general *plan for thinking* which is applied to all kinds of concepts, producing a coherent system of belief.

Not all cultures have such an overall integration or patterning of thought, but modern anthropology suggests that there may be a *limited number of general principles* underlying the ideological and social systems of human societies. The search for these principles is what makes cultural anthropology more than a descriptive or historical discipline. One extremely important approach to this problem is that of Claude Lévi-Strauss. In his recent works, such as *The Savage Mind* and the three volumes of *Mythologiques,* Lévi-Strauss has attempted to demonstrate the coherence of primitive belief systems by detailed examinations of native categories and their relationships.

He begins his book on *The Savage Mind* by rejecting the notion that primitive thought is in any fundamental way different from that of contemporary civilized men. He documents the logical, abstractive, and deductive powers of many primitive peoples, as well as their keen perception and persistence. The development during Neolithic times of the "great arts of civilization—of pottery, weaving, agriculture and the domestication of animals"—is evidence of early man's cognitive capacities, for "there is no doubt that all these achievements required a genuinely scientific attitude, sustained and watchful interest and a desire for knowledge for its own sake."[50]

How, then, does primitive or "mythical" thought differ from "scientific" thinking—which is, after all, a recent development in Western civilization? Myth, Lévi-Strauss contends, is a "science of the concrete," in which man attempts to understand the world in terms of its *sensible qualities*—that is, through his perception and imagination rather than through the abstraction of properties which cannot be directly perceived. Primitive man categorizes his experiences on the basis of what he can see, hear, taste, smell, and feel; he then uses this "repertoire" of categories to build mythical explanations of what he seeks to understand.[51]

Since the elements of mythical thought are never completely freed from their concrete sources, Lévi-Strauss insists that a structural analysis must examine the *detailed contents* of myths in order to comprehend their significance. Only by studying the precise identity of, say, animals mentioned in myths and plants used

---

50. C. Levi-Strauss, *The Savage Mind* (Chicago: University of Chicago Press, 1966), p. 14.
51. *Ibid.*, p. 17.

in rituals, as well as their relations to one another in native thought, is it possible to discover the *principles* underlying a primitive belief system.

The principles which Lévi-Strauss discovers in totemic and other systems of classification always involve an *opposition* of terms: male/female, living/dead, high/low, individual/group, animal/plant. These oppositions function to define categories within a belief system in the same way that phoneme attributes (voiced/voiceless, and so forth) function in phonological systems, and that Murdock's criteria (lineal/collateral, and so forth) function in kinship systems. Careful study is needed to determine which oppositions are involved in a given classification because, according to Lévi-Strauss, it is the oppositions themselves and *not* the categories formed by them which are transferred from one part of a cultural system to another. For example, in a society with totemic clans there are two systems of concepts, one of "natural species" and the other of "cultural groupings."

> Nature: species 1 (bear) ≠ species 2 (eagle) ≠ species 3 . . . ≠ species *n*
> Culture: group 1 (Bear Clan) ≠ group 2 (Eagle Clan) ≠ group 3 . . . ≠ group *n*

Now, according to Lévi-Strauss, the cultural system is *homologous* with (has the same form as) the natural system. However, the homology "is not between social groups and natural species but between the differences which manifest themselves on the level of group on the one hand and on that of species on the other."[52] It is the oppositions (≠) that remain constant. Totemism does not imply that group 1 is like species 1, group 2 like species 2. Rather, it implies that group 1 *differs from* group 2 in the same way that bears *differ from eagles,* and so on. Thus it is essential to discover how each society conceives of the contrasts among crucial species, for bear and eagle can be differentiated by a number of different oppositions (low/high, slow/fast, friend/enemy, and so forth), and it is the particular opposition chosen that is also significant in the social structure and other systems of classification. Animals and plants are important to myth and ritual because they provide a natural model for the categories of culture: "The diversity of species furnishes man with the most intuitive picture at his disposal and constitutes the most direct manifestation he can perceive of the ultimate discontinuity of reality."[53] Oppositions perceived on one level can be transposed to another level and

52. *Ibid.*, p. 115.
53. *Ibid.*, p. 137.

used there to create folk taxonomies. This is also true in societies without totemic institutions.

Lévi-Strauss believes that the integrating principles of ideological and other cultural systems are to be found on the level of unconscious structure, with most of them taking the form of binary (two-way) oppositions. Not all anthropologists accept these ideas, and few can handle them with the elegance and productivity of Lévi-Strauss. But the search for ways to describe the general patterns of cultural systems is continuing, and the contributions of Lévi-Strauss are sure to stimulate discussion for many years.[54]

In the next chapter, we turn to the analysis of value systems. Several of the concepts developed in this chapter will be seen to have relevance for the study of values. As was noted in the Introduction to Part Five, conceptions of what *is* and what *should be* are closely interrelated. It should also be remembered that our conceptions of what exists and our judgments about what is valuable are both largely the product of our cultural tradition.

RECOMMENDED READING

Banton, M., ed., *Anthropological Approaches to the Study of Religion.* London: Tavistock Publications (A.S.A. Monographs, No. 3), 1966. An interesting collection of essays on the nature and social functions of religion as viewed by contemporary anthropologists.

Herskovits, M. J., *Economic Anthropology.* New York: Norton, 1952. A descriptive survey of economic institutions and practices in a large number of the world's societies.

Lévi-Strauss, C., *Totemism.* Boston: Beacon Press, 1963. Probably the most accessible of the works of the French master, reviewing the history of approaches to totemism and adding his own distinctive interpretations.

Pospisil, L., *Anthropology of Law: A Comparative Theory.* New York: Harper and Row, 1971. The most recent major contribution to the analysis of legal systems in a comparative framework.

54. See the recent two-volume collection of essays dedicated to Lévi-Strauss on his sixtieth birthday: J. Pouillon and P. Maranda, eds., *Échanges et Communications* (The Hague and Paris: Mouton, 1970).

CHAPTER 11
Value Systems

Cultural *values* may be briefly defined as *shared conceptions of what is desirable:* they are *ideals* which the members of some social group accept, explicitly or implicitly, and which therefore influence the behavior of group members. Some values relate to very specific objects or events, while other values are much more general and relate to a variety of situations. As with other rules of culture, values may be violated, and individuals may use values to achieve their own private purposes. But since such actions take place within a cultural context, they often testify to an awareness of the very conceptions they violate. It is often the revolutionary who is most aware of his society's values precisely because he wishes to change them.

The *value system* of a society consists of the explicit and implicit ideals shared by the group together with their relative *priorities* and *integrating patterns.* That is, like beliefs, the values held by members of a social group tend to form a coherent system. Despite the presence in many a society of alternative or even conflicting conceptions of the desirable, it is usually possible to demonstrate some ranking of the values found as well as systematic connections among these values. The general conceptions which help to integrate a value system are usually referred to as *patterns* or *orientations* (rather than principles or premises). In this chapter, we shall survey the ways in which several societies *evaluate* the behavior of their members and certain products of that behavior.

THE PROCESS OF EVALUATION

Human behavior frequently involves judgment and choice. We are constantly called upon to respond to our environment by classifying our experiences and/or deciding among alternative courses of action. In daily life, we must answer questions such as: Did he say *pin* or *pen*? Is that Mary Smith or her twin sister? Should I order steak or spaghetti? What kind of book is this? And on occasion we are faced with more crucial decisions: Which of these candidates should I vote for? Should I ask Jane to marry me? Which of these job offers should I accept?

In trying to answer such questions, the individual makes use of various *criteria* or *standards of judgment.* Some of these criteria are highly personal; but most of the categories and standards that we use are socially acquired: they are learned as part of the culture of the groups to which we belong or wish to belong. Culture, then, includes *plans for making decisions;* it provides us with criteria for judging what kinds of evidence are relevant and even how much evidence we need before making a choice. We may not be aware of how frequently we rely upon socially acquired standards. But numerous experiments have shown that even in the artificial setting of the psychology laboratory, most people "give extra weight to stimulus material, or suggestions, attributed to people whom they regard as experts [or] attributed to the majority of a group with whom they identify."[1] (See Figure 11.1.)

The process of evaluation, then, is universal; but the standards by which persons, objects, and events are judged differ according to one's culture. Even in so prosaic a matter as food preferences, we find striking cultural differences. In most societies, there is a staple food which must be included in any meal if the meal is to be judged filling or satisfying. But whether this staple is rice, taro, milk, maize, potato, manioc, yams, or bread obviously depends upon local tradition. Even the judgment that some substance is or is not "food" involves a partly arbitrary evaluation: the insects that one group treats as a delicacy are rejected by another group as disgusting.

This last sort of evaluation is actually a form of categorization. The person making such a judgment must decide whether a given object or event meets the criteria for assignment to a given category. If the ethnographer can discover what criteria are used in making the judgments, he may be saved the trouble of listing all known substances as "foods" or "nonfoods." He may also be able to *predict* how the members of a society would classify some

1. D. Johnson, *The Psychology of Thought and Judgment* (New York: Harper, 1955), pp. 295–296.

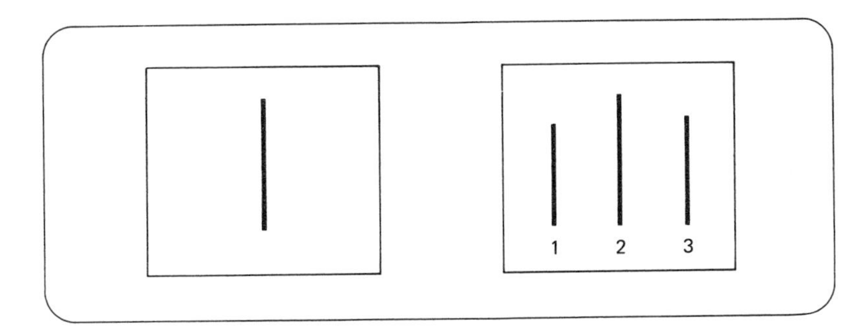

Figure 11.1 **Opinions and Social Pressure. In this experiment college students were asked to match the length of lines (left-hand card) with one of three line lengths (right-hand card). Students were able to do this with few, if any, errors. However, when these students were placed in groups whose other members had been secretly instructed to give the same *wrong* answer, 75 percent agreed, in varying degrees, with the majority. Errors made under conditions of social pressure averaged 40 percent.**

novel substance. Furthermore, it may be possible to discover relationships between food categories and other kinds of evaluation.

E. R. Leach has suggested that every culture divides the objectively edible part of the environment into three main categories:

1. Edible substances that are recognized as food and consumed as part of the normal diet.
2. Edible substances that are recognized as possible food, but that are prohibited or else allowed to be eaten only under special (ritual) conditions. These are substances which are *consciously tabooed.*
3. Edible substances that by culture and language are not recognized as food at all. These substances are *unconsciously tabooed.*

He also argues that these categories and their associated plans for consumption are systematically related to cultural attitudes toward interpersonal relations. Leach notes that there is a "universal tendency to make ritual and verbal associations between eating and sexual intercourse," and he hypothesizes that "the way in which animals are categorized with regard to edibility will have some correspondence to the way in which human beings are categorized with regard to sex relations." He discusses this idea using the example that "from the point of view of any male [ego], the young women of his social world will fall into four major classes," and "the English put most of their animals into four very comparable categories." These classifications are reproduced below, side by side:

Categories of Women (General)	*Categories of Animals (English)*
1. Those who are very close—"true sisters," always a strongly incestuous category.	1. Those who are very close—"pets," always strongly inedible.
2. Those who are kin but not very close—"first cousins" in English society, "clan sisters" in many types of systems having unilineal descent. . . . As a rule, marriage with this category is either prohibited or strongly disapproved, but premarital sex relations may be tolerated or even expected.	2. Those who are tame but not very close—"farm animals," mostly edible but only if immature or castrated. We seldom eat a sexually intact, mature farm beast.
3. Neighbors (friends) who are not kin, potential affines. This is the category from which [ego] will ordinarily expect to obtain a wife. This category contains also potential enemies.	3. Field animals, "game"—a category toward which we alternate friendship and hostility. . . . They are edible in sexually intact form, but are killed only at set seasons of the year in accordance with set hunting rituals.
4. Distant strangers—who are known to exist but with whom no social relations of any kind are possible.	4. Remote wild animals—not subject to human control, inedible.[2]

Finally, Leach suggests that the special importance of certain animals—shown by the elaborate taboos and rituals which surround hunting, racing, or eating them and the use of their names as terms of abuse when applied to human beings—is associated with the *ambiguous* position of these animals in the classification (see Figure 11.2). For example, the dog is "nearly human"; the horse is partly a pet, partly a farm animal; the rabbit is sometimes a farm animal and sometimes game; and the fox is a wild animal treated like game in the ritualized British fox hunt.

Leach's theory that "ambiguous categories . . . attract the maximum interest" enables us to understand the *special value* that attaches to certain forms in a given culture.[3] Species or beings that refuse to fit into our normal categories (good/bad, male/female, alive/dead, and so forth) become the focus of taboo and ritual, be they zombies, hermaphroditic spirits, or virgin moth-

2. E. R. Leach, "Anthropological Aspects of Language: Animal Categories and Verbal Abuse," in E. Lenneberg, ed., *New Directions in the Study of Language* (Cambridge: M.I.T. Press, 1966), pp. 31, 42–44.
3. E. R. Leach, "Genesis as Myth," in J. Middleton, ed., *Myth and Cosmos* (Garden City: Natural History Press, 1967), p. 4.

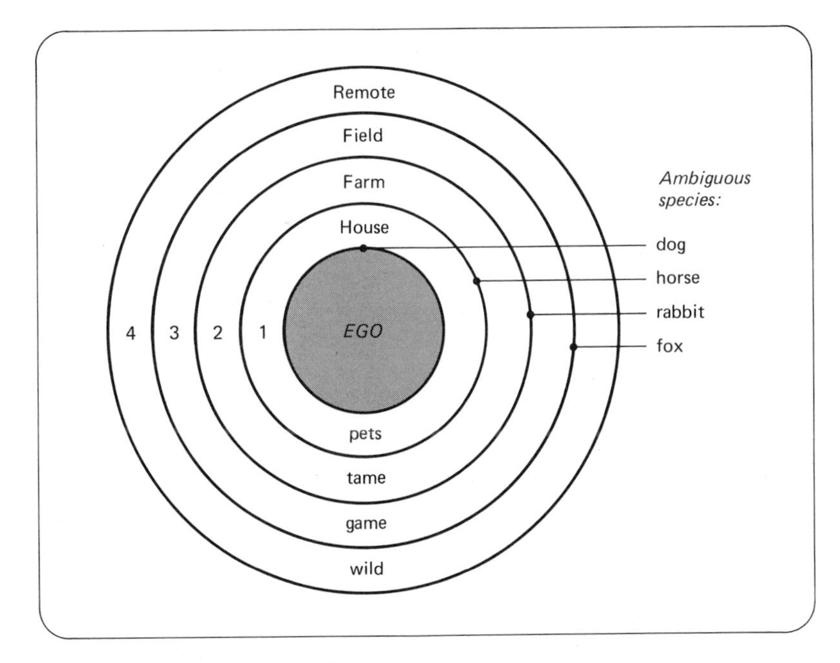

Figure 11.2 **Animal Categories (after Leach)**

ers. Such beings are said to "mediate" between the ordinary categories. This theory is an extension of some ideas of Claude Lévi-Strauss (see above, p. 345) and shows once again the importance of understanding the basis of native classifications. But not all evaluations involve a simple classification. We turn now to some of the more complex types of evaluative processes.

Many kinds of evaluation call for judgments of *equivalence* or of relative *ranking.* Given a series of objects, events, or persons, we are sometimes required to judge which of them are in some sense the same and/or to rank them along some kind of continuous dimension. These judgments are often very difficult to make because they call for the use of a number of different criteria, each of which must be weighted somewhat differently. Because of these complications, it is unusual to find complete agreement among members of even a homogeneous community, and harder still to decide how people are making their judgments. But the sensitive ethnographer can use the *disagreements in evaluation* as clues to what criteria are actually being used.

For example, in his study of native prestige ranking in the Mexican village of Zinacantan, Frank Cancian attempted to judge the relative prestige of Zinacanteco men on the basis of their participation in the religious *cargo* system:

> The *cargos* are public offices, and Zinacanteco men fill them as community service. That is, the incumbents receive no pay and usually make very substantial cash outlays for saints' *fiestas* and ceremonies. The term of service is one year. . . . Almost all Zinacanteco males serve at least one cargo during their lifetime. . . . The cost of cargos varies tremendously, and only the rich can afford the most expensive ones.

However, Cancian found that

> expense is not the only factor that determines the "prestige" (respect, deference) that accrues to a man for his participation in the cargo system. Other factors are important. The most crucial of these seems to be the authority that the incumbent of one cargo has over the incumbents of other cargos in ritual situations. . . . In almost all cases it is difficult to decide how much expense is equivalent to how much authority in calculating the prestige a cargo brings to . . . the person who has completed it. Another difficulty is that the idiosyncratic features of some cargos, e.g., which fiestas they are featured in, seem to have influence on the prestige. In the end I had to construct a prestige ranking of cargos using the cost scale as a base line, changing the rank of some cargos according to my knowledge of the authority of the post and the idiosyncratic features involved.

Since the people of Zinacantan were reluctant to discuss relative prestige, Cancian tried to validate his ranking of cargos by asking his informants which men had completed what cargos and then analyzing the *factual errors* that they made. He found that the errors were not random, but rather that his informants were guessing "in terms of some general impression of the cargo-holder's prestige in the community." That is, when an informant gave an objectively wrong answer, he usually indicated a cargo that Cancian had ranked as very close in prestige to the correct answer. From this material, Cancian concluded that "Zinacantecos, though they will not openly discuss it, actually do perceive cargos in terms of relative prestige; and are apt to remember the approximate prestige of an individual even when they have forgotten the particular cargo he passed in the process of achieving it."[4]

The institution just described is one of the leveling mechanisms discussed in Chapter 10 under concepts of property. That is, the cargo system of Zinacantan both translates individual wealth into socially approved symbols of prestige and prevents excessive accumulation of resources by individuals. But the persons who participate in such institutions are not being uneconomical or irrational. They are using their wealth as a *means* to achieve culturally valued *ends*.

---

4. F. Cancian, "Informant Error and Native Prestige Ranking in Zinacantan," *American Anthropologist*, Vol. 65 (1963), pp. 1068–1069, 1073.

The distinction between means and ends is extremely important to an understanding of value systems. As we shall see, there is far more agreement among cultures about what constitute valuable ends than there is about the appropriate means to achieve these ends. In addition, what constitutes a valid end in one society may be viewed merely as a means to some further end in another group. As Robert L. Heilbroner has pointed out, the *profit motive* or the valuing of gain for gain's sake, which is common in our own cultural tradition, "is foreign to a large portion of the world's population, and it has been conspicuous by its absence over most of recorded history," while the positive "social sanction of gain is an even more modern and restricted development." Heilbroner states that until nearly the start of the sixteenth century in Europe, land, labor, and capital were simply not "for sale":

> Economic life and social life were one and the same thing. Work was not yet a means to an end—the end being money and the things it buys. Work was an end in itself, encompassing, of course, money and commodities, but engaged in as a part of a tradition, as a natural way of life. In a word, the great social invention of "the market" had not been made.[5]

Thus, in trying to understand the value systems of other societies, we must beware of confusing means and ends. This is particularly true with respect to the high value which most Americans place upon *efficiency.* All peoples have some notion of more and less efficient means to an end. If they did not, they probably could not survive. But in most societies, efficiency is only one of a number of criteria used in choosing among possible courses of action. In American culture, this particular value often becomes an end in itself—or at least the sole standard of judgment. This pursuit of efficiency has doubtless contributed to our amazing economic development; but it has also led us to squander many of our social and natural resources, to upset the balance of nature, and to ruin the natural beauty of large portions of our continent.

A similar point can be made about American attitudes toward *education.* As Cora DuBois has observed, "To many Americans schooling has acquired the weight of a goal rather than a means. A college degree is a 'good thing' in itself, whether or not the education entailed is prized."[6]

In the following sections we shall consider the ways in which

---

5. R. L. Heilbroner, *The Worldly Philosophers* (revised edition; New York: Simon and Schuster, 1961), pp. 12–14. Compare M. Spiro, "Buddhism and Economic Action in Burma," *American Anthropologist*, Vol. 68 (1966), pp. 1163–1173.
6. C. DuBois, "The Dominant Value Profile of American Culture," *American Anthropologist*, Vol. 57 (1955), p. 1237.

moral and esthetic judgments are made in a number of societies, with particular attention to the distinction between means and ends. The chapter will conclude with a discussion of the general patterns and orientations which help to integrate value systems.

JUDGMENTS OF GOOD ACTIONS: MORALITY

Every culture provides a set of categories and standards to be used in evaluating human behavior. Some of these standards are ideally the same for all persons: the Golden Rule, the ideal of self-determination, and the ideal of a single law "for you and for the stranger who sojourns with you" (Exodus 15:16); they are *universalistic* standards, intended for all human beings. Other standards are *particularistic*: they are meant to apply only to certain persons within specific social groups—not to outsiders.

Every society has numerous particularistic standards. The most important of these are the role expectations—for example, conceptions of how a good father or a good employer should behave. But even where moral standards are stated in universalistic terms, certain particularistic standards generally take precedence over them. For example, Theodore Stern has analyzed the folklore of the Klamath Indians of Oregon to determine whether their mythology presents "an internally consistent statement of valued behavior." Based on selected myths, Stern concluded that in Klamath society *loyalty to kin* takes precedence over "commitment to an all-embracing ethical code, for it is only with more remote consanguines and neighbors that such a code begins to be expressed." Within the immediate family, warm personal ties may override moral expectations and even the norm of reciprocity. "It is only among neighbors and . . . strangers that a person is judged solely on his performance."[7]

Among the Navajo, the ideal moral pattern was to treat all people as if they were relatives. But even this universalistic standard recognizes that a moral code must be *extended* from the in-group, where it is relatively easy to observe, to an out-group, where it is more difficult to follow. Even in complex civilizations, kinship relations are frequently chosen to *symbolize* the ideal relationship among strangers; for example, the Emperor as the "father of his people," or the use of "sister" among members of the women's liberation movement.

Another useful distinction is that between *absolute* and *situa-*

7. T. Stern, "Ideal and Expected Behavior as Seen in Klamath Mythology," *Journal of American Folklore*, Vol. 76 (1963), pp. 27–28.

tional morality. An absolute standard is one that should apply in all times and places, as, for instance, "Thou shalt not kill." A situational rule, on the other hand, is one whose applicability is explicitly or implicitly limited to specific social settings. There is considerable overlap between the concepts of absolute morality and universalistic standards. They differ in that the latter is an ideal for all kinds of persons, whereas an absolute value may be restricted to particular kinds of persons but applied regardless of the situation. For example, in Western society the doctor is expected to save the life of his patient regardless of the circumstances. The saving of life is thus an absolute value for doctors, but not for the man in the street, and certainly not for the soldier.

The case of Japan shows that a situational morality can be just as demanding as an absolute one. As Ruth Benedict has observed:

> In Japan the constant goal is honor. It is necessary to command respect. The means one uses to that end are tools one takes up and then lays aside as circumstances dictate. When situations change, the Japanese can change their bearings and set themselves on a new course. Changing does not appear to them the moral issue that it does to Westerners. We go in for "principles," for convictions on ideological matters.[8]

In *The Chrysanthemum and the Sword,* Benedict discusses a number of moral categories and standards found in traditional Japanese culture. As she describes it, Japanese morality is organized around the concept of *on,* "indebtedness," and categories of "repayment" known as *gimu* and *giri.* The Japanese assume that each individual incurs at birth a great indebtedness to his Emperor and to his parents, while other kinds of *on* are acquired in the course of his life. All of these debts must be repaid. *Gimu* repayments are considered limitless in both amount and duration: these are obligations to one's parents and to the Emperor, and the Japanese say that "one never repays one ten-thousandth of [this] *on.*" Giri repayments are much more specific: these relate to debts which must be repaid "with mathematical equivalence to the favor received," and within certain time limits to avoid "loss of face." Of the two kinds of obligations, the Japanese say that "giri is hardest to bear." Why should this be so?

The category of giri is a difficult one for Westerners to understand. On the one hand, it consists of giri-to-the-world: obligations to affines, to distant relatives, and to nonrelated persons who have done favors or loaned money, and so forth. On the other hand, it includes giri-to-one's-name: the duty to "clear"

8. R. Benedict, *The Chrysanthemum and the Sword* (New York: Houghton Mifflin, 1946), p. 171.

one's reputation of insult, to admit no professional failure or ignorance, and to fulfill the Japanese proprieties (for example, showing proper respect to superiors, curbing inappropriate displays of emotion, not living above one's station in life). But giri is considered a single virtue. Its two subtypes are, to the Japanese, distinguished by the fact that giri-to-the-world is a consequence of specific indebtedness, whereas giri-to-one's-name is "outside the circle of *on*." But it is *not*, as we might phrase it, a difference between "gratitude" and "revenge." For them, giri is the same whether one is reacting to another's benevolence or to his scorn:

> A good man feels as strongly about insults as he does about the benefits he has received. Either way it is virtuous to repay. He does not separate the two, as we do, and call one aggression and one non-aggression . . . so long as one is maintaining giri and clearing one's name of slurs, one is not guilty of aggression. One is evening scores.[9]

In view of the great horror that Japanese have of losing face, it is interesting to note that they have developed many ways of avoiding situations in which it might occur. These include the minimization of competition, the use of go-betweens, and above all, an elaborate code of *etiquette*.[10] Extreme politeness was characteristic of traditional Japanese culture. It was another expression of care for one's honor and that of others. If one was insulted or shamed despite all precautions, vengeance or self-destruction became necessary to "clear one's reputation." Revenge is an honorable act in Japanese culture. And for a Japanese, as a last resort,

> suicide, properly done, will . . . clear his name and reinstate his memory. American condemnation of suicide makes self-destruction only a desperate submission to despair, but the Japanese respect for it allows it to be an honorable and purposeful act. *In certain situations* it is the most honorable course to take in giri to one's name.[11]

Note again the situational standard: suicide is neither good nor evil in itself, but in certain situations it may be the most honorable action possible. It is a means to the culturally valued end of giri-to-one's-name.

Cultural attitudes toward suicide vary greatly, and the reasons given for these attitudes are even more varied. In some societies, the act of suicide is simply unthinkable—if it takes place, a sorcerer (or mental illness) must be responsible. In many other groups, suicide is the expected response to specific circumstances. For example, in Tikopia, if a man's family refused to

---

9. *Ibid.*, pp. 115–117, 133, 146.
10. *Ibid.*, pp. 156–157.
11. *Ibid.*, p. 166 (italics added). Compare J. Douglas, *The Social Meanings of Suicide* (Princeton: Princeton University Press, 1970).

accept his choice of a wife, the couple might drown themselves. In the Trobriand Islands, a young man hurled himself to his death from the top of a coconut palm when his incestuous relations with a clan sister were made public; this was regarded as the only line of action open to him. The Navajo, on the other hand, regard suicide as undesirable in any circumstances. They are primarily concerned with *this* life, and there is no generally accepted doctrine of rewards and punishments in a future life. (Nevertheless, some Navajos hold the belief that suicides and witches live apart in the afterworld.)

Certain actions, such as witchcraft and incest, are always condemned by the Navajo, while hospitality, courtesy, and deference to age are always kept positively valued. But Navajo morality is mainly *situational*; according to Clyde Kluckhohn: "The Navajo conceives of nothing as good or bad in and of itself. Correct knowledge and following the rules emanating therefrom are good because they lead to long life and happiness. Morals are relative to situation and to consequences rather than absolute. Everything is judged in terms of its consequences."

Kluckhohn made several attempts to reduce the vast body of Navajo prescriptions and prohibitions to several basic moral patterns. Aside from specific forbidden behaviors, the Navajo judge the goodness of an action in terms of its consequences for the individual and his family. Also, the emphasis in Navajo culture is upon deeds rather than words: "Acts rather than beliefs count. Behavior is judged—not verbal adherence to a theological or ethical code."[12]

Moral evaluation of one's behavior and that of one's fellows is a notable characteristic of human beings in all societies. It is one of the characteristics that distinguishes us from other animals. *Man is a maker of tools, rules, and moral judgments.* Some moral principles are virtually universal, and these are presumably necessary to the continuity of organized society. Surely, no society could continue in which indiscriminate murder, theft, and lying were considered desirable. But beyond these functional prerequisites for social life, each culture has elaborated somewhat different patterns of valuing—different both in categories of good and bad actions and in plans for applying these categories. Thus, an action which is considered good in one society may be condemned or ignored in another. Suicide, blood vengeance, and even the accumulation of personal wealth are among the actions which, as we have seen, may be highly valued in one group and strongly disapproved in another. Unless we are prepared, ethno-

12. C. Kluckhohn, "Navaho Morals," in R. Kluckhohn, ed., *Culture and Behavior* (New York: Free Press, 1962), p. 175.

centrically, to maintain that our own values are absolute and should be accepted by all peoples, we are faced with the question: *Is it possible to evaluate value systems?*

A few anthropologists have suggested criteria which might be used in evaluating the moral systems found in different cultures, but none of these formulations is entirely satisfactory.[13] One reason for this is that the criteria proposed are often vague and difficult to apply. We all value "humane" behavior, but it is often hard to decide whether certain kinds of behavior (abortion, imprisonment, euthanasia, and so forth) are "humane."

Some writers have suggested that the degree of *conformity* found in a society between behavior and ideals (whatever the ideals may be) is a suitable index of morality. But this solution simply redefines morality in terms of conformity, and there may be cases in which we want to distinguish the two—for instance, when an individual's violation of his society's moral code seems to involve an appeal to a "higher" moral standard, or at least shows a fuller realization of the ideals of his own group. This is the old problem of the spirit versus the letter of the law, and it has never been an easy one to resolve.

Ruth Benedict once suggested that total cultures differ in the degree to which they promote self-realization of the people who live by them. But this emphasis on the full development of each individual—the avoidance of what Benedict called "human waste"—is itself a value characteristic of a certain social class at a particular time in history.

Most anthropologists, therefore, have adopted some version of the position known as *ethical relativism.* This is the view that we *cannot* evaluate value systems; indeed, we cannot even judge the behavior of an individual outside the context of his own social group and its morality. This view is not without difficulties. For example, an ethical relativist must accept and try to understand actions which are personally distasteful or abhorrent to him, without passing any moral judgment on them. He need not approve of, say, torture or fascism, infanticide or cannibalism, but he must try to prevent his culturally determined emotional response from getting in the way of analysis and understanding.

Although ethical relativism presents many difficulties as a philosophy, as a methodological assumption it is essential to anthropology. Even as a working principle, ethical relativism can be phrased in several ways. Our emphasis here has been on the difficulty of comparing actions or value systems in the absence of any culture-free, absolute standard. Others have stressed the equal validity or the arbitrariness of *all* cultural systems. On the

13. See A. L. Kroeber, *Anthropology* (New York: Harcourt Brace, 1948), sections 127–128.

other hand, Clyde Kluckhohn has suggested that the observed variation in ethical codes may be comparatively superficial, so that the anthropologist should examine questions such as:

> Is ethical *intent* very similar if not identical the world over? Are variations largely related to means rather than ends? Are means and some of the more proximate ends determined by historical accident and local circumstance? Is the whole picture needlessly confused by the local symbolisms for expressing ultimate goals and enforcing standands that are universal or near-universal?[14]

In *The Primitive World and Its Transformations,* Robert Redfield suggests that some kind of *moral evolution* may have taken place through human history, in both the development of more humane standards and the growing extension of moral conduct beyond the immediate social group. He recognizes that there have been frequent and severe lapses from this trend and that a case can also be made for the moral inferiority of civilized man, but Redfield's basic view is optimistic and quite persuasive.[15] (Whether the behavior of civilized man will ever catch up with his highest ideals is another question.)

When they hear the word "morality," most Americans think immediately and exclusively of sexual morality. We have covered some aspects of this topic in the sections on sex roles and concepts of property. Patterns of sexual behavior found throughout the world have been surveyed by C. S. Ford and F. A. Beach.[16] It is probably safe to say that in few other areas of culture do we find such a variety of beliefs and values combined with such frequent discrepancies between ideal and real behavior. Yet behind the mass of mating and marriage patterns, a few basic principles do emerge: the universal prohibition on incest, a general concern for legitimacy of birth, and a few recurrent patterns of social control over marital choices.

Sexual behavior is restricted, to some degree, in every human society; but not all groups condemn the same actions. Nor do all societies regard violations of their conventions as bad or evil. Homosexuality, masturbation, or adultery may be ignored, or viewed as foolish. Or, as in the Navajo view, such acts may be condemned as likely to interfere with normal social relations, but not as immoral in and of themselves. On the other hand, many primitive societies are even more puritanical than our own in regard to sexual deviations, and any variation from the norm of "who

14. C. Kluckhohn, "Ethical Relativity: Sic et Non," in R. Kluckhohn, *op. cit.*, p. 273.
15. R. Redfield, *The Primitive World and Its Transformations* (Ithaca: Cornell University Press, 1953).
16. C. S. Ford and F. A. Beach, *Patterns of Sexual Behavior* (New York: Harper, 1951). Compare P. K. Bock, "Courtship Customs," *Encyclopedia Americana* (in press).

does what to whom'' may be severely punished (if discovered).

We are all aware that American *sex norms* are gradually changing. Although the *behavioral* changes which have taken place in recent decades have been far greater, there has been a general shift from relatively puritanical absolute standards to a set of more flexible situational standards. This trend has been recognized by many popular commentators, such as Hugh Hefner, as well as by religious spokesmen, such as the late Bishop James A. Pike. It has been related by anthropologists to the development in American culture of a ''fun morality,'' the obligation to have fun. Some psychologists associate the change with a growing emphasis on the value of self-realization. However, as we observed in the discussion of Japanese moral concepts, a situational morality can be just as demanding as an absolute code. One popular author has suggested that Americans and Europeans, having finally freed themselves from guilt feelings over their violations of absolute moral standards, now torment themselves about the sincerity of their erotic attachments. In other words, although our sexual *behavior* is more liberated than formerly, we now question our *motives* much more closely, so that the net gain of ''freedom'' may be small.[17]

The study of moral values is increasingly becoming a part of anthropological investigations, and in the future, we shall probably see the development of new concepts and techniques for the study of this important part of human culture. One of the benefits of the women's liberation and the gay liberation movements has been a general raising of consciousness in both sexes about the arbitrariness of conventional sexual morality. But only time will tell what the ultimate consequences of these changes will be.

JUDGMENTS OF BEAUTY: ESTHETICS

Esthetic judgments involve the appraisal of persons, objects, or events in terms of their pleasing qualities or beauty, though, as we shall see, moral and practical criteria sometimes enter into these appraisals as well. The categories and criteria used in making esthetic judgments are mainly implicit, at least in primitive societies, and their application calls for skills of ''connoisseurship'' which can be developed only through a long acquaintance with a culture. For these reasons, esthetic judgments are often difficult for the ethnographer to understand or describe; however, by careful study of native evaluations and through systematic analysis of

17. S. Vizinczey, *In Praise of Older Women* (New York: Bantam Books, 1965).

style and language, it is sometimes possible to discover the more obvious esthetic standards embodied in a culture and to communicate these to an audience of outsiders.

Although esthetic judgments are difficult to study, in a way they typify the nature of culture better than almost any other kind of human behavior. When we think of an ancient or exotic society, one of the first things that comes to mind is the typical artistic style embodied in its material culture. For most of us, ancient Egypt is characterized by its pyramids and paintings, just as classical Greece is thought of in terms of its epics, statues, and architecture, or the Middle Ages as a succession of cathedrals. The art, music, and literature of a society—its "culture" in the narrower sense—embody ideals of form and content which give to a tradition its distinctive flavor. And these art styles are the result of many people judging, choosing, and acting in accordance with shared conceptions of beauty.

All the arts are characterized by a *striving for formal perfection* which goes beyond and is sometimes opposed to practical or utilitarian values.

> When the technical treatment has attained a certain standard of excellence, when the control of the processes involved is such that certain typical forms are produced, we call the process an art, and however simple the forms may be, they may be judged from the point of view of formal perfection; industrial pursuits such as cutting, carving, moulding, weaving, as well as singing, dancing and cooking are capable of attaining technical excellence and fixed forms.[18]

The craftsman not only produces useful objects; he also forms and decorates his baskets, spears, or pots to make them beautiful. The musician or storyteller does not just repeat traditional forms; he also embellishes them and creates new works pleasing to himself and his audience. All such creations and re-creations rest on a basis of traditional techniques and skills. But the artist utilizes these skills to produce improved and/or novel forms—forms which express cultural ideals and which must be judged by *esthetic standards.*

Every human society has some standards of excellence which may be called esthetic. The earliest material evidence for man's esthetic impulses goes back several hundred thousand years to the Acheulian period. During this period we already find beautifully formed hand axes—some tools shaped with an eye for symmetry and balance that went far beyond the utilitarian purposes for which they were employed. During the Aurignacian and Magdalenian periods of the Upper Paleolithic, some 35,000 years ago, we can

---

18. F. Boas, *Primitive Art* (New York: Dover, 1955), p. 101.

Paleolithic sculpture depicting Venus, goddess of fertility. ***Musée de L'Homme***

clearly see the development of distinctive and technically accomplished artistic styles at a time when man was still a hunter of big game. Of course, we can only guess at what has been lost from earlier periods; but the impulse to decorate and to represent forms in various media is surely an ancient one. Folk tales are probably as old as language itself, and music may be still more ancient. Such activities, of course, leave no material traces, but we know from archaeological discoveries that the Neanderthals (and even *Homo erectus)* selected bright red pigments from their environment and transported them to their living places (probably to decorate their bodies).

The key word in understanding the esthetic values embodied in a culture is *selection.* All artistic activities involve a selection of "some specific method, technique, manner, or plan of operations" from among several possibilities, and a development of this chosen style in the direction of formal perfection. According to A. L. Kroeber:

> A style is a way of achieving definiteness and effectiveness . . . by choosing or evolving one line of procedure out of several possible ones, and sticking to it. That means, psychologically, that habits become channeled, facility and skill are acquired, and that this skill can then be extended to larger situations or to somewhat altered ones. [Thus] every style is necessarily prelimited: it is an essential commitment to one manner, to the exclusion of others. . . . The range of its channeled skills will extend so far; beyond, they fail. Then we say that the style has exhausted itself, its characteristic pattern has broken down. . . . The style either loses its skill of touch and its products deteriorate; or it becomes frankly repetitive. . . . A pickup in quality will normally be possible only with a new start toward a new style. . . .
>
> It is a commonplace that all esthetic styles rise and fall and perish. All art has constantly to get itself reborn with a new set of impulses, and then run a new course. . . . [But] the arts are by no means something wholly set apart from the rest of civilization. The same principles of style or method, and therefore of pulsation, tend to hold for most or all cultural activities.[19]

In the following pages, we shall consider the esthetic values held by members of three different societies and their application to a few arts: graphic design, folklore, and music. In each case, it will be evident that esthetic ideas can be understood only in relation to the total value system of the culture.

Esthetic Categories

One way to approach the esthetic values of a culture is by analyzing the linguistic terms used to describe or evaluate esthetic

---

19. Kroeber, *op. cit.*, p. 329.

objects. Harold K. Schneider has made such an analysis of the key esthetic concepts of the Turu, a Bantu-speaking people of central Tanzania. He discusses four main Turu terms: *-ja, luhida, nsaasia,* and *majighana.* The translation of these terms presents special difficulties. As Schneider notes, one Turu grammar defines the suffix *-ja* as "good, beautiful," whereas a Turu informant translated it as "useful":

> *-ja* encompasses all things of value to Turu, including those which are esthetic. The concept does not differentiate things which are man-made and natural objects, though according to one informant, *-ja* occurring in nature are "as if someone had made them," i.e., as if they had been fashioned for man's use. . . . Examples of *-ja* are cattle, cloths [sic], songs, and even the useful actions of people. . . .
>
> *Luhida* may be contrasted to *-ja* as esthetically pleasing ornamentation, i.e., a design *added to* something else. *Luhida* is visible . . . and has spatial continuity and isolation. It is designs which are geometrical or otherwise patterned, having rhythm, symmetry and balance but no precise symbolic meaning.

There are several types of designs which come under the heading of *luhida.* These include *madone,* a series of disconnected round units which are esthetically patterned (OOOOO), and *nsale,* a series of unconnected parallel lines occurring within a spatial field (|||||||). According to Schneider:

> The Turu would not see the parallel lines in a notebook as *nsale* because they run off the edges of the sheet, but if all the lines stopped short of the edge and the same distance from the edge of the page, they would be *nsale.* This design often occurs in the form of scarification of the body and as ornamentation on flour gourds.

The concept of *nsaasia* is more difficult to explain. It is sometimes thought of as a quality of action and sometimes as a quality of things, but in either case it must have a pleasing effect. Furthermore, *nsaasia* is always produced by human skill, whereas *-ja* and *luhida* may occur naturally. "A cow cannot be *nsaasia* no matter how pleasing to the eye, 'because it was born that way,' but a herd can be thought of as *nsaasia* because it is assembled by man." A person cannot look *nsaasia,* nor can an object that is flawless retain this quality:

> The essential qualities of *nsaasia* are regularity, smoothness, symmetry, cleanliness and color. Unlike *luhida, nsaasia* is also wholeness and completeness. . . . A stool which has no ornamentation may still be *nsaasia* because it is skillfully made with integral flourishes and fine lines. It loses this quality if disfigured, even if it is still useful. A clean, pressed shirt is *nsaasia* until it becomes dirty and rumpled or

torn. A house may be *nsaasia* if the builder transcends utility by the use of matched and aligned poles.

The last of the four concepts, *majighana,* is closely related to the notion of *nsaasia* but it refers primarily to "a voluntary action which makes people happy." Actions which are done under duress are outside of this concept; but a "man of *majighana* is one who customarily exercises freedom of choice to do things which make others happy." These may be simple acts such as sharing cigarettes, speaking pleasant words, or visiting with people to establish friendship, but the concept also includes sponsorship of "freely given" feasts and ceremonials such as ancestral sacrifices and fertility rituals:

> Among the activities considered to be *majighana* is the circumcision rite, particularly the initial part in which the initiates are operated on and the feasting and dancing occur. . . . The pain in the act is discounted and the happiness it brings to others is emphasized. The dancing, drinking and eating make those attending the feast happy, and the achievement of social maturity by their child pleases the parents.

The Turu say that *"nsaasia* is *majighana."* This statement is the key to one of the most distinctive features of Turu esthetics, for it discloses their attitude towards the social function of art and the artist. As explained by Schneider:

> Nature can produce valuable and even esthetically pleasing things, but when they are created by men they are something special—*nsaasia. Nsaasia* is an act of *majighana* or altruism. . . . Art is an esthetically pleasing form that is produced by men. An artist is one who is able to perform acts of *majighana* by exercising his *nsaasia* to bring pleasure to others. Artists are one of the class of magnanimous people including any others whose actions bring joy to people.

Running through all of these concepts is a strong element of the practical. Thus, the sky is not *-ja* because, as one Turu said, "When the sky can be seen there are no clouds so there will be no rain." A certain spotted beetle was said not to be *luhida* because it is destructive of crops, while "a well designed cigarette package is not *nsaasia* because when it is empty it is crumpled and discarded."[20]

---

20. H. K. Schneider, "Turu Esthetic Concepts," *American Anthropologist*, Vol. 68 (1966), pp. 156–160.

Turu esthetic concepts, then, are firmy embedded in a social context and they cannot be understood outside of this context. This is also true of the stylistic values embodied in traditional folklore. Samuel H. Elbert examined some nine hundred Hawaiian tales to establish their major stylistic features so that these could be compared with the principal emphases of the traditional culture. The "old culture" of the islands is characterized as "predominantly aristocratic" and as centering on four major areas of interest—physical, intellectual, emotional, and ethical; each of these characteristics is clearly expressed in one or more of the following features of folklore style:

Hyperbole

Exaggerations used in the tales are useful indices of cultural values. The heroes of Hawaiian tales are always described in extreme terms. "These heroes have great powers: they drink the sea dry, leap from island to island, or transform themselves into fish or animals. Their flawless bodies are so beautiful that strangers hasten to wait on them."

Metaphor and Simile

"The richly elaborated figurative language of the tales shows the cultural interest in nature. A bride is a flower, a child a lei, ignorance 'intestines of night' and wisdom 'intestines of day'."

Humor

Word play and scatological jokes are the most frequent forms of humor found in the tales, with sarcasm occurring less frequently. "Punning is a form of aggressive competition between heroes." Joking shows a fascination with the human body, including its deformations. "Adultery and lechery are not sources of humor in the tales because of the lack of taboos on this kind of behavior."

Names

"A striking feature of Polynesian mythology is the fondness for names." All the characters in a tale are listed at the beginning, and full personal names are frequently repeated where we might substitute pronouns. Genealogies were memorized and recited on many occasions. (According to some early missionaries, the

Hawaiians thought that the "begats" in the Bible were the "best parts.")

Details

"Hawaiian tales frequently mention body parts, especially eyes. . . . This is in keeping with the cultural interest in the sacred body, as mentioned previously." Verbal fluency was highly valued and is displayed by the heroes of the tales, often in the form of elaborate insults. "Nature is referred to with the most persistent attention and wealth of detail."

Treatment of Character

The heroic tales illustrate the aristocratic emphasis of Hawaiian culture. Most of the tales deal primarily with persons of high rank; commoners enter the picture only "to illustrate a virtue, such as hospitality, or to wait on or applaud a chief. The slave class is completely unrepresented." Animal characters are scarce. There is a realistic treatment of even the character of heroes, partly for esthetic effect: "The sudden weaknesses of the hero, the fact that his mana occasionally fails, his fears and temporary setbacks, are realistic touches that serve as devices for heightening suspense and enhancing dramatic appeal."

Finally, Elbert describes a number of "nonsemantic elements of style"—devices used less for their meaning than for their inherent esthetic appeal to members of this society. These devices include antithesis, repetition, and catalogs, all of which serve as esthetic embellishments as well as ways of prolonging rituals and prayers in order to please the gods. According to Elbert:

> Antithesis is a feature of nearly every myth. In a chant about the winds, the contrasting pairs little and big, long and short, successively qualify waves, a canoe paddle, and a canoe bailer. . . . Long catalogues or lists provide esthetic satisfaction and afford desired length, as in the case of a triumphant recital of sixty-one victories, or a list of one hundred eleven winds and where they live.

Repetition of key words in successive verses is much admired, and this may be combined with antithesis:

> One rain from the uplands,
> One rain from the lowlands,
> One rain from the east,
> One rain from the west.[21]

---

21. S. Elbert, "Hawaiian Literary Style and Culture," *American Anthropologist*, Vol. 53 (1951), pp. 345–354.

Interest in and delight with long lists of personal names and place names is a characteristic of many folklore traditions (for instance, the catalog of ships in the *Iliad*). These lists and genealogies often have very practical purposes, as when they are used to validate the claim of a descent group to territory or to certain privileges. But the recitation of such lists can also acquire an independent value and come to be enjoyed for its own sake. As Thorstein Veblen pointed out long ago, men frequently come to consider beautiful that which is merely expensive or, we may add, essential to their way of life.[22]

A folklore tradition can be related to its cultural context more easily than can most of the other arts. Music (aside from song texts which may be treated as a kind of folklore) is particularly difficult to work with. Nevertheless, in his study of the Enemy Way chant, David P. McAllester has made a significant contribution to our understanding of Navajo social and esthetic values.

The Enemy Way is a three- or five-day chant, held for the explicit purpose of bringing relief to a person who is being troubled by the ghost of an outsider (a non-Navajo). The details of this ceremonial need not concern us here except to note that, unlike most Navajo chants, the Enemy Way involves an alternation of sacred with secular songs: on each of the nights of the chant, following rituals performed by the singer, all the men present join in singing "sway songs" and various kinds of "dance songs," usually until dawn of the next day.

> An important function of the social part of the ceremony is the "bringing out" of young girls who have reached marriageable age. The interest of the young men is clearly centered in the social singing and drinking and in looking over the available girls. The Enemy Way is felt to be a particularly enjoyable ceremony for the spectators. Any man may join in a good deal of the singing, and women have been known to do so, too. This is one of the rare occasions in Navaho life on which young men may dance with girls, and it is one of the few ceremonies to which a composer may bring his songs for a public hearing.[23]

The difficulties of investigating musical values are illustrated by one of McAllester's experiences. He asked several Indians the quesion, "How do you feel when you hear a drum?" This was intended to evoke an "esthetic response"; but drumming is rarely heard in contexts other than Enemy Way singing. Since feeling dizzy or otherwise peculiar at this ceremonial is considered an

---

22. T. Veblen, *The Theory of the Leisure Class* (New York: Modern Library, 1934), especially Chapter 6.
23. D. McAllester, *Enemy Way Music*, Papers of the Peabody Museum, Vol. 41, No. 3 (Cambridge: Peabody Museum, 1954), pp. 7–8.

indication that the spectator needs to have the chant performed for him, what the ethnographer thought of as an esthetic question turned out to be, "for the Navahos, a most specific ceremonial question. [It] was interpreted by the average informant as an inquiry into his state of health."

McAllester also found it impossible to separate esthetics and religion in any neat way because, for the Navajo, "what is desired in music is an *effect,* primarily magical, whether the song is for dancing, gambling, corn grinding, or healing. When a traditional Navajo is asked how he likes a song, he does not consider the question, 'How does it sound?' but 'What is it for?' "[24]

Although some of McAllester's informants expressed their preference for songs that "make you happy" or that "aren't too rough," the traditional view of what constitutes beauty in music had to be inferred by a detailed musicological analysis of many Enemy Way songs. Only in this way was McAllester able to formulate the *implicit esthetic standards* which appear to govern Navajo music. These may be summarized under the following headings:

Tonality

"Tonality should be consistent. A particular song should not change key while it is being sung, and a group of songs should be in the same key."

Voice Production

"A good voice is somewhat nasal, the vibrato is rather wide; the voice should be as high as possible, it should be capable of sharp emphases, and there should be an easy and powerful falsetto." These values are found more in younger than older singers; but endurance is also valued, and here the older singers seem to have the advantage.

Group Singing

Navajo group singing is characterized by a kind of "wild freedom." Unlike the neighboring Pueblos, there is little emphasis on careful rehearsal and uniformity:

> Not all the singers seem to know the song equally well, nor do they all seem to be singing exactly the same version of the song. . . . The

---

24. *Ibid.*, p. 5.

impression is of a group of individualists who tune their differences to each other at the moment of singing in a dynamically creative way which is very hard to describe.

The singers do not appear to be distressed by this variation within the group.

Rhythm

Navaho rhythms are characteristically fluid. The syncopations, the interrupted double beat, and the intricate variations in beat from one measure to the next evoke a gratified rhythmic motor response from native listeners. It seems that the rhythm is not a steady background for the melody, as in the case of most Western European music, but is as keenly perceived as melody for its combinations and permutations.

Tempo

Most if not all Navajo music is performed at a fast tempo, with a very limited range of note values:

If the most frequent value is indicated as a quarter note, one finds that quarters and eighths predominate overwhelmingly. . . . It is not unusual [in other cultures] to find restrictions in note values for a particular kind of music . . . but it is [unusual] for all kinds of music within the culture to be so similar in this respect.

Melodic Line

"Except in chant singing, the melodic line in Navajo music tends to start high and move down, often over the course of an octave."[25]

None of these standards would be likely to be explicitly formulated by a Navajo; nevertheless, since they can be shown to influence the performance of songs and the creation of new songs, they may be accepted as valid statements of Navajo musical esthetics. In the last part of his monograph, McAllester shows how certain *nonmusical* values of the Navajo are expressed in the performance of the Enemy Way. These values include self-expression, humor, formalism, and individualism.

Alan Lomax and his co-workers at Columbia have attempted to formulate objective descriptions of the musical styles of numerous societies and to relate these styles to other aspects of culture. They call their approach *cantometrics:* it includes both musico-

25. *Ibid.*, pp. 74–75.

logical analysis of the esthetic standards embodied in a corpus of folk songs and study of the social structure of performing groups.[26] Lomax has been able to show several interesting correlations between the *organization of musical performances* in a society (for example, as individualistic or cooperative, democratic or authoritarian) and the more general *beliefs and values* of that society. The work of McAllester and of Lomax illustrates the way in which ethnomusicology is moving beyond the simple description of exotic musical traditions to the study of their relationship to the cultural contexts in which they occur.

ETHOS: INTEGRATING PATTERNS OF VALUE

The term *ethos* refers to general patterns or orientations formulated by the anthropologist to describe the integration of a value system. Ethos, then, stands in the same relation to a value system as does eidos to a belief system. It constitutes an attempt to reduce the complexities of a value system to a few *basic patterns* which influence all parts of the system and to account for the *coherence* among, for example, economic, moral, and esthetic values. Some of the basic premises described in the section on eidos could equally well be treated under the heading of ethos (for example, Banfield's statement of amoral familism and its consequences for social and political behavior). As A. L. Kroeber has written, "Ethos deals with qualities that pervade the whole culture—like a flavor—as contrasted with the aggregate of separable constituents that make up its formal appearance. . . . The ethos includes the direction in which a culture is oriented, the things it aims at, prizes and endorses, and more or less achieves."[27]

One of the earliest attempts to characterize primitive cultural systems in these terms was that of Ruth Benedict in her famous book *Patterns of Culture.* Benedict felt that it was possible to describe whole cultures in terms of their general emotional approach to the world and to human relationships. Borrowing some of her terminology from philosophy and abnormal psychology, she described four very different societies as if each had a unique and consistent personality. Thus the cultural ethos of the

---

26. A. Lomax, "Song Structure and Social Structure," *Ethnology*, Vol. 1 (1962), pp. 425–451. A more comprehensive report of the cantometrics project is A. Lomax *et al., Folk Song Style and Culture* (Washington, D.C.: American Association for the Advancement of Science, Publication No. 88, 1968).
27. Kroeber, *op. cit.*, p. 294.

Zuni Indians is described as "Apollonian"—seeking peace and order through self-control and cooperation, with a high degree of subordination of the individual to the group. The Plains Indians, on the other hand, are characterized as "Dionysian"—valuing violent emotions and stressing the individualistic quest for supernatural power.[28]

In a similar manner, she characterized the Kwakiutl Indian ethos as "megalomaniac" (assertive and self-glorifying), while the Dobuans of Melanesia were termed "paranoid" (hostile and suspicious). Benedict believed that such *configurations* (whole culture patterns) were developed when the members of a society would select a particular character type as their ideal and would then elaborate their arts and institutions in ways consistent with the chosen type. The outcome was a society in which a single "style" dominated the entire culture.

Patterns of Culture was and still is an important book, for it communicates a vivid sense of cultural differences and of the integrity of exotic societies; but many of Benedict's statements have been criticized by later anthropologists as oversimplifications. It has been pointed out, for example, that the "peaceful" Pueblo Indians had a well-developed pattern of warfare, and that the "warlike" Plains Indians were quite capable of cooperative activities (as in their communal bison hunts, p. 335). Also, the Kwakiutl potlaches—which Benedict saw as expressions of the chiefs' craving for power and self-glorification—have recently been shown to have had important economic and integrative functions.[29] In presenting her four societies as unique configurations, Benedict failed to represent the *diversity* of values found in every human group.

For these and other reasons, Morris E. Opler has suggested that cultural value patterns should be described in terms of several *themes*—cultural ideals, "declared or implied," which control behavior or stimulate particular kinds of activity. According to Opler, cultural integration is the result of the dynamic interplay among a number of different themes, some of which reinforce one another while others contradict or limit each other.[30]

Anthony Leeds, whose discussion of Yaruro beliefs was cited in Chapter 10, has tried to sum up the Yaruro value system in a

---

28. R. Benedict, *Patterns of Culture* (New York: Houghton Mifflin, 1934).
29. See S. Piddocke, "The Potlatch System of the Southern Kwakiutl: A New Perspective," *Southwestern Journal of Anthropology*, Vol. 21 (1965), pp. 244–264.
30. M. E. Opler, "Themes as Dynamic Forces in Culture," *American Journal of Sociology*, Vol. 51 (1945), pp. 198–206. Also his article "The Themal Approach in Cultural Anthropology and Its Application to North Indian Data," *Southwestern Journal of Anthropology*, Vol. 24 (1968), pp. 215–227.

number of themelike statements and to relate these propositions to Yaruro cosmology (see p. 315). The major themes of Yaruro culture are:

Cosmic Structure

The cosmos is static, limited, concrete, and internally continuous in that no barriers separate man and his society in the physical world from the nonphysical world.

The Good

Goodness inheres generally in the cosmos as a system. The goodness manifests itself in understood causes and concretely and describably known parts of the cosmos which, whether places, persons, or things, are given exact locations.

The Not-Good

Evil, which is not polar to good, finds its locus in specific persons, things, or events inside or outside the cosmos, and is manifest in specific results. The underlying causes of evil, however, are inaccessible to the sense or to understanding. (Being neither known or localizable, they are not part of the unified kin and cosmic structure in which gods, the dead, and men and their respective lands are tied together.)

The Good Society

In the good cosmos, the good society consists of kin-related gods, the dead, communities and individuals living in tranquility and sharing all things.

Determinants of Action

In the good society, action is guided by precept, suggestion, and by sensibility to the wants of others and of self, but compulsion and hostility are not permissible.

Nature of Precepts and Principles of Action

In the good society, precepts and principles are general rather than specific and prescriptive. [The result is that patterns of behavior and thought in Yaruro society are quite unformalized, unritualized, and unspecified. According to Leeds, all classes of behavior show a great range of variability and flexibility.]

Freedom or Restriction of Will

> The individual . . . is not compelled by the nature of the cosmos nor by the personnel in it to follow any particular path. He has free will with regard to the ordained order of things.[31]

Philip L. Newman has also used the concept of theme in his description of Gururumba culture. One particularly important theme which was isolated early in his study is the people's great "concern with growth and strength." As Newman comments:

> The Gururumba are horticulturalists and the growing of food is much on their minds. Casual conversation frequently turns around the state of one's garden or the health of one's pigs. Many of the songs they sing concern growth. . . . A concern with physical strength is also manifest in everyday life, since a strong body is necessary for carrying out the tasks associated with gardening, hunting, and defending the group. It is a characteristic highly admired in both men and women, amounting to one of the major standards of beauty.[32]

Many Gururumba rituals are intended to promote growth and to ensure the strength of plants, pigs, and people. But beyond the practical basis of their concern, Newman demonstrates that "achieving growth and showing strength have come to be values in their own right":

> The ability of an individual or group to be productive and assertive is among the most general values in Gururumba culture, and to produce food, to grow children, and pigs, to protect the group, to seek out and discharge obligations vigorously, is to demonstrate the presence of that ability. The rituals of growth and strength, then, are not only of importance to the Gururumba because they add to their technical mastery of the physical world, but because they relate to the mastery of affairs in the social world as well.[33]

Newman discusses the ways in which these general values are manifested in ideas and rituals surrounding sexuality and in the people's cosmology. He shows that "much of the character of Gururumba life can be understood as if it were the result of striving to attain" both productivity and assertiveness, while at the same time trying "to achieve some balance between nurturant and destructive tendencies in man . . . to turn strength into nurturant channels":

---

31. A. Leeds, "The Ideology of the Yaruro Indians in Relation to Socio-Economic Organization," *Anthropologica*, Vol. 9 (1960), pp. 1–10.
32. P. L. Newman, *Knowing the Gururumba* (New York: Holt, Rinehart and Winston, 1965), p. 72.
33. *Ibid.*, p. 75.

To a Westerner, daily life among the Gururumba appears to be carried on in a highly aggressive fashion: the constant banter about giving and taking, the frequency of fights and violent emotional eruptions, and the fact that many of the idioms in the language are built around "violent" verbs such as "hit," "strike," or "kill." "I hit him" can mean "I gave it to him," rather than the reverse as in our own language. In most contexts this kind of behavior is not aggression to the Gururumba; it is a display of the strength stemming from vital essence, the strength man draws upon to endure and flourish. Within that part of the social world defined by the sharing of food, assertiveness is not aggressiveness because it creates food and the social channels through which food flows. Furthermore, making a demand implies the obligation to be demanded of, and giving is not a means of overwhelming others because reciprocity will transform givers into takers.[34]

Once again the importance of reciprocity in maintaining social relationships is evident. The Gururumba express their relationships in a violent and unfamiliar idiom; but the social functions of their rituals and their elaborate gift exchanges become clear when we see that local groups and kinship groups are bound together by reciprocal obligations.

Newman also analyzes the Gururumba understandings about *human nature.* These contrast in a striking manner with the Yaruro ideology outlined above. Indeed, the positions of these two cultures almost define opposing ends of a dimension of values, as will be discussed below. The Gururumba believe that their ancestors lived in a presocial era which lacked the institutions of marriage and of gift exchange (both of which are expressions of reciprocity). These ancestors were "strong," but they gave free reign to their impulses; they did not live in villages and had no domesticated plants or animals. "They raped, murdered and stole as whim directed them and ranged freely over the countryside without concern for boundaries."

Significantly, the Gururumba sometimes liken themselves to these ancestors. At other times, they say that people are like their pigs: semidomesticated animals which frequently "tire of the rope and the fence" and break out of these constraints, doing great damage to houses and gardens. According to Newman, the Gururumba understanding of human nature may be summed up in three general statements:

1. *Man has selfish, destructive, and aggressive impulses in himself.* Witches are real people, ghosts and ancestors once were. Death releases harmful tendencies that have always been in man. Ghosts are not harmful because they are attempting to punish man or

---

34. *Ibid.*, p. 89.

subvert his basically good nature; they are harmful in the same way men are.

2. *These impulses are curbed by the forces of society.* This understanding is present in the statement that men would be like ancestors of the presocial era if they did not live in society, and in statements drawing a parallel between men and unwatched pigs. The Gururumba never indicated any particular longing to be like the voracious pig or the presocial ancestor, but their statements indicate an understanding that they would be that way more often than they are if it were not for social constraints. (They are this way toward . . . their enemies, with whom relationships are not modified by reciprocity and obligation.)
3. *Society represses but does not eradicate impulses that cannot be allowed expression within its boundaries.* This is . . . apparent in the attitude toward men who exhibit a behavior pattern people refer to as "being a wild pig." These men run amok, attacking people and stealing objects. There is no attempt to restrain such behavior beyond keeping a watchful eye on it to avoid serious injury and no recriminations are made when it is over. . . . The name given this behavior is instructive since there are no truly wild pigs in the upper Asaro valley, only pigs that have temporarily escaped their masters.[35]

The care and consumption of pigs in Gururumba society are surrounded by many rituals and taboos. In terms of Leach's theory (p. 350), it is interesting to note that pigs hold an *ambiguous position* in native thought, being neither fully tamed nor really wild.

Some anthropologists hold that there are a number of *universal issues* on which every society must take a value position. It follows that we should be able to characterize the value system of a given society in terms of its position on each of these issues. Furthermore, it should be possible to compare different societies by noting their relative positions on each of these value dimensions. We have already touched on this idea in Chapter 6, where the differential emphasis placed on past, present, or future was discussed under the heading of "social time." Florence Kluckhohn has suggested that each society must also take a position on the issue of "human nature," whether men are fundamentally good, evil, or a combination of these. The two ethnographic examples given just above illustrate the extreme positions on this dimension: the Yaruro view man as inherently good, while the Gururumba think of man as evil (unless constrained by society). An intermediate position is represented by the Navajo, who regard good and evil as complementary and ever-present, in both man and nature.

Similarly, we may recognize three positions on the issue of the relationship between man and nature. On this dimension, both the Navajo and the Yaruro represent the intermediate position in

---

35. *Ibid.*, pp. 92–93.

which man and nature are seen as existing in mutual *harmony.* The two extreme positions would be those in which man is viewed as *dominant over* nature or as *subordinate to* nature; they are represented, respectively, by modern American culture and by the culture of the southern Italian peasants described by Edward Banfield (p. 341, above).

In developing this approach, Florence Kluckhohn and Fred Strodbeck found that most societies possess both dominant and variant value orientations.[36] For example, a society like ours which places its greatest emphasis on future time and man's dominance over nature will also contain, though to a lesser degree, variant orientations toward the past and present, as well as some subgroups which emphasize man's harmony with or subjugation to nature. Similarly, although it has always been the orthodox Christian view that human nature is fundamentally evil, this view has been unacceptable to many Christian thinkers, and different Christian sects have attributed varying degrees of goodness to man. Kluckhohn and Strodbeck utilized questionnaires and statistical techniques to establish and compare the dominant and variant value orientations found in different societies. The major dimensions they worked with are summarized in Figure 11.3.

Other attempts to characterize the ethos of various cultures utilize concepts such as "ideal person," "dominant style," and "world view." In each case, the anthropologist attempts to discover and state a few basic patterns that will account for judgments, evaluations, and choices made in various aspects of social life. The approaches differ widely in their use of *materials,* which

Universal Problems	*Possible Value Orientations*		
Human Nature	Evil	Neutral/Mixed	Good
Man/Nature	Subjugation	Harmony	Mastery
Time	Past	Present	Future
Activity	Being	Being-in-becoming	Doing
Relational	Lineal	Collateral	Individual

Figure 11.3 **A Classification of Value Orientations (after Kluckhohn and Strodbeck)**

36. F. Kluckhohn and F. Strodbeck, *Variations in Value-Orientations* (Evanston, Ill.: Row, Peterson, 1961).

range from life histories and firsthand observations to questionnaires, projective tests, and "cultural products" (art objects, folklore, and so forth). But they also differ in their *goals.* Some anthropologists, following Benedict, are content to formulate *unique characterizations* of a culture's ethos which can be compared with others only impressionistically, if at all. Others emphasize *comparability* and, like Kluckhohn and Strodbeck, try to find universal categories of values in terms of which different cultures can be systematically compared. Still others hope to *explain* the differences among value systems by examining patterns of child-training, features of social structure, subsistence, ecological relations, or various combinations of these factors.

Perhaps these fundamental cultural differences cannot be explained. But in a rapidly changing world where intercultural misunderstandings threaten the entire species, it is the responsibility of anthropology to try to understand both the nature and the sources of human values. According to David Bidney, "the most important and difficult task which confronts the cultural anthropologist is that of making a critical and comparative study of values."[37] Clearly, an ethnocentric approach which ranks other value systems as "primitive" or "advanced" to the extent that they approach our own views is unacceptable.

The reduction of ethnocentrism through a widespread appreciation of the integrity of other cultures is an important and practical goal, one that anthropologists are today pursuing. But in the interest of human survival, anthropology must go further, seeking a basis for intercultural understanding and cooperation. Hopefully, we will be able to show how radically different means and cultural idioms can be reconciled so that men can work together toward a common end—the good of mankind.

RECOMMENDED READING

Armstrong, R. P., *The Affecting Presence.* Urbana: University of Illinois Press, 1971. A difficult but rewarding essay on the arts (principally African sculpture and literature) which attempts to define the scope of a "humanistic anthropology."

Kluckhohn, C., *Culture and Behavior.* New York: Free Press, 1962. A collection of essays on diverse subjects by the anthropologist who was most influential in showing the importance of the study of values as a part of culture. The essay on "ethical relativity" is particularly clear and relevant to modern concerns.

Lee, D. D., *Freedom and Culture.* Englewood Cliffs, N.J., Spectrum Books, 1959. Provocative essays by an anthropologist who uses linguistic and psychological approaches to give a deep appreciation of the position of the individual in different cultures, both exotic and familiar.

37. D. Bidney, "The Concept of Value in Modern Anthropology," in A. L. Kroeber, ed., *Anthropology Today* (Chicago: University of Chicago Press, 1953), p. 698.

Lomax, A., *Folk Song Style and Culture*. Washington, D.C.: American Association for the Advancement of Science, Publication No. 88, 1968. A report on the work of the "cantometrics project" which reveals the close connection between song style and various features of social structure. This is probably the most important empirical work now available on the relationship between esthetic and social values.

Pitt-Rivers, J. A., *The People of the Sierra*. Chicago: Phoenix Books, 1961. A case study of a village in southern Spain which illustrates with clarity and charm an approach of social anthropology to the study of moral values.

Turnbull, C., *The Mountain People*. New York: Simon and Schuster, 1972. A disturbing report on an African tribe, the Ik, who seem to put individual survival ahead of any other values, including filial or parental love.

We have now surveyed the evolutionary development of man, the process of enculturation, and the four major subsystems of culture (language, social systems, technology, and ideology). In the following chapters we shall discuss the ways in which anthropologists gather and analyze the data on which their conclusions are based. Our emphasis will not be on theory but rather upon *method*: methods of observation in the field, the kinds of "texts" which are accumulated as permanent records of those observations, and the inferences that can be made from observations and texts.

Although observation and inference are separated in the discussion, it must be remembered that the two always go hand in hand when the anthropologist is at work. It is very difficult for an enculturated adult to observe objects or events without automatically classifying and responding to them in terms of his *own* cultural system of categories and plans. Anthropological training can help us to counteract this tendency. But inferences are still necessary, for it is only by framing *provisional interpretations* of what he sees that the anthropologist knows what questions to ask and where to look (or dig) next. Premature interpretations can lead any investigator astray, but without some guiding ideas he is completely lost. Science does not teach us to avoid inferences but rather to realize that they *are* provisional (hypotheses) and that we must search for data which might contradict as well as confirm our ideas.

The following chapters are not intended as a "how to do it" guide to anthropological field work; rather, it is hoped that this brief discussion will give the reader some idea of the *conditions* under which anthropological data is collected and the *problems* involved in drawing valid conclusions from such data. Anthropology differs from many of the sciences in that, as Robert Redfield once put it, "The anthropologist's own human nature is an instrument of work." This fact is both helpful and problematic. That is, we are able to understand alien cultures partly because at one time we have all had to learn a culture—our own; but it is precisely because we have been enculturated that it is difficult for us to clearly comprehend the patterns of a different way of life. Just as the student of a second language must struggle to overcome his foreign accent, the anthropologist must struggle to overcome his ethnocentric biases, many of which he is not even aware of. It is part of our scientific faith that this can be accomplished.

American Museum of Natural History

PART VI
The Anthropologist at Work

CHAPTER 12
Field Methods

The aim of anthropological research is to discover *regularities* in human social life. To this end anthropologists study and compare all kinds of social groups, living and extinct, small and large, simple and complex. They observe concrete objects, persons, and events, both for their own sake and also in order to discover the shared categories and plans which have guided human behavior in various settings.

When an ethnographer sets out to observe a society, or an archaeologist to dig a site, each is faced with an enormous range of observable phenomena. From this nearly inexhaustible richness, the trained observer selects those events and objects which are most relevant to his purposes. If he has no criteria of relevance, his fact-gathering will be random and scientifically useless. *The primary data of cultural anthropology consist of descriptions of acts and artifacts viewed as manifestations of human culture.* These descriptions (ethnographies, site reports, grammars, and so forth) may be analyzed and reanalyzed for a variety of theoretical purposes; but unless the primary data have been gathered with care and intelligence, the theories will be built upon shifting sands.

Ethnographic field work involves the firsthand observation of social behavior from a relativistic viewpoint. It is an attempt to understand the historical basis and adaptive functioning of a cultural system without evaluating it in terms of ethnocentric standards. Thus the first task of the ethnographer is to *learn the culture* of the group he is studying; in this respect, his task is similar to that of a child born into the group, for both must discover the categories and plans shared by other group members. But whereas the child must also develop the skills appropriate to his position in the society so that he can function as a regular group member, the ethnographer is required to formulate, consciously and explicitly, the rules which appear to guide the various classes of group members in their daily interactions. The ethnographer's learning is thus both *more explicit* and *less skillful* than the child's enculturation.

Of course, not all ethnographers (or archaeologists) set out to describe the total culture of a single group. Often, the anthropologist is concerned with some particular aspect of culture, or with surveying a number of different societies in the same region. Nevertheless, most ethnographers do try to get a general feel for the society they are studying so that they can better judge the significance of their specific data in its total cultural context. In the following sections we shall use the attempt to describe a total culture as our model of field work, keeping in mind the fact that most actual studies deal with limited ethnographic problems.

OBSERVATIONS OF BEHAVIOR

The anthropologist who plans to observe and describe social behavior must, as we have already noted, have some criteria of relevance to guide his observations. These criteria are provided by his professional training, in which he has learned the kinds of facts which have proved significant in previous studies. Since his time in the field is limited, he cannot possibly see everything; therefore, he generally starts with those phenomena he has been trained to observe. For example, in a "primitive" society he will usually begin with the kinship system, the subsistence technology, and the process of enculturation. These studies will lead him into all the other areas of the culture. Ideally, the ethnographer will have been trained to observe and to report accurately on all kinds of phenomena he may encounter, from techniques of housebuilding to religious ritual.

The extent to which he can prepare for the specific phenomena he encounters depends on how much is already known about the region in which he is to work. No ethnographer in his right mind goes into the field cold. He will read the reports of explorers and other field workers, familiarize himself with the history and geography of the region, and if possible, prepare himself in the local language or lingua franca (for example, pidgin English, or in East Africa, Swahili). Such preparations enable the ethnographer to make the best possible use of his time in the field and ensure that he will be aware of some specific problems he will face. His general academic training provides the basic skills, attitudes, and theoretical information needed to increase the reliability and relevance of his observations.

In addition to academic preparation, there are numerous practical problems which must be anticipated by the field worker. Adequate funds, suitable clothing, medical supplies, inoculations, and special equipment (cameras, tape recorders) must be acquired; transportation must be arranged; lines of communication and supply must be established; and in many cases, permission must be requested from a variety of government officials before research can begin. Assuming that all these practical problems can be resolved, the field worker must also be prepared to adapt himself and his research techniques to the local situation, for this is never exactly what he has anticipated, no matter how careful his preparation. *Flexibility* is probably the most essential characteristic of the good field worker if he is to keep his sanity, much less accomplish his planned research.

A classic description of the difficult conditions under which field work must sometimes proceed is given by E. E. Evans-Pritchard in his book *The Nuer:*

> Besides physical discomfort at all times, suspicion and obstinate resistance encountered in the early stages of research, absence of interpreter, lack of adequate grammar and dictionary, and failure to procure the usual informants, there developed a further difficulty as the inquiry proceeded. As I became more friendly with the Nuer and more at home in their language they visited me from early morning till late at night, and hardly a moment of the day passed by without men, women, or boys in my tent. As soon as I began to discuss a custom with one man another would interrupt the conversation in pursuance of some affair of his own or by an exchange of pleasantries and jokes. . . . These endless visits entailed constant badinage and interruption and, although they offered opportunity for improving my knowledge of the Nuer language, imposed a severe strain. Nevertheless, if one chooses to reside in a Nuer camp one must submit to Nuer custom, and they are persistent and tireless visitors. The chief privation was the publicity to which all my actions were exposed, and it was long before I became hardened, though never entirely insensitive, to performing the most intimate operations before an audience or in full view of the camp.
>
> Since my tent was always in the midst of homesteads or windscreens and my inquiries had to be conducted in public, I was seldom able to hold confidential conversations and never succeeded in training informants capable of dictating texts and giving detailed descriptions and commentaries. This failure was compensated for by the intimacy I was compelled to establish with the Nuer. As I could not use the easier and shorter method of working through regular informants I had to fall back on direct observation of, and participation in, the everyday life of the people. From the door of my tent I could see what was happening in camp or village and every moment was spent in Nuer company. Information was thus gathered in particles, each Nuer

> I met being used as a source of knowledge, and not, as it were, in chunks supplied by selected and trained informants. Because I had to live in such close contact with the Nuer I knew them much more intimately than the Azande [another large African tribe of the Sudan], about whom I am able to write a much more detailed account. Azande would not allow me to live as one of themselves; Nuer would not allow me to live otherwise. Among Azande I was compelled to live outside the community; among Nuer I was compelled to be a member of it. Azande treated me as a superior; Nuer as an equal.[1]

The techniques of the field worker, then, must be adapted both to the problem he is studying and to the exigencies of the situation he meets. This is why it is difficult to describe how field work should proceed. The following remarks are simply indications of the kinds of methods which often prove useful.

To begin with, the ethnographer must enter the community he has chosen to study. This sounds much simpler than it is, for entry involves not only physical presence (which may itself be difficult) but also social acceptance, and this means finding a *social position* within the group in which the anthropologist can be tolerated and allowed to carry on his work. By the time an ethnographer reaches a "native group," they have usually had some contact with or information about Europeans, Americans, or some other kind of outsiders such as missionaries or traders; if so, the anthropologist has to deal with the tendency of the group to assimilate him to their prior experiences. Particularly in colonial or formerly colonial areas, he is likely to be taken for a government agent of some kind—a tax collector, policeman, or administrator. Such stereotypes could obviously interfere with the worker's access to many kinds of information; even in fairly open areas, the field worker (either ethnographer or archaeologist) is likely to be considered a spy and to be viewed with great suspicion.

It is, then, up to the anthropologist to explain his purpose in terms which are understandable to group members and to avoid being categorized as a kind of person from whom the community will withhold information. There are so many variables involved in this problem that it is difficult to tell in advance what will work. Some explanations which sound quite plausible may backfire. For example, at the beginning of my field work with a band of Micmac Indians I stated that my intention was to do a "historical survey" of their community. The idea of having someone study their history was quite acceptable to most of the Micmac to whom I spoke; however, a few interpreted the word *survey* too literally, and within two days rumors were flying that I was a government "surveyor" who had come "to divide up the lands." The Micmac, like most

1. E. E. Evans-Pritchard, *The Nuer* (London: Oxford University Press, 1940), pp. 14–15.

American Indians, are extremely sensitive about their reservation lands—understandably, since they have been cheated so often. It took me several weeks to overcome this rumor, and many Indians remained suspicious throughout the period of field work.

The problem of entry can be understood with reference to the concepts used in the chapters on social structure. In order to know how to behave toward the field anthropologist and what to expect of him, the members of a society must somehow fit him into their set of social categories (roles, groups, and so forth). Once this is accomplished, the plans for interaction with him follow automatically. But the anthropologist does not easily fit into the traditional categories—except perhaps on the Navajo Reservation, where it is said that the typical family consists of a man, his wife, their children, and an ethnographer. Nevertheless, he must be given a position in the social structure. In a kin-based society, this means he must be attached to one or more specific kin groups and perform the minimal expectations associated with his kin role; in a caste society (including military organizations), he must be given a temporary rank so that others will know whether to treat him as a superior, an inferior, or an equal; and so on. Any such assigned status will both open some sources of information to the field worker and exclude him from other sources; such restrictions, however, are usually less of a handicap than those experienced by the ethnographer who tries to establish a marginal position on the outside of a social system.

Assuming that the field worker has entered the community and established himself in a social role which leaves him relatively free to gather information, he then has two possible ways of fact gathering available to him: (1) use of *selected informants* and/or (2) *participant observation.* Usually both of these will be employed, though in different proportions depending on the field worker, his research problem, and the field situation. As Evans-Pritchard observed, some societies insist that the ethnographer take part in the social life, while in others such participation is difficult or impossible. In the latter case, the ethnographer has no choice but to work intensively with a few people who are willing to talk to him. This is also the preferred method when time is limited or when the field worker is trying to *reconstruct* an earlier cultural situation. But it is usually possible and desirable to participate to some extent in the normal social life of the group, if only to verify the statements of informants and to resolve discrepancies.

A high degree of participant observation is possible only when the ethnographer has gained general acceptance in a non-restrictive role and when his own temperament enables him to take part in the social life actively and without becoming too emotionally involved. One of the dangers in participant observation is the fact that by performing a specific social role the anthropologist is liable to lose perspective on the total system. Another is the danger of "going native" to the extent of refusing to reveal any information about the group studied; obviously, anthropological science could not progress if this always happened. Nevertheless, participant observation is essential for getting the feel of an alien culture and for experiencing the interaction between its structural rules and the organizational processes through which they are put into action. (See Chapter 7.)

As field work progresses, the ethnographer does not simply add to his collection of facts in a random manner. Rather, as pointed out in the Introduction to Part Six, he organizes his observations and places provisional interpretations on them. These *hypotheses* come from the interaction of his observations with his theoretical training. They guide his continuing observations in a systematic way so that a line of questioning with an informant or a series of participant observations can contribute to his understanding of the cultural system (instead of just adding up to a collection of curious customs). For example, if questioning of two informants reveals a discrepancy between their accounts of some custom, these accounts will not just be left side by side; the ethnographer will try to understand the discrepancy in terms of what he knows about the society and his informants' statuses; he will then question other informants and/or arrange for participant observation either to resolve the discrepancy or to show how the differences between the accounts are related to other social factors (the sex, age, or group membership of the respective informants).

Whenever an ethnographic hypothesis is stated in a *quantitative* form, it is desirable to make enough observations of the phenomenon in question to permit *statistical* treatment of the data. The topic of statistical inferences will be dealt with in the next chapter, but an example should suffice at this point to show what is meant. Let us suppose that our ethnographer is trying to understand the marriage rules in a given society. A number of elderly informants in this patrilineal tribe state that in the past a man *always* married a member of his mother's clan; but the younger informants say that while there is a preference for marriage with a member of the mother's clan, most men today do not consider this important in choosing a wife.

A provisional interpretation of these statements would be that a former strict marriage rule has broken down; however, before trying to explain the reasons for this cultural change, it would be wise for the ethnographer to verify his hypothesis. To do this, he must examine a good-sized *sample* of marriage choices over the last few generations, together with information about each person's clan membership and his mother's clan. For although the informants' statements may indicate a genuine change in attitude, analysis of actual marriage choices may show that marriage with a matrilateral relative was *not* so common in the past as the older people believe (let us say 70 percent rather than 100 percent), while a high proportion of recent marriages (let us say 65 percent) *do* follow this rule; that is, young men still ten to marry matrilateral kin, whether they realize it or not.

Cases of this sort are very common in ethnographic work. They form the basis for a distinction between *ideal culture,* what people say they should do, and *real culture,* how they actually behave in a given situation. Our example shows that there can be a discrepancy between ideal and real, and that the ideal culture may change while the real culture stays pretty much the same. The ideal culture can also remain relatively constant while the actual behavior of persons increasingly deviates from the structural rule. A good example of this latter process is provided by the contrast between American sex norms and, for instance, premarital sex behavior of college students. Nevertheless, I have argued in Chapter 7 that such changes in behavior will *eventually* bring about a change in the structure. For instance, the coeducational dormitories that are now taken for granted on dozens of campuses would have been "unthinkable" as recently as 1960.

COLLECTION OF TEXTS

It is very unwise for the ethnographer to rely too much upon his memory in the field, for the kinds of distortions which affect our memories in everyday life are multiplied many times when one is in an unfamiliar or exotic situation. Most ethnographers, therefore, attempt to collect and record their data in a variety of permanent forms, which we shall call *texts.* In the next few pages, I shall list and briefly describe a number of specific techniques used by the ethnographer in gathering and recording his data. The list is not exhaustive, but it should indicate the usual activities of the ethnographer at work.

I. Field notes

Every ethnographer must keep a running record of his experiences in the field, from his first contact with the group he intends to study through his departure. The only general rule for taking field notes is this: the more detailed, explicit, and legible, the better. These notes should include all of his observations, together with the time and place they were made and the names of others present. He should also write down his provisional interpretations of these observations, keeping the facts and inferences as distinct as possible. Particulary at the start of field work, *everything must be recorded,* for observations which at the time seemed unimportant often turn out to be extremely significant. Part of the ethnographer's continuing education comes from rereading his notes and seeing how his perceptions of the society he is studying have changed with increasing familiarity; but first impressions have a special significance (in field work as in personal relations), and it is essential that they be fully recorded.

II. Informant interviews

These interviews range from relatively informal conversations through all-day (and sometimes all-night) sessions for which the informant may be paid. Notes or tape recordings made during such interviews are most useful, but in many situations this is either impossible or it would interfere with the free flow of information. In such cases, notes must be made as soon as possible after the interview to avoid loss of details or possible distortion in the ethnographer's memory.

Mention should be made here of the very important quality known as *rapport.* Unless the ethnographer is able to establish some degree of rapport with an informant, he must be very cautious in using the information he gets. Rapport involves mutual confidence, understanding, and emotional affinity. There are no general rules for establishing rapport, but it helps if the ethnographer is able to demonstrate his genuine interest in and respect for the native culture; also, he must convince his informants that their personal remarks will be kept confidential. The field worker cannot be a gossip; like any other professional, he must protect his sources of information. Violation of confidence is both poor ethical practice and bad ethnographic technique.

III. Genealogies

Since the pioneering work of W. H. R. Rivers, the collection of genealogies (family trees) has been a standard part of the ethnographer's task. Extensive genealogies are collected from several reliable informants and supplemented by interviews with others. In a kin-based society, knowledge of the genealogical relationships among persons is essential to understanding how the social system works. Genealogies are used in analyzing kinship terminology, descent group recruitment, marriage rules, political organization, and many other social phenomena. Another advantage of

A linguist records the speech of an Amahuaca Indian in Peru. *Cornell Capa/ Magnum*

genealogy collection is that this type of fact gathering seldom meets with much resistance from community members; since genealogical information invariably proves to be valuable, it is a convenient place to start an ethnographich investigation. Not that genealogies are always easy to compile. Among the Tiwi, for example, whenever a woman remarries, her new husband *renames* all her children. Since most Tiwi men marry for the first time at a rather advanced age, a given individual may have four or five different names given by his father and various stepfathers.[2] Elsewhere, there are stringent taboos against even mentioning the name of a deceased person, while in some communities there may be dozens of living individuals with the same name. In Bali, young people are usually addressed simply as "first-born," "second-born," and so forth, and members of a village community may not know of the other names an individual possesses. But it is exactly this capacity for leading into other aspects of the culture that makes genealogies so useful.

2. C. W. M. Hart and A. Pilling, *The Tiwi of North Australia* (New York: Holt, Rinehart and Winston, 1960), pp. 21–25.

IV. Community mapping

Careful mapping of the community and region under study is useful in the study of residential groups, interaction patterns, land tenure, and conceptions of social space. Locating all members of the community is also of considerable practical importance for purposes of sampling and for determining the relationship of locality to other social phenomena. In Latin America, for example, it is common for the homes of influential citizens (as well as political and religious buildings) to be located around the central plaza of a town or village, while craftsmen and the poor are localized in other areas. Large communities are further divided into *barrios* ("quarters"), each of which tends to duplicate this structure on a smaller scale. Mapping of such a community reveals a great deal of information and should prevent hasty generalizations on the basis of data gathered from only one of the subdivisions.

V. Structured observations

A technique increasingly used by ethnographers is the control of their observations by deliberate sampling in space and time—the use of structured observations. For example, once the general structure of a community is determined by mapping, the ethnographer may make it a point to spend roughly equal periods of observation in each of its subdivisions. Another type of control involves brief, intensive periods of observation with an attempt to record many details of the interactions among particular classes of persons. Such observations may be recorded in terms of a predetermined set of categories. For example, in a recent comparative study of child-training in six different societies, the field workers were instructed as follows:

> The fieldworker should make 12 five-minute observations on each child. These observations should be scattered as widely as possible over time and setting. The fieldworker should describe all instances of the situations in which we are interested that occur in each of these five-minute observations.[3]

The situations in which the writers of the guide were interested included the following: instances in which the child hurt himself, had difficulty, broke a rule, or started an interaction, or in which another person assaulted, insulted, hurt, or reprimanded the child. The goal of this study was to obtain comparative material on child-

---

3. J. Whiting, I. Child, W. Lambert, *et al.*, *Field Guide for a Study of Socialization*, Six Cultures Series, Vol. I (New York: Wiley, 1966), p. 94.

hood experience in a representative sample of the child's environment in each society. The main advantages of such structured observations are that they keep the ethnographer from being overwhelmed with data, and at the same time, prevent him from putting too much emphasis on striking but unrepresentative occurrences which he happens to observe.

VI. Trait lists

For some comparative and historical purposes, particularly where time is limited, it is useful for the ethnographer to employ a list of cultural elements (traits) which he can simply record as being present or absent in a given community or society. In a living culture, trait lists may serve as a guide to observation, helping the ethnographer to take note of things he might otherwise neglect. Where an aboriginal way of life exists only in the memories of a few elderly informants, trait lists derived from archaeological or ethnological studies of neighboring groups may serve as a stimulus to the informants' memories and thus aid in the reconstruction of a culture the manifestations of which can no longer be directly observed.

VII. Questionnaires

The use of questionnaires is not very widespread in ethnographic field work; however, in large-scale investigations employing a team approach, questionnaires may be used as part of an attempt to standardize interview procedures for greater comparability of data. When they are well designed, questionnaires can be quite useful, particularly for gathering quantitative data on topics which are already understood in a general way. The major defect in an approach which relies heavily on questionnaires is that a person often gives different interviewers differing responses to the same question. If the investigators have no contact with the respondent except while administering the questionnaire, linguistic and personal difficulties often prevent the establishment of rapport. In any case, it is essential that proposed questions be pretested on a small sample to determine both their *reliability* (the degree to which they elicit consistent responses) and their *validity* (the degree to which they elicit accurate information). Some sociologists have developed methods for deriving interesting data from censuses and from large-sample surveys which were originally gathered for other purposes; anthropologists could probably make good use of these methods, particularly in studying communities within modern nations.

VIII. Psychological tests

The use of psychological tests depends upon both the training and the interests of the ethnographer. Some tests can be given with little preparation, while others, such as the Stanford-Binet intelligence test or the Rorschach personality test, require many months of intensive training before one is qualified to administer (much less interpret) them. Relatively few ethnographers have these skills, though on large-scale projects it is possible to employ a psychiatrist or clinical psychologist to administer the tests. The main problem in their utilization is that of *cross-cultural validity:* that is, where a test has been designed for use with, say, American school children, it cannot be used in other societies without extensive modifications (after which, of course, it is no longer the same test and results are not really comparable). Psychological anthropologists have pretty well concluded that *there is no such thing as a culture-free test.* Even fairly straightforward tests of perception or of memory involve situations and stimuli which are likely to be unfamiliar to nonliterate persons. Although significant work has been done with psychological tests of various kinds, this is one of the most difficult types of ethnographic work, and it should be undertaken only with careful planning and safeguards.[4]

IX. Elicited texts

There are three major areas of study for which it is desirable to transcribe lengthy statements made by informants. The first of these involves recording native language *linguistic texts,* on tape and/or in a detailed phonetic transcription, to provide data for linguistic analysis. Linguistic texts are of many types. Often the ethnographer or field linguist will try to elicit sequences of utterances which will reveal the structure of the language—for example, minimal pairs or sentences which differ only in verb tense or person of the subject. Once the phonology and grammar are fairly well understood, samples of normal speech or repeatable stories may also be elicited.

Linguistic texts often overlap with *folklore texts,* in which the field worker attempts to elicit one or more versions of a traditional tale, legend, or myth. Such texts may be analyzed in a number of different ways (see below), but they are most valuable when they have been taken down in a phonetic or phonemic transcription accompanied by a word-for-word translation plus a relatively free

4. See M. Segall, D. Campbell and M. J. Herskovits, *The Influence of Culture on Visual Perception* (Indianapolis: Bobbs-Merrill, 1966).

translation with remarks on specific cultural concepts necessary to an understanding of the material. Other texts, such as magical formulas, court records, and even recipes, can be profitably treated in the same way.

The third type of extended text most often elicited by ethnographers is the *life history*. Such documents, particularly when accompanied by explanatory notes, can be highly revealing of cultural patterns.[5] A series of brief life histories may also be collected in connection with studies of personality or of culture change. But the elicitation of a reliable life history requires considerable skill and a high degree of rapport between the ethnographer and his informant. In general, it should be attempted only after the anthropologist has been in the field for some time, and such materials must be interpreted with great caution.

X. Photography

If one picture were really worth 1,000 words, most ethnographic reports could be shortened to perhaps fifteen pages of plates. But aside from a few experimental volumes on Navajo, Balinese, and Formosan culture, photography has played a rather minor role in ethnography. Its value as a supplement to written records is unquestioned, but it must be remembered that the camera is selective as well as objective, so that the taking and interpretation of photographs is a difficult affair. In recent years, there has been increasing interest in the potentialities of *ethnographic films,* but these are both difficult and expensive to make. Like life histories and psychological tests, motion pictures can be meaningful only when the fundamental cultural patterns of a social group are fully understood and good rapport has been established. An ethnographic film made for teaching or esthetic purposes will be very different from one intended solely as a record of observations. Good films of any of these types are still extremely rare. The most successful of these films have been the result of intimate collaboration between an experienced ethnographer and an imaginative professional film maker.

A recent innovation in the use of photography involves the analysis of pictures taken by members of the society being studied. For instance, John Adair has taught several Navajos to make and edit motion pictures on themes of interest to them, and Hal Kagan has experimented with having Colombian peasants each take a series of still photographs which they feel express certain cultural values. These "texts" can then be analyzed in a number of ways.

---

5. L. Langness, *The Life History in Anthropological Science* (New York: Holt, Rinehart and Winston, 1965).

In the past, anthropologists have analyzed professional films made in France, Russia, and Japan in connection with the study of "national character," but Adair and Kagan are the first to use this technique in nonliterate societies.

XI. Artifact collection

Many ethnographers bring back from the field an assortment of artifacts which illustrate the arts and crafts of the society they have studied. Such collections may be analyzed by experts in primitive technology, and ultimately find their way into museums of anthropology. An ideal ethnographic collection will include samples of all the major tool types utilized by a society. For the larger artifacts, native craftsmen can often be persuaded to make accurate scale models. The artifacts, however, are nearly useless without careful notes that tell where they were made and that describe the materials, the manner of production and distribution, and the ways they are used.

Artifact collections constitute the principal data for archaeological inferences (see below). The archaeologist is particularly aware of the importance of good field notes which accurately describe the location of and relations among those *traces and products of past human behavior* that he is able to recover. Modern archaeology often aims at the reconstruction of the history and total way of life of prehistoric human communities. For these purposes it requires careful study of every shred and sherd of evidence which can be recovered from a site. The field archaeologist must be a specialist in the excavation, preservation, and restoration of crumbling architectural features, fragile textiles, brittle bones, and all sorts of other cultural remains—from pottery fragments to plant seeds. He must identify and plot the position of each find, labeling and cataloging even apparently insignificant objects. And he must interpret these finds in terms of the reconstructed environment and the archaeological context from which they came.

XII. Document collection

Particularly in working with literate societies, the anthropologist will compile a collection of documents—diaries, baptismal records, epitaphs, graffiti, newspapers, letters, and so forth. Like other forms of evidence, these require interpretation to extract the valid structural and historical information which they contain. Sometimes the relevant documents for ethnohistorical study must be sought at some distance from the society under study. For example, Latin Americanists may consult the royal archives of

Spain or Portugal, and Indianists may need access to the records of British colonial agencies and trading companies.

The preceding list should give some idea of the kinds of records, texts, questionnaire responses, and test protocols that may be produced by a period of field work. The quality of each type of record is a result of the skill of the ethnographer and the conditions under which he has to work. The goal of all these techniques is to reduce observations of human behavior, verbal and nonverbal, to forms which can be analyzed to disclose regularities at various levels of cultural patterning. These texts (in the broad sense of the word) provide the evidence for general statements which the ethnographer makes about the culture of the group he has studied.

INFERENCES FROM TEXTS

In this section we shall consider certain kinds of inferences which the anthropologist can make from field data of his own and of others. It is no doubt true that an anthropologist analyzing his own data makes use of unrecorded memories and of intuitions derived from his period of field research; however, we shall *assume* here that all inferences derive from, and are documented by, written texts, photographs, and artifact collections—that is, from evidence that could in theory be analyzed by any competent anthropologist, with roughly comparable results. The extent to which this assumption is untrue is a measure of the degree of subjectivity which remains, and which perhaps must remain, a part of anthropological inference.

The kinds of inferences made from records of observations depend in part on the nature of the materials; therefore, we shall discuss the methods of linguistic, ethnographic, and archaeological inference separately. We shall be concerned primarily with inferences of *structure*—that is, the categories and plans found in particular languages or social systems. In the following chapter we shall consider the comparative methods which are used to make historical, functional, and causal interpretations of materials from different periods or different cultural systems.

Linguistic Inference

The texts from which the linguist derives his analysis of behavioral regularities have already been described: they consist of records

A		B	
q'an	'ripe'	q'anq'an	'rotten'
suk	'good'	suksuk	'delicious'
ras	'green'	rasras	'very green'
q'eq	'black'	q'eqq'eq	'jet black'
nim	'big'	nimnim	'very big'
kaq	'red'	kaqkaq	'very red'
saq	'white'	saqsaq	'very white'

***Figure 12.1* Part of a Pocomchi Linguistic Text (from W. Merrifield *et al.*, *Laboratory Manual for Morphology and Syntax* [Santa Ana, Calif.: Summer Institute of Linguistics, 1962] Problem 54).**

of speech, elicited or overheard, plus judgments made by native speakers as to the grammaticality and meaning (in translation) of these utterances. For example, part of a linguistic text in Pocomchi (an Indian language of Guatemala) is given in Figure 12.1.

From such a text (which has already been phonemically written), what inferences are possible? For one thing, in this language, it would appear that words such as those in Column *B* can be formed by *reduplication* (repetition) of words such as those in Column *A* and that this plan for word formation produces an *intensification* of meaning. Suppose now that the linguist finds in his text the word *suq,* 'sweet.' Is he justified in forming from this another word, **suqsuq,* with the probable meaning 'very sweet'? There is a temptation to generalize a plan such as reduplication which works for a number of forms; but in this case, the linguist or the Pocomchi child would be mistaken, for the meaning 'very sweet' is rendered in Pocomchi as *mas suq.* If our linguist had access to a native speaker of the language, he would be able to discover that **suqsuq* simply does not occur in normal speech. (As in Chapter 2, the asterisk preceding a word indicates a form that does not occur in normal speech.)

Any language, then, is described in terms of *categories* of sounds and meaningful sound combinations plus the *plans* associated with these categories. The plans make it possible to build words, sentences, and larger linguistic units (speeches, tales, and so forth) from a limited number of units. The linguist identifies significant categories in his text and determines the plans which govern their combination by studying the *form and distribution of similar items.* That is, he goes carefully through his text comparing items which partly resemble one another in form and/or meaning, and he charts their relationships to other such items. All apparent regularities are then stated as provisional linguistic rules (hypotheses) and carefully checked against other texts or elicited utterances. The *minimal goal* of a linguistic description is to account for all of the material in the texts by showing that it is the manifestation of learned rules (plans) operating on learned categories of experience.

From his theoretical training the linguist knows the kinds of units and relationships he is looking for, and he has a number of techniques which help him to determine the units and to state the rules which govern them. The larger the corpus (number of texts) on which a description is based, the more valid a given set of rules is likely to be; yet so long as a linguistic description accounts for all the material in the texts, it meets the minimal goal stated above. (Actually, there are a number of competing descriptive models in modern linguistics, but we shall not discriminate among them in this discussion.)

A more ambitious goal of linguistic description is that of accounting for the *ability* of speakers of a language to produce and interpret an infinite number of sentences (see the discussion of productivity, p. 45). Thus a so-called *generative grammar* is intended not only to describe a finite corpus reliably, but also to state the rules which would generate *all* and *only* those sentences which a native speaker would judge to be grammatical. We know that a finite number of categories and plans can be used to generate an infinite number of sentences because children in every human society learn to speak languages which have these properties; they learn not only a list of morphemes but also rules for forming and understanding new words. Ideally, then, the linguist with a large enough corpus and an adequate theory of language should be able to describe *everything that a native speaker has to know in order to speak and understand his language.* In principle, this should be possible because it involves the same kinds of inferences that children make unconsciously when learning grammatical rules from their observations of adult speech; but in practice we are still a long way from this ideal.[6]

Standard linguistic descriptions are composed of sections dealing with the sound system and the grammatical system, plus a dictionary that lists words (or morphemes) together with their meanings. For the present, we shall limit ourselves to the kinds of rules found in a modern generative grammar. A description of English grammar begins with the series of rules shown in Figure 12.2.

In the three rules in Figure 12.2 we can already feel some of the distinctive features of English syntax taking shape. Note that

---

6. See F. Smith and G. A. Miller, eds., *The Genesis of Language* (Cambridge: M.I.T. Press, 1966).

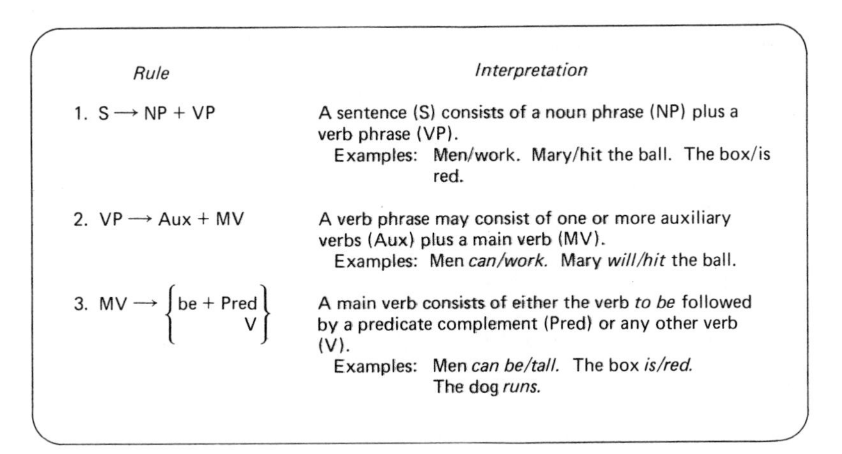

Rule	Interpretation
1. S ⟶ NP + VP	A sentence (S) consists of a noun phrase (NP) plus a verb phrase (VP). Examples: Men/work. Mary/hit the ball. The box/is red.
2. VP ⟶ Aux + MV	A verb phrase may consist of one or more auxiliary verbs (Aux) plus a main verb (MV). Examples: Men *can/work.* Mary *will/hit* the ball.
3. MV ⟶ {be + Pred / V}	A main verb consists of either the verb *to be* followed by a predicate complement (Pred) or any other verb (V). Examples: Men *can be/tall.* The box *is/red.* The dog *runs.*

Figure 12.2 **Some Rules of English Grammar (rules from O. Thomas, *Transformational Grammar and the Teacher of English* [New York: Holt, Rinehart and Winston, 1965], 29-38)**

each of these rules analyzes the left-hand (input) symbols—S, VP, MV—into their constituent parts. In other parts of the grammar, rules are used which transform sentences from one state to another (for example, positive to negative, statement to question, active to passive):

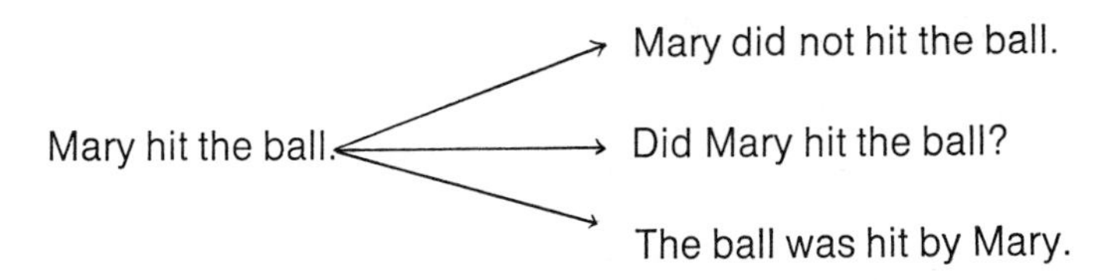

Still other rules combine a number of different sentences into a single sentence; for example:

John went home. + John slept. ⟶ John went home and slept.

Such rules specify both *what kinds of linguistic units can be combined* and *how they must be modified when they are brought together.* There are always some limits to what kinds of combinations are possible (grammatical). Thus, an adequate grammar of the English language should generate the sentences:

I am here.
John is here.

and the combination sentence:

John and I are here.

but not:

*John and I is here.

or:

*John and I am here.

any more than an adequate grammar of Pocomchi should generate:

**suqsuq*, 'very sweet.'

When we say that the rules of an adequate English grammar should not produce sentences such as **John and I am here,* we do not mean that English speakers never produce ungrammatical sentences. Errors of performance, both accidental and deliberate, are extremely common in spoken language, for linguistic rules are only shared conventions for speaking which, like other kinds of social rules, *may be violated.* A grammar or a description of social structure cannot and does not claim to account for actual behavior. Rather, a structural description gives the rules which channel behavior into expected patterns. It seeks to specify the *competence* that members of a society must share if they are to understand one another's speech and actions and that enables them to judge the grammaticality of an utterance or the appropriateness of a social act.

Ethnographic Inference

Ethnography is the description of the structure and organization of single societies. Ethnographic descriptions are usually limited to one period of time; they may employ historical materials when these are available, but the traditional ethnography is a *synchronic* (same-time) study.

The texts on which ethnography descriptions are based consist of records of social interaction together with native judgments of the meanings and appropriateness of such actions. From these concrete cases and evaluative statements, the ethnographer infers the shared expectations (social rules) which govern interaction in the group he is studying. In this section, we shall discuss inferences concerning social systems; but most of the points are equally applicable to technological and to ideological systems as well.

Given a set of texts which constitutes an adequate sample of social interaction, how does an ethnographer formulate his description of the social system? As in linguistic analysis, he must go through his corpus, taking note of the *form and distribution of similar items*. In social analysis, however, the relevant units are kinds of persons (roles), kinds of groups (including institutions), conceptions of social space and time (situations), and the principles of organization which guide the way in which the structure is put into action.

In the brief compass of this chapter, it is impossible to give an extended example of ethnographic inference. Instead, let us consider how an alien observer would go about formulating an ethnographic description of a great American institution, the college football game. To make it harder, we shall forbid him access to the official rules. Having decided upon his subject of study, our alien ethnographer will attempt to observe and ask questions about several different performances of the game. He will learn that football games take place during a particular part of the athletic year (football season) and usually on a specific day of the week. The next Saturday will find him sitting in the stands, busily taking field notes. He will ask questions of his fellow spectators, take pictures, interview coaches and team members, and collect a few documents and artifacts (game programs, an official ball, a penalty flag, and perhaps a model goal post). The coaches probably will not allow him to actively participate in the game, but he may attend a few practice sessions, if he can convince them that he is not a spy. Having built up a sizable corpus of texts, he then will retire to try to make sense out of them.

Any halfway adequate ethnography of the football game would have to include an *inventory of the categories* of persons, times, places, and objects listed in Figure 12.3, together with the features which distinguish each from the other. But in addition to such a listing of categories, one would also have to discover the *plans associated with each category* and the ways in which these are related to one another. That is, the ethnography should state both the general behaviors expected of the category of Players (as contrasted with other kinds of persons present in the situation) and the more specific actions expected of, say, a Quarterback on a third-down play. These plans would be more than just the official rules: they should constitute a "grammar" of the game, indicating what combinations of units are possible (for example, four- and five-man lines) and how different units must be modified in various situations (for example, reaction of each team to an intercepted pass).

Furthermore, the ethnographer should try to specify the mode of *recruitment* to each of the categories of persons: How are

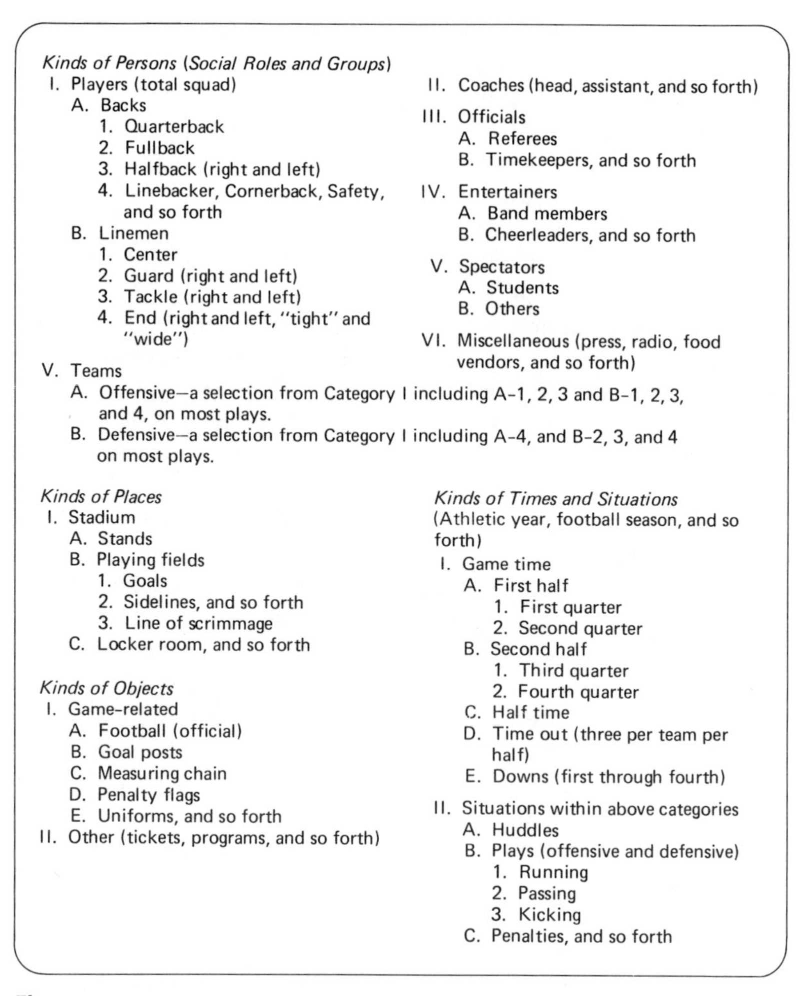

Kinds of Persons (Social Roles and Groups)

I. Players (total squad)
   A. Backs
      1. Quarterback
      2. Fullback
      3. Halfback (right and left)
      4. Linebacker, Cornerback, Safety, and so forth
   B. Linemen
      1. Center
      2. Guard (right and left)
      3. Tackle (right and left)
      4. End (right and left, "tight" and "wide")

II. Coaches (head, assistant, and so forth)

III. Officials
   A. Referees
   B. Timekeepers, and so forth

IV. Entertainers
   A. Band members
   B. Cheerleaders, and so forth

V. Spectators
   A. Students
   B. Others

VI. Miscellaneous (press, radio, food vendors, and so forth)

V. Teams
   A. Offensive—a selection from Category I including A-1, 2, 3 and B-1, 2, 3, and 4, on most plays.
   B. Defensive—a selection from Category I including A-4, and B-2, 3, and 4 on most plays.

Kinds of Places

I. Stadium
   A. Stands
   B. Playing fields
      1. Goals
      2. Sidelines, and so forth
      3. Line of scrimmage
   C. Locker room, and so forth

Kinds of Objects

I. Game-related
   A. Football (official)
   B. Goal posts
   C. Measuring chain
   D. Penalty flags
   E. Uniforms, and so forth
II. Other (tickets, programs, and so forth)

Kinds of Times and Situations
(Athletic year, football season, and so forth)

I. Game time
   A. First half
      1. First quarter
      2. Second quarter
   B. Second half
      1. Third quarter
      2. Fourth quarter
   C. Half time
   D. Time out (three per team per half)
   E. Downs (first through fourth)
II. Situations within above categories
   A. Huddles
   B. Plays (offensive and defensive)
      1. Running
      2. Passing
      3. Kicking
   C. Penalties, and so forth

Figure 12.3

coaches, referees, and players chosen? Which are paid and by whom? What kinds of persons attend the games as spectators or as band members? and so on. Our alien ethnographer might find that his attempts to study the recruitment of players met with some resistance, but this would lead him into a number of significant areas (the scouting system, training methods, athletic scholarships, and league regulations on eligibility) which would then require accumulation of data and careful analysis.

A person who had all this knowledge would know how to avoid breaking rules, but he would *not* necessarily be able to do anything right (for example, block, tackle, or catch a pass). Once again, we are talking about knowledge or competence rather than performance. To *perform* successfully in any of the roles described, one also needs certain *skills* which can be gained only through practice and participation and an *understanding* of organizational principles—in this case, the strategy of offensive and defensive play and team leadership. Although the principles of strategy and leadership can probably be verbally formulated, it is doubtful that they would be of much use to persons without firsthand experience in playing the game. This is true of rules of art and maxims in general: they are of use only to those who have already acquired considerable skill and nonverbal comprehension.[7] We should recognize these limitations of an ethnography (or a grammar) without forgetting its goal: to state the structure within which meaningful human behavior takes place.

An ethnographic description of any social group or institution consists of a more-or-less systematic statement of those categories and plans that guide the behavior of group members. Whether it deals with a college football game or the kinship behavior of the Tallensi, ethnographic inference operates on a series of concrete cases to produce statements of regularities. From records of who did and said what, where, when, and to whom, the ethnographer *infers* the *recurrent patterns of behavior* and states them as plans (expectations) associated with categories of persons, objects, and situations. His first interpretations are hypotheses which he checks against further texts. For example, the provisional interpretation that "only members of category I-B-4, Ends, may receive forward passes" must be modified when he discovers cases in which some Backs may legally do so.

Many social rules are discovered by the ethnographer only when he is able to *observe the consequences of a violation.* For instance, the significance of the line of scrimmage and the rules governing behavior along this movable boundary may become evident only after the ethnographer has recorded and analyzed a number of violations of these rules and the penalties which follow such violations. Informants may disagree as to whether a specific violation has taken place, but there will generally be a consensus as to what kind of behavior constitutes a violation (for example, being on the wrong side of the line of scrimmage when the ball is snapped) and how it should be penalized. Such judgments of appropriateness are among the most important clues that the ethnographer has to the existence of shared expectations.

But this is by no means the whole story, for there remains the problem of the relationship of the group or institution to its environment. A college football game is a highly artificial situation: it contributes only indirectly, if at all, to the biological survival of the

7. M. Polanyi, *Personal Knowledge* (New York: Harper Torchbooks, 1964), Chapter 4.

spectators or the players. Occasionally, a football hero may be enabled to find a mate as a result of his athletic prowess, but this selective advantage is probably overshadowed by the dangers of his profession. For a winning team, victory in a game may be "adaptive" in that it leads to a championship, a good job offer (for players and coaches), and prominence for the college (which may make recruitment of players easier). The college may also benefit from having a winning team, by recruiting sports-loving students and faculty, and by maintaining alumni interest with its accompanying financial support. But these adaptations are primarily on the level of the social environment. (See Figure 7.3.) In analyzing a primitive society, the anthropologist soon becomes aware that every category of person has his part to play not only in maintaining the social structure but also in obtaining and producing the materials necessary to sustain life and to satisfy human needs.

A full understanding of cultural adaptation on all three levels is essential to a complete ethnographic description. This must go beyond the statement of roles, groups, and situations to a consideration of the needs which they serve. Like tools, social structures have definite effects upon the environment in which they operate, though their "technological functions" are not always easy to specify. When a group of men with hoes goes into a field to cultivate the ground, the function of the work group is in part the same as that of the tools: the men use their skills and energy to break up the soil into its component parts so that crops can grow and men can eat. But what about a political party, a church, a college faculty, or a football team? How can we describe their adaptative functions?

We have come to some rather intricate problems of social theory, and all that we can do here is to indicate the nature of the problems. To begin with, in Chapter 5 we defined three major types of group functions—task, control, and expressive—each of which is present in every group, though in varying proportions. We also distinguished between explicit functions (of which the participants were overtly aware) and implicit functions (of which the participants are presumably unaware, but which were detected by the anthropologist). When anthropologists speak of a *structural-functional approach* (or theory), they mean one in which the structure of a group is related to the specific task, control, and expressive functions which it performs. Thus, members of a clan society may give various explicit reasons for the rule of clan exogamy, but the implicit function of producing social solidarity by the exchange of women is seldom recognized by the participants themselves. Clans may also have important functions in relation to the physical/biological environment, as in societies where they control access to land or other resources, and they may function on the level of the internal environment by providing personal security and a sense of identity. All of these possibilities must be considered by the anthropologist.

Within the last fifteen years, ethnographers have increasingly come to use *ecological* variables to explain different forms of social organization. In Chapter 9 we mentioned the apparent relationships between type of band organization and the principal game animal hunted, and between civilization and the development of intensive agricultural technology (such as irrigation). Marshall Sahlins has been a leading exponent of this approach. In one study he has linked a kind of lineage organization (segmentary patrilineages) with an environmental situation in which a large group was undergoing "predatory expansion" into the territory of weaker neighbors. In another study, he has related different Pacific island environments (Polynesian) to varying degrees of social stratification. And Roy Rappaport has demonstrated that both social and religious organization can be better understood when human cultures are viewed as parts of larger ecological systems.[8]

In assessing the functions of a custom or institution, the anthropologist must be particularly on guard against ethnocentrism —he must not judge a custom to be dysfunctional (harmful to the society) simply because he disapproves of its content, or nonfunctional just because he cannot immediately understand its purpose. For example, even if the anthropologist disapproves of race prejudice, he must try to understand the part it plays in maintaining a status quo. Similarly, in his functional analysis of political machines, Robert Merton was able to show that some big-city political bosses provided necessary personal services to their constituents at a time when impersonal bureaucracies were ineffective in meeting genuine needs.[9] And Marvin Harris has recently suggested that the sacred cow of Hindu India—often cited as a destructive and worthless animal—actually performs essential adaptive functions by providing dung for fuel and fertilizer as well as oxen for plowing and transport.[10] This does not mean that the anthropologist has to endorse prejudice, bossism, or superstition, but it does mean that he must avoid judging a practice before he has studied the part it plays in the total culture. For although there may be some *survivals* (functionless customs which have persisted from earlier periods), in every culture the vast majority of customs,

---

8. M. Sahlins, "The Segmentary Lineage: An Organization of Predatory Expansion," *American Anthropologist*, Vol. 63 (1961), pp. 322–345; *Social Stratification in Polynesia* (Seattle: University of Washington Press, 1958); R. Rappaport, "Ritual Regulation of Environmental Relations Among a New Guinea People," *Ethnology*, Vol. 6 (1967), pp. 17–30.
9. R. K. Merton, "Manifest and Latent Functions," in *Social Theory and Social Structure* (revised and enlarged edition; New York: Free Press, 1957), pp. 19–84.
10. M. Harris, "The Myth of the Sacred Cow," *Natural History*, Vol. 76 (March 1967), pp. 6–12A.

groups, and institutions *do* contribute to social continuity and the satisfaction of needs.

The discovery of social functions is only partly based on inferences from texts. When an ethnographer states that a given social ritual contributes to group solidarity or that an institution, such as a university, functions to support the traditional social class structure, he may simply be invoking some theoretical notions which find no direct support in his texts. If, however, he is able to demonstrate that when the ritual is omitted, groups tend to break up, or that admission to the university depends upon the applicants' social class and perpetuates their high status by giving graduates access to prestigious roles, then his statements of social function have a firmer basis. The kinds of structures and functions that a particular anthropologist will detect in his materials depend largely upon his theoretical training and interests. The reader should at least be aware that there are competing theories of description and explanation in modern cultural anthropology, and the choice among these theories is still largely a matter of personal preference.

Archaeological Inference

The processes of archaeological inference are quite similar to ethnographic inference with two important exceptions: (1) the archaeologist is limited to observation of the material remains and other traces of once-living cultures and (2) he is more likely than the ethnographer to be concerned with *diachronic* problems: questions of historical development and relationships. Also, the archaeologist's use of artifact collections is more extensive: his texts consist of a catalog of artifacts (usually available for reexamination) together with a record of their relative spatial positions at the time of excavation. Since he cannot observe these objects actually being used, he must *infer their history and functions from a detailed study of their form and distribution.* But, as we shall see, the archaeologist can also make use of comparable ethnographic materials in forming his hypotheses.

Within the boundaries of a specific site, the archaeologist makes use of descriptive units similar to those we are by now familiar with. He defines significant *categories of objects*: artifact types, buildings, fossil remains of plants and animals, and so forth. He attempts to make sense out of these forms, often by comparing them with known tool types or organisms, and he studies their distribution relative to one another and to features of the natural environment. On the basis of such information he tries to characterize the culture of the people who once inhabited

A church in a Mayan city in the Yucatan Peninsula in Mexico. ***William Fain/ Woodfin Camp***

the site. He asks questions such as: How many people lived here and how long did they stay? What was the nature of their subsistence economy? Were they hunters, fishers, gatherers, agriculturists, or some combination of these? What was their social structure like? Is there evidence of large-scale social cooperation? Of social stratification? Of religious or artistic activity? And so on.[11]

These are the same kinds of questions ethnographers ask about the communities they study. But the archaeologist must

11. See K. C. Chang, *Rethinking Archaeology* (New York: Random House, 1967).

find his answers indirectly, by examining those cultural remains which have survived (due to their composition or the accidents of preservation) and inferring their meaning. In making such inferences, the archaeologist must exercise extreme caution and avoid making unwarranted assumptions. Take the matter of population size, for example. Even where extensive skeletal remains have been preserved (which is not usually the case), it must be remembered that these constitute only a *sample* of the total population; certainly, it must not be assumed that all the individuals represented in a cemetery lived at the same time. Similarly, when population size is estimated from the remains of shelters, the archaeologist must not assume that all of the detected structures were standing during the same period; nor should he estimate the number of persons per dwelling on the basis of modern standards of comfort. The nature of the shelters (materials, construction, form, and so forth) can give some indication of the permanence of habitation at the site; however, even where rather substantial dwellings are found, it is dangerous to assume continuous occupation without additional evidence. We know, for example, that the Eskimo often build large wood and stone dwellings which they occupy only during certain seasons, living in perishable tents or igloos at other times.

Subsistence activities can be inferred from a variety of object types: projectile points, traps, fishhooks, hoes, seed grinders, containers; and the shells, bones, seeds, or pollen of various organisms can all be used as clues to the nature and relative importance of different economic activities. Paleobotanists and zoologists can often identify plant and animal species from fragmentary evidence, and in most cases, can also determine whether organic remains are those of wild or domesticated varieties. The skills of these and other specialists are very important to modern archaeology, for present-day archaeologists are more concerned with understanding the adaptation of prehistoric societies to their environments than were their predecessors, who tended to be collectors or historians. Thus, every scrap of evidence is inspected and items are collected which might formerly have been dismissed or overlooked: pollen samples, bits of charcoal for radioactive dating, broken tools and pieces of pottery—anything that might reveal the nature of human activities.

When he comes to making inferences about the social structure of prehistoric societies, the archaeologist must draw on ethnographic parallels, but only with great care. The presence, for example, of a large-scale irrigation system or of monumental architecture (burial mounds, temples, and so forth) indicates the existence of social cooperation which probably required some kind of overall political organization, but it does not necessarily indicate that the people lived in concentrated population centers. Although this is the case in most contemporary societies, there is considerable evidence that the Mayan civilization was based upon a dispersed population which nevertheless built magnificent ceremonial centers which were fully occupied only on ritual occasions.

The degree of social stratification in an extinct society can sometimes be estimated indirectly from the quantity and quality of grave goods (material objects buried with a person). Thus if most of the burials at a site contain a scattering of poor trinkets, but a few burials contain a variety of finely made weapons, containers, and ornaments, the archaeologist is probably justified in inferring the existence of a wealthy class. Confirmation of this hypothesis may be found in variations in the dimensions and quality of different dwellings.

Change in a culture over time may be inferred in a variety of ways. Within a single site, the most important evidence for length of occupation and for culture change comes from the *stratification of remains.* That is, when a particular location has been inhabited for several generations, cultural evidence tends to accumulate. Although it may be disturbed by later activities, the general tendency is for older materials to be covered by more recent remains. This means that the archaeologist can, with caution, *translate spatial distributions into temporal sequences.* The principle of stratification states that, other things being equal, the lower down in a deposit, the earlier in time are the objects uncovered. Thus in sites such as Olduvai Gorge, the caves of southern France, or the *tels* (mounds) of the Near East, centuries of prehistoric occupation have left stratified remains which, when interpreted, give a clear picture of man's biological and cultural development in these regions.

In the same way, archaeologists can fit together several stratified sites with overlapping cultural sequences to produce a long-range picture of cultural development within a large region. The bits and pieces of the regional picture are gradually fitted into place, with the gaps showing what work remains to be done. Of course, some of the pieces may be lost forever, and at any point a new discovery may call for partial or complete redrawing of the picture. But in areas where the general outline of cultural development has emerged, archaeologists know pretty well what they are looking for and approximately where they will find it. What is required is money, and as with any puzzle, skill and patience.

Not all archaeologists, however, are content with just reconstructing particular historical sequences. The "new archaeology" (like the new linguistics) is much more ambitious. It is concerned with the causes of cultural variation rather than just classification, and with general principles rather than conjecture about "influences" or "migrations." And it insists that archaeologists must adhere to the scientific method of forming hypotheses and testing them against the data. As Lewis Binford has put it, "We attempt to explain similarities and differences in archaeological remains in terms of the functioning of material items in a cultural system and the . . . operation or evolution of the cultural systems responsible for the varied artifact forms, associations, and distributions observable in the ground."[12]

This means that the topics which a new archaeologist can explore are limited only by his imagination in formulating hypotheses and by his ability to devise methods for testing them on available data. It also means that archaeology must "test the validity of explanatory principles currently in use and attempt to refine or replace them by verified hypotheses relating the significance of archaeological data to past conditions."[13] Their goal is the formulation of *general laws of cultural process,* and they often emphasize the role of long-range ecological processes in producing cultural change. This is a goal which will require close cooperation among archaeologists, ethnologists, linguists, and specialists from many biological and physical sciences. It is a vast undertaking, but it does represent one way in which we might someday achieve a unified science of man.

RECOMMENDED READING

Binford, L. R., *An Archaeological Perspective.* New York: Seminar Press, 1972. A collection of provocative essays and personal reminiscences by one of the founders of the "new archaeology."

Casagrande, J., ed., *In the Company of Man.* New York: Harper and Row, 1960. A dozen prominent anthropologists describe their experience in the field, especially their relationships with informants.

Golde, P., *Women in the Field.* Chicago: Aldine, 1970. A dozen women describe their field work with special emphasis on the advantages and liabilities of being a woman ethnographer.

Vayda, A. P., ed., *Environment and Cultural Behavior.* New York: Natural History Press, 1969. A collection of articles illustrating the range and findings of ecological studies in cultural anthropology.

Wax, R. H., *Doing Fieldwork.* Chicago: University of Chicago Press, 1971. A very personal and highly readable account of field work in three different social settings, together with useful warnings and advice for the green ethnographer.

Williams, T. R., *Field Methods in the Study of Culture.* New York: Holt, Rinehart and Winston, 1967. A brief handbook of standard field methods, illustrated from the author's experience among the Dusun of North Borneo.

12. L. Binford, *An Archaeological Perspective* (New York and London: Seminar Press, 1972), p. 120.
13. *Ibid.,* p. 121.

CHAPTER 13
Comparative Methods

Man is the culture-bearing animal, the principal maker of "tools, rules, and moral judgments." The most general goal of cultural anthropology can be stated as the attempt to *understand the similarities and differences among all human cultures and the processes which have produced them.* To achieve this purpose, we must compare all kinds of data on living and extinct societies, languages, technologies, and ideologies. For if we are to understand any culture—including our own—we must see it in relation to and in contrast with other cultures. Otherwise, we may attribute to "human nature" beliefs and behaviors which are only the conventions of a particular society.

At the end of Chapter 12 we saw how archaeologists are able to move from the synchronic description of single sites to the study of historical sequences by comparing a series of sites and/or interpreting the layers of a stratified site in temporal terms. We also noted the development in archaeology of methods for understanding general processes of cultural stability and change. These methods require the archaeologist to think in terms of a total cultural-ecological system, and to test carefully formulated hypotheses by the study of material forms and their distributions.

In this chapter we shall look at some of the comparative methods employed in linguistics, ethnology, and social anthropology. Comparisons can be carried out for at least three different, though related, purposes:

1. Historical—to reconstruct the sequences of development within and relationships among cultural systems. Historical studies may also deal with particular items within systems—for example,

the history and spread of a particular word or technique rather than an entire language or technological system.

2. Functional/Causal—to understand the general principles of cultural development and integration. Although certainly not independent of historical understanding, this involves comparisons among different historical traditions and the use of special, cross-cultural methods.

3. Universals—to discover features which appear in every language and social system. These may be universals of content or of process. The anthropologist also attempts to trace such features to their sources in human biology or psychology, in culture history, and/or in the necessary constitution of cultural systems.

We shall begin with a consideration of comparative methods in linguistics, using language as a model for other kinds of cultural systems, and conclude with a discussion of the responsibilities of the anthropologist to the subjects of his study.

COMPARATIVE LINGUISTICS

In addition to descriptions of particular languages, linguists are concerned with the *history of language change* and with constructing a *general theory of language* which will account for similarities and differences among all human tongues. Both of these enterprises require the systematic comparison of linguistic forms, though the inferences drawn from the comparisons are somewhat different.

Historical inferences about language are necessary because *all languages are constantly changing*; these inferences are possible because *linguistic change is regular.* That is, changes in one part of a sound system or grammar tend to be generalized to other parts of the language. Furthermore, change in a language is systematically related to other changes in the culture of its speakers. These generalizations are most easily demonstrated in the sound system.

Written records which reflect the manner in which a language was spoken at various times can be used to reconstruct the processes of sound change. For example, by comparing our modern speech (=NE) with that of Chaucer (Middle English = ME), it is possible to show systematic changes in the pronunciation of various phonemes and actual changes in the phonemic system. Between Chaucer's time (the fourteenth century) and our own, English has lost only one consonant phoneme—/x/, pronounced

Middle English		Modern English	
Written	Phonemes	Written	Phonemes
wif	/wi:f/	wife	/wayf/
see	/sæ:/	sea	/siy/
hous	/hu:s/	house	/haws/
spon	/spo:n/	spoon	/spuwn/

***Figure 13.1* The Vowel Shift in Some Common English Words (adapted from W. Lehmann, *Historical Linguistics: An Introduction* [New York: Holt, Rinehart and Winston, 1962], p. 151)**

like the German guttural sound -*ch*—and added two new consonant phonemes, /ŋ/ and /ž/. The vowel system, however, underwent a massive change known as the Great English Vowel Shift, which affected nearly every vowel and vowel combination in a complicated way. Some indication of this shift can be seen in Figure 13.1, which is a comparison of a few common words in which NE phoneme clusters (ay, iy, and so forth) have replaced ME long vowels.

Since there also exist written texts for even older literature, such as *Beowulf,* which show a still earlier stage of English pronunciation (Old English = OE), the changes in our sound system can be traced back over a thousand years and their regularities demonstrated. Such sound shifts which affect every part of a language can be stated in a few simple rules. Thus, if you study Chaucer, you can learn to pronounce a reasonable approximation of Middle English by applying these rules systematically.

Vocabulary change is another matter. Careful attention to sound change can help us to decipher many Old or Middle English words (OE wudu > ME wode > NE wood), but where a different morpheme is used in Modern English we have no choice but to learn each definition separately (ME yclept becomes NE named, called). Nevertheless, it has been argued that although word change is unpredictable, it does take place at a relatively *constant rate.* On the basis of this assumption (which is strongly disputed by many linguists), Morris Swadesh developed a method for determining how long two or more related languages have been "separated" from one another. Before we can discuss this method (known as *glottochronology),* it will be necessary to explain just what is meant when we say that languages are "related."

1. M. Swadesh, "Diffusional Cumulation and Archaic Residue as Historical Explanation," *Southwestern Journal of Anthropology*, Vol. 7 (1951), pp. 1–21. See also the series of five papers on lexico-statistic dating (glottochronology) in *International Journal of American Linguistics*, Vol. 21, No. 2 (1955), pp. 91–149.

English can be traced back through its earlier written forms until it is revealed as one of a number of Germanic dialects spoken during the late Middle Ages. Further comparative studies show that these Germanic dialects (whose daughter languages include the modern Scandinavian tongues as well as German and Dutch) are but one branch of a widespread language stock known as Indo-European (see Figure 13.2). The relationships among these languages were discovered by comparative linguists in the nineteenth century, and since then a few more languages (such as Hittite) have been added to the stock. The regular sound changes which produced phonological differences between the various branches of this vast family have been well worked out, and the history of some branches (such as the Romance descendants of Latin, including French, Spanish, Italian, and Rumanian)

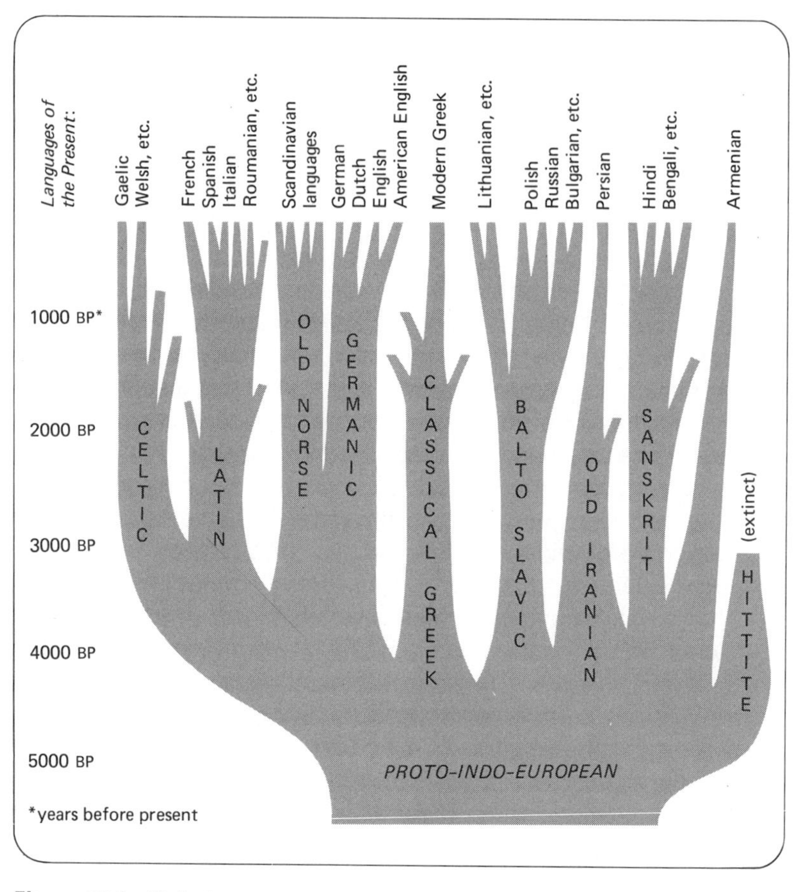

Figure 13.2 Main Languages and Language Families of the Indo-European Language Stock (showing approximate time depth)

is known in great detail. Thus, when we say that two or more contemporary languages are genetically related, we mean that comparative study shows they have been derived in a systematic manner from some earlier language, called a *protolanguage.* Due to the regularity of phonological and grammatical change, the protolanguage can often be reconstructed *even in the absence of written records.*[2]

Vocabulary change is much less systematic than sound change; however, if Swadesh is right that words are replaced at a constant rate, it should be possible to determine the approximate time at which daughter languages separated from one another. In making these comparisons, Swadesh used a list of 100 "culture-free" terms—for example, equivalents of English words such as "sky," "water," "hair," and so forth. The *rate of replacement* calculated for a number of languages with known histories is roughly 20 percent per 1,000 years. That is, 1,000 years after two languages first separate, a comparison of 100 words in the vocabularies of the languages should show resemblances in about 80 of the items, while the remaining 20 should have changed (due to borrowing, and so forth) to dissimilar forms. After 2,000 years, 20 percent of the similar items on the 1,000-year list would be replaced, leaving $80 - (.20 \times 80)$ or about 64 items with resemblances. This process would continue until, after 6,000 years, only a very few resemblances could be detected.

Glottochronology confirms the other estimates that the Indo-European families are descended from a language known as Proto-Indo-European, which was spoken about 5,000 years ago in eastern Europe. The glottochronological method is extremely useful in forming hypotheses about culture history. It can be applied to any two languages for which vocabularies are available to give either an estimate of their time of separation or a judgment that they are probably unrelated. The method is, however, controversial enough that most culture historians regard it as a useful but undependable supplement to their other techniques of reconstruction.

Besides the matter of establishing historical relations between languages and reconstructing their proto-forms, comparative linguistics also aims at a general understanding of the nature of language. This includes the search for language *universals*—generalizations about linguistic change and linguistic structure. A vast number of language universals have been proposed. A few of these are listed below:

---

2. See W. Lehmann, *Historical Linguistics: An Introduction* (New York: Holt, Rinehart and Winston, 1962), pp. 83–114.

1. All human languages make use of a limited number of phonemes from which an infinite number of utterances can be constructed.
2. Sound change is universal. There is a historical tendency toward "phonological symmetry," although there are gaps in every sound system. Every sound system has stop phonemes that contrast with nonstops. The stops always have at least two contrasting positions of articulation (English /p/, /t/, /k/).
3. Among the units of every human language are found proper names and at least one element that denotes the speaker and one that denotes the addressee. Indeed, all known languages have pronominal categories involving at least three persons and two numbers.
4. "If a language has the category of gender, it always has the category of number," and "if either the subject or object noun agrees with the verb in gender, then the adjective always agrees with the noun in gender."
5. "In declarative sentences with nominal subject and object, the dominant order is almost always one in which the subject precedes the object." That is, where S = subject, V = verb, and O = object, the common ways of ordering these elements may be represented as VSO, SVO, and SOV; the three other possible orders (OSV, OVS, or VOS) are either extremely rare or unknown.[3]

These five examples illustrate the kinds of phonological and grammatical universals that linguists have discovered thus far. Some recent work in language universals has been concerned with the questions: What kinds of grammatical *rules* are found in all languages? In what *order* are they learned by children acquiring a first language? These are important questions, for the answers (if they can be discovered) will provide information about the crucial and distinctively human capacity for learning a language and how this capacity operates. Such findings should also be useful in furthering our general understanding of the enculturation process.[4]

It was suggested at the beginning of this section that linguistic changes are related to changes in other parts of a cultural system. Sociolinguists have just begun to explore the factors responsible for phonological and grammatical change; these include such things as bilingualism, dialect prestige, and various kinds of interlanguage influence. But anthropologists have long recognized the

3. J. Greenberg, ed., *Universals of Language* (second edition; Cambridge: M.I.T. Press, 1966), pp. 73–113.
4. See D. McNeill, "Developmental Psycholinguistics," in Smith and Miller, *The Genesis of Language* (Cambridge: M.I.T. Press, 1966), pp. 15–84.

relationship between *vocabulary* change and culture change. Our discussions of folk taxonomies have indicated the close tie between cultural categories and their labels. This means that innovations in any part of a cultural system (social structure, technology, and so forth) will ultimately be reflected in the vocabulary of the language. The development of scientific terminology and other specialized occupational jargons is one obvious illustration of this process in our own society.

The relationship between culture and vocabulary also has important historical implications: since historical linguists can reconstruct extinct protolanguages, they are able to tell us what terms were found in the ancestral tongue, and in many cases, what terms have been replaced or lost in the daughter languages. Thus, from the reconstruction of Proto-Indo-European we are able to tell some things about the environment, the kinship system, and the technology of the people who spoke this language 5,000 years ago. For example, the reconstruction of Proto-Indo-European terms for "beech tree" and for a particular species of salmon have helped in locating the probable homeland of the ancient population. Similarly, many cultural contacts of their descendants can be traced by discovering non-Indo-European terms in the vocabulary of daughter languages. The general use in modern European languages of the term "algebra" (from the Arabic *al-jabr*, literally, 'the reduction') accurately indicates the source from which this form of mathematics was borrowed.

A more recent example is also of interest. In both modern and Middle English, there is a contrast between the terms used for certain animals (cow, calf, pig) and the words used for their meat (beef, veal, pork). Linguistic comparisons show that the former terms are derived from Old English while the latter are descended from Old French (in modern French: *boeuf, veau, porc*). This would be difficult to interpret without historical knowledge of the eleventh-century Norman invasion of England which resulted in a French-speaking aristocracy being imposed upon an Anglo-Saxon peasantry. However, given these facts, it is understandable that the living animals (which were cared for by the peasants) kept their Old English names, whereas the meat which was brought to the table (and consumed mainly by the aristocracy) acquired Old French names.

In cases where we know only the *results* of inter-linguistic influence, it may be possible to infer the social conditions which produced these results. Thus comparative linguistic materials can be sources of hypotheses about culture history. In this respect, they are analogous to distinctive items of material culture (pottery, textiles, and so forth) which may be used to trace ancient culture contacts when found outside of the areas where they were produced. For example, the unique pottery of the Minoan civilization of ancient Crete has been used to demonstrate the widespread trade carried on by these peoples with Egypt, the Near East, and Greece. In the New World, contacts between the high civilizations of Mexico and the American Southwest are confirmed by similar types of evidence; Mexican influence on ancient Pueblo social structure, art, and religion can also be inferred.

CULTURE HISTORY AND CULTURE EVOLUTION

Ethnology is to ethnography as historical linguistics is to descriptive linguistics. Both ethnology and historical linguistics make use of comparative methods in order to draw historical inferences. The ethnologist attempts to infer culture history from the *geographic distributions of social, technological, and ideological forms.* His goal is to trace the source and spread of various peoples and to understand the processes which lead to acceptance, rejection, and modification of cultural innovations. In achieving these aims, the ethnologist makes use of certain assumptions similar to the archaeological principle of stratification. For example, in trying to infer the relative age of different forms from their contemporary geographic distribution, he often assumes that, other things being equal, the greater the spatial spread of a form, the older it must be. This assumption is known as the "age-area principle." (See Figure 13.3.)

As with the principle of stratification, other things are of course *not* always equal, and the age-area principle must be used with great caution. But in the absence of other evidence, it is useful in forming hypotheses about temporal sequences from spatial distributions.[5] In much of Africa, for example, archaeological remains are few, due to the perishability of materials used and the poor conditions for preservation; therefore, inferences from geographic distributions are heavily relied upon in reconstructing culture history. This has also been true until recently in the Pacific islands; but in the last thirty years, increased archaeological activity in this region has led to a reevaluation of many historical reconstructions which were based solely on ethnographic comparisons and native legends. In many cases the previous reconstructions were confirmed, but in some cases they were shown to be inaccurate.

Many of the historical statements in the chapters on tech-

5. See the classic paper, "Time Perspective in Aboriginal American Culture: A Study in Method," in D. Mandelbaum, ed., *Selected Writings of Edward Sapir* (Berkeley: University of California Press, 1951), pp. 389–462.

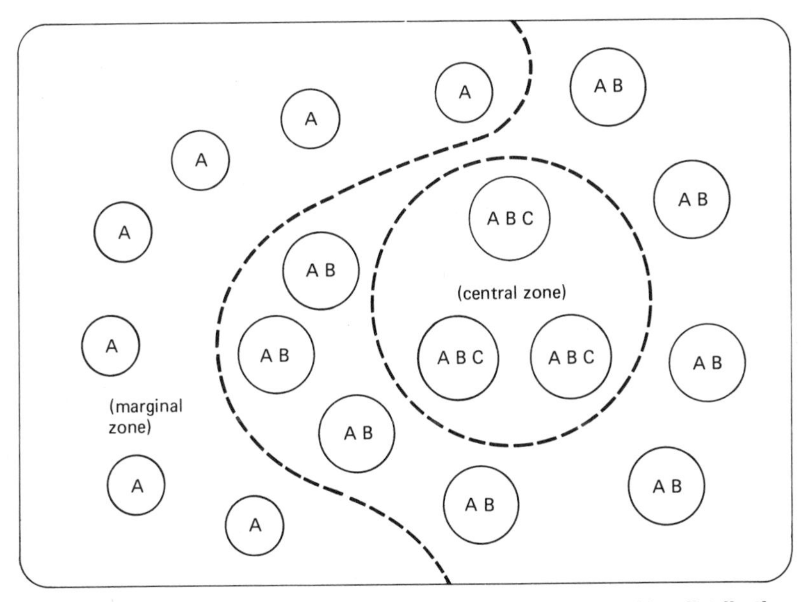

Figure 13.3 **The Age-Area Principle. Mapping the geographic distribution of selected cultural elements (A, B, and C) makes it possible to tentatively infer their relative age. For example, if each of the circles above represents a different community and if A = radio, B = black-and-white television, and C = color television, it might be inferred that radio is the oldest invention (due to its wide distribution), followed by black-and-white television (which has a more restricted distribution and has not yet reached the "marginal" communities), while color television is the most recent, being found only in the central zone.**

nological systems are the result of painstaking comparative research by ethnologists, supplemented by archaeological data when available. For example, the discussions of types of snowshoes, boats, and fire-making techniques are all based on detailed comparative studies of ethnographies. The ethnologist plots the geographic distribution of the forms he is interested in, and analyzes the artifacts or practices into the smaller cultural elements of which they are composed. For example, an arrow is considered in terms of the type of point, shaft, feathers, and so on. Using criteria of similarity and elaboration, culture historians make inferences about the origins and spread of various elements, describing the ways that they have been reinterpreted by borrowing societies and/or combined with other elements. In most culture historical studies, individuals are unknown or unimportant; the focus is upon sequences of cultural developments in regional and sometimes world-wide contexts.

Traditional culture history has been criticized by many contemporary ethnologists for its arbitrary methods, untested assumptions, and insufficient attention to the social and environmental functions of the elements it studies. Some of these criticisms are doubtless justified, but the best culture historians have always been aware of these problems and done their best to control them.[6] What has really happened is that the interests of ethnologists have changed so that they are now asking different questions. In addition to tracing the development of specific regional traditions, the ethnologist is interested in the processes of *adaptive change* and *culture growth.* He asks questions such as: What happens when groups with relatively similar cultures move into diverse environments? Are there any general tendencies which can be found in the development of human culture as a whole? One recent formulation does an impressive job of bringing these two questions together and answering them within a consistent framework. This is the approach suggested by Marshall D. Sahlins and Elman R. Service in their collection of essays on *Evolution and Culture.*

Basic to the ideas of Sahlins and Service is the distinction between *general* and *specific cultural evolution.* The study of general evolution is concerned with the overall progressive trend of human culture as a whole; it is measured in terms of mankind's increasing control over sources of energy (see p. 271, above). "The objectives of general evolutionary research are the determination and explanation of the successive transformations of culture through its several stages of over-all progress. What progressive trends have emerged . . . in economy, in political institutions, or in the role of kinship in society?"[7]

Such studies are concerned with the emergence of new levels of organization or principles of social integration regardless of where they take place and without regard to environmental conditions. The study of specific evolution, on the other hand, is concerned with the particular adaptations made by particular regional cultures to their material and social environments. As Sahlins and Service have noted:

> The cultural anthropologist surveying the ethnographic and archaeological achievements of his discipline is confronted by variety if nothing else. There are myriads of culture types, that is, of the culture characteristic of an ethnic group or a region, and even greater variety of cultures proper, of the cultural organization of given cohesive societies. How has this come about? In a word, through adaptive modification: culture has diversified as it has filled in the variety of opportunities

6. See the discussion by J. Vansina, "Cultures Through Time," in R. Naroll and R. Cohen, eds., *A Handbook of Method in Cultural Anthropology* (Garden City: Natural History Press, 1970), pp. 165–179. Several other articles in this encyclopedic collection also deal with comparative approaches (pp. 581 f.).

7. M. Sahlins and E. Service, eds., *Evolution and Culture* (Ann Arbor: University of Michigan Press, 1960), pp. 28–29.

for human existence afforded by the earth. Such is the specific aspect of cultural evolution.[8]

Thus we are led to a view of cultural evolution which has many similarities to the modern theory of biological evolution: new forms (organic or cultural) arise and survive through adaptation to different environmental situations; but above and beyond this specific process, there emerge new levels or "grades" of organization which may be ordered in an ascending series. Just as the biological "grade" of *monkeys* arose independently in the Old and New Worlds from different groups of prosimian ancestors, so did the cultural "grade" of *civilization* arise, more than once in both hemispheres, from very different cultural traditions.

The notions of general and specific cultural evolution add an important dynamic dimension to studies of culture history. They are representative of a renewed interest among ethnologists and other culture historians in studying regularities of cultural development. At the same time, however, another group of ethnologists has been developing methods for the cross-cultural study of synchronic problems. The subfield of *social anthropology* is concerned with the comparative study of institutions and social relations; its goals include the discovery of cultural *universals* and of *correlations* among variables in both social structures and enculturation processes. Let us examine some of the comparative methods used by social anthropologists in investigating functional relationships among the parts of cultural systems.

CROSS-CULTURAL METHODS

Under the heading of "ethnographic inference" (Chapter 12), we discussed the discovery of functional relationships *within* a given society. There we said that through long and intensive acquaintance with an alien culture, the ethnographer is often able to discover the implicit function of customs and institutions which seem bizarre and arbitrary on more superficial acquaintance. But for the discovery of some kinds of functional relations, comparative study is necessary. For example, the function of a type of kinship terminology or the consequences of some mode of enculturation can be understood only by systematically comparing societies in which the custom or trait is found with other societies in which it is *not* present, and noting what appear to be the consequences for other parts of the culture.

8. *Ibid.*, p. 23.

The social anthropologist constructs categories of customs which can be applied cross-culturally: he studies "cross-cousin marriage," "matrilineal descent," or "dependency training" in a variety of different societies. While recognizing that the actual behaviors in each group are quite different, he still hopes to discover some *regularities of form or process* which will show a functional relationship between the custom under study and some other part of the cultural system.

This kind of study has a long history in anthropology. During the nineteenth century, Sir Edward Tylor coined the term "adhesion" to indicate those customs which were found together in more societies than would be expected if they coexisted just by chance. For example, Tylor was interested in the custom of "mother-in-law avoidance," a social rule which forbids a man to speak to, or in some cases even to look at, his wife's mother. He studied a large number of ethnographic descriptions of societies in which this custom was observed and found that in the majority of them, the rule of post-marital residence was matrilocal—the man was expected to reside with his wife's kin.[9] This adhesion—or as we would say today, *correlation*—does not explain either of the rules, but it does indicate the probability of a functional relation between them, and it indicates that any attempt to understand "mother-in-law avoidance" must take account of residence patterns.

The logic of the *correlational approach* to functional relationships may be demonstrated by the following example. Suppose that an ethnologist has a hunch—based upon theory or on his own field experience—that two customs, *A* and *B*, are functionally related. One way to test its validity is to go to the ethnographic literature and select a *sample* of, say, 100 societies, and then evaluate them for the presence or absence of each of the customs. For any given society, there are five different possible findings:

1. *A* and *B* are both present (+A, +B)
2. *A* is present, *B* is absent (+A, −B)
3. *A* is absent, *B* is present (−A, +B)
4. *A* and *B* are both absent (−A, −B)
5. no reliable information is available

Assuming that information is available on both customs for

9. E. B. Tylor, "On a Method of Investigating the Development of Institutions; Applied to Laws of Marriage and Descent," *Journal of the Royal Anthropological Institute*, Vol. 18 (1889), pp. 245–269. See also H. Driver, "Geographical-historical *versus* Psycho-functional Explanations of Kin Avoidances," *Current Anthropology*, Vol. 7 (1966), pp. 131–182. See also Naroll and Cohen, *op. cit.*, especially pp. 888–1003.

all 100 societies in the sample, the results may then be tabulated in the form:

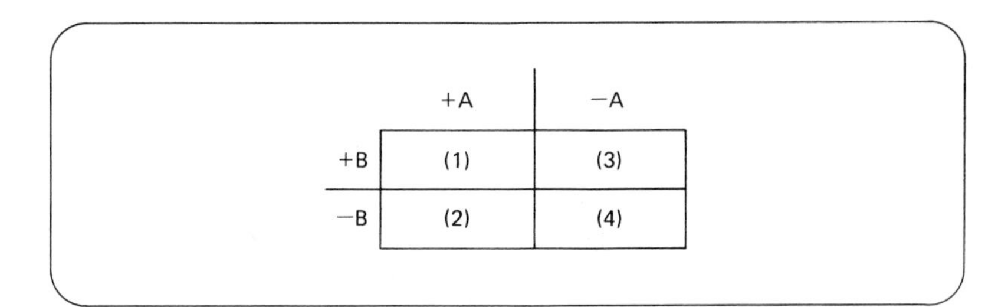

	+A	−A
+B	(1)	(3)
−B	(2)	(4)

Into such a table, the ethnologist enters the *number of societies* which meet each of the pairs of conditions: into cell (1) he enters the number of groups in which both *A* and *B* are present; into (2) the number meeting the second possibility; and so forth. The total of all four cells is equal to the size of the sample. If there is *no* relationship between the customs—that is, if the fact that one custom is present or absent has no effect on the probability of the other being present or absent—and if each custom is found in half of the 100 societies in the sample, the resulting table would look something like this:

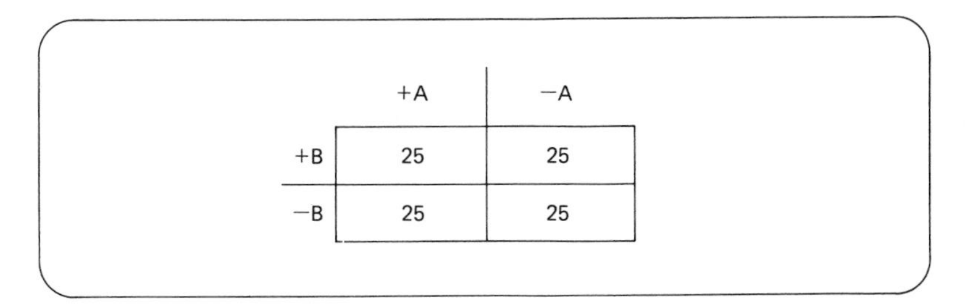

	+A	−A
+B	25	25
−B	25	25

That is, an equal (or nearly equal) number of societies meet each of the four possible conditions. This is the ideal demonstration of *no correlation* between *A* and *B.*

If the two customs are not found in half of the societies, it is still possible to calculate their probabilities of being found together. For example, if *A* was present in only 30 percent of the societies in the sample and *B* was found in 60 percent, the probability of *A* and *B* occurring together *by chance* is found by multiplying the percentages (.30 × .60 = .18); even if there is no relation between these customs, they would be expected to occur together in 18 percent of the cases. The ideal no-correlation table for such a sample would look like this:

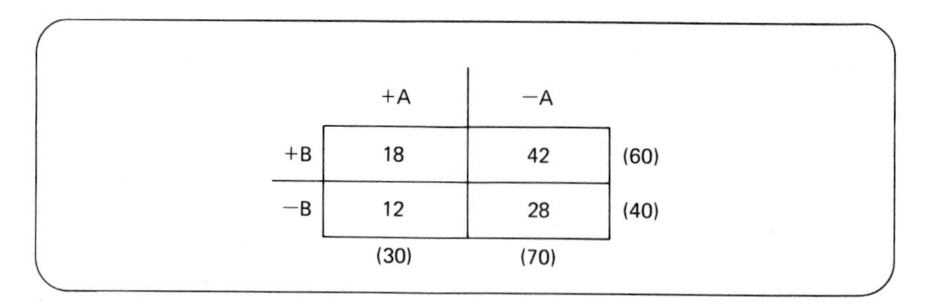

	+A	−A	
+B	18	42	(60)
−B	12	28	(40)
	(30)	(70)	

(The figures in parentheses show the totals adding across or down; the expected number for any given cell is computed by multiplying the total of its row by the total of its column and dividing by the total number of cases, in this example, 100). Slight departures from these ideal tables still do not indicate the presence of an association between *A* and *B.*

If the correlation between the chosen customs is *perfect,* then the presence or absence of one custom in a society allows us to predict with certainty whether the other custom is present or absent. This ideal relationship can occur in two different ways. In a *perfect positive correlation,* the presence of *A* is always accompanied by the presence of *B,* and if *A* is absent, so is *B.* Both of the following tables show a perfect positive correlation:

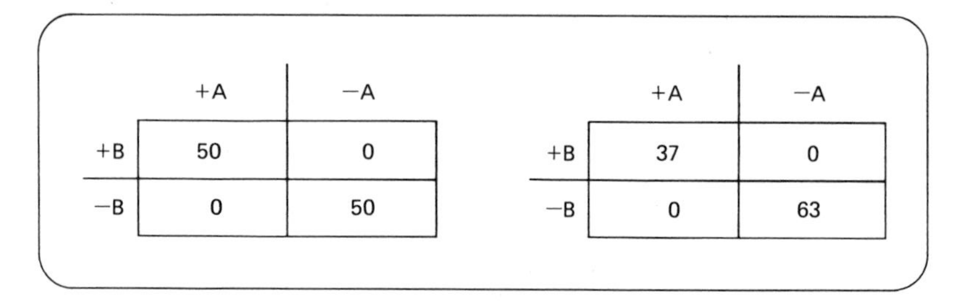

	+A	−A
+B	50	0
−B	0	50

	+A	−A
+B	37	0
−B	0	63

That is, so long as all of the cases fall into cell (1) and cell (4), we have a perfect positive relationship. On the other hand, if all of the cases fall into cell (2) and cell (3), we know that the two customs are "mutually exclusive"—never occur together—and this is called a *perfect negative correlation,* as in the tables below:

	+A	−A
+B	0	50
−B	50	0

	+A	−A
+B	0	14
−B	86	0

It is, of course, very unlikely that one will find any of these ideal cases, except for rather trivial relations; for example, it is hardly surprising that there is a perfect negative correlation between societies (A) having a hunting economy and (B) using nuclear energy. The following three tables are from actual correlational studies and are more representative of typical findings:

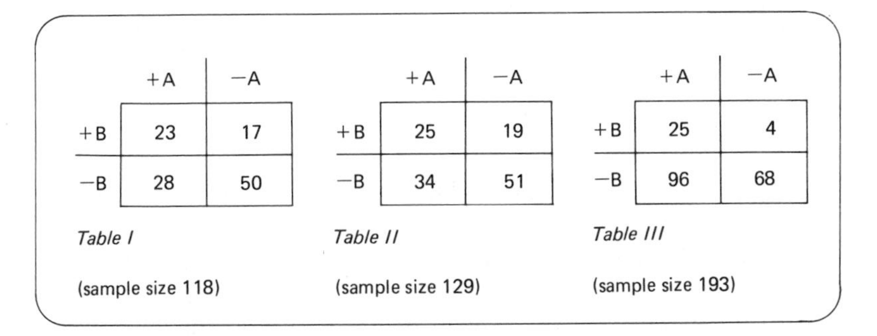

	+A	−A
+B	23	17
−B	28	50

Table I

(sample size 118)

	+A	−A
+B	25	19
−B	34	51

Table II

(sample size 129)

	+A	−A
+B	25	4
−B	96	68

Table III

(sample size 193)

What kinds of inferences can be drawn from tables such as these? Fortunately, there are a number of simple *statistical techniques* which make possible the analysis and evaluation of this kind of data. The mathematics is not essential. The important point is that given *any* two-by-two table, we can estimate the probability that a genuine functional relationship exists between the customs being tested. Statistical analysis shows that the positive associations in Tables I and III could come about *solely by chance* less than 1 in 20 and 1 in 100 times, respectively. The association found in Table II could occur by chance more than 1 in 5 times; it is therefore not considered to be "significant"—that is, the apparent relationship is not to be relied upon.

The most extensive use of the correlational approach in social anthropology is that of G. P. Murdock in his book *Social Structure.*[10] Using a large sample of societies from every part of the world, Murdock systematically tested many different hypotheses including 120 tests on the "determinants of kinship terminology." Many of his findings are highly technical. We shall examine one example of his approach and then summarize his conclusions on the relationship between kinship terminology and other rules of social structure.

Among the hypotheses tested by Murdock is one that suggests an association between the marriage custom known as "sister exchange" and a kinship terminology in which ego uses the same term for his wife's brother's wife as he does for his own sister. As the diagram shows, where this type of marriage is

10. G. P. Murdock, *Social Structure* (New York: Macmillan, 1949).

practiced, these two relationships will often be represented by the same person:

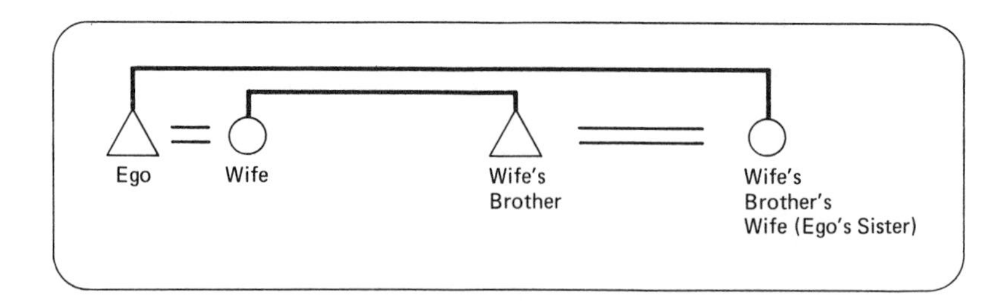

The test of this hypothesis (WiBrWi = Si) for a sample of 65 societies is shown in the table below. Although there were only seven societies in this sample with the custom of sister exchange, the association between this marriage custom and terminology is highly significant (the probability of this table arising by chance is less than 1 in 100) and the functional relationship is confirmed.[11]

		Sister Exchange	*Other Marriage Rules*	
Terms for WiBrWi and Sister	Same Term	6	13	(19)
	Different Terms	1	45	(46)
		(7)	(58)	

It will be noted that there are thirteen societies that have the terminology without the marriage rule and one society with the marriage rule but not the terminology. These exceptions to a perfect correlation may be explained in various ways, but they do not invalidate the association.

Following many such investigations, Murdock reached some general conclusions about the relative effect of three structural factors upon kinship terminology. Although special *marriage rules,* such as sister exchange, have a notable effect upon kinship terminology, the effect of *descent rules* upon terminology is somewhat stronger. Murdock also found that *residence rules,* although they do affect terminology to some extent, are not as powerful as either of the two other factors. In decreasing order of their effect upon kinship terminology, then, we have:

11. *Ibid.*, p. 172.

1. rules of descent (patrilineal, matrilineal, and so forth) and the kinship groups they produce
2. marriage rules (polygamy, polyandry, monogamy, and so forth) and the kinds of families they produce
3. residence rules (patrilocal, neolocal, bilocal, and so forth) and the local groupings they produce[12]

The functional relationships among these three structural factors have also been studied. Murdock concludes that although residence rules have a relatively weak effect upon kinship terms, they tend to be "progressive" rules: in the course of social change, it is the residence rules which are most likely to change *first.* This eventually produces changes in the more "conservative" rules governing descent and marriage, which in turn have strong effects upon kinship terminology. These findings support the conception of social structure as a *system* within which any change in one part has effects upon all the other parts. But since residence rules are most responsive to environmental change, they also caution us to look *outside* of the social system for some of the factors which set change in motion.[13]

Murdock's work was in part made possible by a research aid known as the Human Relations Area Files (HRAF) which he founded at Yale University during the 1930s. These files contain ethnographic information on several hundred societies ranging from primitive tribes to national states. They are organized by culture area and are broken down into categories for indexing. These materials have been duplicated and are now available to researchers at most major universities and colleges. They make possible the rapid inspection of materials from a great variety of societies on any given cultural topic. For instance, if an ethnologist is interested in diet, wedding ceremonies, or clothing in some region of the world, he has only to go to the files, and in a few hours, he can pull out and inspect a range of materials which it would otherwise take him many days or weeks to locate. HRAF also commissions and publishes integrative studies on cultural topics and regions. Summaries of various studies based largely on materials in the files are published in the journal *Ethnology.*

Another area of comparative research in which the cross-cultural approach has been used is the study of enculturation (or, more generally, culture and personality). In some of these studies, the statistical aspects are somewhat complicated by the use of *rating scales* on which the intensity of a custom is evaluated, rather than just its presence or absence. But the principle is the same:

---

12. *Ibid.*, pp. 182–183.
13. See J. Gibbs, "Social Organization," in S. Tax, ed., *Horizons of Anthropology* (Chicago: Aldine, 1964), pp. 160–170.

if one custom or personality trait can be shown to go with another (to a greater-than-chance extent), the hypothesis that they are functionally related is felt to be validated. For example, John Whiting and Irvin Child have tried to show that cultural explanations of illness are functionally related to child-training practices (socialization). Without going into the details of their theory (which hinges on the Freudian concept of fixation), we may describe their general conclusions in regard to "oral explanations" of illness.

By "oral explanations," Whiting and Child mean the custom of attributing illness either to the ingestion of some material (food or poison) by the patient or to verbal spells and incantations performed by other people. They found that *there is a significant relationship between oral explanations of illness and the presence in a society of child-training practices likely to produce considerable anxiety about oral behavior* (sucking, eating, or speaking). The child-training practices believed to produce a high degree of "oral socialization anxiety" include such customs as early or severe weaning as well as excessive punishment in connection with oral behavior. They found that early weaning was highly correlated with the presence in a society of oral explanations for illness—beliefs that illness was caused by something eaten or spoken.[14] The table on which this conclusion was based is summarized below:

		Oral Explanations for Illness		
		Present	Absent	
Age of Weaning	Early	17	3	(20)
	Late	6	13	(19)
		(23)	(16)	

The use of the cross-cultural approach in culture and personality research is very widespread, but thus far it has raised as many questions as it has answered. Among the problems still to be solved in this area are the following:

1. Validity and comparability of the primary data (ethnographic sources)
2. Reliability of the rating procedures

14. J. Whiting and I. Child, *Child Training and Personality* (New Haven: Yale University Press, 1953). The table below is adapted from their Table 9, p. 162.

3. Suitability and randomness of the sample
4. Allowance for geographic factors (control for the possibility of historical diffusion rather than functional relationship of customs)
5. Significance of the results

Each of these points could be discussed at great length, and there are numerous books and articles which attempt to deal with them. We shall comment here only on the last point. In the case of Whiting and Child's data described above, what does it *mean* that early weaning and oral explanations of illness are found together in a high proportion of societies? To begin with, it does *not* necessarily mean that there exists a *causal relationship* between the two customs. A correlation must never be taken as proof of causation. Although it may be argued from this data, given several assumptions from Freudian psychology, that custom *A* (age of weaning) is the "cause" of custom *B* (oral explanations of illness), there are *at least three other possibilities* which must be taken into account in this (or any other) case:

1. The supposed causal relationship between *A* and *B* could be reversed. In this example, perhaps people who believe that illness is caused by ingestion of the wrong kind of material tend to wean their children early as a form of protection.
2. Both *A* and *B* may be produced be some third factor, *C*, which is as yet unrecognized. (There is a high correlation between the flowering of fruit trees and the northerly migration of birds—but most people recognize that there is a seasonal factor which controls both.)
3. The finding may be spurious due to an unintentionally biased sample. Statistical analysis says only how *improbable* a certain outcome is—it can never certify the validity of a finding. Indeed, statistical theory asserts that highly improbable combinations of factors *do* occur now and then simply by chance.

Thus the cross-cultural approach, even with the help of research aids such as the HRAF and techniques of statistical inference, cannot guarantee valid findings. And even the most plausible *post hoc* explanations of correlations must be carefully questioned. It is only when a hypothesis based in theory has *preceded* the testing of a relationship that the correlation can be taken as support for the hypothesis.

For these and other reasons, ethnological inference remains, to a large extent, an *art*. In most arts, valid results are produced only when talented workers apply their knowledge and skills to a vast domain of phenomena. For the ethnologist, this domain consists of the facts discovered by ethnography, linguistics, and archaeology. And these subfields, too, have their "artistic" qualities. As Evans-Pritchard has observed:

> The work of the anthropologist is not photographic. He has to decide what is significant in what he observes and by his subsequent relation of his experiences to bring what is significant into relief. For this he must have, in addition to a wide knowledge of anthropology, a feeling for form and pattern, and a touch of genius.[15]

CULTURAL UNIVERSALS

Anthropologists have been interested for a long time in the question of whether there are cultural universals. It should be obvious that any answers to this question must be based on a wide range of comparative data. But even though we will never be able to study all human societies in detail, the more we know, the better are our chances for arriving at valid generalizations. For example, it is now well established that all human societies have language systems which are entirely adequate to their communication needs; as recently as fifty years ago, however, it was maintained by some scholars that "primitive languages" were crude, incomplete, or unable to express certain kinds of concepts. These ideas are no more valid than the travelers' tales which claimed that members of such and such a group had to supplement their speech with gestures and thus were unable to communicate in the dark—probably because they huddled around a fire at night. Yet without scientific study of primitive languages and cultures, such statements could not be effectively refuted.

Today we have a great deal of ethnographic material on which generalization can be based. Some statements of universals are actually classifications of cultural subsystems which, while useful, do not tell us anything about the *content* of these systems. In this book, we have used an implicit classification which is made explicit in Figure 13.4.

Another classification of the "universal cultural pattern" is that suggested by Clark Wissler in his *Man and Culture.* Wissler classified the "facts of culture" under nine headings: Speech, Material Traits, Art, Mythology and Scientific Knowledge, Religious Practices, Family and Social Systems, Property, Government, and War.

---

15. E. E. Evans-Pritchard, *Social Anthropology* (New York: Free Press, 1954), p. 82.

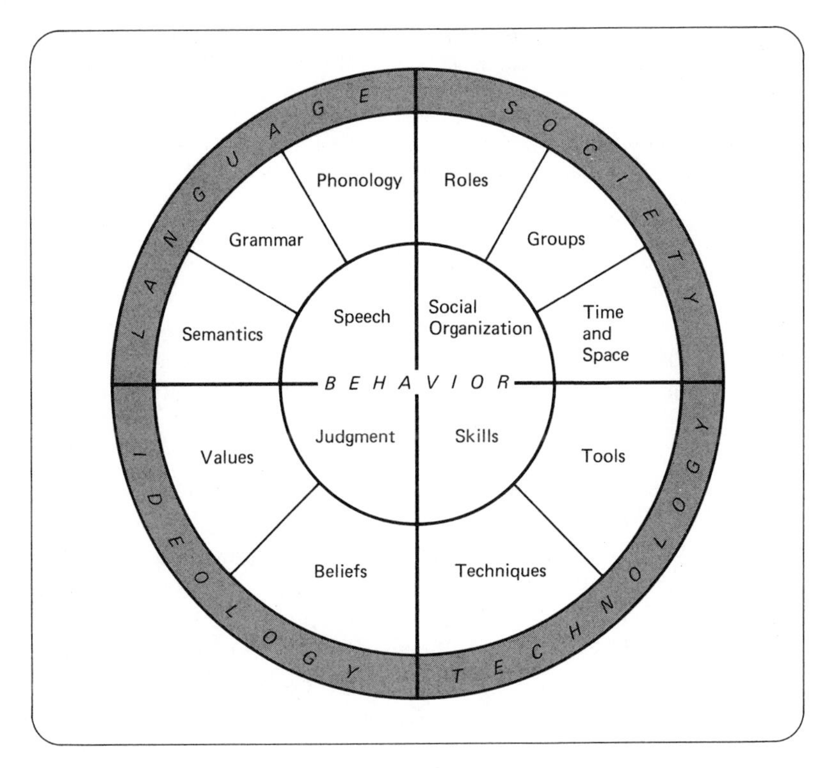

Figure 13.4 **The Major Subsystems of Culture: Language, Society, Technology, and Ideology. The middle ring contains the major structural components of each subsystem; in the center are the behaviors which manifest the various subsystems.**

Each of these headings is subdivided in various ways, of which the following is an example:

6. Family and Social Systems
   a. The forms of marriage
   b. Methods of reckoning relationship
   c. Inheritance
   d. Social control
   e. Sports and games

Wissler also suggested that certain cultural contents are found in all human societies. For example:

> All the historic cultures, however primitive, knew fire. They also knew its value in the preparation of food. In every case they knew, or formerly knew, how to chip stone. The principle of the knife was known and the fundamental idea of the drill. Likewise, the art of twisting

string, or the making of cord; as to weaving, there was not one that did not understand the fundamental step. The fact that some of them went no further is not to the point. . . . We can go even farther, for there were common beliefs. The belief in a soul or spiritual counterpart of some kind . . . is universal. Again, the idea that evil fortune can be avoided by the strict observance of formulated prohibitions, or taboos, as they are often called, is equally so.[16]

Let us suppose that we have discovered a number of valid cultural universals. How are they to be understood? That is, why are certain particular acts, beliefs, or items found in all human societies while others are not? There are at least three kinds of explanations for the universality of a given category of culture. These may be summarized as follows:

1. The universal may be rooted in human biological needs and thus constitute a prerequisite for human social life. For example, food preparation and care of the young, though part of every culture, are also present in the animal world wherever a species is capable of a varied diet and where the young are born relatively helpless. Without *some* way of performing these tasks, the society (animal or human) could not survive; but the human "capacity for culture" elaborates a group's solution into a complex social tradition.

2. The universal may be an exceedingly ancient invention which has had time to spread (diffuse) around the world. For example, the use of fire or the basic techniques of chipping stone-cutting tools are "technicial traits" (to use Wissler's phrase) which were first developed hundreds of thousands of years ago and have had ample time to spread or be carried over the face of the earth—whether from one or several centers of invention. We can, today, see the rapid spread of other traits from the places of their invention (for example, the smoking of tobacco, which spread from the New World to Europe in the sixteenth century and since then over most of the world; and the use of metal cutting tools which is now universal). Diffusion may have been slower in past ages, but it was just as inevitable.[17]

3. Universals may be the result of the "convergence" of cultural forms due to their adaptive advantage. That is, similar traits or techniques may have been independently invented many times and may have survived or replaced other items because of their functional value for the group. This is a frequent explanation for the universality of the incest taboo, the notion being that groups

16. C. Wissler, *Man and Culture* (New York: Crowell, 1923), pp. 73-77.

17. See J. Harlan and J. M. J. de Wet, "On the Quality of Evidence for Origin and Dispersal of Cultivated Plants," *Current Anthropology*, Vol. 14 (1973), pp. 51–55, and the following discussion.

without some such rule would suffer the social and biological disadvantages of inbreeding, while those with such a taboo would of necessity establish cooperative bonds with other social groups—relationships which would operate to their advantage in the struggle for survival.

These three types of explanations are not mutually exclusive. Given a human biological need (say, temperature regulation), the development of a culture trait which helps to meet this need (such as fire, dress, or shelter) is very likely to spread, whether it is invented once, twice, or many times. Similarly, explanations of the historical (2) and functional (3) types are as applicable to regional or nonuniversal traits as they are to true universals. In some cases, one type of explanation may seem more plausible than another. For example, the *norm of reciprocity* has been claimed to be universal (Chapter 7); but even if it is only very widespread, an explanation of its distribution based on its implicit function (production of social solidarity through exchange) is more plausible than one which claims the norm was "invented" at some early time and then spread. Both functional relationships and historical diffusion play an important role in culture history. Some social anthropologists who look only for functional explanations may neglect much more obvious historical ones.[18]

It is not always easy to determine whether a given norm (social rule) is universal, for numerous violations and difficulties of enforcement may obscure the fact that the norm is still highly valued. One such case is the so-called *norm of legitimacy.* According to William J. Goode, this is a universal norm which still remains a desired standard however frequently it is violated in a given society. Goode is fully aware that the rate of illegitimate births in some societies is greater than 50 percent; nevertheless, he believes that these high rates are the consequence of social and cultural *disorganization* which makes it difficult for all but the most prestigious social groups to enforce conformity to the norm.[19] His explanation for the universality of this norm is a functional one; he believes that all social structures operate best if every individual has two socially recognized parents (a pater and a mater) so that the individual can be placed in his correct social position (descent group, class, or category). Goode also points out that every society has some form of marriage, and even in societies with very high illegitimacy rates, it remains the *goal* of most women to marry

18. P. K. Bock, "Love Magic, Menstrual Taboos, and the Facts of Geography," *American Anthropologist*, Vol. 69 (1967), pp. 213–217.
19. W. J. Goode, "Illegitimacy, Anomie and Cultural Penetration," *American Sociological Review*, Vol. 25 (December 1961), pp. 910–925. See also P. K. Bock, "Patterns of Illegitimacy on a Canadian Indian Reserve: 1860–1960," *Journal of Marriage and the Family*, Vol. 26 (1964), pp. 142–148.

sooner or later. Many couples who have lived for years in consensual unions ultimately *do* marry. Like the norm of reciprocity, the norm of legitimacy performs an important social function, and the general disapproval which follows its violation is a measure of its strength.

A final type of universal which has interested some anthropologists may be called a *value universal.* Although cultural anthropology teaches us not to evaluate other societies by an ethnocentric standard, it does not preclude the possibility that at least some values are found in every culture. Indeed, the norm of legitimacy (which places a negative value on birth out of wedlock) and the norm of reciprocity (which positively values repayment of obligations) may be instances of value universals.

One other possible kind of value universal is suggested by the work of Lévi-Strauss (p. 345). It may be that in every culture, there are certain *oppositions* which must be maintained, and although cultures may phrase them in different ways, some kinds of boundaries are essential to individual and social continuity. For example, every culture makes a distinction between the living and the dead, and devotes a good deal of ritual energy to maintaining this boundary. The line between life and death may be drawn in very different places according to social conventions (for example, the dispute in modern medicine as to whether "brain death" or "circulatory death" is the proper criterion of the life/death distinction). But *some* such convention is essential to human social life. Similarly, every culture seems to make and defend oppositions between sacred/profane and between nature/culture. It may well be that the most profound differences among cultures have to do with the ways in which they draw these universal distinctions, while the most profound similarities flow from the common "human nature" which makes us draw them.[20]

RESPONSIBILITIES OF THE ANTHROPOLOGIST

In these chapters we have been concerned with method. But as a wise man once said, an excessive concern with technique, whether in science, art, or love, frequently leads to impotence. Let us then discuss some of the purposes of anthropology, begin-

20. C. Geertz, "The Impact of the Concept of Culture on the Concept of Man," in E. Hammel and W. Simmons, eds., *Man Makes Sense* (Boston: Little, Brown, 1970), pp. 46–65. Also, A. F. C. Wallace, "The Psychic Unity of Human Groups," in B. Kaplan, ed., *Studying Personality Cross-Culturally* (New York: Harper and Row, 1961), pp. 129–163. These two synthetic essays do not take the position stated in the last paragraph, but they are concerned with the nature of man in relation to cultural universals and differences at the most general level.

ning with the responsibilities of the anthropologist. In the Epilogue we will consider some more philosophical issues.

To begin with, the anthropologist has certain responsibilities to his profession. As a social scientist, he is committed to use his critical intelligence, to choose genuine social issues for investigation, and to carry through his research with energy and imagination. In the last analysis, the scientific method means to "do your damndest" while being ready to admit mistakes. The anthropologist also has a responsibility to work for an *integrated* science of man. This is becoming increasingly difficult due to specialization and fragmentation within the discipline. For example, within just a few days I noted (in print) the following designations for "kinds of anthropology":

Structural Anthropology	Psychedelic Anthropology
Psychological Anthropology	Humanistic Anthropology
Applied Anthropology	Educational Anthropology
Economic Anthropology	Political Anthropology
Ecological Anthropology	Urban Anthropology
Behavioral Anthropology	Development Anthropology
Linguistic Anthropology	Radical Anthropology
Cognitive Anthropology	Visual Anthropology
Medical Anthropology	

and these are in addition to the conventional subfields of physical, cultural, and social anthropology! Such specialization is perhaps inevitable, if only because the number of professional anthropologists has doubled in the last ten years; but it also means that our understanding of man and culture will become fragmented if we do not actively strive for an integrated view.

Anthropologists also have certain *ethical* responsibilities to their profession. One good rule for the ethnographer is "Don't mess up so bad that nobody can ever work there again." There are a number of communities (and even countries) where American anthropologists are not welcome because of the alleged misbehavior of their colleagues. Certainly, the anthropologist should avoid becoming involved in dishonest or undercover kinds of research, the results of which cannot be freely disclosed and published. But equally important are the responsibilities of the anthropologist to the people he studies.

Anthropology may well be the study of man, but what if "man" doesn't want to be studied, or doesn't realize the possible consequences for his life of having anthropologists poking around in his society? Times have changed. Natives and third-world peoples have a new sense of their cultural identity, and for many, the anthropologist has become a symbol of imperialism. People are no longer uncertain about his social role—as far as they are concerned, he is simply a "tool of neocolonialism." At the very least, they are asking: Why should we let you study us? What will be the benefits to our community? And they have forced many anthropologists to rethink their notions of responsibility and obligation. We have always hoped that our work would not harm the people we studied; but we must now ask ourselves—given that our own careers are advanced by doing research—whether we should not ensure some positive benefits (intellectual and/or economic) to the subjects of our inquiry. For example, several ethnographers have arranged for any royalties from the publication of their field research to be paid into a medical or scholarship fund for people of the community.

The situation becomes much more complex when the anthropologist, on the basis of his analysis, deliberately attempts to produce changes in the community he has studied. Even when the changes are in line with what "the people" want, there is a great deal of uncertainty about long-range consequences, about the degree of intracommunity consensus, and about the reaction of institutions in the larger society. And when he is undertaking applied anthropology on behalf of some external agency (business corporation, government bureau, or foreign aid group) the anthropologist must carefully consider the uses that might be made of his findings and policy recommendations.[21]

Finally, the anthropologist also has responsibilities to the public which supports his research and teaching efforts, and to the students who sit in his classes. Quite aside from the application of anthropological knowledge and techniques to practical social problems, I believe that the anthropologist has an obligation to make available to the public ("popularize," if you like) the valid findings of his science, and to actively combat the myths and fallacies that threaten our civilization. These include the myth of racial superiority, the ethnocentric assumptions of all peoples, and sensational distortions such as "man, the killer ape." We must also beware of *anthropocentrism:* the assumption that man is the most important species and that "whatever is good for mankind is good for the planet." There are many historical examples of cultures which became extinct because they ignored the relation of human society to the larger environmental system. It will be ironic if our principal "advance" over the ancient civilizations turns out to be our ability to pollute and degrade the environment with greater speed and efficiency.

---

21. See the section on "The Social Responsibility of the Anthropologist," in T. Weaver *et al.*, eds., *To See Ourselves* (Glenview, Ill., Scott, Foresman, 1973), pp. 5–61.

RECOMMENDED READING

Greenberg, J., ed., *Universals of Language.* (Second edition). Cambridge: M.I.T. Press, 1966. Scholarly papers on the important topic of linguistic universals in phonology, grammar, and semantics.

Kaplan, D. and R. Manners, *Culture Theory.* Englewood Cliffs, N.J.: Prentice-Hall, 1972. A good, brief overview of the history of anthropological theory and of its contemporary disarray.

Murdock, G. P., *Social Structure.* New York: Macmillan, 1949. Still the classic example of applying cross-cultural (correlational) methods to the study of comparative social structures.

Oswalt, W. H., *Other Peoples, Other Customs.* New York: Holt, Rinehart and Winston, 1972. A history of ethnography, from early explorers to modern professionals, together with a readable summary of world ethnography.

Weaver, T. *et al., To See Ourselves.* Glenview, Ill.: Scott, Foresman, 1973. An extensive collection of readings on anthropology and modern social issues, from studies of poverty and racism to the social responsibilities of the anthropologist.

Burt Glinn/Magnum

Epilogue

The Proper Study of Mankind

The author of an introduction to a discipline is constrained by various social conventions from intruding too much of his individual personality into his writing. He is supposed to present a reasonably objective and comprehensive survey of his field, including certain facts, theories, names, and dates which his peer group expects to find there. (An overview of anthropology without, say, Malinowski is like a pizza without cheese.) This has become a much more personal book than the usual text; even so, I have repeatedly found myself playing the role of "anthropologist" and hiding behind the pronoun "we." In the few remaining pages, I want to come out from behind this protective shield and discuss, in my own voice, a few general issues that have recurred throughout the text. First, however, let me summarize the major points that I have tried to make in this book.

SUMMARY AND CONCLUSIONS

Man is a product of biological evolution. Examine your body and you will find hundreds of features which attest to our close relationship with the higher primates. Even the gross features of our behavior show many affinities to the apes. (This is one reason we stand fascinated before the zoo cage of the chimpanzee.) Biological evolution has not ceased. In man, however, it has been supplemented with cultural development. A complex relationship between biological and cultural factors has come into being.

The possession of culture gives man a flexibility not available to any other creature, for learned categories and plans can be rapidly altered. They are not built into the nervous system. They are acquired during the process of enculturation, and despite the persistence of habits acquired early in life, they can be modified at any time. Hunters can become farmers, and farmers are swept into industry without any prior *genetic* changes, though such great changes in ways of living will ultimately have genetic consequences.

In this book, language has provided a *model* of what cultural systems are like. I have tried to show that each language system consists of a limited number of categories of sounds and of meaningful elements associated with general plans for speaking. The speakers of a language are capable of using their shared expectations to communicate an infinite number of different messages. Languages operate by imposing conventional and largely unconscious *constraints* on what can be said. By accepting these constraints, however, men gain the ability to communicate with one another—and with themselves. As Dorothy Lee once put it:

> A language is full of regulations and interdictions; yet it is freeing. Through learning the rules, I am enabled to communicate with others, I am free to express myself and often to achieve ends which I could not otherwise reach. I am not hampered by the rigid taboo against using a singular verb for a plural subject; I am not outraged when I am commanded to add *ed* to *wash* when I refer to yesterday. And I do not feel that all my originality is submerged through the need to conform to regulations.[1]

Language, conceived as an abstract system of categories and plans, was contrasted with *speech:* the concrete, observable behavior in which the language system is manifested and from which the system is inferred. This same general viewpoint was then applied to social and technological systems, each of which was described as a system inferred from concrete human behavior.

Social structure is composed of roles, groups, and institutions, each with its own plans for action which often include distinctive ways of dealing with time and space. An integrated social structure makes possible smooth interaction among individuals; without these shared categories and plans, people do not know what to expect of one another. Like linguistic rules, however, social rules can be violated; they influence behavior but do not determine it.

Under the heading of "Social Organization" I discussed the various ways in which social expectations (rules) are translated into action. The social structure is manifested in behavior by indi-

1. D. Lee, *Freedom and Culture* (Englewood Cliffs, N.J.: Spectrum Books, 1959), pp. 2–3.

viduals who anticipate events, evaluate alternatives, and make decisions. They do this under the guidance of general norms such as reciprocity. At the same time, however, individual psychological factors and environmental influences come into play. Although the actions of enculturated humans generally conform to the structural alternatives open to them, we all have some capacity for choice, novelty, invention, and discovery. Cultural *change* is viewed as the inevitable result of these processes of social organization and adaptation.

Cultures are always changing, for reasons which range from defective enculturation to major environmental challenges. Every culture enables those who live it to adapt to their environment, to one another, and to themselves. But in attempting to solve one set of adaptive problems, tensions are created in other areas of the society. Conflicts inevitably arise and are resolved, only to give rise in turn to new conflicts among individuals or groups. The plans for action developed by one generation never exactly fit the needs of the next. Eventually, new patterns of choice emerge which constitute changes in the very structure of the society.

The same general kind of analysis was then applied to technological systems. Tools are viewed as manifestations of abstract categories, while techniques are the plans for their manufacture and use. Tools have adaptive functions: they help satisfy human needs and increase the adaptation of a society to its environment. Techniques of harnessing energy, getting food, curing illness, and making objects were discussed, together with the skills that enable men to employ these techniques effectively.

In Part Five (Ideological Systems), I attempted to give some idea of the tremendous variety of beliefs and values held by different peoples, without losing sight of their common source in human needs and experience. Every culture has its cosmology which places man in a structured universe with a known history. Every culture has certain conventional concepts of authority and property which define who, if anyone, has legitimate control over other persons, objects, and situations. Also, since men constantly evaluate their experiences, every culture provides some standards of judgment—moral and esthetic values. The anthropologist may discover, compare, and try to explain these values, but they can be fully understood only in relation to the integrating patterns (ethos and eidos) of the total ideological system of which they are a part.

Finally, in Part Six (The Anthropologist at Work), I tried to give some idea of the methods used by anthropologists to transform their observations of behavior into valid descriptive statements (texts). I maintained that this differs from the way in which a child learns his own culture only in being somewhat more explicit and systematic. The process of *inference* from ethnographic texts to historical, functional, and universal statements was also discussed.

Throughout the book I have stressed the conventional basis of cultural phenomena. The criteria that we use in categorizing colors, sounds, kinsmen, or diseases, the ways in which we structure time and space, and the standards we use in evaluating goodness or beauty are all creations of our predecessors. They *could have been different.* In some other society they may be either ignored or reversed.

Yet beneath the multiplicity of phonological and kinship systems, we know that there lie a few *basic oppositions,* rooted in the givens of human biology, thought, and society: vowel/consonant, male/female, older/younger, individual/group, sacred/profane, and so forth. Anthropologists have shown the ways in which cultures have erected superstructures of great complexity on these foundations. Perhaps it is not too much to hope that other cultural subsystems will someday yield to a similar kind of analysis.

CULTURE AND FREEDOM

A major concern of this book has been the great *paradox of culture*—the fact that culture frees men by binding them. As with language, the benefits of other cultural systems come only as men accept their constraints. The very process of enculturation, which makes possible communication and interaction among the members of a society, excludes them from participation in other traditions. The child who learns a particular set of linguistc, social, and ideological conventions will probably never feel entirely comfortable with a different set. All too often, he grows into an intolerant adult who is afraid to let loose, even for a moment, of the categories and plans he learned as a child. He is thus disqualified from having a genuinely new experience of the world.[2]

Culture is without doubt a wonderful creation. Words and social roles were necessary inventions. We need categories in order to deal with the complexity of the real world. The inability to form general concepts (to "see the forest for the trees") is a serious block to understanding. But when we substitute the role for the whole person, or when we mistake the word for the thing, there is a danger of losing contact with our direct experiences. Categories are essential to communication. But most categories

2. E. H. Erikson, *Childhood and Society* (second edition; New York: Norton, 1963), p. 404. See also the important writings of Carlos Castaneda such as *The Teachings of Don Juan* (New York: Ballantine Books, 1968), and the collected essays of Gregory Bateson, *Steps to an Ecology of Mind* (New York: Ballantine Books, 1972).

either lump together experiences that share a few attributes while being uniquely different in other respects, or give separate labels to events that are actually different aspects of the same underlying process. For example, the tendency to label all non-Western peoples as "savages" (or all nonconformist youths as "hippies") indicates both prejudice and a striking lack of imagination.

Ernest Schachtel has suggested that most of us cannot remember the first years of childhood because the culture categories (schemata) into which we have learned to force our memories are too narrow to accommodate the richness of those early, direct experiences. In his essay "On Memory and Childhood Amnesia," he says that "the world of modern Western Civilization has no use for . . . experiences of the quality and intensity typical of early childhood." Yet Schachtel believes that "memory cannot be entirely extinguished in man, his capacity for experience cannot be entirely suppressed by schematization. It is in those experiences which transcend the cultural schemata [and] those memories . . . which transcend the conventional memory schemata, that every new insight and every true work of art have their origin."[3]

I agree that genuine creativity and spontaneity depend on being able to break through the labels, stereotypes, and conventions of an arbitrary tradition. Does this mean that cultural categories are merely artificial annoyances to be brushed aside whenever possible and by whatever means (including the use of drugs) are available? No, I think not. And for two reasons.

First of all, breaking through the conventions does not guarantee truth, happiness, or creativity. Without discipline, the results may be just childish, sloppy, or bizarre. The great artist or scientist does go beyond the conventional wisdom of his day. But his insights are based in part upon an understanding of the achievements as well as the deficiencies of his predecessors. He develops his new contributions by contrasting or integrating his ideas with what he has received from the past. Paradoxically, this often restructures traditions and thus revitalizes them, so that they can continue to be of use to the men of each successive "modern" period. Furthermore, the innovator's creations must somehow be communicated to his contemporaries: otherwise they would remain hazy elements of his private world and be doomed to die with him.

This problem of communicating new insights brings us to the second point. In the absence of shared expectations and understandings, people become inarticulate: communication and meaningful interaction quickly break down. This is why revolutionary

3. E. Schachtel, "On Memory and Childhood Amnesia," in his *Metamorphosis* (New York: Basic Books, 1959). See also N. O. Brown, *Love's Body* (New York: Random House, 1966).

and utopian movements, be they political, religious, or artistic, must develop an "in-group" jargon and culture or perish. The sense of loving cooperation and empathy which often occurs during or after a great crisis (what Victor Turner has called "communitas") cannot last indefinitely. Yet if its benefits are to continue, they must be consolidated into institutional forms which seem—to some participants—the exact opposite of the open, equalitarian experience that they valued. This leads some to despise Establishment culture and even to despair of ever communicating through ordinary language. But this, in turn, can lead to a vicious circle of withdrawal, suspicion, failure of communication, hostility, further withdrawal, and so on. The dialectic between person and institution is an unavoidable part of the human condition.[4]

For thousands of generations men have used cultural means to solve their adaptive problems. The reliance on tools and rules in addition to genes has enabled *Homo sapiens* to become the dominant species on our planet. But since one cannot learn "culture" in the abstract, every human being must rely on the traditions of the group in which he is enculturated. This reliance entails many positive benefits for the individual, especially for the powerful and privileged; but even the most exploited castes owe their survival to the society that exploits them. They participate in its traditions even in rebelling against them. In Michael Polanyi's eloquent phrase, "Our believing is conditioned at its source by our belonging."[5]

Does this mean that we are stuck with whatever culture we happen to be born into? Again, I think not. There is a certain nobility in loyalty to a tradition, provided that one tries to develop the best in it. But on the other hand, the more we know and understand ourselves, our own traditions, and those of others, the more free we become—even though we may at first shrink back from the anxiety and responsibility that accompanies such consciousness of freedom. Since cultures are integrated systems, we cannot borrow bits and snatches from here and there and expect them automatically to add up to a meaningful way of life. But the wider our knowledge of other cultures, and the deeper our understanding of cultural processes, the more likely we are to find something beautiful, meaningful, and useful. Human freedom includes the freedom to believe.

I suggest that we should start with our own traditions, developing and adding to them in a spirit of *play,* trying not to take ourselves too seriously, recognizing that the rules are conven-

---

4. V. Turner, *The Ritual Process* (Chicago: Aldine Publishing Company, 1969). Also, J. P. Sisk, *Person and Institution* (Notre Dame: Fides Publishers, 1970); R. Murphy, *The Dialectics of Social Life* (New York: Basic Books, 1971).
5. M. Polanyi, *Personal Knowledge* (New York: Harper Torchbooks, 1964), p. 322.

tional, but striving to create something good and beautiful out of the materials at our disposal. People who speak several languages generally agree that the second and third are the hardest; thereafter, learning a new language becomes easier each time. Speaking many languages does not guarantee scientific insights into linguistic processes; but I believe that it does give the individual greater freedom by making available to him different modes of thought, understanding, and expression. This development of flexibility and potential for creativity also comes from knowing a variety of cultures. (This is the reason I believe anthropology should be part of every liberal arts curriculum.) To quote Dorothy Lee again: "When I study other cultures . . . I am enabled to see my culture as one of many possible systems of relating the self to the universe, and to question tenets and axioms of which I had never been aware."[6]

Ethnocentrism, suspicion of the unfamiliar, and hostility toward outsiders are understandable (and even occasionally useful) in a small, isolated society, struggling for survival. But in a vast civilization built with the ideas and labor of men from every corner of the earth, such attitudes are no longer adaptive. Modern technology can bring the sights, sounds, and thoughts of distant traditions within easy reach in books or on films and records. The truly "cultured" person is free to enjoy these experiences because he *does not feel threatened* by them. He knows his own tradition and recognizes both its values and its limitations. His contacts with alien peoples and places are pursued as much for the esthetic satisfactions they bring as for any practical purpose. As Robert Redfield once observed:

> In coming to understand an alien way of life, as in coming to understand an alien art, the course of personal experience is essentially the same: one looks first at an incomprehensible other; one comes to see that other as one's self in another guise. This widening of our comprehension of the human has been going on, I suppose, since the day thousands of years ago, when some primitive hunter relaxed his suspicion of or hostility to the people over the hill long enough to think to himself, "Well, I guess those fellows have something there after all." It goes on today, in spite of all the hatreds and conflicts between peoples. Slowly, for one or another of us, the vision and comprehension of humanity, both in its extraordinary variety of expressions and its fundamental sameness, is widened.[7]

The "widening of our comprehension of the human" should, I believe, be a continuing goal for anthropology as it pursues the proper study of mankind—man.

---

6. D. Lee, *op. cit.*, p. 2.
7. R. Redfield, *Aspects of Primitive Art* (New York: Museum of Primitive Art, 1959), p. 39.

Glossary

Italicized terms are defined elsewhere in the glossary.

acculturation Culture change as a result of continuous, firsthand contact between societies.

adaptation, cultural Learned *plans* for coping with environmental demands, whether from the physical/biological environment or the external social system.

affinity a *criterion* which separates *ego's* blood relatives (consanguines) from in-laws (affines).

age-area principle In *ethnology,* the assumption that—other things being equal—cultural elements that are widespread are older than those with a more restricted distribution.

age-grading Any division of a social group or *institution* into categories based primarily upon age.

age-set A social group with *recruitment* based upon the similar age of its members; an age-set may move as a unit through a series of age-grades.

agriculture Any system of cultivation making use of the plow, usually in connection with an animal or mechanical source of energy.

American Anthropologist The journal of the American Anthropological Association, published since 1898; soon to be devoted exclusively to general articles and book reviews with a sister journal, the *American Ethnologist,* to contain more specialized articles on ethnology and social anthropology.

anthropocentrism The attitude that *Homo sapiens* is the most or the only important species on this planet. See *ethnocentrism.*

anthropology The study of *man* and his works. It includes physical anthropology, which deals with man as a biological species—his anatomy, physiology, and development—and cultural anthropology, which is concerned with the behavior of men as members of organized societies.

anticipation A principle of *social organization* which calls for the preparation of personnel, resources, and setting prior to the initiation of recurrent social *situations.*

apes The gorilla, chimpanzee, orangutan, and gibbon, plus extinct members of the biological family *Pongidae,* but not including monkeys.

approach, cross-cultural In ethnology, *techniques* for *inferring* culture history by comparisons of several related cultures. In social anthropology, techniques for making functional/causal inferences by comparisons of historically unrelated societies.

approach, ecological In ethnology, examination of the relationship of cultural systems (or subsystems) to the larger environmental systems in which they operate and to which they must adapt.

approach, structural-functional Techniques for inferring the social functions of *relationships* and *institutions* within a society by careful examination of their structure.

archaeology, prehistoric That subfield of cultural anthropology that deals with inferences about extinct societies.

artifact Any portion of the material environment that has been deliberately modified for use by man.

association A social group with voluntary recruitment based on some common interest of its members.

Australopithecinae A subfamily within the family *Hominidae*; contains extinct "man-apes" which lived in the Old World between 1 and 5 million years ago.

authority As part of a leadership role, legitimate command over the actions of others (followers).

avunculocal A *rule of residence* which assigns a couple to the household or community of the groom's mother's brother.

Benedict, Ruth F. (1887–1948) A student of *Boas*, her innovative studies emphasized the unique configurations of each culture and the relation of culture to personality. Major works include *Patterns of Culture, The Chrysanthemum and the Sword,* and *An Anthropologist at Work* (ed., M. Mead).

bifurcation A *criterion* which separates ego's relatives on "mother's side" from those on "father's side," that is, according to the sex of the linking relative.

bilateral A rule of *kinship group* formation which permits membership on the basis of genealogical ties through males and/or females.

Boas, Franz (1858–1942) German-born and trained in the natural sciences, he became the father of American academic anthropology. At Columbia University he trained a generation of major scholars. His works include *Race, Language, and Culture* (collected papers) and *The Mind of Primitive Man.*

career, social A sequence of social *roles* through which some set of individuals is expected to pass.

castes *Endogamous* social groups based on descent and ranked in a rigid *hierarchy,* each caste usually having specific ritual and/or technical functions.

categories, cultural Learned classes of persons, objects, or events, conventionally associated with learned *plans* for action or interaction.

clans *Descent groups* composed of several *lineages*; although clan membership does not require that actual genealogical links be known, there is usually an ideology of descent from a common founder. When the founder is given an animal name, we speak of a totemic clan.

class, social A division of a *societal group* into ranked subgroups with recruitment based on a variety of criteria and with movement of individuals among groups at least theoretically possible.

collaterality A *criterion* which separates ego's lineal relatives (direct ancestors and descendants) from collaterals (all others).

conformity Compliance with the expectations embodied in a given *social structure*; includes choice among legitimate alternatives.

cosmology The part of an *ideology* that is concerned with the nature and origin of the universe and with man's position in it.

criterion, kinship A binary *opposition* used to divide a set of relatives into two subsets. See *affinity, collaterality, bifurcation, decedence.*

cross-cousins Children of ego's mother's brother (matrilateral) or father's sister (patrilateral).

culture Learned *categories* of experience conventionally associated with learned *plans* for action. Refers both to specific cultures of societal groups and to the culture of mankind taken as a whole.

culture, paradox of The inescapable fact that acceptance of any cultural system frees the individual at the same time that it constrains his behavior.

Current Anthropology An international journal containing special review articles with commentary, announcements, and extensive correspondence. Published since 1960 by the University of Chicago and sponsored by the Wenner-Gren Foundation.

decedence A *criterion* which separates those kinsmen who are linked to *ego* by living relatives from those whose links are deceased.

descent groups Kinship groups to which ego is assigned by an automatic recruitment rule. See *patrilineal, matrilineal, double descent.*

diachronic study An examination of cultural systems at two or more points in time, emphasizing history and change. See *synchronic study.*

double descent A kinship system in which

ego belongs to both his father's *patrilineal* group and his mother's *matrilineal* group.

dual organization A division of a societal group into two halves (Fr., moieties), usually with reciprocal social functions and with recruitment based upon descent.

ego The individual, sex unspecified, who is taken as a point of reference in a *genealogy* or kinship chart.

eidos Integrating principles of belief which give consistency to an *ideology.*

enculturation The process of learning one's culture; often synonymous with socialization, though the latter term sometimes refers to deliberate techniques of child-training.

endogamy A *marriage rule* specifying that ego should select a mate from within a given category of persons. See *exogamy.*

esthetics, anthropological Studies judgments of beauty in different societies.

ethnocentrism The attitude that one's own culture is the highest and constitutes a standard for judging all other cultures. See *relativism, cultural.*

ethnography The subfield of cultural anthropology which formulates descriptions of social, technological, and ideological systems.

ethnohistory The subfield of anthropology which uses materials from ethnography and archaeology in conjunction with documentary evidence for the reconstruction of culture history.

ethnology The subfield of cultural anthropology which compares materials provided by *ethnography,* usually to draw historical inferences. See *social anthropology.*

Ethnology Published since 1962 by the University of Pittsburgh, this journal emphasizes studies in Africa and the Pacific as well as cross-cultural studies employing the *Human Relations Area Files.*

ethnosemantics The study of systems of meaning as embodied in other languages with special attention to *folk taxonomies* and *binary oppositions.*

ethos Integrating patterns of value which give coherence to an *ideology.*

evaluation The general process of judging persons, objects, or events relative to some culture standard (for example, of beauty, grammaticality, or morality); may involve classification and/or ranking.

evolution, biological The well-supported theory that by known genetic mechanisms, higher and more recent forms of life have developed, as a result of adaptive change, out of lower and more ancient forms.

evolution, cultural The plausible theory that complex forms of culture and society have developed, as a consequence of adaptive change, out of simpler forms, although the mechanisms are not clearly understood.

evolution, moral The unlikely notion that man's moral behavior (or at least his standards of judgment) have improved in some absolute sense over the million or so years of his existence.

exogamy A *marriage rule* specifying that ego should select a mate from outside of a given category. See *endogamy.*

function, adaptive The way(s) in which a given *tool* helps to satisfy human needs.

function, social The way(s) in which any cultural element contributes to the survival of the society and/or continuity of the culture in which it is found.

genealogy A record of the (alleged) relations of descent, co-descent, and marriage among a set of persons.

glottochronology A technique for determining the dates of separation of related languages descended from some *protolanguage.*

grammar The rules which influence the verbal behavior of speakers of some language; also, a linguist's attempt to formulate these rules, excluding the *phonology.* See *morphology, syntax.*

group, corporate A clearly bounded social group whose members share in some "estate," material or nonmaterial.

group, kinship Any social group to which members are recruited by virtue of kinship connections. See *descent groups.*

group, residential A category of persons who customarily live in the same area of *social space* and who share some *plans* for interaction. Typical residential groups found in most societies are the household (domestic group) and the local community (whether mobile or sedentary).

group, societal The group composed of all the members of a given society.

Herskovits, Melville J. (1895–1963) Best known for his studies of Negro culture in the Old and New World, he founded the first major U. S. program in African Studies at Northwestern University. A student and biographer of *Boas,* he was among the first to appreciate the value of economic theory to anthropology. Works include *Economic Anthropology, Cultural Dynamics, Dahomean Narrative* (with F. Herskovits), and *The Myth of the Negro Past.*

hierarchy Any arrangement of parts from high to low, whether in terms of power, wealth, or prestige.

Hominidae The biological family of *man,* including *Homo sapiens, Homo erectus,* and the *Australopithecinae*; all members of this family except for the modern variety of *Homo sapiens* are now extinct.

Homo erectus The species most closely related to and ancestral to *Homo sapiens;* includes Java man, Peking man, and other extinct varieties which flourished about a half-million years ago.

Homo sapiens The biological label for the human species, including both *Neanderthal* and modern varieties, which have flourished for the last 100,000 years.

horticulture Any system of food cultivation that does not employ the plow, though it may use "intensive" techniques such as fencing, irrigation, or fertilization.

Human Organization The journal of the Society for Applied Anthropology, published since 1941; contains articles and commentary on the application of anthropological theory and methods to social problems.

Human Relations Area Files An extensive, cross-indexed catalog of ethnographic information on more than 600 different societies, used as a research tool in cross-cultural studies.

ideology Cultural subsystem consisting of beliefs and values shared by the members of a social or societal group.

inference In anthropology, reasoning from regularities in the form and distribution of human behavior (and products of behavior) to the cultural elements that *influence* that behavior to produce the perceived regularities.

influence The relationship between cultural *categories* and *plans* and the behavior of persons who share these learned elements.

innovation Any behavior that violates the rules or general expectations associated with a social *situation,* from a slightly novel choice to a completely original action. See *invention.*

institutions, social Relatively self-contained subgroups within which several different social *careers* are organized into a system.

institutions, total Institutions in which at least some persons spend all of their time, such as boarding schools or mental hospitals.

integration, group A quality of solidarity or cohesiveness within or between social groups, generally produced by the exchange of equivalent values among members. See *reciprocity, norm of.*

invention Any social, linguistic, or technological *innovation* which violates cultural rules by the omission, rearrangement, substitution, or combination of expected elements.

Journal of Anthropological Research See *Southwestern Journal of Anthropology.*

Journal of the Royal Anthropological Institute See *Man.*

kindred A *bilateral kinship group,* often vaguely bounded, and with optional *recruitment.* Each individual may be the focus of his own personal kindred, or the stem kindred may revolve around a particularly important individual.

Kluckhohn, Clyde K. M. (1905–1960) A background in the classics gave Kluckhohn (whose wife and son are also anthropologists) a unique perspective on many anthropological problems. He is best known for his intensive studies of the Navajo, and he was an innovator in studies of values, personality, and religion. Works include *Navaho Witchcraft, Mirror for Man,* and *Culture and Behavior* (ed., R. Kluckhohn).

Kroeber, Alfred L. (1876–1960) A student of *Boas,* Kroeber (who had been trained in the humanities) had a lifelong fascination with style in culture and with processes of cultural growth and change. His contributions to all fields of cultural anthropology are enormous. Major works include *Anthropology* (1948), *Style and Civilization,* and *The Nature of Culture* (collected papers).

language a subsystem of *culture* consisting of *categories* of sound associated with *plans* for speaking. See *speech.*

legal system Cultural *categories* and *plans* relating to the settlement of disputes within and among *societal groups.*

lineages *Exogamous descent groups,* often localized, with automatic *recruitment* based on known or fictional genealogical relationships.

linguistics, anthropological A subfield of cultural anthropology which is concerned with the *language* systems and *speech* behavior of all human groups.

Lowie, Robert H. (1883–1957) Another student of *Boas,* he brought careful scholarship and sensitivity to his field studies of the Crow Indians and his comparative studies in the Plains and elsewhere. The Lowie Museum of Anthropology is in Berkeley, California, where he and *Kroeber* taught for many years. Major works include *Primitive Society* (a response to *L. H. Morgan*), *The Crow Indians,* an autobiography, and collected papers (ed., C. du Bois).

Malinowski, Bronislaw (1884–1942) Polish-born and trained in the natural sciences, he became a founder of *social anthropology* and of a variety of functionalism that emphasized the relationship between *institutions* and human needs. Known for his intensive field work in, and publications on, the Trobriand Islands. Major works include: *Argonauts of the Western Pacific, The Coral Gardens and Their Magic,* and *Magic, Science and Religion.*

man "The maker of tools, rules, and moral judgments." *Homo sapiens,* though sometimes used more generally to refer to all of the *Hominidae.* See *anthropocentrism.*

Man Formerly the *Journal of the Royal Anthropological Institute,* this publication includes articles on cultural and social anthropology, and brief but excellent book reviews.

marriage, rule of A *recruitment rule* stating the preferred or permitted *categories* from which a given *ego* may select a mate. See *endogamy, exogamy.*

matrilineal A rule of *descent* which assigns *ego* to the *kinship group* of his or her mother.

matrilocal A rule of *residence* which assigns a couple to the household or community of the bride's parents

method, comparative In linguistics, techniques for reconstructing the parental form or *protolanguage* of two or more related languages. In ethnology, see *approach, cross-cultural.*

morality, absolute Judgment of the rightness of actions according to an unvarying (cultural) standard.

morality, situational Judgment of the rightness of actions according to standards which take account of particular circumstances.

Morgan, Lewis Henry (1818–1881) Pioneering American anthropologist, lawyer, and believer in cultural *evolution,* he founded the comparative study of kinship systems and was a student of the Iroquois. Works include *Ancient Society* and the *Journals* (ed. L. White).

morpheme An ordered set of *phonemes* associated, in a given language, with a minimum unit of meaning; includes roots and affixes.

morphology In linguistics, the study of how *morphemes* are combined into larger meaningful units ("words") and the modifications that they undergo in the process.

Nacirema A societal group in North America having unusually backward customs (and spelling!).

Neanderthal man A variety of *Homo sapiens* that flourished between 50,000 and 100,000 years ago, at the end of the Ice Age.

neolocal A rule of *residence* which assigns a couple to a separate household of their own.

nuclear family A *kinship group* composed of a married couple together with their unmarried offspring; may or may not correspond to a residential group (household).

observation, participant In *ethnography,* the technique of learning and collecting data while taking part in the daily life of the society.

opposition, binary A two-way contrast between categories of persons, objects, or events; for example, vowel/consonant, sacred/profane, raw/cooked, affine/consanguine.

organization, social Processes involving individual *anticipation, conformity, adaptation,* and *innovation,* in response to the requirements of a given *social structure.* See *reciprocity, norm of.*

parallel cousins Children of ego's mother's sister (matrilateral) or father's brother (patrilateral). See *cross-cousins.*

pastoralism A system of food production

based on herding and (usually) husbandry of domesticated animals.

patrilineal A rule of *descent* which automatically assigns *ego* to the *kinship group* of his or her father.

patrilocal A rule of *residence* which assigns a couple to the household or community of the groom's parents.

phonemes Meaningless but significant *categories* of vocal sound which signal differences of meaning in a given *language.* Selections and combinations of these units of sound make up *morphemes.*

phonology The study of the sound system of language, that is, *phonemes*—their distinctive features, variant forms, and distributions.

phratry An association among several clans, often sharing a common *marriage rule* or other social *function.*

placebo effect An apparent cure of illness brought about by the confident administration of a chemically inert medication, as, for example, sugar pills or a salt-water injection.

plans, cultural A set of learned, hierarchically organized expectations, which *influence* sequences of behavior in some social group; conventionally associated with one or more cultural *categories.*

polygamy Any *marriage rule* permitting *ego* to have more than one spouse at the same time. More particularly, "polyandry," which allows a female ego to have plural husbands, and "polygyny," which allows a male ego to have plural wives.

Pongidae A family within the order *Primates,* consisting of the living and extinct *apes.* See *Hominidae.*

Primates An order of mammals which includes *man* (living and fossil forms), the *apes,* the monkeys, and several other species, living and extinct.

productivity In linguistics, refers to the fact that speakers of a language can produce (generate) an infinite number of grammatical utterances; in ethnography, refers to a similar capacity on the part of group members—their ability to behave in novel but socially appropriate ways.

protolanguage The reconstructed "parental" language of a group of related "daughter" languages; see *method, comparative.*

Radcliffe-Brown, Alfred R. (1881–1955) With *Malinowski,* a founder of *social anthropology,* "R-B" was a master of comparative studies of *social structure* (in Australia and Africa). His functionalism is still basic to British social anthropology. Major works include *The Andaman Islanders, Structure and Function in Primitive Society.*

reciprocity, norm of A possibly *universal* principle of *social organization* which demands that individuals should help, and not hurt, those others who have benefited them; a general plan for interaction which can take over in the absence of (or in addition to) more specific expectations.

recruitment, rule of A device for assigning classes of individuals to social *roles* and *careers* according to factors of birth (ascription) and/or other criteria (achievement). See *criterion, kinship; rules.*

Redfield, Robert (1897–1958) Trained in the law and familiar with sociological theory, Redfield pioneered in the study of peasant societies and the civilizations of which they formed a part. His works include *The Little Community, Folk Culture of Yucatan,* and two volumes of collected papers (ed., M. P. Redfield).

reduplication In linguistics, a *plan* for producing words with modified or different meanings by repeating syllables; for example, "mama," "go-go," "aku-aku."

reinterpretation The assignment of new "meanings" to borrowed cultural elements.

relationship, social Any pair of social *roles* for which there exist cultural *plans* for interaction; for example, father/son, doctor/patient, but not *patient/son.

relativism, cultural The attitude that beliefs and practices must be understood in terms of the culture of which they form a part. See *ethnocentrism.*

relativism, ethical The attitude that moral/ethical judgments cannot or should not be made cross-culturally, but must be relative to the standards of a particular social group.

Review of Anthropology, Annual Starting in 1972, a useful collection of articles reviewing recent developments in various subfields of anthropology. Between 1959 and 1971, the Biennial Review of Anthropology (Stanford University Press, ed. B. Siegel and others) was issued in odd-numbered years. This is probably the best single source for evaluation of and bibliography on current ideas and methods.

revitalization movements Social movements which deliberately attempt to "construct a more satisfying culture," often by supernatural means; examples are the cargo cults of Melanesia and the Ghost Dance in North America.

rite of passage A ritual event in which individuals move from one social position (*role*) to another, usually through the three stages of separation, transition, and incorporation.

role, kinship A social role to which *ego* is assigned (recruited) as a consequence of actual or putative genealogical connection.

role, personal A category of persons consisting of a single individual together with his or her style of interacting; the label for such a role is the individual's personal name or alias.

role, social Any *category* of persons which, in a given society, is associated with a conventional *plan* for interaction with one or more other categories of persons.

role, societal The category consisting of all members of a society together with their general rights and obligations as such.

rules, descent These assign *ego* to a kinship group on the basis of the group affiliation of one parent. See *matrilineal, patrilineal, double descent*; compare with *bilateral.*

rules, marriage Specify eligible or ineligible spouses on the basis of ego's social category or group membership.

rules, residence Assign *ego* to some residential group (household, local community, and so forth) at one or more points in his social career; for example, at time of marriage, or when first child is born.

Sapir, Edward (1884–1939) American linguist and ethnologist who inspired many fine students to follow his example of intensive field work in Indian languages and cultures. With *Benedict* he founded "culture and personality" studies. Major works: *Language* (1921), and collected papers (ed., D. Mandelbaum).

semantic differential A technique for measuring the connotative meanings of terms in any language.

semantic space Areas and dimensions of denotative and connotative meaning within which particular terms can be located.

semantics The study of meaning in language; with *grammar* and *phonology*, one of the three major areas of linguistic investigation.

shaman A part- or full-time ritual specialist who performs religious and curing ceremonies in behalf of his clients and social group.

situation, social A unit of *social structure* composed of intersecting areas of *social space* and periods of *social time,* together with the *social relationships* expected to occur within them.

social anthropology The subfield of cultural anthropology which compares materials provided by *ethnology* and *ethnography* to draw functional, casual, and universal inferences. See *approach, cross-cultural.*

sociolinguistics The subfield of linguistics that studies the relationships between language and social systems, including the "ethnography of communication."

Southwestern Journal of Anthropology Published since 1945 by the University of New Mexico, it contains articles on all aspects of anthropology with emphasis on theory-oriented research. In 1973 the title was changed to the *Journal of Anthropological Research.*

space, personal Culturally patterned ways of using the area immediately surrounding an individual's body.

space, social Cultural *categories* of space together with *plans* for behaving in or towards them. See *territory.*

specialization, role Refers to the development in food-producing societies of individuals who devote most or all of their time to ritual, political, or specialized technical activities.

speech Vocal behavior *influenced* by some *language* system(s), and from which the language may be *inferred.*

stratification, principle of In archaeology, the assumption that—other things being equal—the deeper an *artifact* is found, the greater its age. See *age-area principle.*

stratification, social The existence within a society of ranked subgroups. See *castes*; *class, social*; *hierarchy.*

structure, social *Categories* of persons and associated *plans* for interaction characteristic of any social or societal group. See (social) *career, institutions, relationship.*

swidden system A form of *horticulture* that involves cutting and firing of vegetation (slash-and-burn) prior to planting.

synchronic study An examination of a cultural system at one point in time, emphasizing the description of structure. See *diachronic study.*

syntax In linguistics, the rules which specify how words can and must be combined into larger meaningful units (phrases, sentences, and so forth), including rules of order, agreement, and transformation.

taxonomy, folk A "native" classification of some set of objects, persons, or events; for example, color terms, plant names, kinship terms; see *ethnosemantics.*

technique A belief about the relationship between means and ends characteristic of some *social role* or group; includes expected ways of employing the human body and/or tools to modify the environment.

technology The cultural subsystem consisting of categories of *tools* together with plans for their manufacture and use, as well as other *techniques* for producing changes in the material environment.

territory Area of *social space* associated with particular individuals or social groups.

text Any record of observations of behavior (or the products of behavior), including field notes, photographs, test responses, documents, and so forth.

time, social Cultural *categories* of time together with *plans* for during or with respect to them. See *situation, social.*

tool An artifact used to augment man's ability to act upon the physical world.

Tylor, Sir Edward B. (1832–1917) Critical scholarship and encyclopedic knowledge set him off from most of his British contemporaries. Tylor used the comparative method (with statistical verification) to infer culture history and functional relationships, and to postulate universal concepts. Major works: *Primitive Culture, Anthropology.*

universals, cultural Elements or processes that are found in all cultural systems.

universals, linguistic Elements or processes that are found in all human languages.

values, social Conceptions of the "desirable" characteristic of a given social group, often forming a system with integrating patterns. *See ethos.*

Index

A Note on the Type

The text of this book has been set by linotype in a type face called Helvetica—perhaps the most widely accepted and generally acclaimed sans-serif face of all time. Designed by M. Miedinger in the 1950's in Switzerland and named for its country of origin, Helvetica was first introduced in America in 1963.